H. G. WELLS, MODERNITY AND THE MOVIES

Liverpool Science Fiction Texts and Studies

Editor
DAVID SEED
University of Liverpool

Editorial Board

MARK BOULD
University of the West of England

VERONICA HOLLINGER
Trent University

ROB LATHAM
University of Iowa

ROGER LUCKHURST
Birkbeck College, University of London

PATRICK PARRINDER
University of Reading

ANDY SAWYER
University of Liverpool

1. Robert Crossley *Olaf Stapledon: Speaking for the Future*
2. David Seed (ed.) *Anticipations: Essays on Early Science Fiction and its Precursors*
3. Jane L. Donawerth and Carol A. Kolmerten (eds) *Utopian and Science Fiction by Women: Worlds of Difference*
4. Brian W. Aldiss *The Detached Retina: Aspects of SF and Fantasy*
5. Carol Farley Kessler *Charlotte Perkins Gilman: Her Progress Toward Utopia, with Selected Writings*
6. Patrick Parrinder *Shadows of the Future: H. G. Wells, Science Fiction and Prophecy*
7. I. F. Clarke (ed.) *The Tale of the Next Great War, 1871–1914: Fictions of Future Warfare and of Battles Still-to-come*
8. Joseph Conrad and Ford Madox Ford *The Inheritors*
9. Qingyun Wu *Female Rule in Chinese and English Literary Utopias*
10. John Clute *Look at the Evidence: Essays and Reviews*
11. Roger Luckhurst *'The Angle Between Two Walls': The Fiction of J. G. Ballard*
12. I. F. Clarke (ed.) *The Great War with Germany, 1880–1914: Fiction and Fantasies of the War-to-come*
13. Franz Rottensteiner (ed.) *View from Another Shore: European Science Fiction*
14. Val Gough and Jill Rudd (eds) *A Very Different Story: Studies in the Fiction of Charlotte Perkins Gilman*
15. Gary Westfahl *The Mechanics of Wonder: The Creation of the Idea of Science Fiction*
16. Gwyneth Jones *Deconstructing the Starships: Science, Fiction and Reality*
17. Patrick Parrinder (ed.) *Learning from Other Worlds: Estrangement, Cognition and the Politics of Science Fiction and Utopia*
18. Jeanne Cortiel *Demand My Writing: Joanna Russ/Feminism/Science Fiction*
19. Chris Ferns *Narrating Utopia: Ideology, Gender, Form in Utopian Literature*
20. E. J. Smith (ed.) *Jules Verne: New Directions*
21. Andy Sawyer and David Seed (eds) *Speaking Science Fiction: Dialogues and Interpretations*
22. Inez van der Spek *Alien Plots: Female Subjectivity and the Divine*
23. S. T. Joshi *Ramsey Campbell and Modern Horror Fiction*
24. Mike Ashley *The Time Machines: The Story of the Science-Fiction Pulp Magazines from the Beginning to 1950*
25. Warren G. Rochelle *Communities of the Heart: The Rhetoric of Myth in the Fiction of Ursula K. Le Guin*
26. S. T. Joshi *A Dreamer and a Visionary: H. P. Lovecraft in His Time*
27. Christopher Palmer *Philip K. Dick: Exhilaration and Terror of the Postmodern*
28. Charles E. Gannon *Rumors of War and Infernal Machines: Technomilitary Agenda-Setting in American and British Speculative Fiction*
29. Peter Wright *Attending Daedalus: Gene Wolfe, Artifice and the Reader*
30. Mike Ashley *Transformations: The Story of the Science-Fiction Magazine from 1950–1970*
31. Joanna Russ *The Country You Have Never Seen: Essays and Reviews*
32. Robert Philmus *Visions and Revisions: (Re)constructing Science Fiction*
33. Gene Wolfe (edited and introduced by Peter Wright) *Shadows of the New Sun: Wolfe on Writing/Writers on Wolfe*
34. Mike Ashley *Gateways to Forever: The Story of the Science-Fiction Magazine from 1970–1980*
35. Keith Williams *H. G. Wells, Modernity and the Movies*

H. G. WELLS, MODERNITY AND THE MOVIES

Keith Williams

LIVERPOOL UNIVERSITY PRESS

First published 2007 by
Liverpool University Press
4 Cambridge Street
Liverpool L69 7ZU

Copyright © 2007 Keith Williams

The author's rights have been asserted in accordance with the Copyright, Design and Patents Act 1988.

All rights reserved. No part of this book may be reproduced, stored in a retrieval system, or transmitted, in any form or by any means, electronic, mechanical, photocopying, recording, or otherwise, without the prior written permission of the publisher.

British Library Cataloguing-in-Publication data
A British Library CIP record is available

ISBN 978–1–84631–059–1 cased
978–1–84631–060–7 limp

Edited and typeset by
Frances Hackeson Freelance Publishing Services, Brinscall, Lancs

Contents

Acknowledgements		vii
Abbreviations		viii
Introduction: Wells's Prescience		1
1	Optical Speculations in the Early Writings: *The Time Machine* and the Short Stories	24
2	The Dis/Appearance of the Subject: Wells, Whale and *The Invisible Man*	49
3	'Seeing the Future': Visual Technology in *When the Sleeper Wakes* and Fritz Lang's *Metropolis*	73
4	The 'Broadbrow' and the Big Screen: Wells's Film Writing	94
5	Afterimages: Adaptations and Influences	130
Conclusion		178
Notes		183
Bibliography		247
Index		269

To my wife and children, for putting up with me and H. G. for so long.

Acknowledgements

Ian Christie's wonderfully interdisciplinary historicisation of the cultural contexts of early cinema, especially *The Last Machine*, was inspirational to this project, as was the pioneering work of John Barnes. Stephen Herbert and Luke McKernan's *Who's Who of Victorian Cinema* was also invaluable for other leads into the scientific and technological backgrounds too numerous to endnote in every single case.

Special thanks are due to: the Carnegie Trust, for their generous research grant for trips to the National Film and Television Archive; for all the help of viewing and library staff at the BFI, especially Kathleen Dickson and Bryony Dixon; similarly, staff at the George IV Bridge site of the National Library of Scotland, Edinburgh; Jeffrey Richards, for his bolstering faith in the value of this project, and Roger Sabin, who thought I might be on to something; Matthew Jarron for his informed and rigorous scrutiny of various chapter drafts; Eric Cash and John Partington, of US and UK branches of the H. G. Wells Society, and to the interlinked editorial boards at *The Undying Fire* and *The Wellsian*, who gave a platform to formative research on *The Invisible Man*; Godela Weiss-Sussex and Franco Bianchini, for similarly accommodating material on Wells, Lang and future cities in *The Yearbook of European Studies*; all my long-suffering colleagues in English and/or Film at Dundee, especially our Research Committee, for support and extra study leave to get this book finished under mounting collective pressures; Chris Murray, Iain Davison and fellow researchers at the Scottish Word and Image Group, for crucial feedback at presentations from work in progress; students on my 'H. G. Wells, Science Fiction and Film' module, who have acted as virtual research assistants over the years; Laura Marcus for her kind and boosting comments; Karin Littau and Jeffrey Geiger at Essex, for inviting me to speak at their recent conference on 'Cinematicity'; Anthony Cond, for persuading me that LUP would be the best home for this book, Kate Possnett and Frances Hackeson for editing; Jim Stewart for indexing; finally to everyone at Dundee, or elsewhere, who gave help, advice or encouragement in the decade it's taken for the book to mature.

The illustrations are reproduced by kind permission of the Trustees of the National Library of Scotland. In the case of individual illustrations which may still be in copyright, every reasonable effort has been made to trace the current copyright holders, who should contact the publishers to discuss further permission if required.

Abbreviations

BFI	British Film Institute
CGI	Computer-Generated Imagery
SPR	Society for Psychical Research

Works by Wells

CSS	*The Complete Short Stories of H. G. Wells*
FMITM	*The First Men in the Moon*
FOTG	*The Food of the Gods and How It Came to Earth*
IM	*The Invisible Man*
IODM	*The Island of Doctor Moreau*
KWWAK	*The King Who Was a King*
MWCWM	*The Man Who Could Work Miracles* [Film]
MWCWMAFS	*The Man Who Could Work Miracles: A Film Story*
NF	*The New Faust: A Film Story*
SB	*Star Begotten: A Biological Fantasia*
SOTTC	*The Shape of Things to Come*
TM	*The Time Machine*
TTC	*Things to Come* [Film]
TTCAFS	*Things to Come: A Film Story*
WITA	*The War in the Air*
WM	*Whither Mankind? A Film of the Future*
WOTW	*The War of the Worlds*
WTSW	*When the Sleeper Wakes*
WTWIG	*The Way the World is Going: Guesses and Forecasts for the Years Ahead*

Note

For ease of reference, I have chosen to use the new Penguin popular editions of Wells's best-known scientific romances, except in the case of *When the Sleeper Wakes*. Here (to emphasise its prescience about new media) I have referenced the Oxford World's Classics edition, which follows the 1899 text, rather than Wells's 1910 revision, *The Sleeper Awakes*.

1 'Mr Paul and his camera', from Anon., 'The Prince of Wales's Derby Shown by Lightning Photography', *Strand Magazine* (Aug. 1896), p. 134

2 A Phantom of the Living? Opening illustration by Paul Hardy to 'The Stolen Body', *Strand Magazine* (Nov. 1898), p. 567.

"IT HUNG IN MID-AIR—MOTIONLESS."

3 'It hung in mid-air motionless.' Illustration by Alfred Pearse to 'The New Accelerator', *Strand Magazine* (Dec. 1901), p. 626.

4 'Out it flew and became thinner and thinner.' Illustration by A. Wallis Mills to 'The Magic Shop', *Strand Magazine* (June 1903), p. 639

5 'As the camera of the Heat Ray hit the water.' Illustration by Warwick Goble to
The War of the Worlds, Pearson's Magazine (July 1897), p. 113

6 'Ostrog stepped across the room, something clicked and suddenly they were in darkness, save for an oval glow.' Illustration by Henri Lanos to *When the Sleeper Wakes*, *The Graphic* (25 Feb. 1899), p. 233

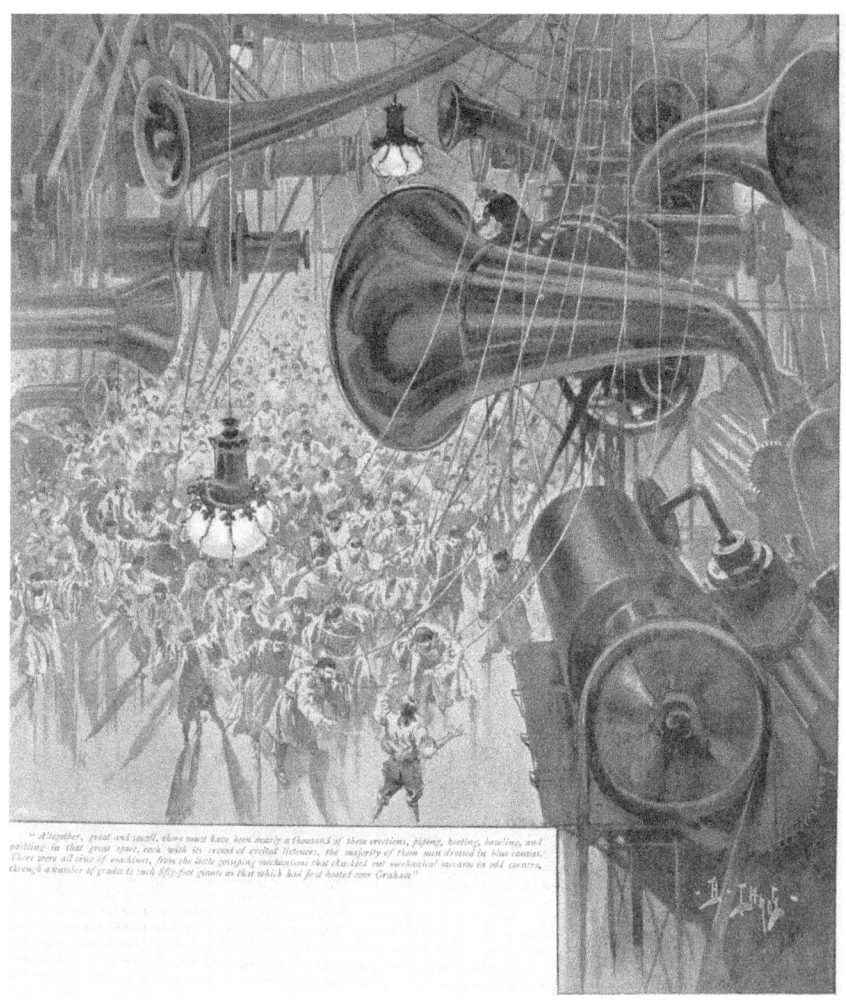

7 'Altogether, great and small, there must have been nearly a thousand of these erections, piping, hooting, bawling, and gabbling in that space.' Illustration by Henri Lanos to *When the Sleeper Wakes*, *The Graphic* (8 April 1899), p. 433

8 'The huge ears of a phonographic mechanism gaped in a battery for his words ...'
Illustration by Henri Lanos to *When the Sleeper Wakes*, *The Graphic* (22 April 1899), p. 497

Introduction: Wells's Prescience

> The motion picture is a triumph over tenses. It is a Time Machine in which we all ride with Lumen.[1]

H. G. Wells's first 'scientific romance', *The Time Machine: An Invention* (*TM*) (1895), was published as a novel the year the Lumière brothers invented their Cinématographe.[2] Though no one could possibly have foreseen the sociocultural impact this would eventually have, the lack of imaginative insight into cinema's potential at the beginning, even by its own makers, seems astonishing to us now, epitomised by Louis Lumière's belief that it had little future.[3] However, the new medium was not a single scientific invention, subsequently hijacked by the Barnumism of the culturally unscrupulous. Its origins and outcomes were complex. As Ian Christie puts it, cinema 'was the invention of an era. A collective progress towards something which turned out quite differently from most expectations.'[4] Writers and artists were, in some respects, more prescient than cinema's inventors. Wells's speculations about, and technical foreshadowings of, cinema and other related new media were particularly remarkable.[5]

The protagonist of *TM* is an expert in physical optics.[6] What I call 'optical speculations' in Wells's early writings and their self-reflexive visuality were also an important culmination of trends in both Victorian science and culture. His fiction was a symptomatic product of a common matrix of factors that seems to render cinema inevitable in retrospect. However, most discussion, by largely restricting itself to historicising Wells's connections with cinema per se – the most obvious outcome of these trends, neglects its embeddedness in the connective tissue of film's wider technical context and cultural prehistory. Wells made a crucial contribution to understanding and advancing not just the possibilities of cinematic narrative, but also the impact of other forms of recording technologies. We need to account for the fuller creativity involved in Wells's response to, and investigation of, one of the shaping forces of modernity. Consequently, this book also examines how his interaction with cinema's wider context makes him a principal pioneer of the media-determined parameters of modern subjectivity.

Significantly, a mere decade later, Wells was already using film narrative as a principal metaphor for his own imaginative method. In *A Modern*

Utopia (1905), he intended readers to follow his protagonists into a parallel world, both mimetic of our own reality, yet also a radical defamiliarisation of it:

> The image of a cinematograph entertainment is the one to grasp. There will be an effect of these two people going to and fro in front of the circle of a rather defective lantern, which sometimes jams and sometimes gets out of focus, but which does occasionally succeed in displaying on the screen a momentary moving picture of Utopian conditions.[7]

Consequently, this introduction sets out some of the principal ways in which Wells's early writings correspond to and critique the 'cinematisation' of his own cultural epoch and beyond.

The Emergence of Cinematic Time

Most obviously Wells had a pivotal role in what Mary Anne Doane calls the 'emergence of cinematic time'.[8] Wells did not invent topical timetravel narrative per se (much in vogue, especially after Edward Bellamy's *Looking Backward: 2000–1887* (1888)), but put it on a *mechanical* basis, so that magical, occult or visionary explanations were no longer necessary, just as the cinema would also technologise the 'miraculous'.[9] Hence mechanised temporal displacement emerged as a crucial theme in the late nineteenth century simultaneously with the advent of film and, as Paul Coates notes, its own specific 'capacity to manipulate the illusion of time'. But it was also linked to the impact of scientific theories such as evolution and relativity with their spatio-temporally expanded and increasingly paradoxical 'multiverse'.[10]

Though the Lumières' first programmes consisted of simple actualities of under one minute such as *Démolition d'un mur*, they quickly discovered (by the serendipity of feeding the reel the wrong way) that cinematic time could run backwards too, so that the wall miraculously recomposed itself from rubble. (Similar effects had already been achieved with Edison's 'peepshow' predecessor, the Kinetoscope.)[11] Reversing, as it became known, was quickly exploited for entertainment value. British pioneer Cecil Hepworth recalled delighting audiences by cranking faster, slower, backwards and even stopping his projector to freeze time altogether at particularly grotesque moments.[12] Such novelties find multiple Wellsian parallels. His fantastic invention makes time itself resemble a movie reel, speeded forwards and backwards, or stopped at will.[13]

Wells's early writing and the birth of cinema were leading and interrelated manifestations of the 'chronotope'[14] of late nineteenth- and early twentieth-century consciousness in its transition to modernity. Indeed, radical transformation in what Stephen Kern calls its 'culture of time and space' characterises that epoch.[15] Time travelling, in literal or psychological senses, is endemic to both 'high' and 'low' Modernism, but seems to derive from a kind of Wellsian relativisation (accelerated, dilated, reversed, subjectivised) towards the turn of the century. Consequently, in this study, I intend focusing on the complex intertextuality between Wells and the movies, not least in terms of parallelism in their respective handling of space and time.

Before the 1880s, time had been set locally by custom, but railway timetabling and the spread of telegraphy and telephony necessitated international reform, segmenting the planet into 24 zones regulated from Greenwich's prime meridian. It was also demanded by capitalism's intensifying industrialisation, by 'sped-up' time-motion efficiencies imposed on factory workers, culminating in the assembly line. Motion pictures were merely the latest in a series of inventions fixing, collecting and commodifying time in the material forms of photographs, sound recordings, etc. Time's problematic nature was at the leading edge of modernity's culture shock, and cinema provided an imaginative space in which to deal with this anxiety. Before Einstein's 1905 Special Theory became widely known, what Christie calls a 'vernacular relativity' of speed and time already existed on screen.[16] Einstein demonstrated that single universal time was a contingent fiction, by showing its dependence on motion and position. The complementarity and interchange of 'space-time' became parameters of the observer's viewpoint and situation. But its emergent plasticity was most dynamically materialised for the wider community in the new narrative medium, with which Wellsian modes of literary visualisation are indivisibly connected.[17] His proto-cinematic metaphors and techniques share common ground by also orientating the reader towards 'post-Newtonian models', as Kenneth V. Bailey argues.[18] Wells's defamiliarising viewpoints are often located beyond normal space and time and frequently observe 'alien' phenomena through lens-like devices. By so doing, the relativistic situation and existential status of his observers are foregrounded, along with forms of mediation enabling them.[19]

A 'triple relationship' between film, the ekphrastically 'cinematic' and the Einsteinian paradigm can be traced back to Wells's early explorations of the theory of alternative dimensions.[20] As Coates points out, the concept of parallel worlds was materialised by photography, because it became virtually possible to shuffle 'the detached surface of one time into another like a card shuffled in a deck'.[21] This was enhanced by frame strips and projection combining in film. Vachel Lindsay (who published one of the earliest critical studies of film in 1915) noted that cinema's capturing of objects in motion over time added a 'mysterious fourth dimension' to photography's 'grace and glory'.[22]

Not only did such potentials inform the subject matter and themes of Wells's work, they also shaped its techniques in ways that help explain its later (albeit problematic) adaptability as screen narrative matured. Commentators have long detected quasi-cinematic effects in both *TM* (accelerated motion/temporal condensation and reversing especially) and *The War of the Worlds* (*WOTW*)(1898) (dramatic dilation and contraction of visual perspective, scale and angle).[23] Similarly, in *The Invisible Man* (*IM*) (1897) Wells perhaps came closest (as Laura Marcus argues) to the 'play of absence and presence' at the ontological basis of cinema.[24]

Realist of the Fantastic

Hence it is more than coincidence that Joseph Conrad's paradoxical 1898 accolade to Wells, as 'Realist of the Fantastic, whether you like it or not',[25] is also applicable to cinema as *the* modern medium containing the greatest potential for visualising the familiar and the impossible on a virtually equal plane of ultra-mimetic or 'simulacral' realism. Wells's view that the method of his scientific romances was to '*domesticate* the impossible', by grounding it in a meticulously constructed impression of everyday material reality, corroborates this.[26] The dual tradition of documentary and fantasy arises almost simultaneously with the moment of film's inception, like conjoined twins sprung from the same techno-cultural matrix, separate yet interdependent life forms. By the autumn of 1896 stage magician Georges Méliès was experimenting with deliberate visual conjuring made possible by editing and 'stop motion effects', following the famous (though possibly apocryphal) incident when his camera jammed in Paris's Place de l'Opéra. The resulting interruption in the continuity of frames seemed instantly to transform a bus exiting a tunnel into a hearse.[27] By November Méliès had shot *The Vanishing Lady* (*L'Escamotage d'une dame*) using this principle of substitution: a young woman is transformed into a skeleton more convincingly than previously achievable on stage. Méliès's film reflected the macabre vogue for unpeeling the body with 'X-rays', discovered by Wilhelm Konrad von Röntgen (also in 1895), but paralleling Griffin's bizarre dis/appearance in *IM* too.[28] From such primitive beginnings film-makers realised that cinema could function as a parallel, 'narrative' reality, with its own peculiar physical laws. The first explorations of the medium's paradoxical potential as 'the Realist of the Fantastic' through stop-motion work find striking visual echoes in stories such as 'The Man Who Could Work Miracles' (1898) or 'The Magic Shop' (1903), as well as the unseen manipulations of *IM*. A similar principle of 'mechanising magic' was arguably key to the imaginative method of Wells's fantastic fiction as a whole.[29]

Albert J. La Valley helps explain the convergence between Wells and cinema as Realists of the Fantastic. Science-fiction film's other worlds must be rendered as ultra-mimetically 'as the more normal one of actors and non-special effects'. However, the technical difficulties were more easily overcome in print during the cinema's primitive phase.[30] Méliès's *Le Voyage dans la Lune* (1902) seems visually far less sophisticated than the Wells novel from which it was partly sourced (*The First Men in the Moon* (*FMITM*) (1901)) because the fantastic novelty of early trickfilms 'overrode any real interest in a technological future' as such. For both technical and cultural reasons, the world had to wait until Yakov Protazanov's *Aelita* (1924) or Fritz Lang's *Metropolis* (1926) for that gap to narrow significantly. Partly because many early film-makers were professional conjurors, sheer visual magic, not narrative plausibility, was the primary fascination. Nevertheless, 'delight in the illusion', granting credence within the narrative context while knowing it for deception, allowed cinema to make the imaginary seem more real than ever before.[31]

Garrett Stewart also argues that there is a built-in optical self-consciousness, or 'videology', in the science-fiction tradition.[32] This is epitomised by Wells, not just in how his writing 'saw the future', but in its synergy with cinema itself, speculating about how the future *might see*. His 'film-minded' texts often waited for the industry to catch up with the potential they foresaw in optical technology, because cinematic versions of them do not just dramatise his thematic materials, they also, inevitably, illustrate the 'state of their own art'. Hence, as La Valley puts it, such films 'hover between being about the world their special effects imply' (i.e. future technology and its social implications), but also about what 'the wizardry' of cinema itself has become capable of at that given moment in its evolution.[33]

Mediating Modernity

Marcus argues that Wells's engagement with film 'was the most complete and complex' among late Victorian and Edwardian writers, his career running 'parallel to the "evolution" of cinema'.[34] Many leading parameters within which the High Modernists' later experimental intertextuality with cinema developed were arguably laid down by him, for example: representation of relativistic 'space-time'; anatomisation of moment and movement; 'eidetic' or virtual visualisation; radical re-envisionings of subjectivity; 'optical' self-reflexivity; 'the cinematised city'; besides anticipatory critiques of film's manifold cultural, political and social impacts.

The generational fruition of the 1870 Education Act created a potential new readership of millions, eager for entertaining but intellectually informed journalism and fiction. Consequently, cinema's rise also coincides with new popular literary genres, such as the 'scientific romance' that Wells exemplified.[35] His serials and stories first appeared in a hospitable plethora of late Victorian magazines. These frequently carried photographic articles popularising the 'wonders' of modern science, its new discoveries and inventions.[36] Looking back in 1911 on his period of greatest imaginative productivity in the short story, he again chose optical metaphors for his own writing process, suggestive of gazing through a cinema screen into a 'parallel' reality with its own distinctive physical logic:

> there would presently come out of the darkness, in a manner quite inexplicable, some absurd or vivid little incident ... Little men in canoes upon sunlit oceans would come floating out of nothingness, incubating the eggs of prehistoric monsters unawares; violent conflicts would break out amidst the flower-beds of suburban gardens; I would discover I was peering into remote and mysterious worlds ruled by an order logical indeed but other than our common sanity.[37]

Wells's sense of the paradoxical scope of the short-story form also suggests the dimensional expansions and contractions of film narrative. His description of easy transition from microscopic close-up to vast panorama is striking: 'it does not matter whether [the story] is as "trivial" as a Japanese print of insects seen closely between grass stems, or as spacious as the plain of Italy from Monte Mattarone'. (*The Complete Short Stories of H. G. Wells* (*CSS*), p. 876) Similarly, in the introduction to his 'film novel', *The King Who Was a King* (*KWWAK*) (1929), Wells explicitly rehighlighted cinema's lack of limitations, in size, scale, depth or distance (see Chapter 4). Moreover, he argued that the ruling themes, concepts and methods of popular fiction, drama and music hall had 'transferred to the cinemas copiously and profitably, and with the greatest possible economy of adaptation'.[38] In a 1935 interview in America promoting his collaboration with Alexander Korda, Wells linked his own practice as a popular writer to cinema's development as a new art form possessing the potential for presenting complex ideas accessibly.[39]

Tim Armstrong has shown how Victorian media technologies became effectively 'grafted' on to the age's physical senses and consciousness, profoundly changing both lived experience and subjectivity. They were 'prosthetic' in the sense of amplifying perception and imagination beyond the body's organic and spatio-temporal boundaries.[40] As a mobile technological extension of sight, theoretically capable of bringing visual impressions back from anywhere (and simulating those it couldn't), cinema typified radical transformations taking place in the relationship between culture and the media. Wells was one of the first 'camera-eyed' writers to try to come to critical terms with, and to exploit, its unavoidable challenge to traditional literary craft.

Through his 'broadbrow' appeal,[41] Wells broke new ground within the discipline of popular form precisely because of the striking 'film-friendliness' of his innovations, which rippled out into cinema, radio and television through adaptations of his themes and methods. His early writings display a visual self-reflexiveness, remarkable for its inventiveness and multiformity. Viewpoint and perspective are always foregrounded. Characters and narrators are constantly seeing or being seen through mediating frames – lenses, screens, windows, doors and apertures of all kinds. Indeed the late Dennis Potter, the most postmodern and 'meta-televisual' of writers, acknowledged his own indebtedness to how Wells's fiction continuously showed the 'frame in the picture', not just 'the picture in the frame'.[42]

In 1893, Wells noted an accelerating trend away from traditionally textual culture to a more visual one, which would make the material forms of 'The Literature of the Future' 'palpitate with actuality'. He cited photography's inroads 'into the very heart' of books and magazines and even wondered whether this trend would eventually make reading redundant altogether (imagining the British Museum's neglected shelves gradually crumbling like *TM*'s 'Palace of Green Porcelain').[43] On the other hand, Wells was instrumental in extending the classical literary principle of 'ekphrasis' – the verbal imitation of visual modes such as paintings or sculptures so that audiences might 'visualise' them without seeing them directly – into the simulacral age of moving images.[44] He strove to imagine forms and techniques of time-based representation that did not, as yet, exist in actual examples from often ingenious but relatively primitive cinema shows of the period. As Bailey notes, the sheer 'eidetic' lucidity of Wells's image-forming functions resembles the means by which films are produced and appear to present realities unmediated.[45] His contemporary, E. M. Forster, considered Wells a 'camera man' for his ability 'of hitting off a person or place in a few quick words' convincing the reader as if with photographic evidence.[46] On the other hand, Wells himself was sceptical about the epistemological truth and purity of photographic virtualism (his cousin Isabel, whom he married in 1891, was a 'retoucher' by trade after all).[47]

Bailey adduces two main kinds of Wellsian visualisation suggestive of analogies with photographic media, but also foregrounding their discursive frames. Besides fantastic visions mediated by advanced optical devices (or metaphors for such), we find detached images or even whole narratives 'floating out of nothingness'. They well up, as if from dreams or the unconscious, but severed from surrounding space and time like screened pictures, often overlapping with or breaking into other deictic contexts.[48] Hence Wells's early fictions 'conjure' with causality, space and time in ways that also became distinctive of film and related media. Studies such as Grahame Smith's show that Wells's predecessors were already beginning to 'dream' cinematic narrative into being ekphrastically, as a new mode of visual imaginary (as Sergei M. Eisenstein also argued in his famous essay).[49] In this, he joined not just Dickens and Verne but also Flaubert, Tolstoy, Zola, Kipling, Rider Haggard, Conan Doyle and others, in pioneering close-ups, slow-motion, moving viewpoints, cross-cutting, etc, on the page. However, Wells's significance lies not just in continuing this process, but also in the astonishing range and accuracy of what he added to it.

The Cinematic Eyes of Science

Victorian writers were increasingly fascinated by mechanisms of vision, such as telescopes, microscopes, photography, magic lanterns and patent optical toys. Their scientific contemporaries' awareness of the camera, as a multi-purpose prosthetic extension of sight for materialising what would otherwise be invisible in space and/or time, was an equally expansive drive behind the invention of the cinema. This is typified by Richard Proctor's 1883 article 'The Photographic Eyes of Science' which noted: the eye's inability to register over-rapid impressions such as a cannon-ball's flight; conversely, its illusion of temporal stasis, as with spinning tops; its inability to see over vast distances; and, moreover, visual memory's lack of total recall. So where the unaided eye was defective, one 'provided by science is practically free from fault'. Proctor celebrated the camera's 'panoptic' potential for advancing knowledge: 'indeed with photography, spectroscopy, polariscopy, and other aids, science promises soon to be Argus-eyed'.[50]

The birth of cinema as an instrument for analysing visual reality was thus the next logical step. The 'persistence of vision' effect, whereby the retina retains images approximately one-twentieth to one-fifth of a second after objects casting them are removed, was scientifically described by Peter Mark Roget in 1824. But Anglo-American photographer Eadweard Muybridge first created the impression of continuous movement using batteries of cameras. Muybridge's 1872 sequences of galloping horses proved that all four legs left the ground simultaneously. Such 'animal locomotion studies' (taken at one hundredth of a second or less using electric shutters) enabled scientists 'to fix attitudes too transitory for the ordinary eye', as Wells recalled.[51] They dissected phenomena in a kind of action replay, but also anticipated the filmstrip. (Muybridge's next step was animating them, combining the zoetrope's rotating drum with a magic lantern projector in his 1879 'Zoopraxiscope'.) Muybridge mutually influenced Étienne-Jules Marey's studies of 'animal mechanism'. Muybridge segmented continuous action, but Marey overlapped it with a 'chronophotographic gun', then high-speed camera on rails. In 1888 and 1890, paper roll and then celluloid film furnished extended strips of black-suited gymnasts, with practically invisible bodies, reduced to outlines of muscular thrust picked out in white. Like Wells's *IM*, Marey's subjects were ambiguously 'dematerialised', fetishistic, but with presence as a physical force. Chronophotography allowed movement to be scrutinised as an abstract object 'developing' in space over time, but also dissolved individual identity into curves of poetic dynamism, anticipating Modernist art. Marey's vast survey, *Le Mouvement*, was published in 1894 and was translated the following year.

However, Edison's commercial success finally pointed towards the film industry. His 'Kinetoscope loops' effectively synthesised the work of Muybridge and Marey,[52] aiming to produce an entertainment machine to do 'for the Eye what the phonograph [patented in 1878] does for the Ear'.[53] This confirms that film's genesis was never independent from recorded sound, something that *IM* also plays on.[54] Edison's researchers, using Eastman-Kodak's celluloid film patented in 1887 (another breakthrough recalled by Wells), created movies between 1889 and 1893 for their peepshow viewer. The 'Cinématographe' itself was finally invented by Auguste and Louis Lumière after their father spotted the kinetoscope's potential for communal viewing, thus gestating cinema as the public projection of moving photographic images.[55] Their resulting combined camera and projector was professionally demonstrated in March. Its famous public debut (28 December) made movies, virtually overnight, an extremely lucrative enterprise.

As a machine to 'convincingly represent empirical reality in motion', as David A. Cook describes it,[56] cinema also became rapidly enlisted as an instrument of many branches of science, from medicine to zoology, anthropology and astronomy, although the impact of scientific films was often as much sensational as instructive.[57] The first filmed operation was by Boleslaw Matuszewski in 1897. Microscope films began the same year, with experiments by Robert Lincoln Watkins and Oskar Messter. By 1903, F. Martin Duncan's series dissected the *Unseen World* of nature with extreme close-ups and microphotography. The Anglo-American Charles Urban was particularly significant in producing scientific films such as Percy Smith's *Secrets of Nature*, equally popular for educational and entertainment purposes from 1911. 'Time lapse' or 'speed magnification' recording plant or crystal growth, cell formation, hatching animals, etc, can also be traced back to 1896 (Messter making some of the earliest of blooming flowers). After the great chronophotographer's death in 1904, the Institut Marey extended his project through X-ray, microscope and high-speed analysis films. Such developments compare closely with Wells's imaginative visualisation of natural processes in time-travelling, as well as *FMITM*'s accelerated lunar ecology.[58] As if to symbolise the 'conjoined' nature of cinema's objectivity and fantastic sensationalism, scientific film caused a scandal in 1902 when an operation on Siamese twins (Eugène-Louis

Doyen's *La Séparation de Doodica-Radica*) was pirated on to the freakshow circuit.[59] Science films opened out and magnified new optical dimensions of fantastic forms comparable to contemporary science fictions like Wells's 'post-historic monster' in *TM*, the cephalopod aliens of *WOTW*, or the giant insects and vermin of *The Food of the Gods (FOTG)*(1904).

The camera's extensive links with aeronautical design are another crucial example of synergy, giving birth to the imaginative possibilities of virtual movement on the one hand and pioneering powered flight on the other. Orville and Wilbur Wright studied Marey's *The Flight of Birds* (1890), alongside glider-maker Otto Lilienthal's *Bird-Flight as the Basis of Aviation* (1889), also known to Wells.[60] Visuality and aviation also converge in Wells's techniques. Graham in *When the Sleeper Wakes* (*WTSW*) (1899) learns to pilot by the aid of film simulations. Bert Smallways and partner in *The War in the Air* (*WITA*)(1908) catch the aviation bug when 'it was driven home to their minds by the cinematograph'.[61]

Besides 'anatomising' natural processes, cinema intensified curiosity about mechanical ones too, especially in industry. Pathé, Gaumont and Biograph were all involved in recording them, as a logical extension of the modern 'operational aesthetic'.[62] Film's visual characteristics stimulated the avant-garde's fascination with the abstract dynamics of processes and forms. The medium as machine seemed to possess a potential for understanding the socio-technological changes of which it was part. This kind of self-reflexive visualisation also figured prominently in Wells's fictions about futuristic machines, mechanised societies and the dubious objective of industrial efficiency as an end in itself, as in the dystopian tendencies of *TM*, 'A Story of the Days to Come', *WTSW*, *FMITM*, etc.

Many Wells fictions first appeared alongside popular scientific articles anatomising such natural and artificial phenomena as conjuring ('sleight of hand'), boxing, ballistics ('explosions'), or action and reaction ('drops and splashes in liquid'), illustrated by rapid photographic series of their subject.[63] Key breakthroughs leading to cinema are similarly reflected in Wells's fictions and recalled by him in his own brief history of the medium's origins.[64] Animal locomotion studies, chronophotography and the kinetoscope are all frequently referenced. Wells alluded to the drive to materialise the transitory for inspection as far back as 'The Chronic Argonauts' (1888), the first published version of *TM*: 'Who can fix the colours of sunset? Who can take a cast of flame?'[65] The *National Observer*'s serialisation (Mar.–June 1894) also compares time travel's acceleration to phenomena too rapid for unaided perception, emphasising the relativity of the in/visible as in photographic studies of ballistics: 'And as soon as the pace became considerable, the apparent velocity of people became so excessively great that I could no more see them than a man can see a cannon-ball flying through the air.'[66] The 1895 novella's psychologist explains the demonstration model's disappearance into the future in similarly paradoxical terms: 'We cannot see it ... any more than we can see the spoke of a wheel spinning, or a bullet' (*TM*, p. 10). Wells explored such processes further in the inverted form of temporal dilation in the 'slow motion' effects of stories such as 'The New Accelerator' (1901).

Wells undoubtedly shared Victorian keenness for optical technology as 'watchdog' of scientific progress and corrector of organic vision, in terms echoing Proctor's. In the January to May 1895 *New Review TM* serialisation, his protagonist argues that 'ordinary human perception is an hallucination'. Contingent upon peculiarities of biological and mental evolution, its construction of reality was limited and defective.[67] Wells wrote about the evolution of the eye from primitive phototropic cells in 'The Origin of the Senses' (1896), using the camera and photographic plate as analogies for explaining its 'mechanism'.[68] However, his earlier *National Observer* version suggests that time travel's proto-cinematic enhancement of vision is a modernisation of perception by artificial means to break out of 'the thought edifice of space, time and number, that our forefathers contrived'.[69] Similarly, David Y. Hughes and Robert M. Philmus note that Wells's early essays disclose secrets of nature as imaginative 'exercises in dissolving the limits of human perception' through microscopic, astronomic or evolutionary lenses, as it were.[70] The first British book on Wells's fiction argued that its distinctive vision was a corrective against the conditioned 'mental astigmatism of the masses'. Wells grounded his fantastic in the mundanely real, to develop a socially critical way of seeing which had much in common with cinema's defamiliarising potential.[71] The study's American counterpart (also 1915) noted Wells's extraordinarily detached way of anatomising human prejudices and presumptions, like a kind of X-ray vision, and the protean transformations of his narrative viewpoint. Like Bessel in 'The Stolen Body' (1898), his writing had 'that double quality' of being actively rooted in life while 'at the same time watching it from a great distance'. It stimulated the mind by perspective switches, 'telescoping ... suddenly' from the microscopic to the planetary, 'expanding and contracting his vision of things at will'.[72]

In 1891, Wells already used one of cinema's key proto-technologies from Victorian popular culture as a metaphor for the new scientific paradigm bursting out of creationism's Newtonian clockwork: 'The neat little picture of a universe of souls made up of passions and principles in bodies made of atoms, all put together so neatly and wound up at creation, fades in the series of dissolving views that we call the march of human thought.'[73] The 'dissolve' was one of many devices that magic lanterns (a method of projection with sophisticated and often moving effects, using multiple lenses and 'slipper' slides[74]) bequeathed to cinema. One image fades lingeringly as it is replaced by another, so they seem briefly to have a simultaneous existence in one space. Its potentials were enhanced in the form of the cinematic 'mix', or 'cross-fade', for transitions between scenes, as well as double exposure and other kinds of 'superimposition', especially for paranormal effects.

In 1906, Wells alluded to dissolving views again in describing his sense of transience contemplating the present order against cosmic processes:

> There are times indeed when it makes life seem so transparent and flimsy, seem so dissolving, so passing on to an equally transitory series of consequences, that the enhanced sense of instability becomes restlessness and distress ... The Pomp and splendour of established order, the braying triumphs, ceremonies, consummations, – one sees these glittering shows for what they are – through their threadbare grandeur shine the little significant things that will make the future.[75]

Wells remained strongly attached to this trope of one picture showing through another for expressing both intellectual scepticism and hope. References litter his early fiction, as we shall see, but in the sub-atomic period of the late thirties he was still using it for Joseph Davis's growing suspicion that his established world-view was becoming 'translucent and a little threadbare', gradually revealing that 'something else quite different lay behind it'.[76]

Although acquiring a popular reputation for (re)presenting objects and events unmediated, cinema ultimately complicated philosophical debate about distinguishing between illusion and reality, which it first promised to settle with scientific precision. After all, its reproduction of living movement was founded on an illusion: the persistence-of-vision effect. Its photographic virtualism opened up the question for Wells of whether the camera also deceived the eye and brain through what Jean-Louis Baudry calls representations 'offered as perceptions',[77] rather than enhancing their powers with objectivity and truth. In 'The Chronic Argonauts' 'Moses Nebogipfel's invention materialises like 'a disordered dream ... a projection of the subjective'. His hapless fellow-traveller, the clergyman, is ejected, as if waking from hallucination back to tangible reality, as the vehicle vanishes again.[78] Similarly, in a warning against the Victorian climate of camera-boosted enthusiasm for new visual certainties, William Kingdom Clifford's study *Seeing and Thinking* (1879) called optical research 'a sort of Clapham Junction of all the sciences'. At this junction, thought trains converged and departed, from physiology, physics, mechanics, but most importantly 'the subject of consciousness – what it is that we see, whether we see rightly, and how it is that we think'. Exploration of vision might be science's perceptio-cognitive terminus, but it was also the point of radical instability in its rationalist epistemology. There, he cautioned (perhaps alluding to impulses behind the Society for Psychical Research), 'more trains of thought ... go off the line' into the speculative, unknown or unprovable than at any other.⁷⁹ In the 1890s, as *both* professional scientist and imaginative artist, Wells's writing focused on this crux. He was only too aware of technologised vision's philosophical ambiguities and discursive tensions, as played out in the 'optical speculations' of his own fiction. Their effects often threaten to decentre radically the subjectivity and worldview of his observers and, by proxy, his readers. They frequently call into crisis what Kate Flint calls 'the binary between the visible and invisible, between the material and the imaginary'. Wells's most sustained protocinematic exploration of that crisis would be *IM*. However, his many and varied other evocations of 'this unstable borderland' implicitly undermine the reader's own epistemological position and confidence about 'what is real and what is not', as subjects of an increasingly mediated modernity.⁸⁰

Transports of Delight

Wells's writing simultaneously reflects both scientific and popular aspects of early cinema. It was filmic narrative's distinctive potential for rearranging space and time which gradually separated it from the traditional unities of merely theatrical discourse, just as its simulatory, Baudrillardian 'hyperreality'⁸¹ opened up new dimensions of vicarious experience. Early viewers reputedly rushed from the path of the Lumières' 'oncoming' locomotive, but simulated movement was soon providing virtual 'transports of delight' (as Christie puts it) which they flocked to hop aboard.⁸² This was foreshadowed in Victorian culture by perception-altering experiences of rail travel and mechanisation. Mobilised and 'framed' viewpoints through train, tram and later motor-car window compressed temporality, foreshortened distance and blurred landscapes, etc. New forms of spectatorship had already been made possible by the rapid succession of images produced by innovations in transport and communications. Dante Gabriel Rossetti visualised an 1849 rail 'Trip to Paris and Belgium' in terms that strikingly anticipate Wells's descriptions of time travel. The 'extreme speed, that the brain hurries with' caused a paradoxical deliquescence of solid space – 'The country swims with motion' – and, conversely, a materialisation of 'Time itself ... consciously beside us, and perceived.'⁸³ Effectively, what Paul Virilio calls cinema's 'static vehicle' culminated decades of magic lantern tours, dioramas, fairground rides and the generalised acceleration of life's tempo. Film's proxy sensation of movement united viewpoint and viewer in what Anne Friedberg calls a 'mobilised virtual gaze' characteristic of modernity's spectacularisation of perception and life.⁸⁴ The 'phantom ride', as it became known, began with 360 degree panoramas, then cameras mounted on vehicles themselves, for vicarious travelling effect, arguably first done by the Lumières in *Jerusalem* (1896), but already widespread by 1897 (including Peter Feather's train ride over our local Tay Bridge).

This inevitable convergence between cinema's spatio-temporal techniques and the cultural effects of Victorian transport are also suggested in the similarly defamiliarising, mobilised and 'framed' viewpoints permeating Wells's writing. Given this background, it is understandable that film pioneer R. W. Paul's 1895 'Time Machine patent' proposed creating a kind of simulator incorporating cinema technology, panorama and diorama sets[85] and a fairground ride that would literally visualise the effects of Wells's novella and give audiences the vicarious experience of a new kind of voyage through the aeons and back. Although it was never built, such hybrid projects became common. Most were cultural dead ends, film proving fittest to survive on its own in the end. However, Pawel Piasecki's hour-long, virtual trip on the Trans-Siberian Railway was one of the hits that Wells might have relished when he visited the 1900 Paris Universal Exposition on holiday,[86] recognising it as a practical realisation of Paul's plan. Raoul Grimoin-Sanson's 'Cinéorama' was another (though malfunctioning) example of the same transportive tendency. Mimicking a Vernian balloon flight, audiences stood in a basket surrounded by a polygonal screen covered by ten projectors. The Expo also featured the Lumières' rival 'Maréorama' simulating a ship's bridge.[87] Alongside these, Wells's 'sphere' in *FMITM* resembles a patent invention for similarly conveying the virtual experience of space travel. With enveloping darkness, broken only by electric shutters revealing multiple sections of a wondrous 360 degree view according to the direction of movement, the sphere mirrors the advanced possibilities of the Expo's attractions. Grimoin-Sanson's clearly may have been one of Wells's topical sources. (Another neatly Wellsian–Mélièsque offshoot of such thrills, a 'Trip to the Moon' in a winged spacecraft, became the principal switchback at the 1901 Pan-American Exposition in Buffalo.[88]) In turn, Hale's 'Tours and Scenes of the World', a global railcar simulator at the St Louis Exposition in 1903, was recognised by Terry Ramsaye as a popular 'flowering' of Paul's prototype, but it was also indicative of virtual travelling to elsewheres and elsewhens quintessentially associated with the medium itself within less than a decade.[89]

Cinema thus simulated mastering every element in submarine, aeroplane or spaceship, through moving 'cycloramas' or porthole views, in parallel with the *voyages extraordinaires* and futuristic vehicles of Jules Verne and Albert Robida, which Wells's fiction succeeded. Such developments testify to its rise as what Christie calls the 'laboratory for the twentieth century imagination', although it also drew on Victorian writers' prior experimentation in a new methodology on the page.[90]

Doors in the Wall

Nevertheless, film rapidly superseded books as *the* medium of vicarious experience, ranging through every then and there (possible or impossible), while spectators remained bodily in the empirical here and now. Again Wells anticipated or paralleled this with the pervasive entertainment screens and videos of *WTSW*'s post-literate future, as well as eidetic views and 'portals' in 'The Remarkable Case of Davidson's Eyes' (1895), 'The Crystal Egg' (1897), 'Through a Window' (1895) and especially 'The Door in the Wall' (1906).

'Authentic' recreations such as *The Last Days of Pompeii* (1908) soon had rival producers ransacking literary history to scale new heights of spectacle. This phase thus opened imaginary 'doors in the wall', into other spaces and times. The 1912 adaptation even began with a very Wellsian effect of travelling back to the Roman world, deserted archaeological ruins suddenly dissolving into a bustling forum.[91] Travel lectures with lantern slides had already raised the desire to enter edifying but also alluring elsewheres.[92] The lantern's transitions between places, states and times are alluded to in numerous tales dealing with overlapping dimensions or multi-temporality, such as 'Davidson's Eyes', 'The Plattner Story' and 'The Story of the Late Mr Elvesham' (the latter both 1896).[93] But, by 1908, writers such as Leo Tolstoy were acknowledging cinema's supremacy in instantaneous scene-shifting, infinitely more virtual than the lumbering machinery of live theatre.[94] Its portable elsewheres and elsewhens had a huge impact in communities with few alternative cultural amenities or contacts with the wider world.[95] However, there were fundamental ideological tensions in cinematic escapism. Audiences might be titillated by pagan decadence and splendour, but reassured by the inevitable triumph of Christian righteousness, just as they were consoled for deprivation by access to the imaginary freedoms of an ideal visual mobility. Like the protagonist of 'The Door in the Wall' or the hypnotic 'regressees' of 'A Story of the Days to Come', they stepped through cinema's portal into simulated elsewheres 'that soon seemed more real than their everyday lives', as Christie puts it.[96] This would have profound cultural and social consequences, as Wells foresaw. Cinema furnished smooth transitions, not just into simulated geographies but also into the 'inner space' of fantasy and dream. It inherited a wish-fulfilling tradition, but added the 'hallucinatory' mimesis of photography, for all the fantastic realism of a waking dream.

Absent Presences

The complementary illusion of transporting cinema audiences into alternative times or environments was materialising desirable or macabre 'others' in theirs. Coates calls ghosts (haunting the present by lingering from the past) 'prototypical time travellers', but cinema also seemed practically able to teleport living bodies through space.[97] Thus a new kind of industrialised celebrity was distributed through moving images, reproducing not just likenesses but virtual corporeal presences of other beings. The star system harnessed the libidinal associations of this effect. Screen charisma's manufactured appeal was dual: playing on the imaged individual as both 'real person' and mediated icon.[98] Arguably, Wells anticipated this in stories such as 'A Dream of Armageddon' (1899) and especially the global cult of Graham's moving image and recorded voice (exploited by Ostrog in *WTSW*). Materialisation of ambiguously absent-yet-present bodies is also fundamental to *IM*.

In his fiction's strange manifestations, Wells also reworked occult themes in (pseudo-)scientific terms. Visual media often feature as 'technology of the uncanny', in Alison Chapman's resonant phrase.[99] Hence Wells also reflects the paradoxical liaison between spiritualism and science in the quest for material proof of the supernatural, as pursued by the Society for Psychical Research (SPR). Founded by leading thinkers and scientists in 1882, it practised filmic and other technological methods of evidence gathering.[100] Victorian notions of spectrality overlapped with Wells's texts, as Flint notes, even when he sought 'allegorical form for abstract mathematical concepts' like four-dimensional geometry.[101] *TM*'s parlour setting, framing its fantastic revelations, resembles an SPR séance.[102] In *IM*, Mrs Hall attributes Griffin's unseen manipulations to the same cause as the 'Tables and chairs leaping and dancing!' which she has read about in newspaper reports of mediums.[103] Theories of telepathy and telekinesis were formulated interdependently with the advent of electromagnetic communications such as telegraphy, telephony, radio transmission and the first tentative experiments leading to television, as studies such as those by Jeffrey Sconce and Marina Warner amply testify.[104] Hence we often find deliberate indeterminacy between scientific or occult explanations for bizarre visual phenomena, as epitomised by 'Davidson's Eyes', 'Crystal Egg' or 'Plattner'.

The contradictory 'paranormal' impact of new science on the popular imagination stemmed from the way it materialised what was invisible to the naked eye, as in the case of Muybridge and Marey's studies, but also the SPR's theory that photography could pick up ghostly 'vibrations', waves from beyond the normal electromagnetic spectrum. This made cameras frequent props in 'techno-Gothic' stories like those by Wells. Similarly, X-rays caused a revolution in perception interconnected with the 'anatomisation' of visual reality made possible by film. Attractions based on their ability to see through flesh and clothes (combining ghostliness and voyeurism) were initially considered far more sensational and were quickly incorporated into *séances* and popular fiction.[105] Many articles about X-rays noted the role played in their discovery by the fluorescent 'Crookes tube' (invented by the SPR president). *Pearson's Magazine* (host of many Wells tales and serialisations) simultaneously featured a grisly story and scientific article on the new 'photography of the invisible' in its April 1896 issue.[106] Edison's own X-ray display blended technological exhibition and showmanship. Dr John MacIntyre first combined X-rays with film, at a demonstration of frog locomotion, before Glasgow's Philosophical Society in April 1897, with an eye to their entertaining possibilities.[107] Pioneer director G. A. Smith quickly employed the theme in his 1897 comedy, in which a professor makes a startling revelation about a pair of lovers just as the American Wallace McCutcheon made *The X-ray Mirror* in 1899.

It seemed logical to many, therefore, that film might settle once and for all the long-disputed existence of the paranormal. Given the Victorians' weird twin obsession with photography and mediums, reflected in 'The Stolen Body', 'Plattner', etc., 'it is scarcely surprising', as Christie puts it, that 'moving pictures seemed supernatural to their first viewers'.[108] Reports of the Lumières' Paris debut proclaimed death's abolition, because we could now see our loved ones again in posthumous life. With its illusion of auto-kinesis, cinema seemed a mechanical *re*-animator par excellence. As in 'The Story of the Late Mr Elvesham', 'The Temptation of Harringay' (1894), etc., film's split subjects and/or artificially animated 'others' reflected a fascination with moving pictures as a discourse in which images appeared to take on a life of their own (at one or more mediated removes from reality), or could 'snatch' likenesses from their owners.[109] The SPR termed apparitional doubles 'reflex men', hinting at the capture of likenesses by 'reflex camera'. Doubling proliferated with new media technology. Indeed, the prevalence of *Doppelgänger* themes in Wells's writing epitomises widespread anxiety about duplication by living pictures within the late-Victorian cultural climate.[110] His most explicitly media-centred exploration of doubling was Ostrog's hijacking of Graham's image and voice, which influenced German Expressionist film-maker Fritz Lang in his robotic extension of *WTSW*'s leitmotif in *Metropolis* (1926).

The Cinematic City and the Invasive Gaze

Movies and urban modernity developed in creative symbiosis. Film-makers and writers quickly saw the city as a kind of fragmented cinematic 'space', with an accelerated, staccato tempo. Wells, as his self-conscious visualisations of mechanised future cities, saturated by media and mass movement, especially in *WTSW*, shows, led the field in this respect too. His vision's dynamic scale and method could not be approximated on the screen itself until a quarter of a century later, although its connections and tensions with Lang's film have never been fully explored hitherto.

More than anything, cinema focused on the city's ambiguous appeal, both glamorising its excitements and sponsoring its mythology as modern Babylon. As in Wells's fiction, the cinematic city was also a key site of ideological struggle to represent and control the socio-economic conditions of modernity, especially its extreme inequalities and mass alienation. Film's cumulative image of the metropolis offered a visual space, as Christie puts it, to help city dwellers 'adjust to the hectic, alluring and dangerous world they inhabited'.[111] Wells's own role in the screening of a city as a battleground for determining the course of modernity would result in the controversial political impact of *Metropolis* in the 1920s and his own riposte to Lang's dystopia, *Things to Come*, a decade later.

The period was also ever more conscious of the camera's intrusive gaze into every aspect of public and private life. Significantly, one of Wells's first essays as a professional writer offered cautionary advice against falling victim to the lens's 'fixing' for posterity.[112] Voyeurism particularly characterised modern urban alienations according to sociologists such as Georg Simmel.[113] The defamiliarised human subjects of Muybridge's studies or early kinetoscope loops created a new kind of voyeuristic appeal, also reflected in the manipulated vision of 'The New Accelerator', or recorded moments of commodified erotic display in *WTSW*'s 'systematised sensuality'. Edison's peepshow temporarily miniaturised the cinematic experience in private view. Nevertheless, the suggestiveness of intimate yet anonymous access remained strongly implicit after projection 'socialised' the movie camera's gaze. However, the medium's privileged intrusion was double-edged, its thrills indivisible from anxieties about potential surveillance. Fictions such as 'Davidson's Eyes', 'Crystal Egg' and *IM* speculate about this sinister reversibility, so watcher might become watched. Most panoptically, Ostrog, 'Big Brother's' prototype, controls his futuristic urban empire through a ubiquitous network of visual and sound technologies.

Moving Image Culture

Saturation of Wells's early texts by visual technology and its effects corresponds to the 'cinematisation' of turn-of-the-century culture. The novelty of moving pictures rapidly pervaded society, weaving 'into the very fabric of daily life'.[114] The Paris Expo of 1900 featured moving pictures of various kinds in 18 displays, including the Lumières' 20m screen, sprayed by fountains for viewing both sides. (Wells probably saw it as confirming his own predictions of giant public projections in *WTSW* and 'A Story of the Days to Come'). The very first film shows were similarly prestigious – at trade fairs, before royalty – but gradually incorporated into established 'low' venues such as fairs and music halls. Cinema was initially seen as a scientific marvel, educational tool or refined entertainment. Deterioration in 'social marking' came with the question of housing regular programmes and the 'moral panic' sparked by touring peepshows.

Arcade parlours appeared to exploit the kinetoscope. London's first was at 70 Oxford Street in October 1894 (where Wells could easily have enjoyed effects anticipated by the *National Observer* serialisation of *TM*). The wave of converting buildings into nickelodeons (penny gaffs in Britain) specifically for projection commenced with the first opening in Pittsburgh, November 1905. The term itself (compounding slang and classical Greek) suggests ambivalence towards mechanised culture, both mass-production cheapness and a bid for credentials. The move upmarket (Britain's first prestige 'picture palace', the Alpha, opened in St Albans in 1908) was the result partly of censorship, but also of the industry's drive for aesthetic respectability. By 1916, there were over three thousand five hundred in Britain. Luxury cinemas usurped some of the exclusive cachet of opera and theatre, but the masses also enjoyed the temporary experience of living beyond their means, at least on screen (again as *WTSW* foreshadows).

Satisfying the huge appetite for cheap entertainment, particularly raised by the new disposable income and leisure of the urban masses, launched the industry on a course eventually determining the leisure habits of the majority of the global population. Although Britain was a very successful technical innovator and exporter in the first decade (as a result of the efforts of pioneers such as Wells's putative collaborator, R. W. Paul), by 1910 between 60 and 70 per cent of films in the West were French, giving Pathé Frères virtual control of the international market. However, the feature boom also coincided with the outbreak of the Great War. This severely curtailed European production and initiated American domination, producing the vast corporations of the post-war years[115] ('pictures by machinery' are integral to *WTSW*'s transatlanticised future economy (see Chapter 3)). US output rose from half that of the world in 1914, to virtually all of it, outside the Central Powers, by 1918. Home-grown films dwindled to less than 5 per cent of British screentime (hence the 1927 Cinematograph Films Act's Canutish attempt to stem the tide with its quota system).

Genres epitomised by the Western exported a distinctively American mythology, apparently democratic and classless, in epic landscapes of moral absolutes. They indicated how rapidly a jumped-up popular form created both its own public and set its own standards, through responsive negotiations between production and consumption. Though Germany and the Soviet Union remained major innovators (until the 1930s when respective totalitarianisms repressed such Modernism), this left Hollywood in a virtually unassailable position over world appetite for *the* mass medium of modernity. This situation also suggested how the movies, as Christie puts it, 'served notice on traditional "high" art', increasingly pressurised into justifying itself in the era of film.[116] Modern writing employed both emulation and critique of its cultural rival to rediscover its own distinctive functions and reinvent its forms in relational terms. Consequently, Wells's engagements with the earliest impact of cinema and related technologies mark him out as one of the most important precedents for both tension and synergy between literature and the new medium.

The Power of the Medium

Cinema's many genres revealed that much more was at stake on screen than new aesthetic potential. Wells already realised that it was going to be an ideological force to be reckoned with in the 1890s. This awareness runs from Ostrog's media manipulations (especially Graham's political 'resurrection' by live world broadcast) and culminated in his own late interventions in film-making itself in the 1930s. Like Ostrog, real heads of state were not slow in grasping the possibilities of film as tool of state, while suppressing its more subversive uses. Kaiser Wilhelm II appointed a personal cinematographer, Ottomar Anschütz, and sponsored footage of Germany's growing naval might. Politicians cultivated their own film personae, exemplified by President 'Teddy' Roosevelt, the most filmed of all pre-Great-War statesmen (William N. Selig's 1909 *Hunting Big Game in Africa* celebrated his safari exploits). Winston Churchill made the first of a lifetime's appearances as victorious Boer War veteran in Warwick Trading Company's *Polo Match between the London Polo Club and the Trekkers* (1901).

Early news films, or 'topicals', catered to modern public appetite for vicarious participation in real events in the most 'hyperreal' form yet available. They also mediated the world in a highly constructed way, while, paradoxically, appearing to present it in the most objective form.[117] Méliès's 1899 pro-Dreyfus '*actualités reconstituées*' of the famous spying trial resulted in one of the first acts of film censorship, showing governments waking up to the infant medium's influence over public opinion.[118] (Like an ironic time machine, Méliès's similar May 1902 film 'reporting' *Edward VII's Coronation* was released before the event, unexpectedly postponed by royal illness until August.) As news medium, film proved as subject to manipulative strategies and faking as any predecessor, although with greater seamlessness. Propagandist reporting of the Boer War (1899–1902) established a precedent for the camera as an official means for managing the impact of events. Walter Lippmann's theory of media 'fictions', representations of facts shaping collective consciousness and memory, was developed as a consequence.[119] By 1914 newsfilm's historic authority and presence were virtually ubiquitous: the Sarajevo assassination was itself partially caught by its lens and British Great War film propaganda would be instrumental in persuading America to abandon neutrality. By the inter-war period, it wasn't just mass audiences who had developed intense relationships with the cinematic imaginary, but the leaders representing or exploiting them. The Great Dictators were also great movie-goers. 'Of all the arts' in the arsenal of Soviet revolutionary persuasion, said Lenin, 'for us cinema is the most important.'[120] To impose their visions of new orders, Hitler and his rivals employed cinema programmatically, mobilising vast studios, whole nations of extras and epic narratives beyond the most megalomaniac dreams of Hollywood moguls. The simulated and censored actuality of their regimes, as Christie concludes, 'would become, vaingloriously and grimly, like being trapped in a movie'.[121] Wells anticipated much of this in *WTSW*'s prototype dictator, and his orchestration of surveillance, celebrity, spectacle and broadcast media to create a 'hyperreality' for mass manipulation.

Similarly, fiction films or 'features' never were pure entertainment and were quickly harnessed for campaigns of various kinds. Interventions by vested interests became particularly influential in shaping cinema's narrative forms. The issue of censorship and control was made more complex than ever before by a mass-entertainment medium bypassing language to communicate directly through the visual sense. Late Victorian moral panic is reflected in *WTSW*'s erotic 'videos', but its advertisements, huckstering evangelical filmshows and giant moving images of the crucifixion also anticipate the other side of the question: a modern medium need not entail use for progressive purposes. The screen was quickly enlisted in the worldwide religious revival, using an apparently materialist technology against itself in a spate of epic features, including Charles Russell's axe-grindingly anti-Darwinian *Photo-Drama of Creation* (1914), denouncing the scientific modernity that Wells and others stood for.

D. W. Griffith's multi-reel features were 'moralised' Hollywood versions of Italian super-spectacles such as Enrico Guazzoni's *Quo Vadis?* (1912), reworked through the innovative devices he refined into a trademark. The director's masterly manipulations of space and time, through a kind of 'proto-montage', made him crucial in finally separating cinematic from merely theatrical discourse.[122] But Griffith was no political moderniser. Like the medium itself, his work was a symptomatic site of transition between Victorian and twentieth-century traditions, between intellectual and popular culture, élite aesthetic standards and mass-produced cheapness. Tension between modern form and ideological reaction was epitomised by his historical epic *Birth of a Nation* (1915). Just as Wells's film-minded fictions often focused on the problems of colonialism and the construction of forms of 'otherness', the movie's acclaim as landmark in cinematic narrative was matched by controversy over racial propaganda, allegedly instrumental in reviving the Ku Klux Klan and inspiring Nazi scapegoat films. *Birth of a Nation* testified to how the medium's power had grown in a mere twenty years, but also its contradictory potentials for both enlightenment and regressive mythologising. In an ironic echo of *WTSW*, Griffith claimed that libraries of the future would replace history books with films. Like truth-telling time machines, they would allow us to 'eye-witness' past events: 'you will actually see what happened. There will be no opinions expressed. You will merely be present at the making of history.'[123] However, Griffith's epic was in no way a faithful reconstruction of 'history as it happened'. It was a state-of-the-art discourse, utilising practically every dynamic and virtual technique to achieve simultaneously melodramatic and pseudo-documentary effect.

Whereas literary texts like Wells's are doubly mediated (manipulating verbal signs which simulate the visible through 'ekphrastic' effects), films are constructed through manipulating shots of photographed reality itself. They are 'hyperreal', in Baudrillard's term, because their discourse makes fiction and actuality appear indistinguishable. Accelerated, synchronic cross-cutting in the rescue scenes, reveals Griffith, like Eisenstein (his brilliant successor at the other end of the political spectrum), as 'a master of sensational manipulation', driving home a point.[124] Precisely because it persuaded through emotional power, rather than rational argument, *Birth of a Nation* marked cinema's emergence as a primary force in the age of mass communications, the perfect medium for indoctrination. It was partly such precedents and the post-Great-War drift back towards national hatreds, remilitarisation of science and renewed global conflict which prompted Wells's re-engagement with cinema on a direct practical basis. This explains the ambitions and style of his 'film novel', *KWWAK*, and scenarios such as his 'brief history of the future', *Things to Come*. To Griffith, God guaranteed the moral 'truth' of filmic method. Later directors, such as the Surrealists, substituted validations like Freud's unconscious or, in Eisenstein's case, Marxist historical dialectics, in pushing formal techniques further. Wells's validation in his 1930s film-making would be his own brand of technocratic progressivism, with its objective of a 'World State'. This, he came to believe, would be communicated more urgently and effectively through the medium itself than the most 'film-minded' literary text. Griffith's next epic, *Intolerance* (1916), with its parallel time zones from different moments of history and Utopian message of universal brotherhood and peace (though prompted by divisive reactions to *Birth of a Nation*), thus also pointed ahead to Wells's attempt at similar interventions and structural principles after the coming of sound.

Friedberg argues that a defamiliarising 'mobilised virtual gaze' is one of the characteristic tendencies of the culture of modernity, as it had developed by the end of the nineteenth century, and that this is epitomised by cinema. Space-time movement was simulated by technological modes of visual representation: 'The *virtual gaze* is not a direct perception but a *received* perception mediated through representation ... a gaze that travels in an imaginary *flânerie* through an imaginary elsewhere and an imaginary elsewhen.' Moreover, because film developed from an apparatus combining the 'mobile' with the 'virtual', cinematic spectatorship changed 'the concept of the *present* and the *real*' in unprecedented ways.[125] Significantly, such a virtual gaze and its often radically defamiliarising effects are also defining features of Wells's early writings. Wells speculated about photography, cinema and telecommunications in ways that play on their paradoxical possibilities as instruments of 'objective' scientific vision and as new forms of imaginary. Hence, in Chapter 1, I want to begin by considering the implications of this in Wells's first scientific romance and a range of early stories, to demonstrate the sheer diversity and prescience of his 'optical speculations' at the beginning of the medium.

1
Optical Speculations in the Early Writings: *The Time Machine* and the Short Stories

Wells's early stories in particular (and this is also true of many scientific romances, though their techniques seem to have been 'tried out' in the stories) display a visual self-consciousness remarkable in its inventiveness and multiformity. Hence his 1890s fictions 'conjure' with causality, space and time in ways that would also become distinctive of the cinema.

The Time Machine

Wells's writing yokes into a striking parallelism with cinema from the outset. The year in which his first great scientific romance[1], *TM*, was published was also when the Lumière brothers invented the cinematograph, a virtual 'space and time machine' itself, in Ian Christie's phrase.[2] Wells's Time Traveller models the theory of time as the fourth dimension in terms that parallel the technological extension of the photograph's virtual stereoscopy into filmic movement:

> You know how on a flat surface, which has only two dimensions, we can represent a figure of a three-dimensional solid and similarly they think that by models of three dimensions they could represent one of four – if they could master the perspective of the thing. See?

He also uses a series of pictures of a man taken at different ages – 'All these are evidently sections, as it were. Three-Dimensional representations of his Four-Dimensioned being, which is a fixed and unalterable thing.' (*TM*, p. 5) – as if imagining the course of a life as one vast chronophotograph.[3] He conceives of intermittent subjective movement in time (mentally 'jump[ing] back' as he calls it (p. 6)) in terms similar to Henri Bergson's contemporary theory of consciousness and memory.[4] The Time Traveller's machine is, in effect, a vehicle for making such movement both possible and prolonged within 'objective' or external time.

To outside observation, the machine's invisible accelerated motion through time is 'presentation below the threshold', a kind of subliminal blurring related to the persistence of vision effect that makes the *kinematic* illusion work.[5] But it is the specific effects on the vision of the Time

Traveller himself which are most cinematic (indeed, many of them were more or less directly realised in the 1960 film, principally using stop-motion object- and graphic-animation, time-lapse camerawork, etc., and in the 2002 version by Computer-Generated Imagery (CGI) (see Chapter 5)). The *National Observer*'s serialised version of Wells's novella explicitly refers to the 'afterimage' effect explained by the persistence of vision theory in this context: 'Then the sun, through the retention of impressions by the eye, becomes a fiery band in the heavens' and 'the tint of the sky … a flickering deep blue'.[6] While voyaging, the Time Traveller, like a film-goer, is paradoxically static, invisible, sitting in the dark, watching things happening outside his own time but proximate in space.[7] He sees his housekeeper, 'Mrs Watchett' (her very name suggestive of spectacularised vision) walk across the laboratory in accelerated motion: 'I suppose it took her a minute or so to traverse the place, but to me she seemed to shoot across the laboratory like a rocket.'[8] At greater acceleration, animal locomotion becomes altogether invisible – 'The slowest snail that ever crawled dashed by too fast for me' (*TM*, pp. 18–19). As the machine's dials spin faster, the effects of temporal condensation increasingly resemble rapid cutting (though the alternation of light and darkness might also suggest the crude flickering of an early projector itself),[9] slow fade-out and double-exposure: 'The night came like the turning out of a lamp, and in another moment came tomorrow. The laboratory grew faint and hazy, then fainter and ever fainter. Tomorrow night came black then day again, night again, day again, faster and faster still' (pp. 18–19). Eventually daylight and dark become indistinguishable. Paradoxically, time is 'spatialised', while space deliquesces into temporality. The sun's motion solidifies as a brilliant arch, whereas what is ordinarily perceived as stable becomes 'misty and vague' as the normally inanimate begins to move. The description seems to suggest early time-lapse films of the growth of plants or architectural (de)construction, but rapidly extends the principle to visualising entire cityscapes and eventually ecologies on an evolutionary timeline:[10]

> I saw trees growing and changing like puffs of vapour, now brown, now green; they grew, spread, shivered, and passed away. I saw huge buildings rise up faint and fair, and pass like dreams. The whole surface of the earth seemed changed – melting and flowing under my eyes … I saw great and splendid architecture rising about me, more massive than any buildings of our own time, and yet, as it seemed, built of glimmer and mist. I saw a richer green flow up the hill-side, and remain there without any wintry intermission. (*TM*, pp. 19–20)

The lunar ecology's daily cycle in *FMITM* may also be an example of cinematically 'sped-up' visualisation, as Bedford watches it through the panes of the sphere in Chapter 8 turn from lifeless desert into aspiring jungle:

> Have you ever on a cold day taken a thermometer into your warm hand and watched the little thread of mercury creep up the tube? These moon-plants grew like that.
>
> In a few minutes, as it seemed, the buds of the more forward of these plants had lengthened into a stem, and were even putting forth a second whorl of leaves, and all the slope that had seemed so recently a lifeless stretch of litter was now dark with the stunted, olive-green herbage of bristling spikes that swayed with the vigour of their growing. (*FMITM*, p. 56)[11]

With a reckless thrill of speed anticipating Marinetti and his followers, the Time Traveller recollects, 'I flung myself into futurity' (*TM*, p. 20).[12] Similarly, the journey back involves an equivalent of 'reverse' and 'decelerating' film motion as the familiar world recomposes itself like the Lumières' miraculous wall: 'I began to recognise our own petty and familiar architecture, the thousand hands ran back to the starting-point, the night and day flapped slower and slower. Then the old walls of the laboratory came round me.' With neatly concluding symmetry, Mrs Watchett's movements 'appeared to be the exact inversion of her previous ones ... she glided quietly up the laboratory, back foremost, and disappeared behind the door by which she had previously entered' (*TM*, p. 86).[13]

Wells's text is replete with analogies suggestive of the experience of film-watching. The eerie silence confronting the Time Traveller at the end of the world (as if the dying planet had lost its soundtrack) recalls that experienced by early audiences – 'It would be hard to convey the stillness of it. All the sound of man, the bleating of sheep, the cries of birds, the hum of insects, the stir that makes the background of our lives – all that was over.' While his stunned dinner-guests are left dazzled by the afterimage of a parallel reality they can scarcely credit: 'I took my eyes off the Time Traveller's face, and looked round at his audience. They were in the dark, and little spots of colour swam before them' (*TM*, pp. 85 and 87).[14] Moreover, the Time Traveller himself is left with a sense of overlapping worlds that don't fit – literally occupying the same space, but radically mismatched in time – and wondering how to ascertain which is more actual or illusory (see *TM*, p. 88). As the 'Realist of the Fantastic', Wells's critical ambivalence about the objectivity of new optical technology arguably comes out in the teasing paradox that his 'cinematic' effects make the fantasy of time travel virtual, while at the same time the existence of that 'future present' cannot be epistemologically authenticated because his protagonist returns without photographic proof. The Time Traveller regrets having no Kodak with flash to record the Morlockian underworld from a safe distance, though packs a camera on the second trip, from which he doesn't return (see *TM*, pp. 54 and 89).[15]

Early movies also displayed a fascination with accelerated mechanical or natural processes, for both scientific study and novelty effect. Just as the Time Traveller witnesses futuristic cityscapes assemble and vanish, and whole ecologies evolve and change, scientific use of the camera and its sensational twin tradition are symbiotically conjoined in the story, as when he is attacked by a 'post-historic' monster. This seems inspired by the extreme enlargements of contemporary microphotography that would later become a standard effect in horror/SF films:

> what I had taken to be a reddish mass of rock was moving slowly towards me. Then I saw the thing was really a monstrous crab-like creature. Can you imagine a crab as large as yonder table, with its many legs moving slowly and uncertainly, its big claws swaying, its long antennae, like carters' whips, waving and feeling, and its stalked eyes gleaming at you on either side of its metallic front? Its back was corrugated and ornamented with ungainly bosses, and a greenish incrustation blotched it here and there. I could see the many palps of its complicated mouth flickering and feeling as it moved. (*TM*, p. 83)

By 1915 Lindsay thought that cinema made time infinitely plastic and variable: 'think of a lively and humoresque clock that does not tick and takes only an hour to record a day'. Allied to its mobilised viewpoint, that made it 'a noiseless electric vehicle, where you are looking out of the windows, going down the smooth boulevard of Wonderland.'[16] Hence the Lumières' invention of the 'world's first static vehicle'[17] naturally also lent itself to the simulation and vicarious experience of more literal forms of mechanised motion. Similarly, relative motion in space features early in Wells in the perspective from a passing train on an experimental flying 'cage' in 'The Argonauts of the Air' (1897): 'From the Leatherhead branch this alley was foreshortened and in part hidden by a hill with villas; but from the main line one had it in profile, a complex tangle of girders and bars' (*CSS*, pp. 116–25, especially 116). And such effects are intensified in Wells's simulations of the viewpoint from aeroplane flight itself. Similarly, his fictional pioneers of aerodynamic design, like their historical counterparts, are guided by the work of Lilienthal and Marey (they use 'a photographic study of the flight of birds'(p. 121)), another of the predecessor technologies of moving images.

As commentators agree, what makes Wells's descriptions of the visual effects of time travel truly extraordinary is that he wrote them *before* he could possibly have seen a film, at least in the cinematograph's sense of the public screening of moving images on a large scale. It's possible, as Terry Ramsaye argued in 1926, that Wells's machine is more like Edison's 'kinetoscope': its motion is controlled by a lever not unlike the kinetoscope's crank and it gives a 'private', individual view (although not a miniaturised one).[18] The kinetoscope also afforded the entertainment novelty of seeing ordinary actions temporally speeded up or reversed. However, even this peepshow predecessor wasn't exhibited in Britain until the first London Kinetoscope Parlour opened on 17 October 1894, at 70 Oxford Street,[19] i.e. after the *National Observer*'s incomplete serialisation (Mar.–June 1894), though arguably around the time of Wells's revision for the *New Review* (published Jan.–May 1895). It's also possible that Wells had read reports of such new optical marvels as Edison's kinetoscope in newspapers or scientific journals.[20] Some commentators date the public projection of motion pictures in Britain to R. W. Paul's first screening on 20 February 1896, at Finsbury Technical College, using his own patent 'Theatrograph' (later the Animatographe), the first commercially viable British film projector, neck and neck with the cinematograph's British debut at the London Polytechnic in Regent Street. However, Paul had already demonstrated his invention at the Royal Photographic Society in January. Both his films and those of the Lumières were soon given prominent billing in Leicester Square theatre programmes.[21]

The early British film-maker R. W. (Robert William) Paul's 24 October 1895 patent application for a film exhibit that would simulate a time journey from present to future and back into the past was inspired by Wells's quasi-cinematic concept and was probably developed in consultation with Wells himself.[22] As Ramsaye put it, that Paul saw the cinema as 'a scientific abstraction which might find concrete utility in the service of art is indicated by the counsel he sought'. Paul was drawn to Wells's text not just for its anticipation of visual effects, but by an instinct that they could be adapted by the camera for 'a new and perhaps especially effective method of narration'. Indeed, Ramsaye argued (somewhat hyperbolically) that 'Paul, inspired by Wells' story ... exactly anticipated the photoplay, which was not to be born yet for many a year.' Every effect that his patent sought would eventually 'be done entirely on screen.'[23]

From 1896 to 1900 perhaps the most important film-maker in Britain, Paul would develop his own camera and projector to become the first independent English exhibitor, as a result of Edison's monopolistic refusal to supply him with films.[24] He instantly spotted the potential synergy between Wells's scientific romance and cinema as, what Christie calls, a virtual 'transport of delight' in his proposal for:

> a novel form of exhibition whereby the spectators have presented to their view scenes which are supposed to occur in the future or past, while they are given the sensation of voyaging upon a machine through time ... The mechanism I employ consists of a platform, or platforms, each of which contain a suitable number of spectators ... leaving a convenient opening towards which the latter face, and which is directed towards a screen on which the views are presented.

Besides the pitch and yaw of the 'vehicle' itself (anticipating today's flight-training simulators), Paul intended alternating light and darkness to suggest passing centuries; projecting landscapes, traversed by vehicles such as hot-air balloons; 'films, representing in successive instantaneous photographs, living persons or creatures in their natural motions' (to be 'faded up' and magnified in size, as the machine gradually decelerated and stopped at any given epoch); slides 'coloured, darkened or perforated' to produce meteorological effects, etc.[25] Finally, for extra realism, the returning spectators would be convinced that they had 'overshot' backwards into the past (just as Wells's protagonist does into the remote future),[26] before their vehicle returned them safely to the present. Wells technologised the fantasy of time travel, but this was symptomatic of a convergence in late Victorian trends which also took the form of cinema. As Jonathan Bignell argues, the experience that the novella outlines 'is a subjectivity to be developed in cinema and in modern consumer culture in general, where technology transports the consumer to a virtual environment primarily experienced visually'.[27] Unlike Wells's Time Traveller, cinema audiences could not literally disembark from their seats to explore alien worlds when the machine stops. However, in Paul's project (derived from Victorian dioramas and panoramas, with added movie technology) this was intended to be the case. Paul's spectators were also to have been virtual passengers able to step out into his scenes, as if oscillating between two and three dimensions like the ambiguous stereoscopy of film itself (a topos that Wells developed in other directions in the parallel but proximate universes of many of his short stories).

In the end, Paul's technically cumbersome and costly attraction was made redundant by the mushrooming growth of the early cinema itself. (Paul produced around seventy films in 1896 for his Theatrograph,[28] shown at London's Olympia and Alhambra Music Hall). But both his patent and Wells's writing, according to Ramsaye, sought no less than 'to liberate the spectator from the instant of Now', to give them 'possession, on equal terms, of *Was* and *To Be* along with *Is*'. Nonetheless, cinematic narration, as it developed, 'was to cut away the hampering fog' of linguistic tenses, just as its ultra-mimetic visualisation seemed 'to cut back to reality through the misty attenuations of language'.[29] Film, as Christie puts it, 'quite literally made time travel a spectator sport'.[30] Wells's Time Traveller experiences the future directly, but the reader and/or film viewer experience it vicariously, mediated by written language in the novella and through the virtualism of moving images (and later sound as well) on film.[31] Paul's patent foreshadowed the virtual travel to elsewheres and elsewhens that would become quintessentially associated with the medium itself.

The cinema would also become *the* medium for creating wondrous spectacles, whereby, as Bignell puts it, the 'absent, novel, distant or unfamiliar became vividly present' as entertainment commodity.[32] As we have seen, there were multiple strands in the visually orientated late Victorian technocultural nexus that simultaneously produced both *TM* and cinema. Blossoming science (fiction), archaeology and optics shared an interest in anticipating futures, documenting pasts or arresting fleeting moments to render them visible for analysis. There were also *fin de siècle* obsessions with memory, mortality and preservation, as well as magic and the paranormal, coupled with the possibilities of exploiting new inventions for mass-cultural consumption. (Félicien Trewey, a professional magician who appeared in many early Lumière films, was also commissioned by them to arrange the cinematograph's London debut.[33]) All these strands are certainly touched on early in Wells's scientific romance (he explored them further in his short stories, as we shall see below). They all converge on the vanishing point of the Time Traveller's model machine. His guests cannot decide whether it's a novelty parlour trick, optical illusion or genuine experiment and consequently doubt the evidence of their own senses. Thus Wells's initial coup as Conrad's 'realist of the fantastic' explicitly focuses on the very boundary between virtualism and reality, just as that ambiguity would come to characterise the visual culture of modernity exemplified by cinema. Similarly, like the medium as it evolved, Wells's machine is, as Bignell puts it, 'a curious mixture of scientific experiment and fairground thrills'.[34] The Time Traveller describes his invention's motion as a kind of 'switchback' (*TM*, p. 19). (Pioneer director D. W. Griffith would use exactly the same metaphor for the interruption of temporal continuity in cinematic narrative by the past.[35]) Thus the connection between Wells and Paul is a perfect illustration of Jean-Louis Baudry's argument that cinema grew out of a cultural desire 'to construct a simulation machine capable of offering the subject perceptions which are really representations mistaken for perceptions'.[36]

Paul's own films continued to conjure with space and time in a variety of playfully Wellsian ways long after their project was buried. Paul's films exemplify the '"vernacular relativity" of speed and time' which quickly developed on screen.[37] In *The*[?] *Motorist* (1905) (his variation on the theme of Méliès's *Le Voyage à travers l'impossible*), a car defies both police and the law of gravity, achieving escape velocity for an interplanetary joyride, including a spin round Saturn's rings. In Paul's *How to Make Time Fly* (1906), the tyranny of temporal standardisation is subverted at will. Characters' motions are speeded up or slowed down by a mischievious child's interference with a clock.[38] Paul also made *An Over-incubated Baby* (1901): a scientist's experiment 'overcooks' a baby into an old man. 'Reversing' also established its own subgenre, as in G. A. Smith's *The Sandwiches* (1899) in which time runs backwards so that a restaurant can retrieve food from a non-paying customer's mouth. One of the most significant elaborations of temporal acceleration and reversing, recalling both the Lumières' *Demolition of a Wall*, and many visual effects of time travel in Wells's novella, such as speeded-up diurnal phenomena and architectural 'de/compositions', was Biograph's 1901 *Demolishing and Building Up the Star Theater*. A New York site was filmed by fixed camera a few frames per hour by Frederick S. Armitage. Although the structure disappears in less than two minutes of projected time, its shadow sweeps in regular rhythm, marking the accelerated passage of four weeks, as well as alternating between sharp outline and fuzziness, so that weather changes are also observable. Finally the whole process is quickly reversed, closely paralleling the Time Traveller's experience of familiar structures recomposing as he returns to the present. In effect a virtual indivisibility developed between such 'trickfilm' exploitation and optical techniques used for scientific research, as in studies of shell trajectories for the War Office ballistics department, which appeared to slow down or even freeze time, or the accelerated motion of 'time-lapse' for studying the processes of nature in the growth of plants, cells or crystals.

The Short Stories

Wells's speculations, about the far-reaching social, political and cultural implications of the new visual technology, proliferated and are *the* conscious imaginative drive of the interconnected realism and fantasy in many early stories. 'I have always been given to paradoxes about space and time', says the narrator of 'The New Accelerator' (1901), which inverts the conceit of Mrs Watchett's briefly glimpsed fast motion. In the *National Observer* serialisation of TM, Wells compared such accelerated motion to phenomena normally too rapid for unaided vision, emphasising the temporal relativity of the visible, which would lead to ultra-high-speed photography and film (see Introduction above). Conversely, the eponymous experimental stimulant of 'The New Accelerator' designed to help cope with the pace of modernity – 'to bring languid people up to the stresses of these pushful days' – is a kind of neuro-physiological time machine which reorganises sight in an effect exactly like cinematic slow motion, to give another privileged insight into ordinary natural or mechanical processes.[39] As its inventor boasts, 'it kicks the theory of vision into a perfectly new shape!' (*CSS*, pp. 487–97, especially 489, 487 and 491, respectively). From the drug-takers' viewpoint, 'objective' time in the surrounding world slows down virtually to a freeze-frame, while alternatively their 'subjective' time speeds up. To the normal eye they blur into invisibility too, like Marey's chronophotographic athletes, or like figures in a movie projected at vastly accelerated speed, such as pioneered by Jean Durand in *Onésime Horloger* (1910). It's interesting to compare this to René Clair's *Paris qui dort* (1923), in which mad inventor Dr Crase freezes time in the French capital with a kind of projector beam (the English translation, *The Crazy Ray*, derives from the original script title, *Le Rayon magique*). The ray allows scope for surrealist mischief and mayhem at will to those who are unaffected, which develops the possibilities for crime only sketched in by Wells.[40] The story also anticipates effects later used in such metaphysical films as Michael Powell and Emeric Pressburger's *A Matter of Life and Death* to suggest a dual time-space continuum,[41] and similar moments in Frank Capra's contemporary *It's a Wonderful Life* (both 1946) when human time halts under immortal scrutiny and intervention, or even today's state-of-the-art 'time-slicing' (also known as 'bullet time'), as in the Wachowski brothers' *The Matrix* (1999).[42]

Relative to these 'tripping' *flâneurs*, the duration of mundane phenomena elongates bizarrely: unlike *TM*'s rocketing snail, a bee hangs motionless. (The story even describes a kind of proto-soundtrack distortion 'synchronised' with its visual effects, which recalls experiments with the phonograph:[43] a band's playing becomes 'a low-pitched rattle, a sort of prolonged last sigh that passed at times into a sound like the slow muffled ticking of some monstrous clock'.) Thus experience becomes literally 'spectacularised' by a paradoxical distance in bodily time while maintaining spatial proximity, again very like the perception of a film audience. As the narrator puts it, 'the whole world had stopped for our convenient inspection' (*CSS*, pp. 493 and 496). Motion and gesture become defamiliarised, as in Muybridge's 'animal locomotion studies', Gargantuanly grotesque, as in screen-filling close-ups like G. A. Smith's 1901 films, or 'candid moments':

> Frozen people stood erect; strange, silent, self-conscious-looking dummies hung unstably in mid-stride, promenading upon the grass. I passed close to a poodle dog suspended in the act of leaping, and watched the slow movement of his legs as he sank to earth. "Lord, look *here*!" cried Gibberne, and we halted for a moment before a magnificent person in white faint-striped flannels, white shoes, and a Panama hat, who turned back to wink at two gaily dressed ladies he had passed. A wink studied with such leisurely deliberation as we could afford, is an unattractive thing. It loses any quality of alert gaiety, and one remarks that the winking eye does not completely close, that under its drooping lid appears the lower edge of an eyeball and a line of white. "Heaven give me memory," said I, "and I will never wink again."
>
> "Or smile," said Gibberne, with his eye on the ladies' answering teeth. (*CSS*, pp. 493–94)

Far from enhancing their sense of reality sympathetically, this alienated viewpoint actually leads to a kind of disgusted detachment, bestowing 'an exultant sense of superior advantage' (*CSS*, p. 494) and tempting Wells's unseen, temporarily 'superhuman' protagonists to cruel interventions as in *IM* (1897). Bailey notes, in many of Wells's early stories displacement in space, as well as time, results in a comparable Invisible Man/cinema-audience effect, as in 'The Crystal Egg' or 'The Plattner Story'[44] (discussed below). Such a perspective was frequently deployed by Wells as a distancing device, but he evidently also regarded film's privileged virtual gaze as ethically ambiguous, even potentially abusive, as the political use of the medium to distort or dehumanise 'others' in twentieth-century propaganda would confirm only too well.

When the Accelerator's effect passes off, the trippers abruptly reappear and the world simultaneously restarts, like a film working again at normal speed:

> The whole stagnation seemed to wake up as I did so, the disarticulated vibration of the band rushed together into a blast of music, the promenaders put their feet down and walked their ways, the papers and flags began flapping, smiles passed into words, the winker finished his wink and went on his way complacently, and all the seated people moved and spoke. (*CSS*, p. 495)

Wells's 1906 fable 'The Door in the Wall' presents a magic portal into another world which furnishes a metaphor for how cinema, in little over a decade, had become a kind of virtual mass-exit into other times and spaces, just as the door reappears in different locations. The politician Wallace first encounters it in a poor district, like the 'penny gaffs' where early films were often shown in the 1890s, then in more upmarket locales, like the picture palaces that were beginning to replace them as cinema bid for middle-class respectability. In particular, the story suggests the photographic medium's powerful virtuality, its status between ultra-naturalistic mimesis and hallucination – 'that undescribable quality of translucent unreality' (*CSS*, pp. 571–84, especially 576).[45] It is left ambiguous whether stepping through this portal enables Wallace to cope with the strain of public affairs, or regresses him into masculine fantasies of women embodying impossibly glamorous or maternal ideals. The screen's 'door in the wall', from what 'The New Accelerator' called the 'stresses of these pushful days', provided temporary wish-fulfilment but sometimes rendered audiences less content with their everyday lives in the long term. Like an early film fan, the disappointed protagonist becomes addicted to a virtual experience of beauty and happiness 'full of the quality and promise of heart's desire', but which then 'made all the interests and spectacle of worldly life seem dull and tedious and vain' (*CSS*, pp. 575 and 572, respectively).[46] Implicitly Wells raises a leading question about modernity:

whether cultural developments such as the movies were beneficial accessories for living more satisfyingly, or compensatory mechanisms for its erosion of authentic experience and selfhood.[47] Wells's protagonist suffers addictive nostalgia for an Edenic place where he may never really have been – 'Heaven knows where West Kensington had suddenly got to. And somehow it was like coming home' – but which nonetheless fills his present with *ennui* and lack. Indeed the story could be read as a prescient allegory of the highly subjective and dubiously 'interpellating' ideological investments that twentieth-century culture would make in cinema (see discussion of the British Film Institute (BFI) adaptation Chapter 5). As a boy, the protagonist was shown a 'living' book in whose pages he believed – 'I saw myself', because it appeared to contain 'not pictures … but realities' (*CSS*, pp. 574–75)[48] – only to be brutally ejected back to mundane existence through another of its frames.

'The Remarkable Case of Davidson's Eyes' (published the same year as *TM*) had already explored the possibility of being perceptually in two places at once and the alienation of splitting between them, 'at home' in neither. The story arguably extends the kinetoscope's private view into 'visual immersion', while preserving sound–vision dislocation. Its speculations about 'seeing and being seen' also predict not just the coming of television transmission in little over thirty years,[49] but, even more far-sightedly, technology's potential to substitute empirical experience with 'holographic' virtual reality, or to dissolve boundaries between public and private space by panoptic systems of surveillance: 'It sets one dreaming of the oddest possibilities of intercommunication in the future, of spending an intercalary five minutes on the other side of the world, or being watched in our most secret operations by unsuspected eyes' (*CSS*, pp. 63–70, especially 70). Through an electromagnetic accident, Davidson loses sight of immediate phenomena, but begins instead to witness events unfolding simultaneously on 'Antipodes Island'. In effect, this resembles the conceit of *IM*, except that the normal physical environment, not the subject, disappears: Davidson passes through solid objects in the 'other' reality (they, in the animate form of penguins, mutually pass through him), but is totally disorientated in this one.[50] Thus the result is visual displacement to 'elsewhere' like cinema, though simultaneously transmitted, like live television, or even today's 'webcams'. In a kind of negativisation, it is day here when night there and vice versa. As Davidson recovers, these (literally) polarised visual fields gradually overlap like double exposure, or 'the changing views of a [magic] lantern', until he learns 'to distinguish the real from the illusory' and elsewhere finally fades out (*CSS*, p. 69). The virtual reality of Davidson's tele-vision[51] is authenticated by the ship's log of the *Fulmar*, which he saw exploring the island. You don't have to accept the fictional explanation (a paradoxical 'kink' in space, induced in Davidson's optic nerves, resulting in a Möbius-strip-like curvature, as explained by the college dean) to appreciate how technology would fulfil the story's prophecy about what the Futurist Marinetti characterised as modernity's 'multiple and simultaneous awareness',[52] enabling one 'to live visually in one part of the world, while one lives bodily in another' (*CSS* p. 70).

In a parallel story, 'The Crystal Egg' (1897),[53] Wells widened this idea to extraterrestrial dimensions: a dusty curio is discovered to be an optical transmitter sent by Martians to monitor human affairs, but through which their alien world is also reciprocally visible (Martian astronomers observe Earth in 'The Star' too (also 1897) (see *CSS*, pp. 281–89, especially 289)). On refracting light from a particular angle, the egg becomes a lens on to 'a wide and peculiar countryside ... It was a moving picture: that is to say, certain objects moved in it, but slowly in an orderly manner like real things, and according as the direction of the lighting and vision changed, the picture changed also' (*CSS*, p. 273). The story contains a naive spectatorial reaction to the sheer 'in-your-face' closeness of stereoscopic simulation, which resembles Wells's putative collaborator R. W. Paul's parody of early film-going, in which country bumpkins peer behind screens in disbelief that approaching trains are not really there:[54]

> And suddenly something flapped repeatedly across the vision, like the fluttering of a jewelled fan or the beating of a wing, and a face, or rather the upper part of a face with very large eyes, came as it were close to his own and as if on the other side of the crystal. Mr Cave was so startled and impressed by the absolute reality of those eyes, that he drew his head back from the crystal to look behind it.[55]

Like an interrupted transmission, the image then 'faded and went out' (*CSS*, pp. 267–80, especially 274). The viewer's name, Cave, recalls Plato's classical allegory about the imprisoning seductions of consolatory illusion, Wells reshaping it for the dawn of the age of telecommunications.[56] In contrast to Cave's cramped, failing shop and dysfunctional domestic life (which resembles the dark kitchens in which Wells's mother slaved away during his childhood), the spacious panoramas of a futuristic and ordered alien civilisation become 'the most real thing in his existence' (*CSS*, p. 278), even though their actuality remains unverified.

One particular branch of Victorian spiritualism was 'crystal-gazing'. A 'rationalist' (i.e. psycho-physiological) explanation for crystal visions was advanced by Edmund Parish in the same year as Wells's story. Parish concluded that they reflected 'what is latent in the percipient's *subliminal* consciousness'.[57] Though ostensibly about extraterrestrial technology, 'The Crystal Egg', as Flint points out, has much in common with Parish's theory, especially its ambiguous status as hallucination.[58] Roland Barthes would view the illusionism of photographs (though generated by material processes developed by science) as a 'modest', 'shared' hallucination,[59] which is conceivably the case with the authentication of the egg's fantastic powers by the assistant demonstrator at a local London hospital.

Conversely, throughout the story there is a similar tension reflecting primitive cinema's dualistic status as disposable gimcrack novelty or revolution in culture and perception. This reworks the Biblical 'pearl of great price', whose unrecognised value might be cast away before swine. After Cave dies, his widow sells his stock indiscriminately, so that, the narrator speculates, 'the crystal egg, for all I know, may at the present moment be ... decorating a drawing-room or serving as a paper-weight – its remarkable functions all unknown' (*CSS*, p. 642).

'A Story of the Days to Come' (1899), a twenty-second-century urban Dystopia similar to *WTSW* (published the same year, and likewise warning against a laissez-faire capitalist version of modernity) is perhaps the early story most saturated with new visual media, in terms of both subject matter and techniques. The narrator says, 'the nineteenth century was the dawn of a new epoch in the history of mankind – the epoch of the great cities, the end of the old order of country life' (*CSS*, pp. 333–98, especially 46). Wells's futurist, Megalopolitan London is a hyper-commodified, publicity-driven corporate state, dominated by colossal moving colour images and broadcast sound recordings. (By 1899, film was already being used to sell anything from soap to dairy products, holidays and the British Navy.) As in *WTSW*, social hierarchy is spatialised in the multi-levelled architecture of the city itself, providing the dynamic visual template for Fritz Lang's *Metropolis* (1926) (see Chapter 3).

Wells associates induced visualisation with oppression and narcosis, rather than cultural stimulation, in this story's post-literate society. Hypnotism (a form of controlled hallucination later used as a leading metaphor for cinema itself in German Expressionism, as in Lang's films) constitutes a kind of virtual time travel, supplying 'artificial dreams'. This allows people apparently to live elsewhere in any historical period they choose. Such vicarious experience of then and there, while remaining bodily subjected to the here and now, parallels contemporary cinematic fantasies of exotic pasts. The hypnotist enthuses idealistically: 'Think of all it opens out to us – the enrichment of our experience, the recovery of adventure, the refuge it offers from this sordid, competitive life in which we live!' But, ironically, this temporary escapism makes long-term entrapment easier. The hypnotist is actually employed by the heroine's father to induce her to forget her underachieving lover. Deceived by this 'novel entertainment', she voluntarily steps through a portal 'into that land of dreams where there is neither any freedom of choice nor will' (*CSS*, pp. 333–98, especially 341).[60] Conversely, the ill-starred young couple yearn for the lost 'authenticity' of a non-urbanised, non-mediated past in a way that anticipates E. M. Forster's 'The Machine Stops' (1909). Such early texts refute the widespread misconception that Wells suffered from a naive enthusiasm for communications technology that blinded him to its dehumanising potential for severing contact with concrete experience and direct human interaction, an alleged flaw that Forster's satire is seen as targeting (see, for example, *CSS,* p. 349).

'A Story of the Days to Come' speculated in particular about the possible marketing applications of moving images, through their infinite duplicability and dimensional elasticity:

> Nineteenth Way was still sometimes called Regent Street, but it was now a street of moving platforms and nearly eight hundred feet wide ... The establishment of the Suzannah Hat Syndicate projected a vast *façade* upon the outer way, sending out overhead at either end an overlapping series of huge white glass screens, on which gigantic animated pictures of the faces of well-known beautiful living women wearing novelties in hats were thrown. A dense crowd was always collected in the stationary central way watching a vast kinematograph which displayed the changing fashion. The whole front of the building was in a perpetual chromatic change. (*CSS,* p. 364)

And visual technology is just as integral in the sales booths, equipped with miniature screens which subtly reshape the body for fitting the latest look virtually. Optical distortion marketing an unattainable consumer ideal of physical perfection is a key drive of this society: 'The moving platform was rushing by the establishment of a face moulder, and its lower front was a huge display of mirror, designed to stimulate the thirst for more symmetrical features.' As they pass this cosmetic surgery clinic, Denton and his companion are, conversely, reflected as living caricatures (like the use of anamorphic mirrors in Expressionist film),[61] visible embodiments of the self-image of the poor and unsuccessful in this chilling future, where human values are measured solely by conspicuous consumption (*CSS,* p. 380).

Not only do images colonise and congest public space, but advertising slogans are even projected all over the urban crowd itself, literally textualising and incorporating them into the spectacle of commodification:

> inscriptions of all sizes were thrown from the roof above upon the moving platforms themselves, and on one's hand or on the bald head of the man before one, or on a lady's shoulders, or in a sudden jet of flame before one's feet, the moving finger wrote in unanticipated letters of fire. (*CSS,* p. 364)

Furthermore, Wells created the whirling spiral motif that would symbolise the publicity-saturated metropolis's alienating dynamic in many key Modernist 'Big City' films of the 1920s and 1930s, such as Walther Ruttmann's

Berlin: Sinfonie einer Großstadt (1927) and Fritz Lang's *M* (1931).[62] With circular irony, a *Tono-Bungay*-like quack medicine markets a cure for the vertiginous process of which it is itself a visual symptom:

> On the *façade* to the right a huge intensely bright disc of weird colour span incessantly, and letters of fire that came and went spelt out –
> "DOES THIS MAKE YOU GIDDY?"
> Then a pause, followed by
> "TAKE A PURKINJE'S DIGESTIVE PILL." (*CSS*, p. 367)

When the couple become destitute and, therefore, serfs of the Labour Company, Denton works at a kind of photographic press, whose mysterious role in the city's culture of simulation and sacrifice of human value to worship of the commodity clearly anticipates the machine idolatry of *Metropolis* (see Chapter 3):

> it was a huge, dim, glittering thing with a projecting hood that had a remote resemblance to a bowed head, and squatting like some metal Buddha in this weird light that ministered to its needs, it seemed to Denton in certain moods almost as if this must needs be the obscure idol to which humanity in some strange aberration had offered up his life. (*CSS*, p. 370)

A related story, 'A Dream of Armageddon' (written in 1899) *CSS*, is not just Wells's *serial* vision of technological apocalypse (watched in nightly episodes, as it were) and an 'If I ruled the world ... ' fantasy, but is also like cinema experienced by the dreamer, Hedon,[63] as so vivid that it renders his ordinary waking world unreal by comparison. Significantly, the verisimilitude is not just down to the dream's capacity to visualise exotic topographies such as Capri, fantastic flying machines and futuristic aerial warfare, but, as in film, its microscopic inclusiveness and indiscriminate specificity as well:

> The vision was so real ... that I kept perpetually recalling trivial irrelevant details; even the ornament of a book-cover that lay on my wife's sewing-machine in the breakfast room recalled with the utmost vividness the gilt line that ran about the seat in the alcove where I had talked with the messenger from my deserted party. Have you ever heard of a dream that had a quality like that? (*CSS*, pp. 547–67, especially 555)

The story is also cinematic for other significant reasons. The unprecented glamour of Hedon's dream lover is 'a sort of radiation' (p. 550), like an anticipation of the charisma built up around the faces of the first generation of stars, such as Mary Pickford, 'the world's sweetheart'. 'To be on film', as Christie puts it, was to be 'desirable and famous in a new way',[64] because of its mass-produced visualisation of the object of desire and the potentially global reach of its market.

Elizabeth Phelps's influential spiritualist text, *The Gates Ajar* (1868), proposed that the temporality of the supernatural world ran parallel to our own, making the absence of the dead a form of simultaneous presence. Bernard Bergonzi notes the 1890s vogue for stories blending occult themes with scientific elements, such as those by Arthur Machen, M. P. Shiel and Vincent O'Sullivan, frequently with bizarre visual implications.[65] For Wells, far from being a rationalist medium, film seems to have been pre-eminently an ambiguous 'technology of the uncanny', which features in numerous ways in his occult narratives too.[66] For example, 'The Plattner Story' (1896) reworks Wells's pervasive topos of spatio-temporal dislocation with yet another optical slant that foregrounds the issue of spectatorship. Plattner abruptly disappears in a flash, like a figure in an early trickfilm, only to rematerialise several days later, in left–right bodily reverse, like a cheap photograph. While in the 'Fourth Dimension', Plattner finds our material world still visible, but ironically now only like a hazy phantasmagoria or double exposure. This parallel universe (chromatically limited to green tinged with red, like a tinted negative) is inhabited by spectral 'Watchers of the Living', passively gawping at, but highly envious of, the human dramas they ceaselessly consume. These 'helpless disembodiments' are themselves little more than heads, with vision but no other sensory contact,[67] like a satire of a wish-fulfilling audience, who desire vicariously through fantasy figures on film (*CSS*, pp. 101–15, especially 112). Appropriately, Plattner encounters a transparent, screen-like membrane preventing contact with the reality from which he is sealed out: 'Whenever he made a motion to communicate with the dim, familiar world about him, he found an invisible, incomprehensible barrier preventing intercourse' (*CSS*, p. 109). The Watchers' phosphorescent world seems virtually two-dimensional (the protagonist's name derives from the German for 'flat'),[68] and ours seems startlingly stereoscopic by contrast, again playing on the dimensional illusionism experienced by cinema audiences. Significantly, their universe only becomes peripherally visible in ours by 'sitting for a long space in a photographer's darkroom at night' (*CSS*, p. 110). Thus Wells alludes (as frequently elsewhere) to 'spirit photography', which catered to the widespread nineteenth-century belief that the mechanical *medium* was also an occult one that could record paranormal presences, invisible to unaided perception, as in William Stead's 1891 discussion of 'The Astral Camera'.[69] (This belief was passed on to film, as parodied in Méliès's *A Spiritualist Photographer* (1903), who 'materialises' a moving woman in a huge photo frame.) Conversely, our universe is visualised from the Watchers' perspective as a kind of projection effect: a dying man's chamber 'came out quite brightly at first, a vivid oblong of room, lying like a magic lantern picture upon the black landscape and livid green dawn'. The deathly 'beam of darkness' which gropes into it is like a forerunner, in negative, of the Martian heat ray (*CSS*, pp. 342 and 344).

There is a distinctive shift in Wells's notion of spectrality in line with the visual signifiers of this new technology of the uncanny. In 'The Red Room', published a year before *IM*, the narrator says, significantly, '"I can assure you ... that it will take a very tangible ghost to frighten me."' (*CSS*, pp. 190–97, especially 190), perhaps hinting at the paradoxical way in which absent presences could be figured so 'substantially' in film at second-hand through the impressions they make on other, visible objects (see discussion in Chapter 2). Conversely, in 'The Inexperienced Ghost' (1902), Wells's gormless spook is semi-transparent just like a superimposition, through which you can see its surroundings, perhaps recalling G. A. Smith's 1897 *Photographing a Ghost*, which quickly applied the Hove pioneer's patent double-exposure process to a supernatural theme (*CSS*, pp. 467–76, especially 470).[70]

'The Story of the Late Mr Elvesham' (1896) is another tale of displaced subjectivity like 'Plattner', but uses quasi-filmic tropes to visualise the process of bodysnatching.[71] Appropriately, Elvesham's young victim, Eden, initially experiences inversions of focus and scale: seeing 'as though ... in a concave mirror' is succeeded by 'an absurd feeling of minute distinctness, as though ... through an inverted opera-glass.' (*CSS*, pp. 126–38, especially 130).[72] He then describes his drugged sensation of being 'in two places at once', or somehow split between them, as a bizarre series of visual distortions. He even thinks about reporting his experiences to the SPR as evidence of 'clairvoyance' (*CSS*, p. 132). Regent Street Polytechnic seems a hallucinatory portal to elsewhere, which he imagines entering 'as one steps into a train'; thus Wells alludes to its reputation for exhibiting the latest optical gadgets and transportive illusions.[73] Alien memories and feelings usurp Eden's consciousness through 'phantasmal' impressions imposing themselves over familiar streets, like a lantern's 'dissolving views' in which one 'would begin like a faint ghost, and grow and oust another' (*CSS*, p. 131). The exchange of identities (anticipating the Robot-into-Maria switch in Fritz Lang's *Metropolis* (1926))[74] is like a kind of cross-cutting between two physically separate objects gradually merging until one superimposes the other: 'It was as if the picture of my present sensations was painted over some other picture that was trying to show through' (*CSS*, p. 132).[75] The story's paradoxical doubling effects are both characteristic of watching the proximate elsewheres of film and would be easily visualised as an effect on screen itself by a variety of techniques, especially in German Expressionist cinema. As Eden is finally evicted from his own body, Wells switches from a subjective to an external 'shot', just as film-makers would gradually discover the camera's capacity to shift between visual equivalents of first- and third-person narrative grammar: 'In [Elvesham's] place, I had a curious exterior vision of myself sitting at a table flushed, bright-eyed, and talkative' (*CSS*, p. 132). Again the concluding effect, of waking to see a hideous old man's face in the mirror rather than his own, is a highly cinematic shock achieved by similarly switching between subjective and externalised perspectives (*CSS*, p. 135).

In the story's speculations about 'man's detachability from matter' (*CSS*, p. 138), it also seems likely that Wells plays on the eerie 'absent-presence' effect of human subjects 'cloned' on screen often experienced by early film-goers (especially in the self-alienation felt by actors watching their own filmed doubles). Elvesham's hijacking of bodies, to create a 'serial' form of eternal youth for himself, resembles the appropriation of likenesses by recordings of roles, which can then be infinitely reanimated, though the mortal self decays. This is Wells's reworking of the posthumously articulate body in Poe's fantasy 'The Facts in the Case of M. Valdemar' (1845) (substituting the uncanny qualities of visual technology for mesmerism), or the corporeal/representational inversion of Wilde's *Picture of Dorian Gray* (1890).

'The Stolen Body' (1898) collides contemporary spiritualist belief in 'emanation' with new visual technology, in another Wellsian variation on the *Doppelgänger* theme. It is arguably another fantasy of animated imaging, where a material likeness takes on a life of its own detached from the living self (as visualised in G. A. Smith's 1898 film, *The Mesmerist or Body and Soul*, which 'projects' a little girl's living soul from her body, then puts it back). Also, like 'Davidson's Eyes', it anticipates televisual transmission. Mr Bessel tests 'the alleged possibility of projecting an apparition of oneself by force of will through space',[76] though Bessel's partner is too astonished by his success to snap a photograph as hard evidence (*CSS*, pp. 512–24, especially 512).[77]

The experiment goes hideously wrong, because Bessel's temporarily vacated flesh is instantly hijacked by another watching consciousness desperately craving physical embodiment, leaving his stranded in another dimension. It is as if Wells comments on how film allows us to 'put on' others' skins, to experience their lives vicariously by identifying with a screen character's viewpoint, though this may be achieved in an egotistically wish-fulfilling or sensationalist way rather than expanding our empathies. Like the protagonist of 'Under the Knife', Bessel also observes his own body and the life of London from a panoptic, aerial perspective of total mobility. Even the most intimate, private space is rendered transparent, as though by X-rays: 'It was like watching the affairs of a great glass hive' (*CSS*, p. 519).[78] Bessel now finds himself only one among a mass of disembodied spectators like the Watchers of the Living in 'The Plattner

Story', part of a shadowy audience gazing enviously at corporeal reality through an impassable, but invisible screen.

In an eerie inversion of the characteristics of early cinema and the phenomenal world on which it is parasitic, Bessel watches reality from this shadow dimension as if *out of* a silent film: 'A thing that impressed him instantly, and which weighed upon him throughout all this experience, was the stillness of this place – he was in a world without sound.'[79] Like film too it is a proximate universe, apparently co-extensive with our own, but lacking real depth or palpability, though, paradoxically, defamiliarising ours and rendering it more visible than ever before: 'a world undreamt of, yet lying so close ... and so strangely situated ... that all things on this earth are clearly visible both from without and from within' (*CSS*, p. 519). In contrast, our pineal gland, the 'third eye' of occult tradition, is the only means by which the presences of this 'shadow of our world' become discernible, when it glows red like a darkroom light (*CSS*, pp. 522–23). Moreover, its population is figured by a montage-like effect of detached faces swarming in a vaporous element. And, as if to confirm the analogy with cinema as a medium of wish-fulfilment and unconscious identifications, these entities seem to represent our own repressed potential for violent lusts and irrational impulses which cannot normally gain access to incarnation or action: 'children of vain desire, beings forbidden and unborn' (p. 520). Indeed, Bessel's situation, as he watches his body on its Hyde-like rampage, is like a kind of nightmare of being lost amid a vast cinema audience, driven hysterical by hero-worship and vicarious thrills: 'And ever an envious applauding multitude poured after their successful fellow as he went upon his glorious career' (p. 522). The demonic *Doppelgänger*, or alter ego (partly under such Wellsian influence), became a frequent subject of early film, especially in German Expressionist cinema, as in Stellan Rye's *Der Student von Prag*, Wegener's Golem films, or F. W. Murnau's *Der Januskopf* (1920), a version of Stevenson's *Dr Jekyll and Mr Hyde*.

Wells investigated other aspects of audience passivity and voyeurism in several early stories. He combined them in 'Under the Knife' (1896), in which anaesthesia induces another kind of 'outer bodily experience', so that the astrally projected subject's vision ranges freely through space, dilating from operating theatre to a cosmic perspective that might have served as a model for similar hallucinations in Expressionist films such as *Narkose* (1929), or the otherworldly scenes of *A Matter of Life and Death* (1946). Also like Powell and Pressburger's film, Wells's story ends with eschatological images 'cross-fading' into mere domestic objects by 'visual matching': a vast hand, wearing a ring and carrying a black rod, accompanied by a tolling bell, turns into the dial of a ticking clock, seen above the bed-rail as the patient comes round (*CSS*, pp. 159–69, especially 169).[80]

At the opposite spatial extremity, in 'Through a Window' (1895) Wells created a rigidly 'framed' narrative about passive spectating that could have furnished the prototype scenario for Alfred Hitchcock's *Rear Window* (1954).[81] The first published version, 'At a Window', is a kind of interior monologue in the first-person narrative present, which has the immediacy of an observing eye fascinated by a spectacle on a screen: 'Here am I, tied to the legs of this couch, and this chequered area of glass is the superficies of the world to me. A world framed and glazed, in which I seem to have little part as if it were a mere painted thing with figures cunningly contrived to move.' This August 1894 version compares what is seen to the cinema's predecessor technology, but also reverses the chromatic relationship between the pictured and the actual: 'Within, in this real world of mine, things are very grey and dull-looking ... Do you wonder I prefer this sunlit phantasmagoria on the other side of the glass?'[82] In 'Through a Window', Wells's protagonist watches the busy world as if merely imaged by a projector beam in a darkened cinema: his 'view outside was flooded with light' (*CSS*, pp. 30–66, especially 30). However, Bailey's viewpoint is exactly like that of a fixed camera, vicariously forcing the reader to experience the story's events in the same way as static observers 'of a moving picture', as Hammond describes it.[83] Although Bailey, immobilised by a broken leg,[84] is a reporter, not a photographer like Hitchcock's hero-voyeur, the story ingeniously makes a narrative virtue by default out of its restricted focalisation in a strikingly similar way to the director's deliberate inversion of the camera's normally mobilised virtual gaze (pioneering variations in distance, angle and focus enabled film to break out of the straitjacket of fixed viewpoint within its first decade).[85] With idle detachment, Wells's protagonist observes a kind of framed cross-section of events on the river outside. As Hammond notes, the initial description of the scene creates the effect of a framed still into which movement suddenly intrudes, throwing the whole into stereoscopic relief: 'Abruptly on the opposite bank a man walked into the picture' (*CSS*, p. 32). Throughout, what Bailey sees is referred to as a 'show' and the impression he gets of the segments of others' life stories, passing briefly into view, appears random, like raw actuality footage without explicatory diegesis. As he says of one man, 'So far as I am concerned, he has lived and had his little troubles ... merely to make an ass of himself for three minutes in front of my window' (*CSS*, p. 32). Paradoxically, the inconclusiveness of these segments of visual experience (an effect which Ford Madox Ford considered characteristic of 'the modern spirit')[86] is more frustratingly suspenseful than Dickens's unfinished mystery fiction – 'Worse than Edwin Drood' (*CSS*, p. 34). Also like *Rear Window,* Wells's text even features a nurse popping in intermittently to share the protagonist's curiosity, as well as a dysfunctional married couple who turn violent. Though their story cuts off tantalisingly (rather than developing into the central murder plot), there is a further crucial resemblance to Hitchcock in that Bailey finally becomes endangered by a killer, who abruptly transgresses his frame of spectatorial impunity by climbing into the room. Wells's visualisation of the intruder's entrance (preceded by 'off-screen' sound effects) resembles the kind of startling, synecdochic close-ups soon experimented with by early innovators, such as G. A. Smith in *As Seen by Telescope* and *Grandma's Reading Glasses* (both 1900), or Edwin S. Porter's enormous revolver firing point-blank 'into the audience' in *The Great Train Robbery* (1903):[87] 'In another moment a hairy brown hand had appeared and clutched the balcony railings, and in another the face of the Malay was peering through these at the man on the couch' (*CSS*, p. 35). Then, in contrast to the narrative's claustrophobic viewpoint, tension is temporally dilated by another subjective 'slow motion' effect not unlike 'The New Accelerator':

> It was Bailey's impression that the Malay took about an hour to get his second leg over the rail. The period that elapsed before the sitting position was changed to a standing one seemed enormous – days, weeks, possibly a year or so. Yet Bailey had no clear impression of anything going on in his mind during that vast period, except a vague wonder at his inability to throw the second medicine bottle. (*CSS*, p. 35)

In its experimental visualisation, 'Through a Window' epitomises what Dennis Potter recognised as Wells's optically self-conscious tendency to put not just the picture in the frame, but the *frame* itself into the picture (see Introduction).

Another 1890s story (which would eventually be realised on film in Wells's own 1937 script for Alexander Korda (see Chapter 4)) was 'The Man Who Could Work Miracles' (1898). The verb in the title itself suggests operation of the marvellous by artifice and the status of film narrative as a parallel reality, but with its own separate physical laws. Hence, full of 'interference with normal causation' (*CSS*, pp. 399–412, especially 305), this comic text was a gift for stop-motion special effects which 'edit out' manipulation by human agency, as in *IM*, especially for object animation which was a staple of primitive trickfilms but highly sophisticated by 1937 (both are also satires of the overreaching 'little man' dictator, a theme that would also be pervasive in film fantasy in the thirties (see Chapters 2 and 4)). For example, the first of Fotheringay's miracles inverts an oil lamp telekinetically. Later he metamorphoses a walking stick into a rose bush, tripping the village constable. In the ensuing altercation Fotheringay 'blasts' the policeman through space to Hades, hastily revised to San Francisco. Fotheringay's ambitions grow, egged on by the local preacher's Utopian ambitions (the reader is cinematically forewarned about rising megalomania by the latter's firelit legs throwing 'a Rhodian arch of shadow on the opposite wall' (*CSS*, p. 404)).⁸⁸ Fotheringay consequently overreaches himself by stopping the Earth's rotation in a bid to freeze-frame time, so that they can carry out their plans for world reform. The result is instant global devastation described in terms also closely realised by the film (see, for example, pp. 409–10). The closing temporal reversal undoes the chaos (again like a film run backwards), but also replays the opening in the pub. In Korda's version, Fotheringay's attempt to conjure with the lamp now fails, because he has wished away his powers. However, Wells's short story leaves the ending open, creating a *mise en abyme* suggestion that the narrative might endlessly replay itself, just like a film-loop (see *CSS*, pp. 411–12).⁸⁹

Significantly, Wells's Time Traveller has also been a conjuror of sorts. The Medical Man suspects that he is using a magic lantern for phantasmagoric effects, after his demonstration model vanishes into futurity: 'Are you perfectly serious? Or is this a trick – like that ghost you showed us last Christmas?' (*TM*, p. 11).⁹⁰ 'The Magic Shop' (1903) was Wells's playfully Mélièsque tour de force of stop-motion illusionism and 'trickfilm' effects – dis/appearances, metamorphoses, doors into other places, expanding and contracting dimensions, fairy creatures, animated objects, etc.⁹¹ Film was the modern medium in which the conjuror's art became consummately invisible and it was no wonder that magic shops became frequent subjects of early British stop-motion animation.⁹² Nevertheless, as Wells acknowledged, it rendered the most fantastic impossibilities paradoxically 'hyperreal'. As the assistant says with teasing ambiguity, handing over the shop's business-card, '"Genuine" ... with his finger on the word ... "There is absolutely no deception, sir"' (*CSS*, pp. 429–37, especially 431).⁹³

For Wells, cinematically enhanced vision did not necessarily provide cast-iron epistemological guarantees that phenomena truly exist, nor that space and time are constants. As the narrator says about this *boutique fantasque*, 'There was something vaguely rum about the fixtures even, about the ceiling, about the floor, about the casually distributed chairs. I had a queer feeling that whenever I wasn't looking at them straight they went askew, and moved about, and played a noiseless puss-in-the-corner behind my back' (p. 435). Indeed, Wells's trickfilm playfulness sometimes sways queasily into hints of perceptual anarchy, as when the shop assistant's features distort elastically like clay or cartoon animation: 'First of all it was a short, blobby nose, and then suddenly he shot it out like a telescope, and then out it flew and became thinner and thinner, until it was like a long, red, flexible whip.'⁹⁴ After his son vanishes down a magic tube, the narrator makes an involuntary final exit through 'utter darkness' on to the pavement outside, from which the shop's frontage has disappeared too, only to recover the rematerialised child (pp. 435–36).

Sometimes, Wells's early texts are based on one highly cinematic, visual trope, which controls the narrative's subject and plot, most famously in the 'living' metonymy of *IM*. Similarly, 'Pollock and the Porroh Man' (1895) elaborates a single conceit, in this case a paranoid 'visual match', the synecdochic 'absent presence' of a body part, giving ample opportunity for close-up and superimposition effects.[95] The story reworks Poe's 'The Black Cat' (1843) in a Kiplingesque or Conradian setting. Pollock gets involved in a deadly vendetta with a witch doctor, only to be haunted by the image of his severed, inverted head, both in dreams and any object which recalls it:

> whenever a round black shadow, a round black object came into his range, there he looked for the head, and – saw it. He knew clearly enough that his imagination was growing traitor to him, and yet at times it seemed the ship he sailed in, his fellow-passengers, the sailors, the wide sea, was all part of a filmy phantasmagoria that hung, scarcely veiling it, between him and a horrible real world. The Porroh man, thrusting his diabolical face through that curtain, was the one real and undeniable thing. (*CSS*, pp. 178–89, especially 187)[96]

In effect, Pollock's guilt draws him into a kind of parallel, visual dimension, inverting the normal dominance of empirical reality over the symbolic. It is even possible to see Wells's story as a prediction of the hallucinatory 'fugue states', or flashbacks, of those traumatised by the horrors of the Great War. That kind of psychological time travel and its disturbance of subjectivity would coincide closely with the cinematic interests and methods of the High Modernists themselves.

There is no doubt that Wells was ahead of most contemporaries in grasping hold of and speculating about the equivocal potential of new visual technology for shaping the narratives of modernity, seeing it as a challenge that traditional literary practices could scarcely ignore. In this light, 'The Temptation of Harringay' (1895) was a cautionary tale about the need for careful negotiations between forward-thinking writer and unknown new medium.[97] The story involves the diabolic seduction of a mediocre artist by a, literally, moving and talking picture (significantly in the likeness of an Italian organ-grinder, practicant of an older catchpenny mechanical art) which promises him masterpieces. As Harringay tries to make the face ('snapped' from actuality) as vivid as possible, Wells's phrasing is deliberately ambiguous, suggesting that the image takes on a lifelikeness which the artist struggles to control: 'The face on the canvas seemed animated by a spirit of its own' (*CSS*, pp. 37–41, especially 38). This seems allegoric of the principle of visual autokinesis, but also witnesses the birth of a kind of cultural Frankenstein's monster. Walter R. Booth's *The Devil in the Studio* (1901) is a stop-motion film taken on Paul's animatographe, with a parallel scenario. Mephisto tempts an artist by making instant living likenesses of models appear on his canvas without the intervention of paint.⁹⁸ Similarly, not unlike one of the early 'lightning sketch' films of live cartooning by Edison, Méliès or Acres (which probably gave rise to graphic animation in the first place), artist and image interact. Though Harringay tries to blot it out, '*The diabolified Italian before him shut both his eyes, pursed his mouth, and wiped the colour off his face with his hand*' [Wells's italics] (*CSS*, p. 39). The story suggests Wells's own uncertainty about what this questionable new art might be and how it might drag traditional literary practices and cultural values into the unknown, about whether any suspiciously Faustian compact, indenturing talent for the promise of future achievements, would indeed be worthwhile.⁹⁹

Wells himself gradually practised the short story and scientific romance less and less in the 1900s, owing (as he admitted in the Introduction to *The Country of the Blind*) to 'a diversion of attention to more sustained and more exacting forms': i.e. the realist novel and the speculative socio-scientific treatise (*CSS*, p. 873). Simultaneously, Wells lost much of his practical interest in the medium of cinema to his growing role as self-appointed prophet of the World State, until the two realigned in his 1927 project for a 'peace film' (published as *The King Who Was a King: The Book of a Film* (1929)) and his subsequent screenplays for Korda. Nonetheless, he kept some kind of critical synergy with cinema alive in the intervening time. Wells was a founding member of the London Film Society in the 1920s and signed major contracts with two studios to adapt his work (British Gaumont in 1914 and Stoll in 1922), though in 1923 he replied brusquely to a magazine questionnaire on 'The Novelist and The Film' and did not return to the idea of scripting himself until later in the decade (see Chapter 4). Some commentators argue that British cinema wouldn't have lost so much ground formally and commercially to Hollywood and others between the 1910s and 1930s, after its pioneering creativity, if modern writers such as Wells had sustained their practical interest in the industry, beyond its initial catalysing of their notions of space-time, perception and narrative techniques.¹⁰⁰ Ramsaye argued in 1926, that it had taken the cinema a quarter of a century to catch up with Paul and Wells's 1895 conception of its optical capabilities for a new dramatic art, and that Wells was the first writer to confront these implications of the new medium.¹⁰¹ If we accept such a case, then Wells becomes the early British screen's great lost opportunity, but also symptomatic of its eventual failure to develop the narrative feature swiftly enough to compete with the rise of Hollywood, especially after the Great War. Ramsaye speculated about what might have happened if Wells and Paul had continued to collaborate, instead of going their separate ways when they achieved unexpected success within their respective media: 'If [Wells] had given attention to the motion picture and its larger opportunity of mastery over Time by translations into the present he might have set the screen's progress forward many a year.'[102] In part this was the challenge that Wells responded to belatedly in *KWWAK*, after Ramsaye reminded him of Paul's patent. But to consider how cinema history might have been otherwise is to step into yet another parallel dimension – that of cultural hypothesis. Suffice it to say that, in the 1890s, the striking convergences between Wells's scientific romances and stories and the new visual technology established a slender but vital critical synergy between literature and the upstart, popular medium, which much two-way traffic has re-energised ever since.

2
The Dis/Appearance of the Subject: Wells, Whale and *The Invisible Man*

In *IM* (1897) Wells arguably devised something just as aesthetically ahead of its time as any of the optical speculations of his earlier fiction: the generation of a whole fiction from a single trope – metonymy – in a way that created a brilliantly reflexive match between form and theme. This particular novella also characterises the intertextuality of Wells's early work with the narrative grammar and manifold philosophical and political implications of what would become the great popular medium of the modern period. It was in *IM* that Wells both came closest to the editorial basis of film narrative and, in turn, created one of his most intriguing commentaries on, and opportunities for, cinema itself.

As in *TM*, Wells modernised an occult theme with roots in ancient myth and folklore, in this case found from Plato's story of the regicidal Gyges's invisibility ring, which he uses to seize power surreptitiously, to the caps and cloaks of Celtic fairytale and medieval romance.[1] As in *TM*, he did this in terms which are symptomatic of the problematisation of visibility and presence in Victorian science and popular culture, using theories about 'optical density' and lowering the 'refractive index of a substance ... to that of air', probably influenced by C. H. Hinton's scientific romance about an invisible woman, *Stella* (1895).[2] In this sense, altered states of vision and/or equivocal forms of in/visibility are essential to Wells's media-decentred exploration of modern subjectivity.[3] They provide a means of assault on the concept of 'objective' social identity. The 'whole fabric of a man', as Griffin explains, 'except the red of his blood and the black pigment of his hair' is largely made up of colourless tissue in different states: 'So little suffices to make us visible one to the other' (*IM*, p. 91).

The contradictory impact of new optical science on the popular imagination stemmed from the way it materialised what was invisible to the naked eye. The uncertainty of the visible was an underlying motive for the anatomisations of motion which provided the scientific drive towards moving pictures. Significantly, the discrete phenomena of the normal human visual field had to be artificially defamiliarised, or even largely *disappeared* before that goal was achieved, as in Muybridge's revelations about how animal locomotion really functions and Marey's chronophotographic strips of black-suited gymnasts' bodies reduced to angles of muscular thrust picked out in white. They allowed physical movement to be scrutinised, but also blurred the fixed identity of individual subjects into curves of dynamism, suggesting modern subjectivity's ambiguous manifestations and displacements. The discovery of X-rays added to photography's materialisation of the normally unseeable and its reputation as an uncanny medium, spawning a whole plethora of scientific articles and sensational fictions shortly before Wells's novella was serialised in *Pearson's Weekly* (June–Aug. 1897) and published as a novel in September. *Pearson's Magazine* featured X-rays as both sensational fiction and science in the same April 1896 issue. Symptomatically, the story came first: George Griffith's 'A Photograph of the Invisible'. A tale of 'purely scientific' revenge, it has overtones of Hinton's and Wells's fantasies of literal invisibility and the ethics of the gaze, as well as eroticised 'unclothings' of the body in trickfilms by Méliès and others. A renowned beauty and jilt is tricked into exposure to a mysterious apparatus. 'Professor Grantham', well practised in making 'spirit photographs' of ghostly doubles, invites her to a '*séance*'. He 'wound[s] her in the tenderest spot in such a woman's being' by literally revealing her mortality, penetrating her with uncanny new rays. Instead of the promised society portrait by new process:

> Above were her features, perfect in their likeness, and the wreathed crown of golden brown hair of which she was so proud, but they were the face and hair not of a living woman, but of a ghost and, beneath all, sharp in outline and perfect in every hideous detail, a fleshless skull – her own skull – poised on the jagged vertebrae of her neck, and supported on the bare bones of her chest and shoulders, grinned at her through the transparent veil of flesh, and seemed to stare at her out of the sockets in which two ghostly eyes appeared to float.

So shocked is she that she 'vanishe[s] utterly from the gaze of her worshippers', locked up in the dark room of an asylum, convinced that she has been transformed into a living skeleton.[4] The rational explanation of the story's spectrality followed: H. J. W. Dam's 'A Wizard of To-Day', an extended interview with Röntgen himself, illustrated (among other X-ray images) by the famous skeletal hand of Professor Paul Spies's wife, with a speck of glass clearly embedded under her flesh, the first instance of their incalculable value to surgery and diagnostics. Dam's article stressed Röntgen's discovery as a revolution in vision by artificial means: 'the world … will have to entirely revise its ideas with regard to the most familiar phenomenon within the scope of human consciousness – light'. Traditional boundaries between the opaque and the transparent, between the visible and the unseen, had been dismantled. X-rays were 'the last new mystery that human genius has summoned across the border between the known and the unknown'.[5]

'The Photography of the Invisible', in *The Quarterly Review*, noted that no scientific discovery had so quickly electrified the media and popular imagination before in so many ways.[6] The most widely published photographs of 1896 were probably of skeletal hands, rendered transparent. These and other X-rays of babies and adults had a radically 'othering' effect on the relationship between the viewer and the spectrally subtracted presences of living human bodies.

Early commentators noted a comparably ambiguous and alienating dilution of human 'thereness' on early films. Theatre had the obvious confirmation of actual bodily proximity, but film critic Iris Barry recalled how spectators felt an eerie 'loss of the physical presence' of actress Sarah Bernhardt when she appeared in *Queen Elizabeth* (1912): 'Her acting was Bernhardt's acting. But it was not merely her voice that lacked: it was an emanation of personality. She of course did not know how to "express" herself in a strange and novel medium: but, even if she had, she still would have been "absent".'[7] In a complementary way, the idea of a visually equivocal 'presence' may also have been suggested to Wells by the widespread Victorian interest in spirit photographs, i.e. the belief that the medium was also a 'medium' that could mechanically record paranormal phenomena invisible to unaided perception. Before the advent of high-speed photography in the 1860s and 1870s, long exposures often registered fidgety sitters or casual passers-by as semi-transparent blurs against solid backgrounds instead of materialising them fully. (Julia Margaret Cameron made this lack of instant focus her aesthetic trademark for 'spiritual' portraits of mid-Victorian celebrities such as Thomas Carlyle.) *Séance* is also the French term for a photographic sitting. At first accidentally, through reusing badly cleaned plates, then deliberately by masking and double-exposure, diaphanous images of the dead could be inserted into 'spirit photographs' alongside the living. Such Victorian interest, typified by Georgiana Houghton's *Chronicles of the Photographs of Spiritual Beings and Phenomena Invisible to the Material Eye* (1882), led to scientifically minded ghostbusters such as Lewis Carroll, Conan Doyle and William Crookes seeking to catch real evidence of 'manifestations' on camera, while at the same time debunking fraudulent ones.[8] (The last, a prominent chemist, as well as SPR president, developed the Crookes tube, essential to Röntgen's discovery. This seemed to bring proof of clairvoyance one step nearer with its disturbingly penetrative gaze by invisible radioactive 'vibrations'.)[9]

Jacques Derrida called cinema 'a medium of spectres' and its early association with equivocal in/visibility and im/mortality led to all kinds of ghostly manifestations from this optical machine.[10] Whether they believed that film could manifest literal spooks, early commentators, such as Lindsay, were enthralled by what he called the movie camera's 'Hallowe'en witch-power'.[11]

As shown in Chapter 1, Wells seems to allude to this occultist–mechanical association with the camera in numerous early writings, such as 'The Plattner Story'. Its negativised world only becomes peripherally visible from ours by 'sitting for a long space in a photographer's darkroom at night' (*CSS*, p. 110). 'The Red Room' (published a year before *IM*) hints at the paradoxical way that absent-presences could be visually figured in film at second hand, through the impressions they make on other objects (despite having no appearance, Griffin is similarly a 'tangible antagonist' (*IM*, p. 130). This shift in the notion of spectrality was more widespread in late Victorian optical culture, as in Sir Herbert Stephen's 'No. 11 Welham Square' (published in *The Cornhill Magazine* (May 1885). Because his ghost is manifest only in terms of its voice and all-too-palpable traces, this produces quasi-cinematic effects anticipating those in *IM*:

> As I looked at this chair it struck me that the seat was considerably depressed, as though some one had recently sat down upon it, and the seat had failed to resume its ordinary level ... I looked at the antimacassar. Towards the top it was pushed up in wrinkles. As I looked, it occured to me that it was impossible for it to hang in such a manner by itself. It looked for all the world as if an invisible but substantial human frame was then actually sitting in the chair ... In an access of frenzied terror, I hurled the book I was reading at the chair ... The next instant the seat of the chair rose up audibly to its normal level and the antimacassar fell out into its usual folds.

Moreover, the final battle with this substantial vacancy closely resembles Wells's villagers' climactic subduing of their unseen antagonist: 'They saw me struggling, partly on the floor, and partly kneeling apparently on space. They rushed to my assistance. Both of them felt the thing, both of them grappled with it.'[12]

Significantly, ex-stage hypnotist, alleged telepath and private secretary to successive SPR heads, Hove pioneer G. A. Smith patented a double-exposure process for his 1897 supernatural films, *The Corsican Brothers* (in which a twin's ghostly sibling shows him how he was murdered), *Photographing a Ghost* and *The Haunted Castle*, to exploit the medium's capacity for absent presences. *Photographing a Ghost*'s comic spook was noticeably transparent, so that objects could be seen through its body. Similarly, the disappeared Griffin is nonetheless outlined in semi-see-through by weather: 'Rain ... would make me a watery outline, a glistening surface of a man – a bubble. And fog – I should be like a fainter bubble in fog, a surface, a greasy glimmer of humanity' (*IM*, p. 114).[13] Likewise, the spook of Wells's 'The Inexperienced Ghost' (1902) resembles a superimposition (see Chapter 1). Equivocally visible subjects, made diaphanous by technological displacement in space or time, featured in diverse contexts in Wells's early writings, suggesting how his interest in the possibilities of optical technology budded off in various philosophical directions. In 'The Chronic Argonauts' (1888), time-travelling Nebogipfel appears in a flash out of nowhere, leading to superstitious speculations about his identity similar to those by the villagers in *IM*. The presence of Wells's prototypical scientist-*Übermensch* is strangely diaphanous, as if only partly materialised like the dis/appearing Griffin with his subcutaneous organs on show: 'the idea of something ultra human was further accentuated by the temporal that pulsated visibly through his transparent yellow skin'.[14] At the end of Wells's novella version, the narrator glimpses the Time Traveller disappearing into the future as 'a ghostly, indistinct figure sitting in a whirling mass of black and brass for a moment – a figure so transparent that the bench behind, with its sheets of drawings, was absolutely distinct; but this phantasm vanished as I rubbed my eyes' (*TM*, p. 90). While voyaging, the Time Traveller sits invisible to the ages through which he passes, like a film viewer. The effects on his own vision involve a paradoxical in/visibility too. Processes beyond the temporal scope of unassisted sight become seeable, while normal animal locomotion disappears altogether (see Chapter 1). In 'The Remarkable Case of Davidson's Eyes', Wells inverts *IM*'s optical conceit, so that the normal physical environment, not the subject, disappears.

As we saw in Chapter 1, the motif of unseen watchers with an artificially privileged, potentially abusive gaze occurs in many Wells stories with media connections. The protagonists of 'The New Accelerator' speed up their bodily time to blur into invisibility and enjoy a dangerously superhuman viewpoint like that of Griffin.[15] As Christian Metz has argued, one of the characteristics of cinematic pleasure is precisely the ambivalent sense of transcendent voyeurism, that the spectator masters or controls the visible action, while being excluded from any responsibility for it.[16] The Invisible Man is thus a metaphor for the ultimate voyeur, who could pry into our most intimate lives, for whom everything becomes transparent: Kemp's 'He may be watching me now' is emblematic of such paranoia (*IM*, p. 135), also stressed in the foregrounding of the camera as 'seeing but unseen eye' by James Whale and others. As Christopher Priest points out, perhaps the characteristic anxiety of the modern world is unwitting technological surveillance: 'we fear the silent wire-tappers, the Internet spies, the identity thieves, the Trojan software that surreptitiously enters our computers – all of which use the invisibility of electronics to invade our privacy' (Introduction to *IM*, p. xvii). (Indeed anxiety about observation may indicate that Wells was technologising another invisibility story, James Payn's *The Eavesdropper* (1886).)

Similarly, Frank McConnell argues it is because the Invisible Man is 'a walking emptiness', a violation of the natural visual order, that he is such 'a peculiarly virulent threat' to the assurances and inhibitions of normal life, in which social subjects are mutually kept in place by seeing and being seen (a brazen selling-point for Paul Verhoeven's recent cinematic remake, *Hollow Man* (2000), advertisements for which were titillatingly captioned, 'What would you do if you couldn't be seen?')[17] McConnell also points out that Wells inverts realist fiction's tendency to bestow ever greater visibility on its heroes, in the social sense of augmenting their subjectivity as bourgeois individualists and, thus, the ideology of success which underpins this[18] (a tendency carried over and, arguably, apotheosised by the personality cult of the movie star in the twentieth century). Early cinema's often unsettling reformulation of the viewer's perspective, through its mobilised virtual gaze, also implicitly raised questions about subjectivity with close parallels in literary Modernism, which would arguably culminate in the self-conscious style and themes of German Expressionist film. In this respect also, Wells's novella anticipated how, in its influential practice and legacy, Expressionism would revisualise the subject as equivocal, disembodied, displaced, divisible and duplicable. The protagonist's deviation from the optical norm is itself foregrounded in both Wells's text and Whale's film, by the huge opaque goggles he wears.[19] The fact that Griffin has rendered sight unreciprocal, like Plato's Gyges, means that he can evade the ancient function of the superego, as a godlike 'all-seeing eye', as McConnell points out.[20] Thus (as Plato anticipated) he threatens to deform the ideological structure of morality and restraint in ways also explored by the contemporary writings of Stevenson, Wilde and Nietzsche.

Both written and, in particular, film texts are 'depthless' media, but function, to a greater or lesser degree, by the illusion of being otherwise, i.e. within them meaning seems profound and presence seems stereoscopically actual. Their effect articulates apparent distinctions between surface and depth, between inside and outside, between something manifest and something concealed. But in both Wells's novella and Whale's film, the most philosophically vertiginous conceit is that nothing is being concealed at all except for vacancy itself. The clothed protagonist hides the fact that, as a subject (in both social and literary senses), he isn't there – he is, literally, an absent presence, an empty signifier of a being, created from things that humans have manufactured.[21] (Appropriately, in the novella, Griffin's end is in his beginning – as an equivocal *sign*. His final posthumous dis/appearance is on the renamed village inn board: 'empty ... save for a hat and boots' (*IM*, p. 149).) Derrida defines deconstructive 'freeplay' as 'always an interplay of presence and absence'. Similarly, the proto-Derridean term 'trace' is Wells's favourite expression for signs of an agency that cannot be located in any visible cause, e.g. hand- or footprints, or the objects that Griffin manipulates (Dr Kemp's forensic alertness picks up drops of blood, depressed bedclothes, etc, in his house, well before Griffin announces that he is there).[22]

IM's optical paradox also upsets what Derrida terms the 'phonocentric' assumption of speech as a guarantee of authentic self-presence, since he becomes a disembodied voice out of nowhere, a discourse without apparent origin.[23] In third-person narratological terms, Griffin does not exist except as *mediated* by the perceptions of other characters or at second hand through, as McConnell notes, eye-witness accounts and newspaper reports.[24] Unlike other characters, he is never given the ontological guarantee of private moments of introspection when he is merely 'self-present' (even his own 'backstory' is audited by Kemp, rather than recollected as internal flashback). Similarly, the mediation of words by Victorian electrical communications technologies, of course, predated the cinema. Each new development foregrounded an increasing displacement of the presence of a live, speaking subject, to the point where language appeared to reproduce itself autonomously, as Jeffrey Sconce and Steven Connor have recently shown in historical detail.[25] Similarly, to the Iping villagers, 'It was the strangest thing in the world to hear that voice coming as if out of empty space.' Marvel the tramp thinks that Griffin is 'ventriloquising' him, quite literally projecting a voice from nowhere (*IM*, pp. 39 and 44). As Flint points out, such 'invisible' means of transmission 'served to collapse the boundaries between the material and immaterial modes of circulation about which Carlyle had been able to write with such confidence'.[26] Moreover, the science of such 'voice' technologies quickly accumulated uncanny associations parallel to moving images. Verne had already predicted their synchronising potential for materialising the absent or resurrecting dead pasts in his phono-cinematographic 'ghost from the machine' story, *Le Château des Carpathes* (1892). The inconsolable admirer of a diva discovers her 'spirit' is merely combined sound recording and projection in the castle of his rival. R. L. Stevenson's 'The Beach at Falesa' (also 1892) evokes uncanny presences by similar tricks of sound. Bram Stoker's *Dracula*, published the same year as *IM*, is also symptomatic of a growing culture of eerily 'disembodied' speech, what Lucy Westenra, hearing the call of the vampire, calls 'distant voices which seemed so close to me'.[27] *Dracula* features other forms of modern communications: typewriters, telegrams and even a 'phonographic diary' (electrical engineer Cecil Wray had suggested it in lieu of a shorthand secretary only in March 1896). There is a particularly intriguing parallelism between Dracula's materialisation from 'earth boxes' and the acoustic reproduction of Dr Seward's voice from wax cylinders. Kipling's 'Wireless' (1902) initiates the haunting of radio by featuring the mediumistic channelling of Keats's 'voice' in Morse. It is likely that *IM* also reflects distanciations of the speaking subject through telegraph, telephone, phonograph and the at least theoretical possibility of radio (Heinrich Rudolf Hertz discovered radio waves in 1887 and Guglielmo Marconi's first successful transmission by wireless telegraphy was actually the same year as Wells's text).[28] The telegraph is mentioned prominently in *IM*.[29] Hence technology progressed through written replicas and then virtually instant 'simulacra' of distant speech without visible source. Moreover, from Thomas Edison's invention of the phonograph (the year following Bell's telephone in 1876), media pioneers strove to create its visual counterpart which would coordinate the recorded word and the moving image in virtual simultaneity and apparently reunite the replicated body with its voice. Edison's own 'kinetophone' was a primitive product of this drive, conceived as a moving-image accompaniment to phonograph recordings (see Introduction and Chapter 3). Auguste Baron produced experimental sound films as early as 1896. At the 1900 Paris Expo, Wells might have seen and heard the '*Phono-Cinéma-Théâtre*', short performances by leading stage stars, including Bernhardt as Hamlet, using film synchronised with recording cylinders. François Dussaud's 'Phonorama', on the other hand, presented the sounds and 'cries' of Paris itself. The Expo also showed an experimental '*portrait parlant*' of Léon Gaumont, and his Chronophone system, which filmed performers miming to music, was on the market in 1902. In Britain, Walter Gibbons produced a series of 'Phono-Bio-Tableaux', presenting music-hall artistes, such as Vesta Tilley. Charles Pathé pursued experiments with opera and music-hall '*phonoscènes*' between 1904 and 1912. Ernst Ruhmer and Eugène Lauste were already pioneering the optical soundtrack by 1910, although it would not be perfected for at least another decade and a half.

Obviously, Wells's text could not have been adequately realised on screen before the full development of the soundtrack (despite such lively silent versions as Pathé's *The Invisible Thief* (1909)),[30] but it was, effectively, a statement on the implications of this further technological quest and the inevitable 'convergence of the twain'. According to Gilles Deleuze, the widespread adoption of synchronised speech with the coming of the talkies, thirty years after Wells's novella (*The Jazz Singer* was released in 1927), made both speech 'visible' and moving pictures 'readable' in a very special sense. In effect, the talkies 'constituted a fourth dimension of the visual image', supplementing its stereoscopy. The speech act '[i]n being heard, is itself seen as tracing a path in the visual image', whether its actual source is out of frame or not. Silent film had various spatial means of representing the utterance and transmission of words, but 'it is now the heard voice which spreads in visual space, or fills it'. This is why, in his view, Whale's film was a talkie masterpiece, because it rendered speech 'all the more visible',[31] in a way which actualises Wells's prophetic foregrounding of a crisis in language and subjectivity through technological displacement. (In his famous 1935 interview, Wells singled out such '[e]xtremely remarkable effects' as one of the spurs to his own practical re-engagement with cinema: 'After that I pricked up my ears. There was something that I could do with the films.'³²) It is perhaps in its implicit anticipation and critique of the consummated co-ordination of dialogue with image that *IM* has its most subtle bearing on cinematic technique and 'self-presentation'.

Even more so than the simulacral moving picture, the perfection of the synchronised soundtrack was promoted as a guarantee of the medium's faithful mimesis of bodily reality, an extension of its tendency to offer representations as unmediated perceptions, as Armstrong documents.³³ It was argued that whereas film-images can never be anything more than illusions of movement in three-dimensional space, projected from static frames on a two-dimensional surface, recorded sound when played back was an *actual* vibration of air layers authentically apprehended by the ear, even if its original source was absent. However, the necessary synchronisation of image with dialogue meant that the Modernist potentials of cinema's spatio-temporal plasticity, and its possibilities for radically reformulating subjectivity, had to be subordinated to continuity editing. Thence emerged the worries of Eisenstein and other avant-gardists that the soundtrack would remortgage cinema to naturalistic priorities.³⁴ They were concerned that its effect of real action and sound produced by live human subjects, taking place in an uninterrupted, stable space-time continuum, mimicked direct perception ever more closely and effaced the cinema's artifice as a discourse. However, Whale's film at once depended on the resurgent naturalism of the soundtrack and subverted it from the inside. In the film, even more than the novella, speech is the foregrounded means of denoting Griffin's simultaneous presence and absence. Paradoxically, it only guarantees the subject's authenticity through his lack of corresponding image, thus materially undoing what it sets out to prove. Whale's talkie exploits the most extreme form of *a*-synchronisation between sound and picture, recuperating (albeit in an equivocal way) Modernistic possibilities ostensibly forfeited by the introduction of vocalised language into a once-silent medium. The aesthetic and philosophical radicalism of Wells's text, dormant until technology caught up, was brilliantly triggered by Whale like a kind of delayed action device.³⁵

Whale was, of course, not the only Hollywood director in the early days of the talkies to explore radically other possibilities in the soundtrack, although the generic licence of SF/horror features obviously allowed greater scope for this. There is a parallel, though more fleeting, dislocation between word and picture in Tod Browning's 1931 *Dracula* (also from the Universal stable). Because of the vampire's uncanny lack of reflection, visual absence is used by Professor Van Helsing, paradoxically, as 'proof' of his real identity and presence. Hence the eerie scene which alternates Dracula, seen charming potential victims, and a mirror-view of the same living group, with his undead figure subtracted, though his dialogue continues.³⁶

We still think of film as a primarily visual medium. But playing Whale's Griffin, reduced to a bodiless voice, paradoxically called for an approach from Whale's actor unexpectedly closer to radio drama, because of the role's dependence on virtuoso inflection and rhythm for emotional expression. In his *Frankenstein*, by contrast, the monster was famously embodied by Boris Karloff as Expressionistically mute like Wegener's Golem (aptly, the German word for silent movie, *Stummfilm*, connotes 'dumbness'). After its phenomenal success, Universal wanted Whale's next picture to be another Karloff vehicle. However, the star, who lisped, balked on discovering that his face did not appear until thirty seconds before the end. The unknown Claude Rains on the other hand, although he failed the visual hurdle of the screen test, impressed Whale vocally. Hence, in a strange kind of doubling effect, the visual absence of the protagonist in Wells's tale was reproduced in terms of the literal lack of an established star in the filmed version. This is a particularly significant point when considered in the context of Benjamin's theory that it was precisely on the illusion of charismatic presence that Hollywood's commercial mystique was built.[37]

As mentioned, the dominant trope which makes the theme and form of Wells's tale so mutually reflexive is metonymy, the construction of meaning not by comparisons between different things (as in metaphor), but by their physical contiguity. David Lodge has argued that, in language, metonymy is a condensation of contexture whereby in a figurative phrase such as 'the crown' to mean 'king(ship)', a human subject or quality can be substituted by an object associated with it as a kind of semiotic shorthand.[38] In *IM* Wells visualised metonymy literally, condensing contexture to the point where the agent of an action and/or subject of the sentence disappears altogether. A perfect example is: 'Kemp stared at the devouring dressing gown' (*IM*, p. 81). In film (though it can also use montage to create metaphor), narrative is often based on the metonymic principle of editing together discontinuous shots of action into visual links, breaking up space and time into fragments and reconstituting them into coherent sequences which also condense the context of action into significant detail and which can focus on clothes or objects, rather than the people wearing or using them. As shown in Chapter 1, 'Pollock and the Porroh Man' (also 1897) is generated from metonymy's related trope, synecdoche, creating in this case an equally quasi-cinematic symbolism, resembling repeated close-up and/or visual matching. It revolves around the ghostly absent presence not of a *whole* body, but of *part* of one.

The Soviet director Pudovkin once observed, 'The playing of an actor which is connected with an object and is built around it ... is always one of the strongest methods of cinematic construction.'[39] This is because film levels, or even interchanges, distinctions between subject and inanimate object, a tendency commented on by early critics such as Lindsay. He also observed that the complementary tendency of this animism was the objectification of people: in 'all photoplays ... human beings tend to become dolls and mechanisms, and dolls and mechanisms tend to become human'.[40] As Keith Cohen explains, this is because, once filmed, self and object 'share the same artificial, ambiguous existence. The image of a sailing ship has just as much existential immediacy as the image of its captain.' Thus cinema 'creates a world in which objects, like human beings, seem endowed with some innate dynamism', mirroring a 'similar reversal' in Modernist literature of consciousness.[41]

It was inevitable that early film-makers would quickly discover that the illusion of movement produced by the 'persistence of vision' effect could be logically extended from people to objects and even drawings. Lindsay noted that the literal animation/personification of objects rife in early film was the consummate visualisation of ancient superstition and wish-fulfilment. Indeed, no early cinema-goer could have failed to notice the medium's fascination with *autokinesis*, the basic principle of moving images. Everyday objects, fantastically animated for poltergeistly or comic impact by methods such as stop-motion animation or double exposure, became a staple. As Lindsay wrote, 'Mankind in his childhood has always wanted his furniture to do such things ... This yearning for personality in furniture begins to be worked upon in the so-called trick-scenes.' Significantly, Wells's terrified landlady screams, 'He's put the sperrits into the furniture' (see *IM*, p. 32) in Chapter 6, with its Lindsayesque title, 'The Furniture That Went Mad'. Lindsay exemplified it with the Pathé one-reeler *Moving Day*, in which household effects obey removal men's 'wireless orders ... with military crispness', flying out of the windows and processing down the street to their new home. As in *IM*, clothes become literal metonyms for their invisible owners: 'The most joyous and curious spectacle is to behold the shoes walking down the boulevard, from father's large boots to those of the youngest child. They form a complete satire of the family, yet have a masterful air of their own, as though they were the most important part of a human being.'[42] Indeed, animation technique became common on both sides of the Atlantic in the early twentieth century, allowing both graphic elements and objects to come to life, with comic and/or supernatural effect. In Méliès's 1897 *The Bewitched Inn* (same year as *IM*), a guest at a haunted house finds that his clothes take on a life of their own after he has undressed.[43] The Anglo-American J. Stuart Blackton's international hit *The Haunted Hotel* (1907) used a single-frame exposure technique to move things around by 'unseen' agency, thus inspiring the Frenchman Émile Cohl's classic object animations. The Cohlesque masterpiece of the genre, *Le Garde-Meuble automatique* ('The Automatic Moving Company' (Pathé-Comica 1912)) is probably the film referred to by Lindsay.⁴⁴ The broom which sweeps up (accompanied by Dukas's *Sorcerer's Apprentice*), after the furniture has decamped, is a self-conscious allusion to its own visual wizardry. However, Lindsay admitted that this was a crudely 'material' or fetishistic use of a technique more subtly, but just as characteristically, employed in mainstream features in which objects are given a dynamically poetic role in relation to the doings and feelings of human actors. By means of repeated visual contiguity, affect could be displaced on to things and complex symbolism created.

Precisely because grotesquely visualised metonymy is the dominant rhetorical trope of Wells's novella, it abounds with such quasi-cinematic effects. This kind of object animation is epitomised by the revolver 'hanging between Heaven and earth, six yards away' with which the Invisible Man threatens Adye, the police chief (*IM*, p. 139). *IM* was adapted by Cyril Twyford and Leslie Lombard for London's Coliseum Theatre in 1913.⁴⁵ However, as was recognised by commentators such as Lindsay, stage magic was already being surpassed by cinema's ability to conjure in ways which rendered its technological legerdemain invisible in the trick itself. Victorian conjurors developed ingenious routines which appeared to create invisibility on stage, with panes of glass at oblique angles, mirrors, lighting effects and black-clad assistants camouflaged against dark backdrops. References to stage magic are liberally strewn through *IM*, as when the vicar tries to rationalise Griffin's uninhabited but mobile clothes as an optical trick: 'Suppose a mirror, for instance – hallucinations are so easily produced. I don't know if you have ever seen a really good conjurer?' (*IM*, p. 54). As Erik Barnouw demonstrates in his classic study of the connection, widespread filming of conjuring acts for the early screen was rapidly followed by the development of stop-motion camera and editing trickery by professional magicians to enhance their marvels (also, ironically, eventually making their own manual skills redundant).⁴⁶ In-camera tricks allowed strange displacements of human presence, like 'ghosts, headless men and Doppelgängers', to 'fraternise with the living' (in Paul Hammond's words), all the more easily.⁴⁷ This meant the literal dis/appearance of human agency in the early trickfilm genre itself, because the magician no longer needed to be present: the machine performed for him! Film consumed stage magicians' 'peculiar heritage of hanky-panky', as Barnouw puts it, while simultaneously 'finding new opportunities for it' as they retired behind the lens and into the cutting room.⁴⁸ As seen in Chapter 1, the mechanisation of magic by cinema seems to be reflected in many early Wells stories, epitomised by 'The Man Who Could Work Miracles'. This comic text was a gift for stop-motion special effects which render human manipulation invisible. These had become highly sophisticated by the time a version of the story was finally made four years after Whale's film in 1937 (see the detailed discussion of *The Man Who Could Work Miracles*

(*MWCWM*) in Chapter 4).

The discovery and refinement of the stop-motion principle meant that anything could suddenly disappear on screen, be instantly substituted with something else or be moved, as if under its own volition. Consequently, innumerable vanishings were transferred from stage acts. Méliès was first with *The Vanishing Lady* (1896).[49] By 1904 the technique was already refined enough for a tour de force like Cecil Hepworth's *The Bewitched Traveller*. A guest at a haunted inn witnesses his table, fellow passengers, train and finally even himself disappear in puffs of smoke.[50] By 'matting' and/ or double exposure it would also become possible to disappear portions of human beings, or animate items of apparel. In Méliès's *Terrible Turkish Executioner* (1904), a torso frantically tries to reattach its legs, 'like a child learning to put on his pants', after being sliced in half by its own scimitar.[51] Early films exhibited positive delight in dismemberment, nonchalantly anatomising the living body and reassembling it.

Hammond notes that numerous invisibility effects in Whale's film also bear a particular resemblance to the earlier roots of such cinematic marvels in the stage wizardry of John Nevil Maskelyne, who founded a theatrical dynasty that also migrated into film-making.[52] The theatre where Maskelyne performed from the 1880s, Piccadilly's Egyptian Hall, became world-famous as 'England's Home of Mystery': Méliès studied his methods as an apprentice sorcerer and Wells knew the master too, at least by reputation.[53] Maskelyne specialised in occult illusions, often moving objects 'telekinetically' by the manipulations of an assistant, invisibly clad in black against ebony drapes. Hammond also notes that a particular gag in Whale's film, where the policeman turns a white cat black with a paint spray because he's mistaken it for the Invisible Man himself, derives from music-hall encounters between black and white, quickly taken up by film, as in G. A. Smith's *The Miller and the Sweep* (1898). Indeed, 'Whale's film has an air of buffoonery and vaudeville', very probably influenced by his early career in British theatre, a popular culture familiar to both the French father of the trickfilm and native literary prestidigitators such as Wells.[54] Whale's proportionally greater visual horror is mitigated by the way in which his medium also enhances the novella's vein of proto-surreal slapstick, as exemplified by the sequences with floating garments (which give rise to village bobby Jaffers's immortal line: '''Ow can I 'andcuff a bloomin' shirt?'), or the self-pedalling bike. Such moments exemplify how the film neatly transcribes Wells's formula of generating black comedy from the collision of stolid habit and the incredible, and how it extends stage routines and early trickfilm treatments of invisibility themes.[55] But whereas a sense of verbal fun is completely lacking in Wells's protagonist, Renzi notes how his filmic counterpart's deliberate facetiousness makes 'him at once more sinister and more humorous'.[56] As he gleefully informs Kemp, 'We'll begin with a Reign of Terror. A few murders here and there. Murders of great men, murders of little men, just to show we make no distinction', before going on to 'wreck a train or two'.

IM also had broader narrative aptitudes for screen-visualisation as a product of Wells's precocious speculations about the discursive possibilities of the new medium. This is supported by the frequency of textual injunctions such as 'You must figure ...', and strikingly directorial strategies, as when Wells alternates panoramic scenes with extreme close-ups, such as the mass-panic at Iping followed by a synedochic 'shot' of a single eye staring out in terror from the corner of a windowpane (*IM*, p. 60). The narrative also has a framed 'flashback structure', in which Griffin relates the backstory of his transformation.

Many of Wells's examples of quasi-cinematic effects were actually reproduced directly in Whale's film, proving that film-minded technique as much as sensational storyline must have caught the director's notice. Particular examples of the dis/appearance of agency, such as the animated suit of clothes and uninhabited shirt (*IM*, pp. 39–40), must have seemed too good to miss; likewise, as mentioned above, the implications of the landlady's horrified exclamation, 'He's put the sperrits into the furniture' (*IM*, p. 32). The fact that foreign substances such as undigested food can be seen moving within Griffin's transparent body is also described quasi-cinematically, although it also alludes to X-rays: 'It was strange to see him smoking; his mouth, and throat, pharynx and nares, became visible as a sort of whirling smoke cast' (*IM*, p. 82).[57] For its climactic *coup de cinéma* – Griffin's simultaneous rematerialisation and death – Whale's movie simply followed the detail of Wells's text, virtually word for image, as a kind of anatomisation in reverse motion (early trickfilms often featured bodies 'undressed' into skeletons).[58] Compare the carefully phased re-appearance of Griffin's skull (a real skeleton was used), subcutaneous tissue (a sculptured dummy), then finally skin, in the film's closing moments, with Wells's verbal rendering of the same process:

> First came the little white nerves, a hazy grey sketch of a limb, and then the glassy bones and intricate arteries, then the flesh and skin, first a faint fogginess and then growing rapidly dense and opaque. Presently they could see his crushed chest and his shoulders, and the dim outline of his drawn and battered features. (*IM*, p. 148)[59]

The film's equivalent special effects were devised by John P. Fulton, in collaboration with cinematographer John J. Mescall (a moniker appropriately echoing the Maskelynes, as well as the notorious hallucinogenic). They were jealously guarded in case of pre-release espionage by rival studios, like an industrial secret – literally Universal's formula for a highly profitable new commodity that would return the Depression-hit studio to solvency. Fulton later wrote an account of his academy-award-winning methods in the *American Cinematographer*. Scenes of total invisibility were simply done with wires. Partially clothed ones were more problematic, so Fulton resorted 'to multiple printing – with variations'. In the first stage, scenes were filmed minus the protagonist, who would be introduced later by co-ordinated 'double-negative' work. The second stage was carried out (adapting an old stage-magic technique) against a black set, walled and floored with non-reflective velvet. The actor was also garbed in black velvet, including gloves and headpiece, just like Maskelyne's assistant, or one of Marey's chronophotographic models, in order to render motion in the abstract visible, by fading individual human subjects 'out of the picture'. Over this, the actor wore whatever was required to picture unsupported clothes moving naturally. A print was then superimposed upon the original frame in a complex matting process.[60]

Because his outline is solely sustained by fabricated materials, the Invisible Man appears an assemblage of animated objects rather than a person, but though his disguise renders him grotesque, he believes it 'not more so than many human beings' (*IM*, p. 120). At the same time, Griffin's objectification raises the unsettling question of the role linguistic and material fetishism might play in producing normal social subjects and their representation in cultural texts. According to Lucien Goldmann, cultural levelling between human subjects and inanimate objects corresponds to the commodification which characterises both economic and technological change under capitalist modernity, in which film plays such a major part.[61] Hence Karl Marx's original theory of the 'spectral' life of goods in circulation, from Chapter 3 of *Das Kapital* (1867), has striking parallels with the rhetorical strategy that Wells uses, as well as with the notion of stardom as the ultimate expression of commodity fetishism. Marx argued that, by virtue of the way that capitalist ideology mystifies how value is created, real conditions of production, which are relations between people as makers and consumers, become 'reified', taking on a fantastic appearance, as if the world were ruled by impersonal forces. In Georg Lukács's words, 'Its basis is that a relation between people takes on the character of a thing and thus acquires a "phantom objectivity", an autonomy that seems so strictly rational and all-embracing as to conceal every trace of its fundamental nature.'[62] Thomas Richards argues that in the exponential Victorian culture of advertising and spectacle, 'the commodity became the living letter of the law of supply and demand. It literally came alive' in semiotic terms which parallel the absent presence and unlocatable agency of *IM*.[63] It is almost as if Wells is parodying the significance of this reification process by pushing his use of metonymy to a grotesque extreme, so that manufactured objects, including clothes, do literally become autokinetic, with an apparent life of their own, and the human agency behind them vanishes.

It is highly significant that a department store named 'Omniums' – emblematic of the whole late Victorian imperial economy – is where the disappeared Griffin first fabricates a new identity for himself. Only after dressing does he 'beg[i]n to feel a human being again' and ventures back out into society (see *IM*, p. 110). Stolen clothes become, paradoxically, the things which both conspicuously manifest – literally objectify – his extreme otherness, and, at the same time, disguise it.[64] Wells pushes this economic theme further by playing on the tendency to reify money, the symbolic medium of exchange values, as an entity capable of acting on human subjects as if under its own volition, as when a sailor encounters

> a 'fistful of money' (no less) travelling without visible agency, along by the wall at the corner of St Michael's Lane ... He had snatched at the money forthwith and had been knocked headlong, and when he had got to his feet the butterfly money had vanished ... And all about that neighbourhood, even from the august London and Country Banking Company, from the tills of shops and inns ... money had been quietly and dextrously making off that day in handfuls and rouleaux, floating quietly along by walls and shady places. (*IM*, p. 69)

Similarly, in Whale's film, Griffin flings stolen cash about the street while singing the pawnbroking rhyme 'Pop Goes the Weasel'. His voice then rapidly yells 'money' five times, in a kind of defamiliarisation of the cliché 'money talks', before braining a policeman with a till drawer for emphasis.

However, Whale's film not only reflects the process of reification, it is equivocally caught up within it as an industrial commodity itself. In Marx's theory, human labour and the web of social relations that produce exchange value disappear into the commodity as fetish. But this also means that the commodity is itself a kind of metonymy from which these condensed but still latent contextual relations might be reconstituted, or made visible again. It was for this reason that Benjamin viewed commercial cinema's naturalistic 'realism' (an effect redoubled by the synchronised soundtrack, as we have seen) as apotheosising fetishistic production for culture in the modern age of mechanical reproduction. Unlike Modernist film-making, which strove to make production processes visible, including its own, the highly 'finished' Hollywood product erased the very means by which it was made, substituting a mystifying transparency:

> Its illusionary nature is that of the second degree, the result of cutting. That is to say, in the studio the mechanical equipment has penetrated into reality so deeply that its pure aspect freed from the foreign substance of equipment is the result of a special procedure, namely, the shooting by the specially adjusted camera and the mounting of the shot together with other similar ones. The equipment-free aspect

of reality here has become the height of artifice; the sight of immediate reality has become an orchid in the land of technology.⁶⁵

The ambiguous discourse of Whale's feature, though not overtly avant-garde, is nonetheless potentially subversive in this respect. With its phantasmal manipulation of objects, from which human agency equivocally dis/appears, and its dislocation between word and image, it simultaneously epitomises and parodies the reification process in a kind of *reductio ad absurdum*.

Detailed comparison between the themes and structure of text and film yields further insights. Whale knew Wells personally through bohemian London theatre circles and had admired his writing from his youth. The possibility of projecting his own dilemma into the enigmatic space at the narrative's centre may have been a more personal reason that it held a fascination for Whale, according to some commentators. Anne B. Simpson argues that the scientific romances are shot through with a critical 'discourse of otherness', highlighting ambivalent 'themes of identification and rejection'.⁶⁶ Dissident sexuality in a homophobic society was, arguably, another kind of equivocally invisible 'otherness' (before the bandaged stranger reveals his actual condition, Griffin's identity is a space into which the small-minded villagers project anxieties and prejudice about difference and folk demons of all kinds, fuelled by sensationalising popular media (see *IM*, pp. 20 and 22–24). This internalisation is highlighted in the carter's name, 'Fearenside', i.e. fear inside, and the children's belief that Griffin is 'the Bogey Man'). Born in Dudley in England's industrial West Midlands in 1889, Whale's sense of contradiction about his working-class origins, as well as his sexual orientation, inevitably influenced the subtext of his films (he also made a version of Alexander Dumas's *The Man in the Iron Mask* in 1939, another 'overdetermined' classic of disguise). As well as being traumatised as a young officer on the Western Front, as a 'would-be gentleman' expatriate, he endured the strain of maintaining a respectable public front to keep his personal history invisible to scandal, according to Mark Gatiss.⁶⁷ Whale's first Hollywood directing break was filming R. C. Sherriff's Great War play *Journey's End* (1930). Hence Whale approached Sherriff to write a screenplay from Wells's novella. As in *Frankenstein*, Whale wanted a narrative about someone trapped in circumstances of his own making over which he loses control, but minus the Gothic horror and overt monstrosity.⁶⁸ The problem was that Whale's casting choice, Rains, was completely unknown to American movie-goers. But Whale's enthusiasm for the state-of-the-art effects demanded proved so infectious that (along with the quality of Sherriff's script) he persuaded producer Carl Laemmle Junior that the picture would still be a money-spinner.

The ongoing debate about the role of science in modernity and its implications for both new media technology and politics is the key theme common to both Whale's adaptation and Wells's original. Wells's own ambivalence about science's double-edged progress is encapsulated in the name 'Griffin': the mythical gryphon was both a builder of golden nests and a chimera – a potential benefactor and a figment of deluded vision. Griffin's exultation after his disappearance, 'I felt as a seeing man might do, with padded feet and noiseless clothes, in a city of the blind' (a metaphor equating privileged vision with power developed by Wells in yet another optical story, 'The Country of the Blind' (1911)), transforms his sociopathic isolation and sense of rejection as albino 'freak' into megalomaniac fantasies of omnipotence. When Kemp objects, 'But– ! I say! The common conventions of humanity', Griffin replies, Nietzscheanly, that scientific genius isn't bound by them (*IM*, p. 118). Through Kemp, Wells underlines the need for science and its technological products to be tempered by ethics, as a Promethean force for technological, social and cultural change.[69] In the novella, Griffin's science is egotistical, not philanthropic. He jealously hoards his knowledge, encoding it in cipher. This means that his experiments succeed only at the cost of complete detachment from common humanity, from which there is no return. However, Whale's Griffin, now humanised with the forename Jack, is only anti-social *after* his transformation (he isn't even albino, thus arguably letting the community off the hook for any complicity in 'othering' him, prior to becoming invisible and insane). His normality is almost overstressed. Griffin's outlook is linked to a stereotypical 'love interest': he wants to prove himself to his girl, to transcend poverty and nonentity by gaining conventional wealth and fame. Like his post-transformation madness, Jack's murderousness was not volitional, but an aberration of 'monocaine' – a portmanteau of monomania and cocaine – his invisibility drug. The motivation for his ambitions is rendered intelligible in terms of the discourse of popular romantic features. In this context, as Renzi argues, the significance of Jack's christening is explained: he is no longer a sociopathic genius with a grudge, but an Everyman, punished for breaking traditional injunctions against 'forbidden knowledge'. Because of this, the shock of the simultaneous death/materialisation scene is a reversal which makes the Invisible Man seem martyrlike. In effect, the film's atrocities are not committed by 'Jack the man, but Jack the Monster'.[70] In terms of another classic (filmed by Hollywood the year before), they are blamed on Mr Hyde rather than Dr Jekyll. This renders Whale's Invisible Man more conventionally tragic and Kemp (a cowardly, sleazy bounder who tries to steal Jack's girl), *more* of a conventional villain. But to what extent Whale was making genuine concessions to Hollywood clichés and box-office formulae in such changes or producing a camp parody of them is open to question.

 The antagonistic relationship of both Invisible Men to their respective

Kemps[71] is fundamental to the difference in the presentation of science between novella and film. Wells contrasts Kemp's sceptical but also largely theoretical, 'armchair science' (as Renzi puts it),[72] with Griffin's driven experimentalism (Kemp has just written a paper that 'demonstrated conclusively' the impossibility of becoming invisible (*IM*, p. 80)). Abstract learning, both social and safe, clashes with Griffin's trangressive blend of the imaginative and the practical, so that the two, while critiquing each other, also become dangerously divorced. In the film, Kemp's science is also conservative. His hack research on preservatives for the company pits him against Jack's private and radical ambition. But in both novella and film, Griffin's post-transformation 'monstering', like that of Frankenstein in Mary Shelley's novel, is not simply a question of corporeality (or lack of it), but of his attitude both to his creation and to the rest of humanity, exemplified by his plans for a reign of terror to seize power. And it is this connection between politics and science that also makes Wells's text so prescient about the relations between technology and terrorism in modernity.

Griffin's absent presence seems to critique ideological contradictions within subjectivity and economics, but on the negative side, it threatens to 'modernise' a social structure which he sees as effete and corrupt with a programme of extreme violence. This alienates scientific rationality from every ethical consideration as much as the literal aliens of *The War of the Worlds* do. Thus the figure of Griffin in some ambiguous sense represents the unleashing of (in his case literally) 'naked', Nietzschean will-to-power, a totalitarian potential in the conditions of modernity. Such power is normally invisible because diffused, as Foucault argued, throughout the social system and its discourses, so that it is at once nowhere to be located and everywhere present.[73]

Although there were silent precedents of literary origin on the same theme (including notable versions of both *Frankenstein* (1910) by J. Searle Dawley and *Jekyll and Hyde* by F. W. Murnau (as *Der Januskopf* (1920)), symptomatically Hollywood produced a plethora of 'Mad Doctor' movies in the 1930s. The transgressive scientist figured in all three of Whale's classic SF/horror films, *Frankenstein* (1931), *The Invisible Man* (1933) and *The Bride of Frankenstein* (1935), which suggests that he was gripped by the renewed topicality of the theme before and after adapting Wells's novella. However, Whale's film is unique in picking up and expanding the all-important nexus between modern science, politics and the *media* in Wells's early optical fantasies.[74]

In his 'brutal dream of a terrorised world' (*IM*, p. 129), Griffin most closely prefigures the totalitarian dictator, according to McConnell.[75] Wells's protagonist can be viewed as a proto-Fascist demagogue both threatening, and promising great things to, the dispossessed (personified by the tramp Marvel) if they believe and follow him with blind obedience. Griffin's manifesto, though merely written on a scrap of paper, prefigures in miniature the promise by Hitler of a Thousand Year Reich: 'Port Burdock is no longer under the Queen, tell your Colonel of Police, and the rest of them; it is under me – the Terror! This is day one of year one of the new epoch – the Epoch of the Invisible Man' (p. 134). However, his superhumanity, like the Martians' lack of earthly immunities, is disastrously flawed. Nakedness, the condition of his absolute invisibility and power, also means bodily vulnerability, inescapable community with the 'little men' he strives to transform into instruments of his will. Wells's 1890s political critique is topically intensified in Whale's movie because of the 1930s context of its making, and, I would argue, primarily because it expands the novella's insights about the dissemination and mystification of power by the discourses of the technological media. Epitomised in cinema, these had, of course, penetrated ever deeper into social life with highly developed forms of propaganda by the time of Whale's movie.[76]

Significantly, Joseph Conrad's own study of the emergence of the 'invisible' menace of modern political terror, *The Secret Agent* (1907), was dedicated to Wells, and is highly intertextual with *IM*.[77] Conrad's letter, addressing Wells as 'Realist of the Fantastic', was written after reading it.[78] McConnell notes that the effectiveness of the condition of unease disseminated by Wells's self-appointed minister of apocalypse depends precisely on being unseeable, impossible to pick out from the normative crowd and able to strike anywhere at any time.[79] In this sense, Conrad's explosive-toting professor, the original suicide bomber, 'passing, unseen' out of the final page of the novel 'like a plague among men', is Wells's symbolic figure made literal. Wells also showed incredible foresight about the irony that agents of new orders often attempt to advance their causes through depersonalised forms of technological violence, 'scientifically' rationalised by Final Solution logic. But the novella is perhaps most foresighted about the way developments in the media would make the ubiquitous psychological power of modern terrorism and dictatorship possible. (This specific link between the analyses of Wells and Conrad was not lost on Alfred Hitchcock. The bomb-planting anti-hero of his own film of *The Secret Agent* (released as *Sabotage* (1936)) is an anonymous picture-house proprietor, whose profession literally screens his activities.)[80]

When Griffin creates mayhem at the village (attempting to retrieve his formulae from the inn) he is initially worried that his secret will be reported: 'It's all about. It will be in the papers! Everybody will be looking for me; everyone on their guard' (p. 62). However, on second thoughts, he realises that publicity is a *symbiotic* asset rather than a handicap in his bid for power. It 'broadcasts' his proposed reign of terror ahead of him – 'I heard a magnified account of my depredations, and other speculations as to my whereabouts' (p. 113). Like a modern politician, he realises that available media discourse can be manipulated to his advantage. The panic of his absent presence is, ironically, disseminated elsewhere far more quickly and effectively as information than it ever could be in person. Moreover, newspaper reporting is not perceived by the credulous as mediation, but as an authentic 'voice' of truth, transparently identical with the real. This irony parallels and becomes satirically enmeshed with the Invisible Man's own paradoxical ontological status as discourse, his reduction to a mere voice independent of the visible fact of a body of evidence.

The year of Whale's film (1933) also saw the Nazi Terror begin in earnest, following Hitler's victory in the German state elections at the end of the previous year. Interestingly, Sebastian Haffner, in his provocative biography of the *Führer*, characterises Hitler's personality as an absence, a nonentity who only became 'visible' in his demagogic media persona, quoting Kurt Tucholsky's opinion that 'The man does not really exist – he is only the noise he makes.'[81] Similarly, the anonymity and shadowy organisation of master criminals in early serials, such as Feuillade's *Fantômas* and Lang's *Dr Mabuse* films (beginning with *Der Spieler* (1922)), have intriguing parallels with Wells's novella and anticipate the psychological methods of modern political gangsters. Lang seems to have consciously explored this, as well as the dictator's symbiosis with the media. His last film, before escaping Hitler's Germany, *Das Testament des Dr Mabuse* (1933), is an allegorical warning about the illegitimate intentions of the embryonic Nazi state. Mabuse wants to create a boundless '*Herrschaft des Verbrechens*' (Dominion of Crime) through posthumous acts of sabotage and psychological terror. Significantly, he orchestrates this campaign as a kind of Invisible Man, issuing instructions while apparently hidden behind a curtain which actually just conceals his empty silhouette and phonographic voice.[82] Like many Expressionist villains from *The Cabinet of Dr Caligari* (1919) onwards, Mabuse exercises mesmeric powers over his victims, a recurrent meta-cinematic motif in Weimar German film-making for the vicarious control of vision by the gaze of the camera itself. In Lang's 1933 feature, Mabuse's power-crazed subjectivity is also disengaged from the presence of his own body: the film literally visualises it as passing into the psychiatrist whom Mabuse has chosen as its host to carry on his work after he dies, by hypnotising him into believing he is the criminal genius himself.[83]

We find a similar topical allegory in Whale's film. Rains, during his ranting speeches, uses gestures instantly recognisable from newsreel footage of orating dictators: he theatrically saws the air like Hitler and even momentarily holds up his hand in Nazi-like salute; Rains also thrusts out his chin pugnaciously and folds his arms like Mussolini. By the 1930s, the technological media were more than fulfilling Wells's early suspicions about their potential for serving dubious political ends and simultaneously mystifying their means. In this respect, Whale's film stands as an implicit deconstruction of the calculated personae of aspiring political supermen, broadcast through technology. The movie's self-reflexive tropes extend Wells's critique of reporting to other media, including their own. Significantly, Griffin enters Kemp's house just as he simultaneously hears a broadcast newsflash about collective hysteria among villagers hallucinating about an 'Invisible Man', the camera also mimicking his observation of Kemp in (to recollect that phrase from Davidson) his 'most secret operations by unsuspected eyes'. Griffin suddenly switches the broadcast off, but continues its terror-inducing effect, mimicking the announcer's voice. Similarly, after his existence is publicly confirmed as fact, Griffin is later shown causing mass panic when a dance is interrupted by a newsflash, without needing to be there even in the special sense understood in his case (he's sleeping peacefully at the time). The equally invisible presence of Whale's camera cleaves through the crowd (as if we were seeing through Griffin's own eyes) to a key close-up of the radio now reporting his latest atrocity as 'fact'. Its loudspeaker then expands into a screen-filling close-up, followed by a rapid cross-section of horrified individuals simultaneously listening to the same bulletin in diverse contexts elsewhere. Crucially, this foregrounds the parallel with Griffin's *own* voice and its equally disembodied and invisible origin: two kinds of scientific–technological displacement with the potential to broadcast hysteria – one imaginary, but the other only too actual in the 1930s – symbolically converge in an unmistakable way.[84]

As we saw in the Introduction, manipulation of the power of virtual presence by politicians was almost as old as the cinematic medium itself. Being filmed rapidly became a novel kind of public 'life mask', as Christie puts it, for statesmen and celebrities at the turn of the century and many began self-consciously to 'play themselves', as it were, off-screen.[85] However, it is arguable that explicit politicisation of the Invisible Man theme came to permeate the culture of the 1930s, especially where critical intertextuality between literature and the media is concerned. So much of the writing of the time is (for understandable reasons) anxious to expose the artifice of the public personae which politicians projected and, correspondingly, the hollowness of the causes they espoused. For example, Archibald MacLeish's radio parable play *The Fall of the City* (1937) (originally broadcast by CBS in America, but also by the BBC) is about the complicity of the masses, panicked into capitulating to 'irresistible' dictatorial power through terroristic propaganda. At the climax, the superhuman conqueror, advancing on the prostrate citizens, is revealed as an animated suit of armour. He is literally a hollow sham, an 'empty signifier', resonating only with their amplified repressions and wishful thinking. By means of the play's eye-witness correspondent narrating events as if they were a breaking news story, radio both creates and then unmasks this false agency, simultaneously baring its own devices.[86] A similar duality in the potential of film to de/mystify itself is implied in Whale's movie and the paradoxical dis/appearance of its central subject and agency. It was no coincidence that the commentator in *The Fall of the City* was played by Orson Welles, who first became famous to 1930s radio audiences as *The Shadow,* a comic-book serial avenger, with the power of making himself invisible through auto-suggestion.[87] (Kemp also protests disbelievingly, 'this *must* be hypnotism. You must have suggested you are invisible' (*IM*, p. 80).) Welles would soon show that atavistic superstitiousness played no small part in the public credibility invested in the scientific media of the Modern period. His own notorious radio treatment of Wells's *WOTW* (also for CBS) caused actual mass panic on the night before Hallowe'en 1938, by using the same persuasive eye-witness device, framed as if it were a live newsflash interrupting a music programme, as in Whale's movie. Moreover, management of public opinion by such means was a matter of concern in liberal democracies as well as states already totalitarianised, or teetering on the brink of it, as Roosevelt's cosy radio 'fireside chats' with the American nation and Chamberlain's cultivation of his image in British newsreels bear out. Welles also intended filming *Heart of Darkness* in 1939 by intra-diegetically aligning Marlow's viewpoint with the camera's gaze, so that audiences would look vicariously through his eyes instead of merely seeing him on screen, effectively making Conrad's narrator a meta-filmic Invisible Man too.[88]

Although converting *IM* for the screen had defeated a number of Hollywood writers, Sherriff (assisted by the uncredited John Weld) wisely decided that the best strategy was to be faithful to Wells's original, because it was already so cinematic in methods, themes and motifs.[89] This was achieved despite tactical concessions to box-office commercialism, such as the interpolated heterosexual romance and significant departures centred on the protagonist's personality and scientific project. As in *Frankenstein*, the main character was deliberately made much more sympathetic. Wells's anti-hero's coolly calculated plans for domination contrast with the unpremeditated nature of his filmic counterpart's designs, despite the latter's greater success as a terrorist compared with the novella's handful of (albeit graphic) murders. Although Wells protested about Whale's device of rendering Griffin insane by means of the drug,[90] he praised the movie's excellence in other respects, perhaps recognising how his own foresight was finally so brilliantly visualised in both sound and image. Largely thanks to Whale, the tale remained 'read as much as it ever was. To many young people nowadays I am just the author of the *Invisible Man*.'[91] The film's special-effects formula was consequently aped in numerous spin-offs into the 1940s[92] and continues to be refined today, through CGI (as Verhoeven's remake, plot aside, impressively exemplifies). Nonetheless, Whale's achievement remains remarkable under the pressures of 1930s Hollywood and its studio system. This is not just for the extent to which it realised the possibilities of Wells's quasi-cinematic style (as a self-conscious comment on the editorial trickery of film), but also for the imaginative way it fulfilled his hunches about the displacement of subjectivity as 'electronic presence', in the complex interaction of modern science, politics and media technology in the coming century.

WTSW's vision is in many ways an extrapolation of *IM*'s radical dislocation in 'seeing and being seen' and the potency and pervasiveness of 'electronic presence'. Wells projects such developments forward into the media-saturated and commodified future of the year 2100. This is, therefore, the focus of the next chapter.

3
'Seeing the Future': Visual Technology in *When the Sleeper Wakes* and Fritz Lang's *Metropolis*

A year into the Great War, Lindsay's *Art of the Moving Picture* alluded to Wells's role in shaping how cinema came to image mass-modernity and its Utopian possibilities: 'The World State is indeed far away. But as we peer into the Mirror Screen some of us dare to look forward to the time when the pouring streets of men will become sacred in each other's eyes, in pictures and in fact.'[1] However, *WTSW* (1899) shows how Wells first projected the implications of sound and image recording into a totally urbanised dystopian future where public and private space are saturated with advanced systems of marketing and control. Effectively, it gathers together diverse 'optical speculations' into an organised social system. Wells's insights into displaced subjectivity and wish-fulfilment in the consumer and into the construction of charismatic electronic presence by 'hyperreal' means are crucial aspects of this.[2] Moreover, this chapter addresses the principal legacy of Wells's early critique in the self-reflexive 'videology' of the science fiction film genre (to use Stewart's term[3]), from Fritz Lang's silent epic *Metropolis* (1926) onwards. Strangely, key transactions between *WTSW* and related texts and Lang's film have been unexplored until now.[4]

WTSW is crucial to understanding Wells's method of 'seeing the future' and its speculations about how media technology would shape the way urbanised modernity might see. John Logie Baird referred to Wells as the 'demi-god' of his youth and was inspired by *WTSW*'s predictions of television and its effects on viewers in his own pioneering experiments.[5] Philmus and Hughes point out that the lost revisions of *TM* seem to resemble the world of *WTSW* more than other versions of his first scientific romance.[6] Indeed, Wells began *WTSW* early and was continuously drawn back to it, tinkering and raiding it for ideas to develop for the rest of his career. Nicolletta Vallorani argues that reworkable potential also makes it 'the most popular of Wells's scientific romances in terms of cinematic exploitation', even though there has never been a named adaptation as such.[7]

Wells has undeservedly acquired a popular reputation for gung-ho technophilia and optimism about the inevitability of social and material progress through scientific change. However, *WTSW* warned that the use of media technology in a globalised, corporate tomorrow might not be driven by political progress and enlightenment, but by managerialism and commodity culture.[8] Its anti-capitalist dystopia envisions not just two-way TV broadcasting to, but panoptic surveillance of, whole populations, among other sinister developments in the year 2100. As such, it is perhaps the most important of what Tim Armstrong calls 'the fantasies of control' produced by an emergent modernity'.[9] In a 1921 Preface, Wells called his Sleeper 'the average man, who owns everything – did he but choose to take hold of his possessions – and who neglects everything'. But Graham awakes to a future which is 'a practical realisation of Mr Belloc's nightmare of the Servile State' (*WTSW*, p. 3). His miraculous trance has been another kind of paradoxical 'absent presence', like that of the Invisible Man, involving spatio-temporal displacement and conspicuous visual defamiliarisation: 'It's a sort of complete absence,' said Isbister. 'Here's the body, empty. Not dead a bit, and yet not alive. It's like a seat vacant and marked "engaged"' (*WTSW*, p. 15). In effect, over 203 years, Graham gradually becomes an iconic ideological space into which a whole civilisation projects its values, especially economically. His cousin Warming's speculations in patent road surfacing ('Eadhamite'), with Graham as (literal) 'sleeping' partner, start the ball rolling for a globalised system to invest in him. Significantly, Graham's parallel American fortune is derived from visual technology ('something about pictures by machinery'). Thus Wells combines rapid transport with communications media, modernity's infrastructural essentials (*WTSW*, pp. 90–91). Eventually the oligarchic White Council rule the future as Graham's trustees. His presence and image become of supreme significance, because of their ambiguous reproducibility. On the one hand, a 'fac-simile' of his signature guarantees the future's currency, while on the other his physical identity can only be authenticated by two-hundred-year-old sepia photographs (*WTSW*, pp. 73 and 90, respectively).

As in 'Through a Window', 'A Dream of Armageddon', 'The Door in the Wall', etc., Wells seems to play on the pleasurable virtualness of cinema as what the text calls 'a phantasmagoria, a new and more vivid sort of dream' (*WTSW*, p. 85), while ambiguously breaking the frame of safety around the spectator's vicarious experience of fantastic elsewheres. At first, Graham relishes this future's wish-fulfilling scenario and the privileged perspectives it affords from glittering skyscrapers, but after the rebellion in the underground ways he gradually realises he is trapped in a nightmarish moving picture of days to come:

> In actual fact he had made such a leap in time as romancers have imagined again and again. And that fact realised, he had been prepared, his mind had, as it were, seated itself for a spectacle. And no spectacle unfolded itself, but a great vague danger, unsympathetic shadows and veils of darkness. Somewhere through the labyrinthine obscurity his death sought him. (*WTSW*, pp. 84–85)

In this hyper-urbanised world state, of which a megalopolitan London is capital, media technology is an overwhelming ideological force: 'After telephone, kinematograph and phonograph had replaced newspaper, book, schoolmaster and letter, to live outside the range of the electric cables was to live an isolated savage' (*WTSW*, p. 117). Ominously, for Wells's film-minded ambitions, in its largely post-literate culture, creative talent is confined to 'factories where feverishly competitive authors devised their phonograph discourses and advertisements and arranged the groupings and developments for their perpetually startling and novel kinematographic dramatic works' (*WTSW*, p. 119). Cinema's early reputation as downmarket escapist entertainment is hypostasised into a principal opiate for masses hired by the day: 'If they have worked well they have a penny or so – enough for a theatre or a cheap dancing place, or a kinematograph story, or dinner, or a bet.' Synchronised words and images on the 'kinematograph-phonograph' simulate voluptuous elsewheres of distant pleasure cities, but only the rich can afford to visit the real things.[10] In the spiritual market place, evangelical sects tout for punters with 'vast and glaring' kinematograph transparencies, presenting New Testament scenes (*WTSW*, pp. 160, 119 and 172, respectively). The mediated cult of the Sleeper itself also plays on Christlike associations. One of Henri Lanos's illustrations to the *Graphic*'s serialisation pictured a vast moving image of the crucifixion.[11]

Wells showed particular prescience about how visual technology would assist in constructing the modern subject as consumer. The naked Graham is kitted out by a tailor, using a miniaturised screen rather than a fashion-plate book, on which a virtual manikin can be posed at will: 'He flicked out a little appliance, the size and appearance of a keyless watch, whirled the knob and behold – a little figure in white appeared kinetoscope fashion on the dial, walking and turning' (*WTSW*, pp. 30–31). Similarly, 'A Story of the Days to Come' (published the same year from material hived off from *WTSW*) elaborates this imagined marketing role. The story's equally megalopolitan London is publicity-saturated, by colossal moving colour advertisements and broadcast sound recordings (see Chapter 1).

In *WTSW*'s parallel future, not only have screens replaced windows on the world outside the city's domed glass roof (halfway between a futuristic Crystal Palace and a vast twenty-second-century shopping mall),[12] videos have superseded texts as windows on the past in the city's mass culture. In a video library, on a series of 'double cylinders', Graham finds versions of Kipling's 'The Man Who Would be King', Conrad's *The* [sic] *Heart of Darkness* and Henry James's 'The Madonna of the Future', although 'this thing before him was not a book as he understood it'.[13] Similarly, Graham gleans the history of this machine-dominated state through watching a 'feature' on the video player. This suggests that Wells foresaw how the coming movie culture might be decoded as an ideological index of its times. About an angry young man from the white silk-clad elite, protesting against socio-economic injustice, the hero of this 'miniature drama' seems embryonic of Freder in *Metropolis*:

> On the flat surface was now a little picture, very vividly coloured, and in this picture were figures that moved. Not only did they move, but they were conversing in clear small voices. It was exactly like reality viewed through an inverted opera glass and heard through a long tube. His interest was seized at once by the situation which presented a man pacing up and down and vociferating angry things to a pretty but petulant woman. Both were in the picturesque costume which seemed so strange to Graham. 'I have worked,' said the man, 'but what have you been doing?'
>
> 'Ah!' said Graham. He forgot everything else, and sat down in the chair. Within five minutes he heard himself named, heard 'when the Sleeper wakes,' used jestingly as a proverb for remote postponement, and passed himself by, a thing remote and incredible. But in a while he knew those two people like intimate friends.
>
> At last the miniature drama came to an end, and the square face of the apparatus was blank again.
>
> It was a strange world into which he had been permitted to look, unscrupulous, pleasure-seeking, energetic, subtle, a world too of dire economic struggle. (*WTSW*, pp. 49–50)

Lang's Freder is also a kind of Sleeper, awakening to generations of economic injustice. He learns the truth of the workers' underground lot, about which his privileged conditioning made him oblivious. Like Graham too, he is heir to the future, because his Ostrog-like father is its master, and faced with the same moral choice: accept the system or change it. Graham meets Helen Wotton, who, like Lang's Maria, awakens his social conscience. As does Maria too, Helen inspires Graham to visit the underworld of the dispossessed third, enslaved by the Labour Department, disguised in their blue canvas uniform (*WTSW*, pp. 155–59 and 170).[14]

Wells created a kind of proto-Debordian 'society of the spectacle' which forewarns about the collusive triumph of commodity culture and media 'hyperreality'.[15] Exploitation of communications technology has created a 'universality of power' (*WTSW*, p. 50). Information is transmitted instantly by videophone to manage the emergency of Graham's unexpected awakening (see *WTSW*, pp. 29–30). Just as the workers' levels are saturated with mind-numbing 'babble machines' (giant phonographs blaring propaganda and commands),[16] 'The Boss', Ostrog (manager of the wind-vane company, on which the city's Edisonian modernity of electric power and light[17] depends), operates a ubiquitous network of surveillance and intelligence-gathering for repressive ends half a century before Orwell's all-seeing 'Big Brother' and his 'telescreen'.[18] Ostrog opportunistically raises rebellion against the Council in the Sleeper's name, but it is a media-created fake, boardroom takeover by violence, exploiting social discontent through agitprop (see *WTSW*, pp. 163–64), only to suppress it on achieving dictatorial power. Clusters of mobile camera-like 'specula' (Wells's term from telescope reflectors (see *WTSW*, p. 114)) enable Ostrog to monitor his *coup d'état* panoptically from his 'crow's nest' above the city, as when the Council's defeated forces are marched away:

> Ostrog stepped across the room, something clicked, and suddenly, save for an oval glow, they were in darkness. For a moment Graham was puzzled.
>
> Then he saw that the cloudy grey disc had taken depth and colour, had assumed the appearance of an oval window looking out upon a strange unfamiliar scene ... He distinguished an orderly file of red figures marching across an open space between files of men in black, and realised before Ostrog spoke that he was looking down at the upper surface of latter-day London. The overnight snows had gone. He judged that the mirror was some modern replacement of the camera obscura, but that matter was not explained to him. He saw that though the file of red figures was trotting from left to right, yet they were passing out of the picture to the left. He wondered momentarily, and then saw that the picture was passing silently, panorama fashion, across the oval. (*WTSW*, p. 102)

For added visual impact, one of Ostrog's aircraft abruptly cuts across the lens, too near to be in focus: 'There was a gleam of metal, a flash, something that swept across the oval, as the eyelid of a bird sweeps across its eye, and the picture was clear again' (*WTSW*, p. 102). Wells also gives a vividly stereoscopic effect of disproportion between the scale of real objects and those on screen: '[Ostrog] stretched a huge black arm across the luminous picture, and showed the room whence Graham had escaped, and across the chasm of ruins the course of his flight' (*WTSW*, p. 104).

Ostrog wants the Sleeper as his 'telegenic' persona, a benign public screen for his repressive new regime (significantly one of Baird's first experimental transmissions was of a ventriloquist's dummy).[19] If lost or killed by the Council, Ostrog intended to replicate Graham physically, endowing a photographically matched double with his identity by hypnotically implanted false memories, to save 'the difficulty of acting'. Hence what matters is not Graham's authentic existence, but the effect of his moving, transmittable image: 'The whole of this revolt depends on the idea that you are awake, alive, and with us' (*WTSW*, p. 100). Specifically, 'At any moment a crisis may arise needing your presence' (*WTSW*, p. 210). Having been a public spectacle lying inside a transparent box, like a stereoscopic still which is suddenly animated and bursts its frame, now Ostrog wants Graham's figure and voice to be duplicated and broadcast simultaneously round the world, as a virtual electronic presence, a ubiquitous simulacrum testifying to the 'miracle' of his awakening, the sign of a new political millennium.[20] Thus Wells predicts the coming role of optical and auditory technology in propaganda and news-management, mass spectacle and the manufactured mystique of media celebrity:

> 'Paris, New York, Chicago, Denver, Capri – thousands of cities are up and in a tumult, undecided and clamouring to see you. They have clamoured that you should be awakened for years, and now it is done they will, scarcely believe –'
> 'But surely – I can't go ...'
> Ostrog answered from the other side of the room, and the picture on the oval disc paled and vanished as the light jerked back again. 'There are kineto-tele-photographs,' he said. 'As you bow to the people here – all over the world myriads of people, packed and still in darkened halls, will see you also. In black and white, of course – not like this. And you will hear their shouts reinforcing the shouting in the hall.' (*WTSW*, p. 106)[21]

Forty-three years later, Wells wrote of the kind of world that had come about specifically as a result of instantaneous communication's shrinking of space and time, globalising individual voices and presences: 'messages that take practically no time at all, loud voices which are heard simultaneously from end to end of the earth, and such contrivances of transmission that the face of a man who was unknown yesterday can become a familiar presence everywhere tomorrow'.[22] *WTSW* also comments presciently on the hyperreal's virtual intimacy. Watching videos, Graham's selfhood became alienated, though quickly offset by what psychologists call 'para-social relationships' with characters on screen: 'he ... passed himself by, a thing remote and incredible. But in a while he knew those two people like intimate friends' (*WTSW*, pp. 49–50). Similarly, not only does Ostrog intend magnifying the Sleeper in gigantic close-up, so 'even the farthest man in the remotest gallery can, if he chooses, count your eyelashes',[23] but, like a prototypical spin-doctor, he also proffers a sloganising 'soundbite': 'Not what you used to call a Speech ... just one sentence, six or seven words. Something formal. If I might suggest – "I have awakened and my heart is with you." That is the sort of thing they want' (*WTSW*, p. 106). Thus the novel's anticipations of radical changes in 'seeing and being seen' (or heard, for that matter) intensified Wells's speculations about the future relationship between politics, subjectivity and media technology in the displacements of *IM* (see Chapter 2).

Eventually Graham sees through Ostrog's electronic cloning and promotion of himself as the ultimate 'branded' signifier and refuses to be puppeted any longer. Nonetheless, he still experiences radically alienated subjectivity faced with the necessity of once again 'playing himself' to studio cameras (rather than to a reciprocally visible public), in order to stir genuine popular revolt by another global broadcast. Ironically the good faith of Graham's new-found political autonomy remains dependent upon mediated image. The distanciation between being recorded and being seen, which unnerved early film actors (as Benjamin recalled),[24] is emphatic:

> the quivering circle of light, the whispers and quick noiseless movements of the vaguely visible attendants in the shadows, had a strange effect upon Graham. The huge ears of a phonographic mechanism gaped in a battery for his words, the black eyes of great photographic cameras awaited his beginning, beyond metal rods and coils glittered dimly, and something whirled about with a droning hum.

Moreover, the surrounding arc-lamp glare is described so as to place readers virtually in Graham's position: 'He walked into the centre of the light, and his shadow drew together black and sharp to a little blot at his feet' (pp. 205–6). Wells shows extraordinary foresight in Graham's realisation that this unprecedented situation demands radical rethinking of the political persona and how it is projected:

> The vague shape of the thing he meant to say was already in his mind. But this silence, this isolation, this withdrawal from that contagious crowd, this silent audience of gaping, glaring machines, had not been in his anticipation. All his supports seemed withdrawn together.

Anxious not to appear merely 'theatrical',[25] Graham tries to adjust to paradoxical disproportionalities – 'the stupendous realisation of a world struggle between Ostrog and himself, and then this confined quiet little room with its mouthpieces and bells and broken mirror!' (*WTSW*, p. 212) – so that he can exploit their potential for intervention in a globalised informational space.[26]

The Videology of SF Film: Wells, Lang and *Metropolis* (1926)

Wells's influence made the question of seeing the future part of the critically self-conscious 'videology' of SF film itself. The role of reproduction technologies was, virtually from the beginning of the screen genre, both part of its subject matter and metacinematic awareness of the state of its own art. The Russian Alexei Tolstoy's very Wellsian SF novel, *Aelita* (1923),[27] is arguably even more saturated with futuristic optical devices of various kinds than *WTSW*. Yakov Protazanov's 1924 adaptation is both a rare example of Soviet 'Cubo-Futurist' propaganda and another strong stylistic influence on Lang. Near the beginning, Aelita, nominal Queen of Mars, disobeys Tuscoob, dictatorial head of the Council of Elders, in order to observe Earth through engineer Gor's interplanetary telescope in the 'tower of radiant energy'. Tuscoob has forbidden knowledge about other worlds, which might spread discontent and subvert the repressive Martian system. What Aelita sees is a montage of documentary views of different countries on Earth, including the newly created USSR, as if projected in a *Kino Pravda* newsreel. Hence the film uses cinema self-reflexively – framing screen within screen – to raise the question: who controls media technology and how it will shape the political consciousness of the future?

This is also the case in comparable sequences from *Metropolis*, scripted by Lang in collaboration with Thea von Harbou, from her 1926 novel.[28] The powerful monopolise access to media technology, shown as integral to what Stewart calls its 'mechanically transmitted chain of repressive command'.[29] Joh Fredersen, Master of Metropolis, surveys his urban business empire panoptically, through a telescreen in his skyscraper HQ, epitomising voyeurism as a key theme and device. This converts to videophone, as he communicates with machine-room foreman Grot, again raising the question of how media technology is managed and for whose benefit. (Closed-circuit television monitors had featured as Wellsian gadgets in Fritz Lang's early serial *Die Spinnen* (1919).[30]) Lang's foregrounding of the camera's gaze typifies his films' tendency towards what Tom Gunning calls 'allegories of vision and modernity', a self-consciousness also pervasive in the many screens and mediating devices in Wells's fiction.[31] Moreover, as Stewart points out, mesh criss-crossing Lang's monitor suggests 'its imprisoning effects'. The viewer's perspective is deliberately aligned with its miniaturised and incarcerated screen-within-screen, framed by the film's warnings against selling out optical science 'to surveillance and enforcement'. Fredersen's videophone is the private counterpart to his robotic 'false' Maria (discussed below), the latter a public spectacle, by which visual entertainment is equally perverted 'into hypnotic delusion'.[32]

Such sequences contrast with Wells's idealistic riposte to Lang's pessimism in his own film *Things to Come* (*TTC*)(1936) (see Chapter 4). This features multiple forms of visual technology in the service of Wells's enlightened 'world state' of 2036, which is saturated with chrome and plexiglass screens and hologram tubes of every shape and size, cut, as Stewart puts it, 'to the eclectic measure of the state's democratic tolerance for the airing of any view'.[33] Optical technology is a benign educational device in Wells's underground technotopia, as demonstrated by a child learning about the superseded 'age of windows' through a screen itself, as a universal, mind-expanding portal on to any elsewhere or elsewhen. Ironically, a sequence near the end shows how even the 'irrational' opposition have access to it, to transmit their protest against unremitting scientific progress (see Chapter 4).

Lang turned back to Wells's early method of seeing the urban future for many reasons, which gave his text renewed topicality within a Weimar German context both class-riven and increasingly polarised around political extremes threatening its fragile social democracy. Besides its technological 'videology', Wells's writing appealed to Lang for stylistic reasons. *Metropolis* was the most monumental epic produced by Universum Film Aktiengesellschaft (UFA), at its Neubabelsberg studios. The film's technical innovations had a pervasive and enduring influence on the development of the screen SF genre (especially its ingenious combination of live scenes and scale models using mirrors, through the pioneering 'Schüfftan process', a prototype of today's 'blue screen' technology).[34] *Metropolis* took 16 months to shoot, required over 37,000 extras, and cost over 7 million marks. Set around the year 2000 in a kind of futuristic New York, *Metropolis* is a hyper-urbanised and -mechanised anti-capitalist dystopia like *WTSW*.[35] Joh Fredersen is its Ostrog-like magnate-dictator, while his son, Freder, assumes Graham's naïve playboy role.

In Wells's fiction, hierarchy is literally embodied in the city's multi-levelled built environment. Social class is also stratified in *Metropolis*'s architecture: above, élite penthouses and orgiastic nightclubs; below, 'monstrous' machine rooms with expendable human components; subterranean, the brutally stylised 'workers' city'. *Metropolis*'s visualisation is perhaps the highpoint of Expressionist cinema's fascination with the city. The scale of Wells's architectonic imagery inspired its groundbreaking sets.[36] *WTSW*'s London, with its vast, teeming, artificial canyons, was a principal model, particularly because of the filmic dynamism with which Wells constantly switches between close-up human scale and the depersonalising, limitless space of its cityscape:

> [Graham's] first impression was of overwhelming architecture. The place into which he looked was an aisle of Titanic buildings, curving spaciously in either direction. Overhead mighty cantilevers sprang together across the huge width of the place, and a tracery of translucent material shut out the sky. Gigantic globes of cool white light shamed the pale sunbeams that filtered down through the girders and wires. Here and there a gossamer suspension bridge dotted with foot passengers flung across the chasm and the air was webbed with slender cables. A cliff of edifice hung above him, he perceived as he glanced upward, and the opposite façade was grey and dim and broken by great archings, circular perforations, balconies, buttresses, turret projections, myriads of vast windows, and an intricate scheme of architectural relief. (*WTSW*, p. 35)

This 'gigantic glass hive' (itself like a huge optical device) with its 'kaleidoscope' pattern of masses, is traversed by 'moving ways', giant conveyor belts crammed with human traffic (*WTSW*, pp. 63 and 36, respectively); the space above, by aircraft and advertising blimps, as in Lang's sets (see *WTSW*, p. 116, for example).

Abrupt symbolic contrast between above and below was one of Expressionist cinema's chief strategies for dynamizing literal *and* social space.[37] *Metropolis*, like *WTSW*, is riddled with all kinds of staircases, shafts and lifts, most famously the '*Pater-noster Maschine*', the central tower's vertebrae, transporting shifts of workers in its cages. However, Lang's relatively sparing use of mass movement against his cityscape is one of the film's technical deficiencies, since (despite the patent Schüfftan process) it wasn't feasible to project sustained crowd action on to scale model sets until Wells's own *TTC*.

WTSW's method of narrating also frequently brought the 'frame-into-the-picture', not least in how Wells's dynamic visualisation of megapolitan London transforms static 'scenography' into a cinematically stereoscopic space, with a constantly angled, refocused and obstructed viewpoint conditioned by the built environment. Everywhere the reader 'sees' vicariously through Graham's mobile intra-diegetic gaze (see Introduction), through transparent panes, or partial structures. Wells alternates panoramic with claustrophobic effects, among crowds and buildings, with subjective 'shots' from Graham's disorientated perspective. These fragment the imaginary visual field into fluctuating three-dimensionality:

> There came a passage in twilight, and into this passage a footway hung so that he could see the feet and ankles of people going to and fro thereon, but no more of them ...
> Presently he was in a lift that had a window upon the great street space ... he saw people going to and fro along cables and along strange, frail-looking bridges.
> And thence they passed across the street and at a vast height above it. They crossed by means of a narrow bridge closed in with glass, so clear that it made him giddy even to remember it. The floor of it also was of glass ... He stopped, looked down between his legs upon the swarming blue and red multitudes, minute and fore-shortened. (*WTSW*, pp. 40–41)

Such descriptions anticipate moving camerawork in *Metropolis*, but also Modernist 'montage' urban documentaries, such as Ruttmann's *Berlin*, with its high and low shots through windows, lift cages, moving trams and girder frames and its collective synecdoches such as commuters' hurrying legs.

Later, after the Council's attempt to suppress the Sleeper sparks a violent uprising, Wells presents scenes of agitated mass movement, complete with lighting effects suggestive of similar sequences in *Metropolis*, when the crowd is visualised from both without and within, i.e. en bloc, or with individuals momentarily highlighted by close-ups:

> He heard the green weapons crackling. For a space he lost his individual will, became an atom in a panic, blind, unthinking, mechanical. He thrust and pressed back and writhed in the pressure, kicked presently against a step, and found himself ascending a slope. And abruptly the faces all about him leapt out of the black, visible, ghastly white and astonished, terrified, perspiring in a livid glare. One face, a young man's, was very near to him, not twenty inches away. At the time it was but a passing incident of no emotional value, but afterwards it came back to him in his dreams. For this young man, wedged upright in the crowd for a time, had been shot and was already dead.

A flare bursts, so that 'This time the picture was livid and fragmentary, slashed and barred with black shadows' (*WTSW*, p. 80). Wells contrives other moments of astonishingly expressive chiaroscuro. For example, when the Council searchlights the city roof over which Graham is escaping, the movement of gigantic wind vanes creates a 'strobing' effect: 'In a score of seconds they were within a tracery of glare and black shadows shot with moving bars beneath the monstrous wheels' (*WTSW*, p. 64).[38]

WTSW also features highly cinematic examples of narrative analepsis. When Graham first awakes, in his disorientated state he experiences 'a panorama of dazzling unstable confluent scenes'. Later he undergoes an accelerated montage, as it were, of recollections, as he tries to piece together 'kaleidoscopic impressions' into some kind of comprehension of the strange world he finds himself in. There is a similar effect in the 'maze of memories, fluctuating pictures', by which Wells recaps Graham's eye-opening visit to the labyrinthine passages of the workers' levels (*WTSW*, pp. 19, 46 and 191).

Wells literally gives wings to Graham's mobilised virtual gaze in climactic scenes of kamikaze tactics against Ostrog's airforce. These are both aerodynamically prophetic and highly cinematic in their simulatory thrills, increasingly sought after in the medium itself as Virilio argues:

> [Graham] swept round in a half circle, staring at this advancing fleet. It flew in a wedge-like shape, a triangular flight of gigantic phosphorescent shapes sweeping nearer through the lower air ... He touched a lever and the throbbing effort of the engine ceased. He began to fall, fell swifter and swifter. He aimed at the apex of the wedge. He dropped like a stone through the whistling air. It seemed scarce a second from that soaring moment before he struck the foremost aeroplane. (*WTSW*, pp. 223–24)

But even amongst such dizzying manoeuvres Wells interposes a mediating visual frame, as the following close-up suddenly reminds us: 'The big machine heeled and swayed as the fear-maddened men scrambled to the stern for their weapons. A score of bullets sang through the air, and there flashed a star in the thick glass wind-screen that protected him' (p. 225).

WTSW presents what Ostrog calls 'this great machine of the city' (*WTSW*, p. 165) as a vast interlocking mechanism. *Metropolis*'s opening montage superimposes working gears and pistons over the cityscape to suggest the same interchangeability. Wells's contemporary, Ford Madox Ford, also described London as an integrated machine in which specialised individuals 'work one into another like the teeth of cogwheels revolving antithetically'.[39] The fascination and fear of modern machinery and its implications for social organisation were given literary form by writers such as Wells and Kipling in the ambivalence of the contemporary 'operational aesthetic'. But this grew out of the power and mystery of new technologies which film visualised in operation, par excellence because it was one of them, as Expressionist and avant-garde documentary cinema would epitomise. Film extensions of the dystopian city-as-machine metaphor satirised 'rationalising' industrial policies such as the efficiency drive through Frederick Taylor's 'time and motion studies'. Taylor's system is attacked by Lang when Freder takes over a worker's shift. He literally fights the clock, crucified on the hands of a gigantic dial. Freder's agonised intertitle, 'I never realised ten hours could take so long', visualises a paradox familiar from stories such as 'The New Accelerator' (see Chapter 1): the simultaneous speeding-up and dilation of temporal consciousness under modern conditions at their most alienating. Lang famously choreographs workers into titanic machines, as organic components, to symbolise dehumanising mass-production. This makes explicit his opening Wellsian suggestion that the city itself is interchangeable with the machine. Lang's *coup de cinéma*, doubling Maria's living features on Rotwang's android, remains the most influential screen embodiment of the artificial slave-workers from Karel Capek's play *RUR* (*Rossum's Universal Robots*) (1920) (despite their bio-synthetic origin). It is also the symbolic terminus of the effects of his mechanised city on bodies and minds.

Wells's Reaction: 'The Silliest Film'?

Despite *Metropolis*'s creative debt to *WTSW* and related writings, Wells was notoriously unflattered by Lang's intended homage, believing that he had outgrown such alarmism about the future. His review of the 1927 New York premiere declared, 'I have recently seen the silliest film. I do not believe it would be possible to make one sillier.' Its depiction of urban modernity compounded 'almost every possible foolishness, cliché, platitude and muddlement about mechanical progress and progress in general, served up with a sauce of sentimentality', though he reluctantly acknowledged 'decaying fragments of my own juvenile work' in the mix.[40]

Wells argued that where the film-makers couldn't plunder someone else's foreseeing, they fell back on the contemporary. Hence *Metropolis*'s aircraft showed no technological advance (they weren't even helicopters) and its cars were 1926 models (*The Way the World is Going*)(*WTWIG*, p. 180). Similarly, it was excusable to 'symbolise social relations' by vertical urbanisation in the 1890s, but the centrifugal tendency to suburbanisation was taking effect even in New York. UFA clearly hadn't read *Anticipations of the Reaction of Mechanical and Scientific Progress upon Human Life and Thought* (1902) and was, therefore not a hundred years ahead, but 'a third of a century out of date' (*WTWIG*, p. 181). Hence, long before this scathing review, Wells revised *WTSW*'s demographic predictions. *Anticipations* marks the point when he renounced the inevitability of the 'systematic enslavement of organised labour', also swapping megalopolitan London for decentralisation, through electrification, telephonics, etc.[41] His dystopian warning about a future 'World State' was also reconfigured as a *positive* project for global integration. This was then elaborated in *Mankind in the Making* (1903), as a proposed 'New Republic', organised on what would become familiar Wellsian principles of technocracy, eugenics, social engineering, mass communications and education, leading to *A Modern Utopia* (1905). Wells rubbished Lang's outdated economics too. Mass production and commodity culture without widespread disposable income and, therefore, mass consumption, would be self-defeating rather than enriching (see *WTWIG*, p. 182).[42] *Metropolis* even clashed with Taylorian efficiency, working machine-minders to death and squandering material resources in preventable explosions.

Lang probably felt wounded on reading Wells's syndicated review in the *Frankfurter Zeitung* of 3 May 1927.[43] In Lang's defence, it's arguable that Wells took symbolic exaggerations of style (Expressionism, by definition, eschewed naturalistic mimesis and proportion) rather literally. With retrospect, it is also arguable that Wells's case was exaggerated, even myopic, coming only two years before the meltdown of transatlantic capitalism in the Wall Street Crash, causing worldwide economic collapse and apocalyptic consequences for Germany particularly. He optimistically opined that industrial advances required more highly skilled workers in ratio, that the *lumpenproletariat* and mass unemployment were no longer inevitable: 'We did not know what to do with the abyss. But there is no excuse for that to-day' (*WTWIG*, p. 183).[44] More understandably, he ridiculed *Metropolis*'s sentimental Christianity. Maria's Babel sermon warned against hubristic 'progress', but reconciliatory 'love' was hardly an effective solution to modernity's complex problems. Conversely, Rotwang's robot-prototype, originally designed to replace drudge labour, was a humane invention in principle (*WTWIG*, pp. 184–85). The 'crowning imbecility' was hijacking this project to convert 'Futura' into Fredersen's agent provocateur (*WTWIG*, p. 186).

Significantly, Wells recognised that the figure of Rotwang owed as much to the Faustian–Gothic tradition as to modern science: '[a] quaint smell of Mephistopheles is perceptible' (*WTWIG*, p. 186). But he also conveniently forgot that so much of his own early writing transformed the occult into SF themes, both in the 'paranormal' marvellousness of its speculations and in its scepticism towards progress through rationalism alone.[45] It is tempting to infer that one reason for Wells's extreme reaction was that his own past was coming back to haunt him. Less surprising was Hitler's enthusiasm for *Metropolis*'s unsettling blend of mysticism and futurity. In 1937, Arthur Koestler described fascism's appeal as an 'ultra-modern form of reaction', because it opportunistically hijacked advanced technologies for irrational ends.[46] Ironically, the template for actual things to come was slipping from Wells's grasp. Though noting that English intertitles called Joh Fredersen 'John Masterman' (*WTWIG*, p. 181), he neither detected topical parallelism with Nazi doctrines, such as 'mastery' ('*Herrschaft*'), nor anticipated their imminent realisation after Hitler won the German state elections a mere five years later. Ominously, *Metropolis*'s intellectual overreaching and narrative incoherence (aggravated by the butchered version released) made it a box-office flop, causing the studio's American bankrollers to pull out.[47] UFA was consequently snapped up by media tycoon Alfred Hugenberg, one of Nazism's principal backers. Subsequent events make Wells's conclusion that *Metropolis* had 'nothing to do with any social or moral issue before the world' seem baffling today (*WTWIG*, p. 187). Wells seems not to have considered (as the Nazis instinctively did in admiring its Wagnerian–apocalyptic pretensions and salvationary politics) that *Metropolis* might be symptomatic of the struggle in Germany itself between reactionary and progressive forces.[48] These were just waiting for economic collapse to catalyse them into a crisis, leading to the most extreme form of authoritarian solution. Ironically, like many of Wells's own texts, *Metropolis* proved to be less about the future than about where the present was heading.

Nonetheless, he conceded that *Metropolis* wasted 'some very fine possibilities', because the Weimar Republic, above all European states, appeared committed to industrial modernity (*WTWIG*, p. 188). Thus at the end of his review we can clearly see the idea for his answering 'technotopia', *TTC* (1936), germinating: 'it would have been … far more interesting to have taken some pains to gather the opinions of a few bright young research students and ambitious, modernising architects and engineers about the trend of modern invention, and develop these artistically'. Coupled with cutting-edge views on communications, labour organisation and politics, such a film would make it possible to bring 'these things ... into touch with the life of to-day' and make them 'interesting to the man in the street' (*WTWIG*, p. 188).⁴⁹ However, Wells's actual scripting came nearly as close to producing a Babelian crash for London Films as *Metropolis* had for UFA (see Chapter 4).

Unrecognised Transactions

Nevertheless, it is revealing how key themes and methods in *WTSW*'s vision of the future, though disavowed by Wells, were developed by Lang. Most tellingly, Wells did not recognise Lang's extrapolation of his themes of proto-totalitarian political control, especially the cloning and projection of charismatic 'electronic presence' through the media. As Joh Fredersen's prototype, Ostrog contemptuously rejects mass democracy – 'the Crowd as Ruler', he calls it – as liberal anachronism versus evolutionary necessity. Urbanisation and technology have inevitably rendered such ideas redundant in the vast interlocking mechanism of the metropolis: 'The common man now is a helpless unit. In these days we have this great machine of the city, and an organisation complex beyond his understanding' (*WTSW*, p. 165). Ostrog believes instead in Nietzsche's mastering 'Over-man', that modern conditions automatically lead to, and justify, dictatorship (*WTSW*, pp. 166–67).⁵⁰ However, Wells's 1921 Preface claimed that Ostrog's plutocratic conspiracy 'gave way to reality' in the shape of *Tono-Bungay*'s uncle Ponderevo: 'Much evil may be in store for mankind, but to this immense, grim organisation of servitude, our race will never come' (*WTSW*, p. 4). The entrepreneurial monopolist of his 1909 novel, nonetheless, inherited undeniably Ostrogian habits, not least wielding the propagandist power of media advertising. Hence the eponymous patent medicine on which Ponderevo founds a global consumer empire. Similarly, Ostrog packages and broadcasts the 'miraculous' cult of the Sleeper as 'endorsement' for his political solution, though its effect on the common good is purely placebic.⁵¹

Other connections merit consideration. As Michael Minden points out, Lang's biblical (as well as Gothic) imagery, which visually puns together archetypal barbarity and the modern, is comparable to the 'mythic method' of High Modernist urban texts such as Joyce's *Ulysses* or T. S. Eliot's *The Waste Land* (both 1922). But Babel and Babylon became current as 'metaphors for the vast and indeterminate nature of the city, ever since it became too large for easy assimilation, in the first half of the nineteenth century'.⁵² *Metropolis*'s most famous biblical allusions are Freder's superimposed vision of the 'heart machine' as the jaws of Moloch, continuously devouring fresh human 'Futter', and Maria's sermon about Babel.

Both are filtered through Wellsian associations. The name of the sacrificial idol and that of *TM*'s troglodytic cannibals – the Morlocks – resonate with proximity. The 'mouth' to their mechanical underworld is also surmounted by a monumental Sphinx (see *TM*, p. 21).[53] The Sleeper cult is embodied in statues of Atlas, nobly shouldering the sky, although the ruling idol is actually the Syrian god of riches: as Helen Wotton says, 'Every city now is a prison. Mammon grips the key in his hand' (*WTSW*, p. 158). Similarly, Babelian imagery (towering architecture, ubiquitous 'babble machines', etc.) and sacrificial machine-idolatry saturate not just *WTSW* and 'A Story of the Days to Come', but also 'The Lord of the Dynamos' (1894), 'The Cone' (1895), etc. (see Chapter 1).[54]

The most important transposition of Wells's optically self-conscious style and themes can be seen in what Stewart terms *Metropolis*'s 'metafilmic allegory'.[55] Wells noted that *Metropolis* was the acme of Expressionism's preoccupation with artificial life: 'Capek's robots have been lifted without apology, and that soulless mechanical monster of Mary Shelley's, who has fathered so many German inventions, breeds once more in this confusion' (*WTWIG*, pp. 179–80). However, he didn't recognise Lang's android as an analogue for film itself, developing his own insights about media technology and charismatic electronic presence.[56] In Expressionist film, simulation or duplication of images of the living (reanimation from undeath or catatonic trance, synthesis as Golem or Homunculus) are widespread and self-reflexive motifs. These are anticipated not just in *WTSW*, but also in many other Wells texts about doubling (as we saw in earlier chapters). Though the subjective distortion of its characteristic style was particularly suited to the morbid or paranormal themes of horror movies (*Schauerfilme* epitomising film as 'technology of the uncanny'), in virtually every genre Expressionism sought out cinema's potential for exploring the psychological and social implications of optical processes, especially those involved in making and watching film itself. Consequently, Lang's voyeuristic tropes (not least Fredersen and Rotwang spying on Maria) foregrounded the camera's mobilised virtual gaze and its positioning of the spectating subject, with all its suggestion of manipulation and consumption. However, *Metropolis*'s specific analogue for the mechanical simulation of life in moving images takes the form of Rotwang's robot. Although Lang and von Harbou were certainly influenced by a skein of media-related intertexts (besides those noted by Wells),[57] in effect, they took up *WTSW*'s underdeveloped motif of the hypnotic double to preserve Graham's likeness for televisation, but displaced it on to their female android. Significantly, Rotwang mesmerises the real Maria (accompanied by repeated close-ups of his controlling gaze, as she is frozen in the projector-like beam of his torch) before he grafts her captive appearance on to his robot (by literal superimposition) in one of the most famous special effects sequences: 'it is time to give the machine your face'.⁵⁸

In reworking Wells's doubling motif, Lang had a precedent in another filmic take on *WTSW*'s themes, Marcel L'Herbier's *L'Inhumaine* (1924) (*The Inhuman Woman*), as Vallorani notes.⁵⁹ With geometric designs by machine-minded Cubist Fernand Léger, *L'Inhumaine* is set in a futuristic Paris (*'Ici dominant la ville'*, an intertitle stresses), where Einar Norsen (Jacque Catelain) practises *'la féerie du science moderne'*. Awakening to a new technological 'life' and mediated absent-presence are ambiguous leitmotifs. Apparently commiting suicide because of unrequited love for diva Claire Lescot (Georgette Leblanc), Norsen suddenly rematerialises to haunting gramophone music besides his own 'corpse'. He wins 'L'Inhumaine' over to the cause of science by showing how her impending world tour could be replaced by television: 'LE MONDE ENTIER EST ICI ... DÉPLACEZ VOUS par TSF' appears over a screen-within-the-screen.⁶⁰ Singing into a microphone, the diva watches a cross-section of images of peoples across the world transmitted back to her. They are simultaneously listening on speakers in all kinds of locations, beyond the traditional stage (*'Elle voyage sans bouger à travers l'espace aboli'*).⁶¹ Norsen sets about literally resurrecting his object of desire, after she is subsequently murdered by his rival, in his laboratory full of whirling discs, tubes, dials, spirals and pendulums, with assistants in shiny black overalls and visors. The visual process of 'L'Inhumaine's' 'rebirth' is thus also an uncanny technological simulation of celebrity womanhood, a point made self-reflexive by effects such as superimposition and the duplication of images of human and machine, rapid montage, flashes of colour even. Norsen's sparking apparatus prefigures the electrical power lines radiating from Rotwang's robot, whose metal face also recalls the diva's inhumanly masked servants. (Wells was so impressed by Legér's designs that he approached him to supply concept sketches for *TTC*. The world broadcasting sequence of his original treatment was also modelled on *L'Inhumaine* (see Chapter 4).⁶²)

Likewise, *Metropolis* responded to Wells's speculations about the undemocratic use of media technology and virtual spectacle by counterfeiting Maria, minister to the masses.⁶³ Rotwang thus disguises his machine of metal parts as 'a "celluloid", an illusory *dea ex machina*', sent forth to subvert discontent, in Stewart's terms.⁶⁴ This is crucial for fomenting a manipulated revolt like Ostrog's, by which his counterpart, Joh Fredersen, stirs discontent into violence to create a pretext for subjugating the workers once and for all. As J. P. Telotte also argues,⁶⁵ like the illusion of cinema itself, the robot is a mechanical 'replication', from which, paradoxically, all appearance of artifice has disappeared in the process and which doubles a reality concealed or elsewhere: Maria remains imprisoned in Rotwang's laboratory while her stolen likeness runs amok. Both cinema and robot are inventions. Both simulate the appearance of living human beings. Both create spectacles moving mass audiences in emotionally charged and/or propagandistic ways. Thus Lang's response to *WTSW*'s prescient media critique had a key impact on subsequent SF cinema's self-referential themes. Postmodern mutations of their joint legacy, into the existentially undecidable 'replicants' inhabiting the 'tech noir' urban sprawl of Ridley Scott's *Blade Runner* (1982) and ever more state-of-the-art CGI cyborgs of more recent 'retrofitted' dystopian environments, testify to that.[66]

However, this narrative of media politics also has a gender flipside. The Weimar German constitution was arguably the most modernising in Europe in terms of sexual equality. But the polarisation of Maria's image may echo Wells's own ambivalence about the emerging 'New Woman' of the 1890s.[67] Cinema would be a symptomatic medium for renegotiating femininity as social product and cultural icon in the modern city, especially its implications of patriarchal panic. (In both novella and film, the false Maria is associated with visions of Revelation's Whore of Babylon.)[68] Significantly, Helen Wotton, Ostrog's radical niece, politicises Graham about the system's oppression, thus catalysing the 'real' revolution. Similarly, *WTSW* replaces maternal functions and responsibilities by faceless automata – 'mechanical figures, with arms, shoulders and breasts of astonishingly realistic modelling' and counterpart machines 'that sang and danced and dandled' – (*WTSW*, pp. 179–80) in corporate crèches. Thus 'liberated', women are able to lead more independent lives, but, it is hinted ironically, primarily as sexual consumers themselves (*WTSW*, pp. 182–83). Wotton's counterpart, Maria, is a more traditionally feminine heroine. Demurely dressed, she first appears leading poor children into the privileged levels, to interrupt Freder's frolics with scantily clad courtesans in the Eternal Gardens. His partner's flirtatiousness prefigures the frenzied 'shamelessness' of the false Maria's nightclub dance (consumed by a tessellated screenful of disembodied male eyes). Both echo *WTSW*'s commodification of desire, which late Victorian Graham finds so shocking. The 'musical fantasia' he watches with its virtual eroticism – 'These were no pictures ... but photographed realities'– alludes topically to cinema's rapid exploitation by pornographers. Consequently, the future's mediated culture is dominated by 'systematised sensuality' (see *WTSW*, p. 51).[69] In line with cinema's ambiguous origins, the robot's maker, Rotwang, is both scientific genius and huckstering showman. In von Harbou's novel he first shows off his creepily 'living' creation to paying crowds in his workshop, like a backstreet 'nickelodeon' proprietor exhibiting the latest risqué novelty.[70] Similarly, during the transformation scene, the robot's electrically generated aura symbolises the synthetic appeal of 'star charisma', already a mass commodity by the 1920s.

Futura's mechanised spectacle (simultaneously erotic entertainment and covert agitprop) unleashes a sensation as Maria appears to betray the workers. However, Fredersen's strategy backfires when, Golem-like, she runs amok, inciting them to destroy the 'heart machine' on which the city depends, and leaving the 'real' Maria (rescued by his son), to save its children from the consequent apocalyptic flood. Labour is then symbolically reconciled with capital. Both recognise common human interest, through the 'mediator', Freder, and his love for Maria. Between these two poles – neo-Victorian domestic saint and synthetically 'modernised' vamp – the new image of femininity was arguably also played out on the early twentieth-century screen.[71]

Wells derided Lang's 'mediator' plot as hokum, though it also derived from the Sleeper's millennial iconography. In the Expressionist terms into which the film transforms Wells's themes, Freder fulfils Maria's prophecy about the individual who will heal divisions inherent in this managerial society's flawed foundations. Her intertitle reads, 'Between the brain that plans and the hands that build, there must be a mediator ... it is the heart that must bring about an understanding between them.' As Lang admitted later, such a *Märchen* ('fairytale') was incompatible with 'socially aware' film-making.[72] But this downplays *Metropolis*'s own pointing-up of the camera's potential for the demystifying treatment of modern urban civilisation. Through Freder's explorations, like Graham's, *Metropolis* makes visible underlying relations between upper and lower socio-economic strata, the spectator/reader 'discovering' these vicariously with respective protagonists. Freder starts in ignorance of what Storm Jameson in the 1930s would call 'the relation between things (men, acts) far apart in space or in the social complex', mystified by modern capitalism. In her view, it was the primary objective of art to document and reveal their reality.[73] In German, *Mittler* can mean mediator or 'medium'. Hence it suggests analogy with Lang's visual technique, whether *intra*-diegetically aligned with Freder's viewpoint (as when he visits the central machine room to witness toil at first hand), or used in *extra*-diegetic, 'third-person' perspective. Lang's camera suggestively links zones of experience alienated from each other, by modes of production and ideological distance, a principle soon extended to representing actual metropolises, through cross-cutting montage films by avant-garde documentarists.

One of the most influential of them, Ruttmann's *Berlin: Sinfonie einer Großstadt*, also marked the swing away from studio-bound Expressionism in Weimar film-making to the location style of *Neue Sachlichkeit* ('New Objectivity') in the treatment of urban themes. Although Lang's film lurches between banal romance and universalising socio-economic critique, the central preoccupation of the 'big city' films of the later twenties would be showing populations amid contemporary metropolises' built environments, in all their complex integration, more mimetically and concretely. Indeed, Wells himself praised *Berlin*'s style as an alternative mapping of the urban mindscape of modernity (for Wellsian connections with Ruttmann, see also Chapters 1 and 4).[74]

Visionary SF similarly continued to battle over shaping the future, with greater urgency as the Weimar Republic reached its crisis. German film became increasingly subservient to nationalist and anti-Semitic propaganda campaigns after Hitler's takeover.[75] Most ominously, *Der Herrscher* (1937) took up where *Metropolis*'s mystical resolution to the problems of modernity ended so ambiguously. Its Berlin was now the integrated, hyperefficient, techno-industrial powerhouse of a reflated and militarised economy. It was watched over by upstanding Aryan men and their superhuman leader, custodians of a future Nazi world order.[76] However, even if Wells disowned Lang's creative revival of his earlier text, their joint influence on seeing the future nevertheless quickly inscribed an international template for the anxieties and aspirations which topical urban SF articulates. For example, *High Treason* (dir. Maurice Elvey, 1929), Gaumont British's first (retrospectively dubbed) sound feature, was a futuristic thriller set in a high-rise London. The adapted Wells–Lang template is clearly visible in the key role that hi-tech media play in imaging the social totality and in political life.[77] London is the capital of the 'Federated States of Europe'. The plot concerns frictions (secretly fomented by a multi-national armaments ring by acts of terrorism) with the 'Atlantic States', a rival superpower centred on New York. *High Treason* prefigures *Things to Come* by predicting the outbreak of another war with a surprise aerial attack in 1940 (it also featured an uncredited Raymond Massey, who would play Wells's lead, as a prominent member of the Peace League). World conflict is prevented by the timely subversion of a televised declaration of war and by mass urban feminist revolt against the air force (daughter of Peace League President, Evelyn Seymour (Benita Hume) playing a Maria-like leadership role). Conversely, Hollywood's *Just Imagine* (dir. David Butler, 1930) countered European scepticism about an 'Americanised' future. It dreamt a technotopian USA of 1980, in which a Depression citizen miraculously revives to delighted astonishment at the cloud-piercing proportions of its built environment, vast urban motorways, aerial traffic and, especially, hi-tech consumer electronics – videophones and televisions. As that rarest hybrid, an SF musical comedy, it set the tone for romantic modernist sets in other genres throughout 1930s Hollywood, although an expensive box-office disaster in its own right.[78] However, the film's optimism (to offset the context of its making) was echoed ironically in Aldous Huxley's *Brave New World* (1932). Huxley updated the media-saturated urbanism of *WTSW* to satirise the potential global triumph of inter-war transatlantic corporatism. Significantly, its most potent form of cultural narcotic was the 'feelies', an extension of *WTSW*'s systematised sensuality into virtual tactility.

Undoubtedly, Wells's ambivalence about the visualisation of 'Wellsian' themes in the cinema of the 1920s stimulated his own belated desire to re-engage with the medium in practical terms. Films such as Lang's opened his eyes to film's potential for reaching a wider audience with his urgent socio-scientific message. His own scripting is therefore the subject of the next chapter.

4
The 'Broadbrow' and the Big Screen: Wells's Film Writing

Silent Wells

Sylvia Hardy argues that Wells is a kind of paradigm of literary involvement in cinema's first decades because he simultaneously reflected and contributed to how film made use of and saw itself as relating to fiction.[1] Demographic, cultural and class parallels between the new mass audiences for both cinema and the kind of fiction that Wells practised are manifold. In his 1929 introduction to *KWWAK*, he noted with satisfaction the pressure that cinema put on the traditional bastions of art, both challenging their social exclusiveness and raising alternative aesthetic possibilities:

> It has been interesting to watch the elegant and dignified traditions of the world of literature and cultivated appreciation, under the stresses and thrusts produced by the development of rapid photography during the past half-century. Fifty years ago not the most penetrating of prophets could have detected in the Zoetrope and the dry-plate camera the intimations of a means of expression, exceeding in force, beauty and universality any that have hitherto been available for mankind. Now that advent becomes the most obvious of probabilities. (*KWWAK*, p. 8)

The early industry resorted to literature to stake its own claims for aesthetic respectability and prestige, mostly through adaptations rather than commissioning original scripts. However, according to Wells, the indiscriminate appetite for scenarios didn't necessarily either enhance the texts it devoured or progress its own technical evolution:

> It bought right and left; it bought high and low; it was so opulent it could buy with its eyes shut. It did. Its methods were simple and direct. It took all the stories it could get, and changed all that were not absolutely intractable into one old, old story, with variations of costume, scenery and social position. (*KWWAK*, p. 11)

Although the screening of Wellsian themes and motifs (if not whole narratives as such) goes back as far as Méliès, and invisible men were rife in the late 1900s, it is unlikely that they were legally sourced, copyright law lagging behind the new medium.[2] Sometimes Wellsian material was mixed in with others, as in Walter Booth's *The Airship Destroyer* (1909), publicised as 'War In The Air! Possibilities Of The Future! An actual motion picture prediction of the ideas of Rudyard Kipling, H. G. Wells and Jules Verne.'[3] *WITA* had been published the year before and this British film gives an effective impression of what aerial conflict might be like, with combatants and civilians alike on the front line. Massed zeppelins destroy a city (including, shockingly, its cathedral) causing widespread panic and casualties, like a technically cruder version of the opening of *Things to Come*. Tank-like mobile guns prove ineffective, though the day is finally saved by a Wellsian inventor with a prototype, wireless-controlled anti-aircraft missile. Arguably silents of the 1900s and early 1910s were saturated with uncredited Wellsian influences. Capitalising on the scaremongering 'invasion' fiction trend (see Chapter 5), they often featured futuristic vehicles, 'inhuman' foes and super-weapons such as airships, Martians, flying torpedoes and death rays.[4] Joë Hamman's *L'Île d'épouvante* (1913) may well be the prototype of all adaptations of *IODM*'s vivisective acceleration of animal evolution. *A Blind Bargain* (1922), in which Lon Chaney's demented scientist creates a monstrously humanised ape, is arguably Hollywood's earliest stab at the same theme.[5] Anti-gravity was also much in the air. Films influenced by Wells's 'Cavorite' may include Cecil Hepworth's *The Professor's Anti-Gravitational Fluid* (1908), in which a predictably mischievous boy wreaks mayhem with people's clothes and possessions. Similarly, anti-gravity powder provided slapstick propulsion for Edwin S. Porter's *A Trip to Mars* (1910).

Because of such unlicensed borrowing, Wells's agent was soon touting exclusive rights to production companies. Wells's first major contract was significant enough to be announced in *The Times* in January 1914: 'world rights of representing the works of Mr. H. G. Wells upon the cinematograph have been secured by Gaumont British'. The paper also noted that Wells's texts were already 'admirably suited for the purpose' of adaptation, but also hoped he would now 'construct stories especially for cinematograph production', as a patriotic opportunity for boosting the home-grown industry.[6] Despite the lengthening hiatus since Paul's Time Machine project, a sense of expectation about Wells's potential contribution was still palpable in 1922 in *Kinematograph Weekly*'s claim that he was 'one of the biggest forces in the world today'.[7] However, Wells did not begin retraining as a professional scenarist for another decade.

Though film-makers evidently recognised the cinematic potential of the scientific romances, because of the special effects demanded, they mostly told Wells's agent that production would be prohibitively expensive. It was precisely the inadequate visualisation of fantastic phenomena which reviewers complained about in Gaumont British's version of *FMITM*.[8] Shooting was put on hold until the Armistice (because key film ingredients were reserved for munitions) and the film was released only in 1919, when expectations about production values would have risen further because of Hollywood's cornering of the international market during the Great War. Surprisingly, given the patriotic climate of the time, the imperialistic Bedford was now an explicit cad, trying to steal the formula for Cavorite and poach the inventor's niece, Susan, from her fiancé, a radio operator picking up interplanetary signals. Director Bruce Gordon Leigh introduced a 'love interest', casting starlet Heather Thatcher as the first woman astronaut, in effect. This may have influenced Wells's decision to institute sexual equality among the crew of his space mission in *Things to Come* (*TTC*), but it was certainly a box-office strategy revived by Hollywood in Nathan Juran's 1964 *First Men in the Moon* with American Martha Heyer.

In the 1920s outside Hollywood, only pariah nations (the newly created USSR and defeated Germany) had big enough production bases to make 'Wellsian' SF epics. Hence technical landmarks such as *Aelita* and *Metropolis*. In Britain, his 'social realist' fiction was more frequently adapted to the mould of screen naturalism: *Kipps, The Wheels of Chance* (dir. Harold Shaw, 1921 and 1922) and *The Passionate Friends* (1922, dir. Maurice Elvey, who went on to make *High Treason*) were all productions in Stoll's 'Eminent Authors Series'. (*Marriage* was also filmed by Roy William Neil for Fox in the USA in 1927.) Such adaptations largely eviscerated Wells's radical commentary on the 'Condition of England', as reviewers noticed at the time[9] (setting a precedent for Hollywood's political elisions in the Cold War (see Chapter 5)). However, they weren't always cinematically unadventurous (there was some very creative flashback and superimposition in Elvey's *Kipps* for example, representing the pull of boyhood affections).[10] Of course, Wells was acclaimed not only for fiction, but also for popular, 'progressive' studies such as *The Outline of History* (1920). Griffith, notorious for 'writing history with lightning' (in President Woodrow Wilson's phrase), came to Britain in 1922 to promote *Orphans of the Storm*, but also to discuss filming *Outline*, although at a proposed 'seventy-two reels' this might have been hype as much as serious endeavour. *Photoplay* wryly asked how the sentimentalising director was going to work in 'his innocent injured heroine and his bold bad villain', but was confident, 'He'll find a way.'[11] Arguably, from *KWWAK* onwards, Wells would wrestle with the opposite problem: how to work his view of historical dynamics into the feature's entertainment format.

Apart from watching *Kipps*'s socially cringing dinner scene being filmed at the Savoy, Wells kept his distance from productions, nonetheless gamely playing 'Reverend Jeremiah Honeydew' in Rebecca West's amateur short, *They Forgot to Read the Directions* (1924). (This bigamy comedy echoed some of the themes of Wells's own social criticism about sexual mores and the subjection of women, by poking fun at Victorian attitudes and sentimental melodrama. Lord Beaverbrook plays its serial seducer, whose vengeful wives are wiped out with poisoned cocktails by the clergyman, who believes murder to be less immoral than public scandal. The Reverend's hypocrisy is nicely highlighted by point-of-view shots of their legs in short 'flapper' dresses. Their 'ghosts' come back to haunt him through crude double exposure.) But, despite his offhandedness, by the end of the silent era he had benefited substantially from film deals.[12] Nevertheless, he bit the hand increasingly feeding him, by attacking shallow commercialism and crude visual clichés, calling film-makers 'utterly damned fools, beneath the level of a decent man's discussion'.[13] Just before the release of *TTC* in March 1936, he recollected, 'I wouldn't then associate myself with any of the big companies because I did not consider their work particularly edifying.'[14] Such comments recalled *KWWAK*'s complaints about cinema's disappointing dearth of technical innovation and enlightened social purpose in the late 1920s. However, although blaming the lack of creative rapport with writers, he didn't seriously begin exploring the practical techniques of scenario writing until 1927, when producer Edward Godal approached him with the idea behind *KWWAK* itself.

Before this, though, Wells made a slenderer contribution to boost his son Frank's career at Ivor Montagu and Adrian Brunel's editing company. Their American backer offered to finance three comic shorts, if he provided scenarios. Wells agreed on condition that putative starlet Elsa Lanchester be cast in the lead.[15] Nevertheless, Wells didn't exactly jump at this chance of scripting at long last. Although the films were promoted on the prestige of Wells's name, the creative graft of developing his scribbled synopses was left to Montagu and Frank.[16]

Bluebottles, *Daydreams* and *The Tonic* (filmed at Gainsborough's Islington studio) were ready by December 1928. However, release was held up by the dithering of the distributors, Ideal Pictures, for virtually a year, a crucial one given the arrival of the synchronised soundtrack (Montagu attributed box-office disappointment to this).[17] *Bluebottles* concerns a nosey servant who blows a lost police whistle, inadvertently foiling a gang of pantomime burglars. It is notable for montage parodying cause and effect. Lanchester's seemingly insignificant action instantly ripples across the globe, as police scramble, armies muster and battleships steam ahead, reflecting the kind of cosmic absurdism found in 'The Story of the Last Trump' (1915), etc.[18] *Daydreams* visualises Lanchester's bodice-ripping fantasies: marriage to a French count; abduction by an amorous rajah; plane, car and yacht chases; marooning; and, finally, becoming Europe's merriest widow. Its overblown romantic clichés gently satirise the feverish wish-fulfilment of movie audiences, as do stories such as 'The Door in the Wall', 'The Stolen Body', etc. In *The Tonic*, Lanchester's employers bank on her ineptitude, leaving her to mix up Great Aunt Louisa's medicines and thus save them from having to poison her themselves. Instead, after the doctor expounds the benefits of 'shock treatment', Lanchester restores the old lady to rude health by leaving her on a level crossing to get knocked out of her bath chair by a train. When these shorts were finally released, they were generally successful with the critics, even if audiences did not mob them as such.[19]

Jamie Sexton argues that experimental film-makers of the time tended to 'deconstruct existing styles' and genres. The Wells–Montagu shorts, reworking British cinema's classbound slapstick, typify this.[20] Such critical self-reflexiveness is consistent with long-standing tendencies in Wells's writing. In *Daydreams*, there are knowing asides at the medium's 'Wellsian' ability to telescope space and time: Elsa's continuous peering through binoculars instantly transports the audience visually from one glamorous location to another, though continents apart. Dimensional relativity is also humorously invoked when Elsa faces the count's disapproving relatives: figures enlarge and shrink in proportion to their social assertiveness. Arguably, *KWWAK*, Wells's novel written as what Marcus calls a 'discursive film scenario', shows a similar intention to engage with popular forms and subvert them for its own ends.[21] How successfully it does this is debatable: Wells's 'Ruritanian' plot sometimes teeters on collapsing into the romantic clichés for which he castigated the industry. Whether the climax is more like 'a conventional woman's picture' than 'political statement', as Hardy argues, is a moot point.[22]

Mary Pickford allegedly remarked that great silents make the lack of words seem like a deliberate artistic choice rather than a handicap. Hardy makes the point that the 222 'shots' of Frank's *Bluebottles* script correspond in every detail to the finished movie. However, *KWWAK* depends far more on textuality (its first part alone containing 62 expository and 211 dialogue titles, plus inserted posters, newsbills, banners, telegrams, etc.) This indicates Wells's difficulty in finally abandoning narration for visualisation, or 'telling' for 'showing'. From this standpoint, her conclusion that, despite the ekphrastic brilliance of his many anticipations of film technique, Wells presents something of a paradox in relation to silent film is right.[23] It didn't dampen his rekindling enthusiasm, however. (He was a founder of the London Film Society (at pioneering critic Iris Barry's invitation), which introduced many of the European avant-garde to Britain at the New Gallery Cinema, Regent Street, and Tivoli Palace in the Strand. Wells remained a member throughout its existence (1925–39).) Nor did it prevent his eventually going on to script elaborate sound epics in the 1930s, albeit with mixed success.

After the bruising experience of *TTC*, Wells would retrospectively dismiss *KWWAK*'s technical experiments as 'entirely amateurish'.[24]

Nonetheless, it contains many ingeniously ekphrastic strategies which emulate camera movement and editing and prefigure key themes, motifs and techniques in his 1930s film-scripting. Furthermore, although *KWWAK* was also originally conceived as 'silent' in 1927, by publication Wells had incorporated a reaction to the coming of the soundtrack. As we saw in Chapter 2, he shared Modernist hostility towards remortgaging cinema's creative fluidity to the naturalistic continuity demanded by synchronised dialogue. *KWWAK* specified recorded words selectively, according to the impact required: 'The incessant tiresome chatter of the drama sinks out of necessity ... with the film the voice may be flung in here or there, or the word may be made visible and vanish again' (See *KWWAK*, pp. 16–17). Only in this way, for example, can we account for nationalist slogans emitted by 'gramophone voices', or audible responses to Dr Harting's controversial lecture (*KWWAK*, pp. 75 and 78). Hence a detailed reading reveals a key moment of transition in Wells's ongoing relationship with the medium.

The King Who Was a King

In advertisements for the book, Wells was quoted wishing, like his character Elvesham, to live life over again so that 'I might devote myself entirely to working for the cinema ... There is nothing more fascinating than the work that goes on in a big studio. And it is at present in its infancy.'[25] He finally nailed his colours to the screen and declared it to be 'the Art Form of the Future', but also had a virtually Leninesque belief in its potential as the most powerful propaganda discourse yet. Being reminded of his part in Paul's patent by Ramsaye's book spurred him to reconsider his own practical role (see *KWWAK*, pp. 8 and 10). The sense of expectation about what Wells might achieve in the text is epitomised by Chaplin's express hope that it might still show the way forward:

> A giant of limitless powers has been reared, so huge that no one quite knows what to do with it.
> I, for one, am hopeful that Mr Wells shall settle the question for us in his next novel.[26]

In 1923, Wells declared himself 'tired of talking in playful parables to a world engaged in destroying itself'.[27] In the late 1920s, he had the opportunity to address the issue directly in a medium capable of having the greatest reach and impact. He was approached by Godal to script a film, *The Peace of the World*, based on a series of his own newspaper articles. Wells embraced the chance to promote his World State solution. Planning went rapidly ahead, but Frank, as industry insider, sounded the alarm about Godal International's impending bankruptcy.[28] Luckily, Wells managed to salvage the script rights before the collapse, converting it into *KWWAK*.

KWWAK's Introduction reveals much about how Wells's ideas concerning the creative interaction between literature and film had evolved. '[B]ottling-up and decanting' stage drama had always been possible, but cinema's inherent narrative capabilities were only gradually being realised, despite the public appetite for visual story-telling it raised. This made cinema's relationship with literature parasitic rather than mutually energising (*KWWAK*, pp. 10–11). But the missed opportunity for collaboration wasn't one-sided, he admitted ruefully: 'These honest pioneers were for the most part young and unknown people, and they got little help or encouragement from those of us who had achieved any popular standing as novelists or playwrights.' Writers had been reluctant to relearn their craft from first principles, or slow to realise that 'a greater depth of intimation, a more delicate and subtle fabric of suggestion, a completer power and beauty, might be possible' (*KWWAK*, pp. 14–15). Wells didn't think he would live to see the new art's masterpieces, but intended *KWWAK* as a contribution to helping it escape from conventional naturalism 'with a theme of world-wide importance', yet within the grasp of ordinary audiences (*KWWAK*, pp. 17–18). In other words, he saw himself negotiating between the parameters of the popular and radical avant-gardism. Film might suture the 'mass civilization/minority culture' schism running through critical debates of the inter-war years. Wells argued that its socially divisive notions of High-brow and Low-brow needed supplementing with the new concept of 'Broad-brow', open to raising formal standards while connecting with wider tastes (*KWWAK*, p. 22).[29]

Wells took Thomas Hardy's 'unstageable' Napoleonic epic, *The Dynasts* (1904–8), as a model. Its panorama of earthly events and motives, surveyed from space, cut between locations and perspectives with proto-cinematic mobility (see *KWWAK*, p. 19).[30] Theoretically there was no spatio-temporal limitation 'of scene, stage or arena', size or scale, depth or distance, to cinematic spectacle: 'It may be the convolutions of a tendril which fill the picture, or the bird's-eye view of a mountain chain, or a great city. We can pass in an instant from the infinitely great to the infinitely little.' Equally it could flex between ultra-naturalism and abstraction: 'The picture may be real, realistic or conventionalized in a thousand ways; it may flow in and out of a play of "absolute" forms' (*KWWAK*, pp. 15–16).[31] Experiments with colour could pick out and intensify details at will (red, for example, is used in recurrent close-ups of maps on pp. 49 and 74 to highlight 'calcomite' deposits). Similarly, soundtracking could be used creatively to compose films as audio-visual 'symphonies' (*KWWAK*, p. 17).[32] *KWWAK* makes elaborate suggestions for such patterning, varying between subtle and clunky. For example, the 'Claverian Leopard rampant', heraldic symbol of all militaristic nationalism, recurs in numerous forms and contexts, on expanding and contracting scales: gigantic carvings, uniforms, flags, clockwork toys, tiny coins, Blackshirt badges, etc. Its auditory counterpart is the strident national anthem. After peace breaks out, this menacing leitmotif shrinks from screen-filling image into 'grotesque' diminuendo of a lampstand (see *KWWAK*, p. 87 and notes on pp. 103 and 237).

Wells admitted the specific problem of making an exciting scenario about a 'negative' concept such as World Peace (*KWWAK*, p. 23), one shared with *High Treason*.[33] He would experience similar difficulties with *TTC*'s post-apocalyptic Utopia: i.e. of dramatising a conflict in which victory seems a morally foregone conclusion. Wells thought that the solution lay in exploiting film's antithetical capacities for the intimate and the epic, to personify a global problem through an individual protagonist that audiences might identify with. He would embody their 'will to abolish war' by casting 'the common intelligent man as king' (*KWWAK*, pp. 27–28). Hence *KWWAK* was to be a psychological drama demystifying its audience's suggestibility to a conditioned 'war complex' comprising a cocktail of ideological pressures and reflexes, rather than any tale of traditional heroic action (*KWWAK*, p. 40). His ambitions show the influence of both Modernist fiction about the unconscious[34] and 'Freudian' cinema (see below). *KWWAK* was also politically advanced in recognising distorted relations between the sexes as a key factor. The heroine couldn't just be a formulaic romantic interest, because that would be patronising 'triviality' or fatal distraction (*KWWAK*, pp. 30–31). Wells groped towards some new conception of women as both actors and spectators, so that they might collaborate in the 'task of cleaning up all that now festers towards a renewal of war' (*KWWAK*, pp. 34–35). Though his archetype ('Woman the Protector and Sustainer') may seem disappointingly domestic, elsewhere *KWWAK* presents individual women renouncing traditional roles as abetting the ends of aggressive nationalism (see, for example, pp. 155 and 243).[35]

Wells intended *KWWAK* to be as ekphrastic as possible, 'very much as one would see it on the screen' in a cinema of the imagination (*KWWAK*, p. 21). He had some success with a diversity of devices and modes, although too many for inclusion in any single feature. A key element in his audio-visual patterning were the archetypal contraries (foregrounded in various guises throughout): Man the Maker, accompanied by a rhythmic tapping and clinking theme, and his *Doppelgänger*, Man the Destroyer. Wells's Prelude reveals a flint-tool-maker through the mists of time (perhaps recalling Griffith's prehistoric narrative, *Man's Genesis* (1912), in which Weak-Hands invents a weapon to defeat his Neanderthal rival, Brute Force).[36] Man the Maker evolves into metal-worker, then symbolically splits into technology's dualistic applications (pp. 45–47). This strikingly anticipates *2001: A Space Odyssey* (1968) and its fight between ancestral apes.[37] Similarly, like Stanley Kubrick's film, it is followed by a characteristic spatio-temporal shift, demanding the most advanced technical expertise to realise: a visual approach to Earth from outer space (also recalling Hardy's method in *The Dynasts*). This planetary perspective then fractures into the competing viewpoints of national interest as it zooms in on a boardroom meeting:

> The world grows larger and the familiar outline of the Western hemisphere comes round ... until North America fills the screen, a hand appears and points to New York ... an aeroplane view is superimposed upon the screen. This view recedes and a window-frame about it becomes visible. We are in the intimate conference-room of a great business organization in lower New York. (*KWWAK*, p. 47)

KWWAK's imaginary camera pans around to a man poring over a map, revealed as Clavery and neighbouring territories. Thus we are introduced, with breathtaking visual fluidity, to Clavery's dispute over strategic mineral rights with Agravia. Behind this are two great powers, the USA and Britain, making Clavery the potential flashpoint of a new world war. International tension is visualised by simultaneity, shifting the scene in and out of the conference space to rival forces:

> Then C. says, '*The British are too fond of blockades and strangleholds.*'
> There is a vision of a British fleet steaming along some blockade coast, and then this fades out to be replaced by a great American battleship, flags flying and coming full speed ahead towards the audience, which fades also to show the Conference, ruffled, uneasy, perplexed. (*KWWAK*, p. 51)

The weight of national pasts bearing down on Wells's 'war suggestion complex' is then represented in accelerated montage, giving 'glimpses of pages' from rival American and British history, 'if possible from well-known pictures' (*KWWAK*, pp. 53 and 61–62). Wells alludes to film's ability to simulate the past in convincingly 'immediate' form, just as Griffith deliberately animated Brady's Civil War photographs and created 'historical facsimiles' (such as the assassination of Lincoln) in *Birth of a Nation*.

The Prelude's 'tapping and clinking' returns to identify car plant engineer Paul Zelinka in American exile, as the latest embodiment of Man the Maker's progress, to be played by the same actor for a 'reincarnating' effect, a principle realised in *TTC*. His rival archetype's visual profile is also matched with scheming Minister for War, Monza (see pp. 116 and 157). Paul is unexpectedly summoned to the Claverian succession, but, under the influence of peace campaigner Dr Harting and daughter Margaret, refuses to be the great powers' pawn and start a war for calcomite. Metaphors of international manipulation are materialised. As Paul asks, '"*Am I a King or a chess-man?*" the alternatives become visible'. As he gains control,

Britain and America become pieces on *his* board (*KWWAK*, pp. 128 and 188–89).

With similar anti-naturalism, mounting subjective pressure is personified in 'ghostly' presences. Consequently, Paul's struggle to escape the hold of the 'Old World' goes into full-blown Expressionist mode. This seems to reflect both literary influences, such as the fantasies of the 'Circe' chapter of *Ulysses* (1922), with Joyce's teeming cast of animated shibboleths, and the shifting psychoanalytic dreamscapes of Pabst's *Geheimnisse einer Seele* (1926), much admired in British film circles.[38] Over Paul and Margaret in the mimetic present, the palace of Clavopolis is grotesquely superimposed 'through a distorting lens'. The reporter, who rumbled Paul's secret identity, 'appears like an impish gnome' outing him to court officials, his deceased predecessor and American high society, as commanding titles stream through the air (reading 'NOBLESSE OBLIGE', etc.). Paul and Margaret flee, pursued by a threatening cloud like 'an armed figure'. Their tiny pioneers' wagon heads towards 'a splendid dream city', before it 'swallows up the prospect'. '*I fear the Old World*' flashes across the screen, before the couple (still talking over Margaret's car) are restored to the naturalistic present (*KWWAK*, pp. 70–72).[39]

Other sequences are so metaphorical that their fantastic transformations could only have been realised using stop-motion, or even the 'polymorphous plasticity' of cartoons.[40] As Paul resists press warmongering, newspapers fly like thistledown: 'Wherever they alight, a little plant grows and spreads, bristling with bayonets and carrying bombs like fruits' (*KWWAK*, p. 146). In another, a monstrous smoke leopard hatches from a shellburst. Paul's struggle with it – 'such as one sees when the animated cartoon mingles with real figures' – confirms Wells's interest in mixing live action and graphics, developed to a sophisticated degree by the late 1920s (see *KWWAK*, pp. 177–79). Animator Anthony Gross was employed to make an insert sequence for *TTC*, although this was eventually scrapped.[41]

Wells's visualisation of the cityscape again shows the influence of Ruttmannesque documentary montage[42] to symbolise what is at stake in the tension between modernity and a brooding past:

> The scene returns to the Square before the Cathedral. It is twilight passing into night. Black groups of people moving about. Trams lit up at the corner. Illuminations begin and spread. The squat citadel, uphill on one side, is outlined in light, but the huge bulk of the Cathedral façade towering up out of the picture into the night remains unlit, black, sombre and portentous.

In startling reverse, his imaginary camera then picks out the palace loggia, flipping into a panoramic view from inside. As it recedes through 'pillars and parapet', it reveals Paul in silhouette, observing his capital (see *KWWAK*, pp. 123–25). This sophisticated sense of moving or framed viewpoint, so prevalent in Wells's fiction, is foregrounded in many other ways: for example, the border observed through field glasses (p. 141).

Wells also uses cinematic visualisation as an optical 'time machine'. A temporal shift back to the Great War emphasises the horror of mutilation with before-and-after close-ups of a soldier's face and hands suddenly blinded and shrivelled. It is likely that such effects would have been too much for film censors, but their irony is reinforced by the leopard crest picked out on the veteran's pension book, sole lasting recognition of his sacrifice. The veteran's face flashes back again as Paul argues against reasserting 'National honour' against Agravia (*KWWAK*, pp. 137–38 and 151). This ministerial crisis meeting is overshadowed by split-screen effects of coming mobilisation, then literally blotted out by a doomsday weapon against which there is no defence, lethal forerunner of *TTC*'s 'Gas of Peace' (*KWWAK*, pp. 158–62).

The central section, 'A Vision of Modern War', comprises Paul's meditation on the consequences of giving in to siren voices and hidden agendas, epitomising Wells's campaigning internationalism. It's an imaginary 'Temptation of St Anthony' (a frequent subject of early film from Méliès), or surreal Apocalypse, not unlike Stephen's climactic vision during the fracas with drunken squaddies in 'Circe'. Wells abandons narration altogether for symbolic metamorphoses (in violently contrasting tints). As Bailey puts it, they 'simply take over the screen',[43] though always spiralling (as in Joyce and Pabst) in and out of naturalistic settings and action. Swirling newspapers transform into bombers. Monza, sporting 'Japanese-reptilian' armour, thrusts Paul forward to 'the Test' – of his resolve to resist the overdetermined pressure to prove national virility: Princess Helen of Saevia, Clavery's ally, proffers a sword, an eroticised Joan of Arc taunting him with cowardice (*KWWAK*, pp. 168–70). Paul becomes subject to a force in which individual will is lost in mass hysteria, as his outline literally dissolves into a background of cheering crowds (*KWWAK*, pp. 170–71). As in *Birth of a Nation*, Wells picks out an exemplifying young couple in patriotic farewell, then shows his death at the front, with an effect of telepathic simultaneity as his fiancée wakes in shock. With the gender neutrality of modern, total war, she now finds herself in an air raid (*KWWAK*, pp. 172–73). That, with ensuing stylised scenes of tank battle, prefigures *TTC*'s 'Everytown Blitz' and 'Endless War' sequences. A single face, also highlighted from the crowd, fills the screen with dumbstruck disbelief at jingoism's consequences (*KWWAK*, pp. 174–76), before a 'wipe' back to Paul's decisive 'no' to this nightmare (pp. 178–79).

Wells was keenly aware of the difficulty of making his final sequence on global transformation (after the international treaty to manage calcomite) believable and exciting, especially since it followed the traditional screen clinch of the victorious couple. He faced a similar task in *TTC* after the old order was defeated, though with the advantage of a futuristic plot justifying spectacular special effects as the devastated world was reconstructed. Nonetheless, Wells's climactic face-on 'shot' of Paul and Helen flying off in their two-seater plane (*KWWAK*, pp. 242–43) prefigures *TTC*'s final scene with its symbolic reaching-out to the stars, as Wells's capsule containing another hopeful young couple is tracked through space. However, Wells also knew his project was unlikely to find another backer (*KWWAK*'s concluding chapter is 'Difficulties in the Way of Production'). Nevertheless, it remains a notable contribution to discussion about the future of popular but innovative cinema. Far from 'dumbing down', or selling out Culture to 'mass civilisation', Wells remained committed to the belief that the screen could state a 'fairly complex argument ... more clearly and more effectively' than any other medium. Like Griffith, he saw its potential for promoting 'the common interests of mankind' (*KWWAK*, pp. 248–49) and idealistically wanted to harness its powers of mass persuasion for progressive ends. Features normally perpetuated a stereotype of modern conflict as a matter of individual heroics in which 'the best man wins'. They played a role in making future war inevitable by concealing the fact that it had become depersonalised, mechanical 'massacre, aiming at demoralization' (*KWWAK*, p. 250) as he predicted in his fiction.

According to Wells, the most likely obstacle to challenging generic anachronism was the British Board of Film Censors' taboo on 'controversy',[44] which would sense that such a film was 'in some obscure but offensive way "political"'. Literary fiction was freer from control, precisely because it was not a mass medium with equivalent reach and impact: 'Unhappily not one in a thousand who would see this gladly on a screen will ever read it as a book' (*KWWAK*, p. 254). Wells may, however, have taken his potential wider audience for granted. The appeal of his own message of technocratic, authoritarian socialism, as well as practical screenwriting skills, would be rigorously tested by the production difficulties and box-office fortunes of *TTC*. Critical reaction to *KWWAK* was also mixed. Kenneth MacPherson, editor of *Close-Up*, thought that Wells's Prelude risked looking 'like a tableau at a World Fair', unless visualised with genuine flair. However, he was struck by Wells's selective use of colour and montage-like cutting showing 'the *Russian* touch'. Wells managed to show British film 'the way it ought to go', but needed to ditch his titles in favour of more creative soundtracking.[45] Dorothy Richardson approved of *KWWAK*'s symphonic conception as 'Music-Drama', rather than naturalistic talkie, and acknowledged that Wells's ekphrastic 'film-seeing' was modernising literary technique. However, she also pointed out the future-orientated Wells's uncharacteristic 'dilatoriness' in acting on his instinct that film was the art form to come. Richardson chided him for exaggeration in suggesting that film might eventually replace literature altogether. Collective cultural experience (no matter how impressively virtual) could never entirely replace the private and reflective.[46] Paul Rotha deflated expectations like Chaplin's with a bigger thumbs-down: 'Mr Wells has written that novel, but the question is no nearer being answered.' He acknowledged that *KWWAK* teemed with ideas gleaned from international movies, but contained little 'that had direct bearing on the position' of cinema itself. Ultimately, its 'outlook' remained 'literary and not filmic'.[47]

Things to Come (1936)

Though *KWWAK* 'dented some of the faith in Wells's powers of resolution', as Marcus puts it, he nonetheless 'retained a significant status' in relation to this new technological art.[48] Wells eventually made his breakthrough into major scripting in the 1930s, partly because both industry and cultural climate had become very receptive to his themes and techniques. As Jeffrey Richards points out, in terms of both specific adaptations and wider influence, the 1930s 'were undoubtedly the Wellsian decade'. Hollywood filmed seminal versions of *IODM* (as *Island of Lost Souls*, dir. Erle C. Kenton, 1932) and *IM*; Britain filmed *TTC* and *MWCWM*, as well as minor ventures, such as a 1936 experimental (four-minute) short based on Wells's story evoking the invisible presence of 'fear itself', 'The Red Room' (Herbert Kosower's *Extinction*). Moreover, critics applied the term 'Wellsian' to a much wider range of fantasies and futuristic technological epics.[49]

With Godal out of the frame, Wells offered his services to any producer willing to rise to his challenge. It was eventually taken up by a great admirer, instrumental in reviving the fortunes of the British industry with films such as *The Private Life of Henry VIII* (1933) and *The Ghost Goes West* (1935). Hungarian émigré Alexander Korda met Wells in 1934.[50] Together they decided to film a text even more ambitious than *KWWAK*, Wells's vast 'Outline of the Future', *The Shape of Things to Come* (*SOTTC*)(1933). Effectively, *SOTTC* was a 'quintessence of Wellsism', comprising his cumulative thinking about the course of world events, the volatile forces driving them and prescribed solutions. Wells even planned to issue audiences with a programme, functioning as a kind of manifesto.[51] Unpromisingly, *SOTTC* was also one of the least ekphrastic of Wells's fictions, with only sketchy clues as to how its futures might be practically visualised.[52] The fraught history of his treatment and revisions showed that though as gifted amateur he often emulated film techniques and speculated about their possible development, this did not automatically make him an experienced scenarist.

It seems that awe for Wells and the conviction that he could provide a 'serious' epic to meet his own ambitions of outdoing Hollywood led to an unwise contract which Korda lived to regret. Its terms conferred virtually dictatorial rights over how the film would be made. In his autobiography, Raymond Massey wrote, 'No writer for the screen ever had or ever will have such authority as H. G. Wells possessed.'[53] Wells was on set almost daily, giving opinions on every aspect of production – design, acting, editing, music, casting, even costumes[54] (perhaps unsurprisingly, given his integrated specifications for *KWWAK*). His final script was the last three revisions, his original 'prentice effort' *Whither Mankind?* proving (by his own admission) 'quite impracticable' (*TTCAFS*, pp. 11–12). Korda, exasperated by arguing and swallowing further misgivings, more or less accepted it intact (although the published version (1935) still shows significant differences from both the release script and the final form on screen). The result suffers as much from Wellsian weaknesses as strengths. Wells's eve-of-release account confirms that Korda 'offered to make a film which was, as far as humanly possible, exactly as I dictated'. However, he confessed that the task of putting the story into screen form took far longer than anticipated: 'how little I knew about the cinema when I wrote the scenario. Many of the sequences which slipped quite easily from my pen were extremely difficult to screen, and some were quite impossible.' Nevertheless, Wells insisted (in public at least), 'The film has emerged spiritually correct', though after many alterations suggested by producer, director and 'a score' of others.[55] Wells's private diary gives a less sanguine account, as did production team members, who found he could be a testy control freak challenging their professional competence. Need for changes had to be pointed out tactfully. His (uncredited) collaborator on the screenplay, Lajos Biró, acted as general emollient, as well as working tirelessly to convert grandiose abstractions into workable dialogue and directions. Despite this stormy relationship, Wells publicly thanked the 'friendly generosity' of Korda's team, especially for innovating new techniques to meet his elaborate specifications (*TTCAFS*, pp. 11–12).[56]

With its unusually high production values, *TTC* took over a year to make, required three studios for sets and effects and cost around £300,000, a huge sum in 1930s film-making and more than any Korda production hitherto.[57] Its unique collaboration aroused huge critical and public expectation. In the full supporting programme on its release was a *March of Time* article ('England's Hollywood'), fanfaring *TTC* as a distinctive national product able to compete in markets at home and overseas, setting the pattern for the future of British cinema. Against a clip of huge futuristic bombers zooming over, the voice-over announced that London Films were 'even teaching Hollywood new tricks'. Against shots of *TTC*'s production team, it identified in their ranks 'one of Great Britain's foremost imaginations'. Getting carried away, it mistakenly reported Wells as having 'now given up writing books entirely in favour of the cinema'. Wells himself addressed the camera about *TTC*'s topical context and aims:

> There's the onset of war, there's the increase of power, there's the change of scale and the change of conditions in the world. And in one or two of our films here, we've been trying, without any propaganda or pretension or preachment of any sort, we've been trying to work out some of those immense possibilities that appeal, we think, to everyman. We are attempting here the film of imaginative possibility. That, at any rate, is one of the challenges that we are going to make to our friends and rivals at Hollywood.[58]

Nevertheless, the project failed to fully rekindle the wondrous optical speculativeness of Wells's early writing and realise its enormous promise. The reasons are complex, but perhaps there are three main ones: a) as imaginative writer, the 69-year-old could not travel backwards to his moment of greatest possibility; b) he wanted the film consciously to subserve a creed, discarding parabolic subtexts for top-heavy didacticism, creative ambiguity for an overreaching socio-political programme; c) Wells had given up fantastic invention for more limited technical feasibility. Nonetheless his reversion to a Vernian *From the Earth to the Moon* style of launch method in the 'Space Gun' (thus avoiding comparison with the despised Lang's *Frau im Mond* (1929)) was considered distinctively unscientific,[59] albeit providing a productive contrast to the weapons technology pushing the world of Part One to the brink of destruction. Ironically, therefore, *TTC*'s futurism seems more dated than other Wellsian narratives, locked into its own time by the relative myopia of current concerns. It may also simply be much harder (if not impossible) to make good SF films which are ultimately optimistic about the future.

Nonetheless, contemporary reviewers were greatly impressed (with qualifications), though, like Lang's epic, *TTC* was hardly a box-office smash either.[60] Most rhapsodic was Sydney W. Carroll in *The Sunday Times*:

> It is a leviathan amongst films. It makes Armageddon look like a street row. It shows science flourishing the keys of Hell and Death, and creating from the ruins of Everytown crazy labyrinthine cities radiant with artificial light, teeming with crowds of art-starved people craving for old excitements and former thrills. A stupendous spectacle, an overwhelming Doréan, Jules Vernesque, elaborated 'Metropolis', staggering to eye, mind and spirit ...
>
> ... as a scathing commentary on the martyrdom of man and the vanity of human wishes, there will never again be a film of greater significance than this.[61]

Alistair Cooke, BBC cinema critic, considered it 'as visually exciting a film as ever came out of a British or any other studio', though astutely identifying its flaws (see below). The *Observer*'s C. A. Lejeune thought, it 'would go out into the world stuck full of Lilliputian arrows'. However, whether you agreed with its thesis or not, that did not alter the fact that *TTC* used film 'for the first time to state a hard and fairly complex argument ... with a force and beauty that gives you no choice but to follow and attend'. Elizabeth Bowen believed it to be the first picture to convincingly represent sheer spatio-temporal scale, though this often rendered dialogue and characterisation trivial in inverse ratio. The women especially 'could have stayed ciphers' but turned into 'bores'. She zoomed in on a major weakness: 'If this film fully came off, it might knock one flat; it does not come off because of a constant conflict between moral and poetic intention.'[62] Audiences on both sides of the Atlantic, as Richards notes, were less likely put off by central ideas – opposition to war and state planning as panacea were mainstream to 1930s thought in many countries.[63] However, many found the expression of an argument through an episodic time structure confusing (as they had done with similar experiments by Lang and Griffith before). They also found its characters coldly unsympathetic and some dialogue ponderous to the point of boredom (so much for Wells's disarming statement about eschewing 'preachment of any sort'). Similarly, despite what *March of Time* boasted about sound as 'a natural new advantage to British film', for Americans it was more a handicap to plausibility, given the cut-glass elocution of *TTC*'s actors. As one US distributor complained, 'Nobody is going to believe that the world is going to be saved by a bunch of people with British accents.'[64]

Though *TTC* was Wells's long-awaited riposte to *Metropolis*, as Richards stresses there are nonetheless key points of resemblance.[65] Effectively, they indicate Wells's ongoing argument not just with Lang but his own more sceptically dystopian phase. *Metropolis*'s opening, semi-abstract montage of machines and buildings is arguably echoed in *TTC*'s reconstruction sequence; both films feature 'Luddite' mobs, though choreographed crowd movement in both ultimately derives from *WTSW*'s 'kaleidoscope' pattern of masses (as when they stream together radially seen from above to destroy the Space Gun, symbol of hated mechanical progress). Cabal is also a benign avatar of *both* Ostrog and Joh Fredersen, though in similarly austere and autocratic mould. The character of Theotocopulos alludes to both rabble-rousing 'false Maria' and the 'dark side' of Rotwang, associating scientific inventions with madness and superstition. Most ironically, Theotocopulos also echoes Graham, a literally 'anachronic man', who similarly leads the people against a technocratic regime, using its advanced media against it. Moreover, both films raise central questions about women's roles in modernity.

Nevertheless, art direction, sets and effects (employing cutting-edge designs, as Wells suggested in his *Metropolis* review) certainly make *TTC* visually stylish and, in that sense at least, one of the most influential films in the genre. Korda chose veteran American William Cameron Menzies more for aesthetic flair than for specifically directorial skills. Art direction was given to Korda's gifted brother Vincent, assisted by Wells's son, Frank; editing was given to Charles Crichton and Francis Lyon; special effects were directed by Ned Mann assisted by Wally Veevers; and camerawork on them overseen by Edward Cohen, with trick photographers Harry Zech and Ross Jacklin. The suggestions for visual effects, architecture and structure of *Whither Mankind? A Film of the Future* (*WM*), though more specific than *SOTTC*, were nonetheless still very impressionistic.[66] Accounts vary about who exactly was responsible for transforming them into finished designs. However, as Frayling shows, they were probably worked out from successive treatments by Vincent in collaboration with Menzies and Mann.[67] Wells initially approached Fernand Léger to supply concept sketches for the city and costumes of the future. Expecting designs like those for *L'Inhumaine*, Wells found what Léger supplied to be more like his 'semi-abstract animation', *Ballet Mécanique* (also 1924).[68] Le Corbusier was approached instead, but, ironically, turned Wells's Utopia down as insufficiently future-orientated for his taste.[69] Nonetheless, Vincent Korda based his geometrically planned garden city on Le Corbusier's *Vers une architecture* (1927), along with other details such as the Basra hangar. Erich Mendelsohn and Sergei Chermayeff's recently completed De la Warr Pavilion at Bexhill inspired 'New Everytown's' clean, curvilinear forms and elegant galleries. The Basra bombers probably originated from Norman Bel Geddes's streamlined airliners in *Horizons* (1932), along with Everytown's rebuilt city square. The result was a fusion of Modernist 'international' style appropriate to Wells's vision of a future beyond nation states.

Thematically, however, the film largely omits *SOTTC*'s central anti-capitalist and anti-nationalist critique of history that the competitive industrial system and pursuit of profit, leading to the First World War and the Great Depression, was inevitably going to self-destruct in another global conflagration before a new scientific social order emerged. This is unsurprising, as Richards points out, given that the British film industry 'was an integral part of the capitalist system' itself (epitomised by *March of Time's* crowing about its revival). Thus *TTC* concentrates more narrowly on the evils of war, stripping away their motivating context (along with Wells's diatribe against religion).[70]

TTC has a tripartite narrative structure, with 'accelerated' linking sequences, transporting audiences between key moments in future history like a cinematic time machine. Each episode witnesses the struggle between progressive and reactionary forces. Like *TM* (apart from the brief Basra and coal-pit inserts), action is located around a particular topography, undergoing dramatic metamorphoses. It begins in 1940, predicting the start of the Second World War, with aerial blitzing of 'Everytown' and social order shattered by modern war. Thus, as Kim Newman notes, Wells introduces the theme of 'the post-holocaust world to the cinema'.[71] Over thirty years' continuous attrition, civilisation reverts to barbarism and a mutated plague rages. Tribal warlords fight over scarce resources and surviving technology. This dire situation is unexpectedly transformed by the 'ultimate revolution' of 'Wings Over the World', a global alliance of airmen, engineers and scientists, led by John Cabal. Their futuristic air fleet and paratroops (from Basra of all places!)[72] subdue the forces of regression with the 'gas of peace', positive alternative to the poison gas of Part One. All awake from this 'Pacificin', apart from 'the Boss', personifying the death of the dinosaur order of combatant 'sovereign states'. A triumphant interlude of planned reconstruction lays the foundations of the airmen's rationalist 'technotopia'. The result is the final sequence set in 2036.

Wells's 'Introductory Remarks' to the published script, describe it as showing that scientific social order is the only 'alternative to perpetual conflict' (*TTCAFS*, pp. 9–10). The film compresses the global space and time of the novel (originally covering 1929–2106) and personalises its complex narrative in dramatic terms through a few central characters in generational reincarnations (like those in *KWWAK*). Most particularly it focuses on John Cabal, 'the air dictator' (young and old)[73] and his great-grandson, Oswald (an unfortunate resonance for us now, echoing another wannabe 1930s superman, Oswald Mosley, leader of the British Union of Fascists).[74] Both men are marked by the hereditary tic of drumming fingers, visualising dynamic impatience. Oswald becomes president of the 'World Council of Direction', which John founded, a modernised version of Plato's oligarchic 'Guardians'. The last part concerns Oswald's struggles with the resurgent forces of reaction.

Everytown was emblematic of the 'great town of our times' (though also recognisably London, especially Piccadilly Circus, with a dome like that of St Paul's in the background). Wells's focus on the modern metropolis (going back to *WTSW*) showed his continued interest in montage documentary's construction of the city by symphonic 'cross-sectional' editing: *TTC* continually repeats and juxtaposes landmarks and routines, traffic, public places, office buildings, department-store window displays and cinemas (cf. *TTCAFS*, pp. 20–21).[75] But neon warning signs, headlines and sandwich men ('Europe is arming …', etc.) increasingly intrude into the Christmas festivities, and carols are intercut with a staccato theme of mounting alarm. Citizens are indifferent: 'Only the camera calls the attention of the audience to the brooding threat' (*TTCAFS*, p. 21).

The film switches to an interior scene at the home of aviator John Cabal (significantly, the only newspaper reader we see), the photograph of a Douglas DC3 prominent over the mantelpiece. It omits the boys' squabble over bombarding the model railway (a Wellsian allegory of constructive co-operation versus destructive competition (*TTCAFS*, p. 26)), though retaining his satirical bite at militaristic immaturity: the grandfather remarks of a model cannon, 'I wonder if sometimes perhaps they don't find these new toys a bit too much for them.' Similarly, *TTC* points up Cabal's ironic riposte to the cliché of Passworthy (Edward Chapman) that war propels progress: 'Yes war's a highly stimulating thing. But you can overdo a stimulant. The next dose may be a fatal one' (*TTCAFS*, p. 27).

Wells's visualisation of the outbreak of total war, with civilians on the aerial 'home front', is closely realised, in jagged, Eisensteinian montage.[76] It had a huge impact in convincingly simulating what the saturation bombing of a city would be like before Guernica or Madrid. The sequence begins with searchlights scissoring the sky and the radio announcing a Pearl Harbor-like sneak attack on the fleet. Everytown is mobilised with 'None of the elation of 1914' (*TTCAFS*, pp. 31–32). Eerie 'shadowgraph phantoms' from the Great War build up behind Passworthy's play-marching son. (As Wells prescribed, the same boy is later buried under rubble, in one of the film's most shocking close-ups.) Anti-aircraft guns are wheeled into place, a loudspeaker van warns people to take cover and truckloads of gas masks are frantically handed out, panic increasingly visible in the reaction shots of faces picked out in crowds, as in *KWWAK*. Invisible bombers are heard homing in. Everytown's 'dreamhouse' (advertising the unfinished Korda production, *Lucretia Borgia*) is one of their first targets, in a metacinematic comment on escapism.[77] The film presciently shows civilians rushing to shelter in the Underground, but omits Wells's surreal mix of shop-window dummies and dead bodies, a scene that would be just as familiar in the Blitz (*TTCAFS*, pp. 32–34). People swarm over bombed-out cars and buildings to escape the terrible rain. According to Michael Korda, the sequence was so effective that *TTC* 'became gospel for both sides in the dispute over armaments and foreign policy', contributing to the expectation of breaking the enemy's will by bombing them back to the Stone Age.[78] Defence preparations focused on this 'knock-out blow', typified by PM Stanley Baldwin's fatalistic slogan, 'The bomber will always get through.' *TTC* was in fact re-released in 1940, to re-exploit its salutary foretelling of what had all but come to pass.

Quasi-documentary focus gives way to a stylised sequence of silhouette armies, battleships and futuristic tank warfare (models designed by Frank Wells, along with the prefabricated wall machine in the reconstruction sequence). Dover's iconographic cliffs below present no barrier to bombers choking the skies. Modern war's pyrrhic nature and Wells's solution in international technocratic alliance are symbolised in another brief set-piece, showing Cabal's humanity to a crashed opponent: 'Why should we murder each other? Why does it come to this?' The enemy pilot confronts the sick joke of impersonal massacre from the sky compared with the natural impulse to give up his gas mask to a choking girl whose distress is visible to him on the ground. Wells's next sequence, 'The Unending War', was to have been temporally condensed by a rapid montage of front pages, symptomatically deteriorating. Perhaps too reminiscent of *KWWAK*'s excessive textuality, the film-makers opted instead for brief scenes of eroding battlefield conditions (military machines disappearing altogether) and superimposed dates. However, they kept Wells's final touch for slowing down into a new narrative present (1966): a shabby news-sheet catches on a branch for the audience to read about the zombie-like 'Wandering Sickness', horrifying symptom of society's traumatised and rudderless state (*TTCAFS*, pp. 37–38). Succeeding shots of desolated landmarks (grown familiar from key repetition) recall the 'dead London' of *WOTW*; parabolic Martians no longer needing to stand in for technologised humanity's own potential for self-destruction.

Conversely, Old Harding personifies the regression of science, working desperately in a dilapidated laboratory to cure this new Dark Age pestilence, without the medicines taken for granted in 1940. The ruthlessness of putative 'Boss' Rudolf, shooting victims on sight to prevent infection speading, signals the restoration of a questionable order (cf. *TTCAFS*, pp. 45–46). *TTC*'s cinematic time machine then 'fast forwards' to 1970 and this 'Patriot Chief' ruling Everytown. His 'combatant state' has miniaturised back into tribal brigandage: telecommunications have broken down, motorised traffic is horse-drawn and industry is at a standstill. The *National Bulletin* is no longer national and is scrawled in chalk. A market scene, with scavenged detritus alongside neo-medieval products, is wittily 'postmodern'. This is a makeshift economy patched together from civilisation's ruins, capitalistic nationhood in its barest essentials. Sole continuity with Part One is, ironically, ongoing warfare, with the local 'Hill People' (*TTCAFS*, pp. 47–48).

In both text and film, the Boss parodies 1930s militaristic rhetoric and pomp (his grotesque combination of tin-hat, sheepskin and bemedalled uniform epitomises the fetishism which Fotheringay lambasts in *MWCWM* (see below)). Actor Ralph Richardson modelled him on the original 'Great Dictator', Mussolini (Rudolf's rosette crosses Tudor device with Fascist emblem). According to some critics, he is the sole light relief in an otherwise dry film, whose main roles were overloaded with symbolism and creaky acting.[79] Despite his swagger, the Boss still depends on coercing master mechanic Richard Gordon to get his antique squadron flying again. The coming of the futuristic scout plane, piloted by the now white-haired

John Cabal, presages the return of 'Law and Sanity' to Everytown. Dismounting against the sky with a vast domed helmet, he is 'a tall portent' (*TTCAFS*, p. 56). Cabal's silhouette deliberately echoes the alien, 'cephalopod' appearance of the Martians, with their distended brains. Like them, he is the harbinger of a new intellectual and political 'commonweal of mankind' (see Chapter 5) after apocalyptic destruction. However, a reviewer in *The Times* drew attention to the miraculous convenience of this 'change of heart': 'Quite suddenly the airmen – presumably the same people who caused so much destruction in the second world war – emerge from the ruins endowed with such wisdom, detachment and nobility as would put Socrates to shame.'[80]

The mouthpiece for Wells's technocratic solution, Cabal's dialogue follows his text closely:

> we, who are all that are left of the old engineers and mechanics, have pledged ourselves to salvage the world. We have the air-ways, all that's left of them. We have the seas and we have ideas in common ... the Brotherhood of Efficiency – the Freemasonry of Science. We're the last trustees of civilisation when everything else has failed.

However, Gordon's response ('I have been waiting for this. I am yours to command' (*TTCAFS*, p. 60)) rings hollow in light of Orwell's criticism that men of science don't necessarily think rationally about questions outside their immediate professional field, evidenced by how many fell into line behind totalitarian ideologies. Orwell sounded the alarm against tempting assumptions that anti-democratic revolution (however benevolent in intent) could ever be a progressive step.[81] The 1941 documentary *They Met in London* (by Paul Rotha Productions for the Ministry of Information) sheds a sharp historical sidelight on the outcome of trust in the rationalism of scientists, though endorsing global thinking. It concerns a key wartime conference at the Royal Institution, at which Wells famously chaired a session on 'Science and the World Mind'. Over footage of Heinkel bombers and other advanced weaponry, the film shows German scientists conscripted as 'mechanics of the Nazi war machine'. Against this it ranged an alternative 'commonwealth of scientists', including China and the USSR. During prominent close-ups of Wells, the voice-over talked about 'a world to be reconstructed' by science 'so that all men may be free from want and free from fear' and noted the conference's pledge never to permit its misuse again for mass murder and enslavement. Nevertheless, as Orwell also noted, the Cold War and the atomic age would soon split the same community again along national–ideological lines.[82]

The allusion behind the Boss's contradictory rhetoric about a war to 'End war ... to make victorious peace' perhaps shows Wells's contrition about his own false prophecy regarding the First World War ('Cabal: "I seem to have heard that phrase before."') More overtly it refers to the punitive Treaty of Versailles, which cranked up the system of national conflict to a yet more explosive level (*TTCAFS*, p. 62). However, with the arrival of Wells's emissary for 'Wings Over the World' (and the sense of a foregone conclusion that this brings), the film diverts attention into the temporary visual excitement of the battle over the Floss Valley coal-pits with the rival 'hill people', then a Boys' Own contrivance to save Cabal's mission: the urgent need to get the ramshackle squadron airworthy requires his technical knowledge, helping Gordon escape to Basra to fetch his fleet of twin-hulled 'flying forts' and end the Boss's parochial tyranny.

Wells originally scheduled the ensuing reconstruction to cover 1970–2054, but the film ends in 2036 (neatly setting concluding scenes a century ahead of its release). Mann's team produced some of their most pioneering effects to realise Wells's instructions for a new industrial revolution of giant boring and blasting vehicles, power plants and dynamic forms of barely imaginable construction processes. Significantly, *WM* suggested that they took his own descriptions of watching future cityscapes arising in *TM* as their template.[83] By blending models against live-action (with tiny operatives on hovercrafts, wearing astronaut-like suits) and semi-abstract, Ruttmannesque patterning, they condensed decades of titanic activity:

> The shots dissolve rapidly on to one another, and are bridged with eccentric mechanical movements. The small figures of men move among the monstrosities of mechanism, more and more dwarfed by their accumulating intensity ... A fantasia of powerful rotating and swinging forms carried on a broad stream of music. (*TTCAFS*, pp. 91–93)[84]

Vincent Korda's original ambitions for this five-and-a-half-minute 'work' sequence included switching from monochrome to colour and from standard to wide screen. *Bauhausler* Lázló Moholy-Nagy was also invited to contribute. As in his experimental film *Light-Play* (1930), he used the principles of Constructivist sculpture – semi-transparent moving materials and shapes – to suggest a new reality, rather than representing it in concrete form. However, this proved too abstract for Wells's emphasis on an inhabitable future. Only flashes of his work remain.[85]

To the correspondingly mechanistic rhythms of Arthur Bliss's score, Wells's anti-Langian blueprint of a future metropolis was fleshed out. It was excavated into the hills of an ecologically re-engineered countryside, the very inverse of *Metropolis*, revealed in cutaway view (*SOTTC* had rendered skyscrapers ironic, by insisting that aerial warfare would transform cities into vast reinforced bomb shelters). Its brightly lit and air-conditioned galleries, elevated 'moving ways', monorails and perspex lift-tubes were, nonetheless, a benevolent version of the multi-levelled, teeming Babylon of *WTSW*. With ornamental trees and running water, New Everytown was literally a hi-tech 'garden city'. Backgrounds and live action were more convincingly combined than had been possible in *Metropolis*. Mann and Veevers (who would advise on Kubrick's *2001*) overlaid full-sized ground-floor sets with maquettes and projected images of crowd movement on to tiny screens in miniatures.[86]

In an obvious exposition device, a great-grandfather (110 years young) teaches a Templesque little girl (seven-year-old Anne MacLaren), privileged to live in an age of continuous invention where life gets 'lovelier and lovelier', about the 'Age of Windows'. A screen-within-the-screen displays a montage of New York skylines ('a funny sticking up place'), thus rendering 1930s modernity laughably antique. Expounding the awfulness of the dark, unhygienic past, he switches to 'a brief fantasia on the theme ... done in the Grierson style' (*TTCAFS*, pp. 94–95).[87] However, the overall visualisation of Wells's Utopia seemed disciplinarian and clinical to many. It gave an impression of 'Puritan Tyranny' (as *SOTTC* calls it), diametrically opposed to the fleshly pursuits which Wells himself relished, as Michael Korda points out. Actor Cedric Hardwicke, playing Theotocopulos who heads opposition to the regime, found the script arid.[88] The presentation of Oswald Cabal's panoramic viewpoint from his eyrie, above antlike crowds, compounded the film's sense of superhuman remoteness for many.

Nonetheless, Wells's memorandum against *Metropolis* stressed that advanced technology must be visualised as a liberation from past social forms and practices. The whole point of machinery was to supersede the 'mechanisation' of human beings by drudgery (*TTCAFS*, p. 14). Like *WTSW* and *Metropolis*, *TTC* features multiple forms of media technology, but now serving Wells's 'enlightened' global state, which even its opponents can access to broadcast their protest against unremitting 'progress'. 'World Communications' was the alternative title of the airmen's organisation, but it is precisely because of them that sculptor Theotocopulos is able to stir up revolt with his speech on 'Art and Life': 'Talk. Radio is everywhere. *This modern world is full of voices.*' Theotocopulos's speech is instantly transmitted from television studio[89] on to a giant transparent screen, lowered into the vast public square. He is also duplicated ubiquitously in viewers (some apparently holographic)[90] of all sizes and contexts in a montage of locations, though those in the text are more elaborate and varied (see *TTCAFS*, pp. 119–20). *TTC* now visualised as technical 'reality' what *WTSW* had foreseen in the power of simultaneous broadcasting. By 1937, Wells's own face and distinctive voice were already familiar to millions from newsreels and radio broadcasts, along with the world leaders who received him as a thinker of renown.[91] As *TTCAFS* puts it, the reality of a single person being able to speak to the whole world, so far as it is interested and will listen, and the swiftness with which a common response can be evoked at the same time in every part of the earth where listeners can be found, is made plain. (*TTCAFS*, p. 119)

TTCAFS also makes it explicit that, through Theotocopulos, Wells is countering Aldous Huxley's 1932 dystopia: 'I will *go* for this Brave New World of theirs – tooth and claw' (p. 93). Wells gives him a Pythonesque – 'What have the Romans done for us?' – line on the benefits of scientific progress. His irrational but romantic nostalgia for the good old days, 'when life was short and hot and merry and the devil took the hindermost', is intercut in *TTCAFS* with scenes of robust senior health, nurseries without infant mortality, benign genetic engineering and personally fulfilling scientific work (replacing factory and office boredom) on a mass scale (pp. 124–26).[92] However, the film gives the impression that machines now do all the meaningful work, and Wells's counterbalance is more weakly verbalised by an argument which follows, between the reincarnation of the time-serving Passworthy and Oswald Cabal, about the generational dynamics of progress. Cabal's daughter, Catherine, and Passworthy's son, Maurice, have volunteered for the Space Gun. Its risks as 'human sacrifice' to technological progress (Theotocopulos alleges) nonetheless raise the spectre of the machine-idolatry of *Metropolis*, just as Wells's motif of interplanetary New Adam and Eve is another hidden echo of *Frau im Mond*.

Cabal's response to Passworthy's objections is intended to answer *Brave New World*'s crux: how to meet the basic human need for a *raison d'être* greater than mere mass-material welfare once it is secured by 'taming' nature. Cabal stresses that whereas the old order condemned people to suffer for destructive and exploitative reasons, 'Our revolution ... simply made death and danger worth while.' Consciously directing what *TTCAFS* calls the 'surplus energies of the race' (p.10) into a new stage of positive evolutionary development will prevent bodily and intellectual entropy from technological comforts. This clearly refers to anxieties about 'posthuman' degeneration from *TM* onwards. In the past our need to strive manifested itself as warlike aggression. Now it is the danger of our own success turning us into consumerist lotus-eaters (*TTCAFS*, pp. 107–8). Wells's belief in perpetual 'evolutionary dynamism' is thus symbolised by space exploration. Against it, he poses a strange kind of revolt by 'more aesthetic types' (*TTCAFS*, pp. 10–11). However, the contrived presentation of this conflict is easily misunderstood as an attack on artistic creativity itself, rather than on the indolent decadence of the privileged he embodied in the Eloi.[93] The necessary streamlining of characters and issues makes the film's plot seem like a stacked game that only one side can win, rather than the more open-ended philosophical debate driving good drama. Moreover, as Cooke's review noted, there is an all-too-visible faultline between *TTC*'s argument and the combined aesthetic appeal *and* utility of its designs. This deconstructs the anachronistic dichotomy between artist and scientist on which the film ostensibly rests: 'It is the gayest mockery of the whole piece that Mr Korda's sets relegate Mr Wells's dialectic to the last and not the next century.'[94]

In a key difference from past insurrections (there are no Morlocks or *WTSW* Labour Department serfs now), the uprising is not by the 'Have-Nots', but by the 'Doers attacked by the Do-Nots' (*TTCAFS*, p. 135). Their cliff-edge appearance at the launch site develops into a form of 'Griffith climax'. While Cabal and Theotocopulos duel by loudspeaker, the Space Gun is launched with only seconds to spare. Cabal warns about the concussion, thus avoiding *SOTTC*'s mass death which might have turned film audiences off-message altogether: *TTC*'s rioters merely look ridiculous in the blast wind. The coda at the observatory presents a stark choice to continue to conquer space and time or to resign ourselves to animal insignificance: 'Which shall it be, Passworthy? Which shall it be?' echoes out into choiring voices against a background of stars. However, Michael Korda argues that this closing problem is 'much more Wellsian than human' and finally dissociates his missionary scientism from the ordinary life which might have helped audiences identify with it.[95]

Whether *TTC* articulates dissident viewpoints convincingly remains controversial. Karol Kulik suggests that Wells deliberately made Oswald's cabal 'smug, cold and unsympathetic' to emphasise the dangerous triumphalism of science untempered by more humane considerations. It is certainly arguable that there are unconscious intimations of Wells's ambivalent conclusion (after future-orientated totalitarianism had ignited the next world war) that 'Our elite is our necessity and our menace.'[96] Moreover, some of Wells's complex dialectics were diluted or cut, especially their sexual politics. In her post-industrial finery, Roxana (Margaretta Scott) hesitates between the ideologies represented by the Boss and John Cabal, like *KWWAK*'s allegorical figure of 'Woman' (see *TTCAFS*, p. 73). However, the film omits much of her dialogue about female subjection. She chafes against her trophy-concubine role, recognising a new power which might transform gender limitations (see *TTCAFS*, pp. 74–75). But she also questions Cabal's patronising rationalism: 'If this new world – all airships and science and order – comes about, what will happen to us women?' Moreover, against Harding's daughter's confidently egalitarian reply, 'We shall work like the men', Roxana suspects that all visionary agendas ultimately derive from the masculine desire for prestige and control, however sublimated, and that sexual motivations can never be ruled out (*TTCAFS*, pp. 80–81). In *WM*, her viewpoint is stressed meta-cinematically, as she 'break[s] through the film so to speak' to address the audience directly.[97] *TTCAFS*'s Oswald Cabal also has a failed marriage to Rowena, Roxana's descendant (played by Scott again, though these scenes were cut).[98] Rowena indicts his lack of fatherliness in not protecting their child from the dangers of the lunar flight: 'You and your kind are monsters. Your science and your new order theories have taken away your souls and put machines and theories in the place of them' (*TTCAFS*, p. 112). But Oswald counters that techno-social change has revolutionised sexual relations ('Do you think that everything else in human life is going to alter, scale and power and speed, and men and women remain as they have always been?' (*TTCAFS*, p. 115)). *TTCAFS* certainly features women taking professional roles alongside men, such as aerial-combat crews and paratroops (images survive from corresponding scenes which were cut), but also explorers and experimenters, as well as astronauts (*TTCAFS*, pp. 85 and 122–23). *TTC* is less bold about what Wells called the need to 'unspecialize women', so they could participate in the human project 'for the good of the race', rather than just 'men's satisfactions'.[99]

In historical retrospect, after the militarisms of the 1930s wreaked planetary havoc and seeded their Cold War legacies, prophecies of bad dictatorship – the Boss – being swept away by the 'good' totalitarianism of black-suited airmen raises ironic associations (even though *SOTTC* is an explicitly internationalist and anti-racist text).[100] Though the 1930s cult of flying was politically multivalent (like thinking on eugenics), aviation was a particularly powerful icon in Fascist film propaganda, as epitomised by Hitler's messianic descent into Nürnberg in a Junker's trimotor, in Leni Riefenstahl's *Triumph des Willens*, the same year in which audiences saw Cabal land in Everytown.[101] But if Wells ever admired Hitler or Stalin, it was not for themselves but for the potential power they wielded through state-planning and command economies. He certainly lost all sympathy as their regimes degenerated into systematic repression and genocide.[102] Moreover, the film's future can also be seen as open to active making rather than passive prediction (as Wells argued in an interview with *Film Weekly*).[103] *Nature* thought *TTC* had proved that the motion picture was the best means today of transmitting a universal message 'warning of disaster unless human purposes were determined by reconstructed principles', because science had 'put into the hands of civilised man the power to destroy himself or to make the world a celestial dwelling place; and the sooner this [was] realised the safer the world [would] be'.[104] However, as Richards points out, since the invention of atomic weapons in 1945 the popular image of scientists is more often as bogeymen than saviours; likewise, the notion of wholesale re-engineering of a fragile ecological balance may seem anathema now.[105]

There is also a key structural problem about sustaining suspense through *TTC*'s tripartite structure, which violates Sam Goldwyn's dictum that the ideal film starts with an earthquake and builds to a climax. As Kulik observes, narrative logic seems to demand a peak for each episode, the final being the most powerful. However, it is arguable that the Blitz sequence is the 'high point of the entire film', which 'the manufactured dramas' of the others fail to match. Victory over the Boss appears both inevitable and comically disproportionate, while the last episode rests on questionable premises.[106]

Despite high hopes, unforeseen difficulties had disillusioned and ground Wells down by the date of release. In his diary, he expressed simmering resentment at the apparent inability to follow his intentions: 'I grew tired of writing stuff into the treatment that was afterwards mishandled ... in the end little more of *The Shape of Things to Come* was got over than the suggestion of a Cosmopolis ruled by men of science and affairs.'[107] In *Star Begotten*, he incorporated negative audience reaction to *TTC* in a self-parody about the impossibility of ever visualising credible Utopian futures. As Professor Keppel explains,

> World peace is assumed, but the atmosphere of security simply makes them rather aimless, fattish and out of training. They are collectively up to nothing – or they are off in a storm of collective hysteria to conquer the moon or some remote nonsense of that sort. Imaginative starvation. They have apparently made no advances whatever in subtlety, delicacy, simplicity. Rather the reverse. They never say a witty thing; they never do a charming act. The general effect is of very pink, rather absurdly dressed celluloid dolls living on tabloids in a glass lavatory.[108]

Susan Sontag points out that SF film's most obvious advantage over the most ekphrastic literature is its instant capacity for 'sensuous elaboration'.[109] But this can also be a drawback. In chastened mood in 1938, Wells noted that for realism of the fantastic the devil was in apparently trivial particularities demanded by a medium of unforgiving visual specificity: 'But directly you come down to real persons seen close-up, you meet what is the final and conclusive defeat of futuristic imagination and that is – the small material details.' *TTC* had brought this home: 'It was easy to write of a Dictator, splendidly clothed, seated at the head of his council, and then go on with the speeches. But when it came to the screen, you have to show him from top to toe. And how was he going to dress his hair?' Most ironically, Wells effectively admitted that *TTC*'s design was scuppered by the same shortcoming for which he castigated *Metropolis*. Though cutting-edge in style, it quickly became yet another of yesterday's tomorrows: 'We did our best, but in fact we could never get beyond contemporary modernism.'[110]

The Man Who Could Work Miracles

Audiences were lured to *TTC* at least as much by the apocalyptic effects as by any interest in the urgent choices confronting humanity. In that sense, Wells had failed seamlessly to fuse popular entertainment with intelligent stimulation. Nevertheless, his next film (contracted before its release)[111] was supposed to ride along in the wake of expected acclaim. *MWCWM* presents a very different view of Wells as both scriptwriter and Utopian thinker. Having enthused about rule by technocratic élite, he turned his attention back to the anonymous 'little man', ostensible benefactor of such state reform, who had often been the more sympathetic subject of his social realist fiction. Wells also turned away from high design back to popular culture, with a story appealing to Korda's love of folklore and visual trickery. As we have seen, Wells was very much aware of the logical translation of stage wizardry to the screen. Full of 'interference with normal causation' (*CSS*, p. 305), this comic text was a potential gift for stop-motion special effects, a staple of primitive trickfilms, but highly sophisticated by the 1930s. Following the story, Fotheringay defines miracles as 'something *contrariwise* to the usual course of nature done by an act of Will' (cf. *CSS*, p. 399). His first one inverts a burning lamp telekinetically. The film's visualisation of this (as in *TTC*, the special effects director was Ned Mann) deliberately recalls the transferral of magic into a medium of more convincing illusionism, hinted at in the pub landlord's reaction as he chucks Fotheringay out: 'Come on, Mr conjuror, we don't want any more bother.' (In the film novel (published 1936), one of the regulars even exclaims, ''E did it with wires.')[112]

Back in his digs, Fotheringay even considers a career 'on the music 'alls' and flourishes minor miracles – levitating furniture, magicking a kitten from a conical hat, making objects vanish and materialise, etc. – in front of an imaginary audience, until his bed is covered in all the clichés of stage trickery. In a later scene (recalling the Sorcerer's Apprentice folktale with its bewitched household utensils working themselves),[113] the film employs its most impressive object animation: Fotheringay orders the draper's shop's commodities and displays to tidy themselves away, described in Wells's film novel thus: 'In an instant rolls roll up, goods fold themselves, stacks of goods straighten up and everything leaps to its place' (*The Man Who Could Work Miracles: A Film Story Based on the Material Contained in his Short Story 'The Man Who Could Work Miracles'*) (*MWCWMAFS*, p. 31). The movie is highly self-referential about its paradoxical processes and effects. After Fotheringay makes a tiger appear and vanish, Mr Maydig refutes the evidence of his senses, explaining it in scientific terms as 'joint hallucination. The thing is quite well known', although he is unable to dismiss the claw marks. Roland Barthes saw photographic referentiality as shared hallucination (see Chapter 1). Early film developed a tradition of using hallucination self-referentially, especially in Expressionism: for example, the desert 'caravan' visualised in the theatre scene of *Dr Mabuse: Der Spieder*, and the wanderings of the Israelites conjured up before the court in *Der Golem* (1920). In that sense, 'joint hallucination' seems an accurate description of the realities which cinema virtually materialises in front of our eyes.

MWCWM also conjures self-reflexively with space in effects of simultaneous elsewheres. Fotheringay inadvertently sends Winch to 'blazes', hastily revised to San Francisco, making for much comic cross-cutting, as the bobby copes with incongruous materialisation in hooting Californian traffic and subsequent problems explaining himself to the American authorities.[114] Fotheringay instantly teleports retired imperial Colonel Winstanley to his stamping grounds in Bombay and back again. The text refers to the effect in terms long familiar from Wellsian praise for modern communications and media, from *Anticipations* onwards: 'Talk about abolishing distance!' (*MWCWMAFS*, p. 69). The movie also recalls cinema's fundamental connection with *TM*, when Fotheringay reverses the town clock, for an extra twenty minutes wooing Ada.

Such tricks are arguably a Faustian 'trivialisation' of superhuman powers. With his Kippsian level of education, Fotheringay isn't imaginative enough to realise their full possibilities yet. He embodies humankind with the 'miracles' of modern technology at its disposal[115] – 'All the saints and science that ever was; it's nothing to what I can do now' – yet is unable to deploy them with sufficient understanding, organisation and imagination to solve fundamental common problems of the species. Fotheringay's expression is 'halfway between inspiration and idiocy', as Wells puts it (*MWCWMAFS*, p. 32).[116] As well as alluding to cinema's popular narrative history, Wells's film also comments on the squandering of its cultural potential to pursue the distractions of cheap sensation.

The movie was released in February 1937, directed by Lothar Mendes. Kulik argues that, having learned from bitter experience, Korda, with the connivance of Wells's son, Frank, kept Wells away from the actual production as much as possible.[117] However, the film novel (apart from fine-tuning dialogue and occasional scene and effect changes) indicates far fewer interventions from his screenplay collaborator, Biró than was the case with *TTC*. The fact that Wells had the opportunity to expand and elaborate an already very ekphrastic short story, rather than cutting down a nebulously panoramic 'history of the future', accounts for this.

The most obvious interpolation was the new interstellar framing narrative based on a trio of 'elementals': Player (Giver of Power), Indifference (spot the hellenically naked George Sanders) and Observer. Hardy's *The Dynasts* also started with similar Immortals surveying conditions from space.[118] The metaphysical frame was indispensable 'to broaden out the reference' and make it 'a proper companion piece to *Things to Come*' (*MWCWMAFS*, p. 10). Wells seemed to point up ironic references to its serious predecessor's pretensions. Player decides to give a random individual superhuman power for change, in order to test whether earthlings can cope with it. A gigantic hand reaches down to Fotheringay, on his way to the Long Dragon in Dewhinton. He is now, as yet unbeknown to himself, able to do anything except influence people's innermost feelings (a handicap for any dictator attempting psychological persuasion).

The paradoxical method of a realism of the fantastic is key to Wells's intended effect in this comic parable, according to his 'Introductory Remarks' about domesticating the miraculous. Everything had to be '"actual", matter-of-fact, up to the last phase of the world catastrophe' (*MWCWMAFS*, p. 9). Consequently, sharing Wells's middle-name, George, Fotheringay (Roland Young) is now a more socially realised character, an assistant at Grigsby and Blott drapers. His author pursued the same apprenticeship before his talents were recognised and there are emphatic parallels with the semi-autobiographical *Kipps* and Shaw's 1922 film (with their miraculous windfall radically transforming Arthur's life). George experiences similar frustration in a dead-end job, with suggestions of compensatory wish-fulfilment. Starlet Joan Gardner plays flirtatious Ada Price, Fotheringay's unattainable 'muse' (he eventually transforms her into a personification of vicarious eroticism, 'like Cleopatra in the movies'), contrasted with Maggie Hooper, his mundane fiancée. Fotheringay begins clearing complexions and healing sprained arms, but co-workers suggest expanding his ambitions. Thus he becomes torn between self-gratifying and philanthropic ends: foreseeing the Derby winner,[119] on the one hand; creating hospitals, on the other. His fellow assistant, Bill Stoker, finally proposes that he should 'run the world' for the common good.[120] But as yet he is held back, like Wells himself, 'distracted between his new sense of power and his old sense of inferiority. He is typically the human being with a gift' (*MWCWMAFS*, pp. 40–41).

Fotheringay seeks advice about his dilemma from Mr Maydig. Ernest Thesiger plays him as a reforming but also power-hungry Baptist minister. Maydig wants to create a priggish Utopia, a parody of Wells's own World State (in the film novel, he flaunts daringly 'progressive' books (*MWCWMAFS*, p. 54)). But he is also a hypocrite, hiding fleshly weaknesses when company calls, though vindictively insisting that Fotheringay turn the colonel's whisky to water. Maydig envisages the future as a rhetorically glib new Eden – 'Sweep it *all* away. A world glowing with health – newborn' – although Fotheringay (instinctively alarmed after conjuring the carnivorous beast) asks for time to think and not act precipitately.[121]

Maydig concedes, 'There's an inertia in things that has to be considered.' Hence the ending plays on the double-meaning of this running theme in both political and physical senses.

As in *TTC*, the film's other new principal characters personify rival interest groups competing for Fotheringay's attention. They either want to exploit miracle-working for their own ends, or prevent him upsetting the status quo. For example, Major Grigsby (Edward Chapman again) represents monopoly capitalism, offering partnership in the glittering future of 'Grigsby, Blott and Fotheringay': 'Just scattering miracles. Cheap as dirt. But canalised – concentrated! Monopolised! Then it can be an immense thing!' He and banker Bamfylde argue performing them free would result in over-production, undermining business and the motivating work ethic. The film novel puts their viewpoint more emphatically (and perhaps too satirically for the film's backers): 'It would ruin everything. Universal bankruptcy. Lassitude. Degeneration.' After Fotheringay is swayed by Maydig's socialistic plans to replace 'a Want System' with one of 'Plenty', Bamfylde squeals, 'He'll kill credit.' Conversely, Fotheringay's fellow workers see management's plans for a 'Miracle Draper's' as a threat of redundancy like automation.

Squire Winstanley (Ralph Richardson reprising his Blimpish role) represents imperialistic militarism. He first becomes alarmed on discovering his weapons collection metamorphosed into symbolic ploughshares and sickles: 'What's this – this blinking Bolshevik thing?' Fotheringay (effectively quoting the title behind *KWWAK*) says it will 'prepare your mind for the Peace of the World'. Winstanley waxes apoplectic at the casualness (and grammar) of Fotheringay's announcement, 'I suppose we shall start the Golden Age somewhere in the afternoon', but especially Maydig's Eloish replacement of manly activities with 'go[ing] about Loving one another!' After appeals to traditional decency fail, the colonel tries assassination, but Fotheringay wishes himself invulnerable in the nick of time.

Like *TTC*, the denouement is shaped by topical context. Fotheringay loses patience with quarrelling factions, and, intoxicated with the possibility of power (much of which is clearly libidinal: 'My world's going to be full of pretty women'), seizes absolute control and sets his own agenda for the future: 'It's going to be the world of George McWhirter Fotheringay ... All of you – you wanted to use me. Now I'm going to use myself.' Fotheringay's accent has suitably modulated from vernacular diffidence to commanding RP. In the film novel, his new status as comic dictator is even more explicit, posturing Napoleonically before the mirror and enlarging his stature. He also calls himself 'Master of the World', invoking Verne's aerial megalomaniac. Wells leaves no doubt about his dangerousness: 'Close-up of his excited and glowing face advancing with an effect of exultant menace towards the audience' (*MWCWM*, p. 82). The movie alludes less directly to Hitler's 'little man' inferiority complex and Stalin's fondness for ruthless 'Five Year Plans'. In a very impressive effects sequence comparable to *TTC*'s reconstruction scenes, Fotheringay magics up a grandiose, neo-classical palace, suggested by the print over Maydig's mantelpiece.[122] (It is arguable that Wells also echoes Joyce's surreal 'mockalypse' and petit-bourgeois reformist fantasies of the 'New Bloomusalem' from 'Circe'.) He then assembles bankers, businessmen, opinion-formers and world statesmen (by kaleidoscopic superimposition) into a kind of conscripted League of Nations Union chamber, without option to withdraw, as the Fascist powers had done to pursue nationalist ends.[123]

Fotheringay insists that world leaders become genuinely answerable to the needs of the 'common man' who invests in them politically: 'Chaps like me have had to trust you, willy-nilly. And what did you do for us? What sort of a deal did you give us?' (The film novel makes it abundantly clear that they already possessed the technological and economic means to eradicate misery *before* miraculous intervention.[124]) Most vehemently, Fotheringay indicts their failure to prevent war because of an addiction to displays of power: 'A trenchful of dead chaps like me? *That* made you feel more real and important, eh?' However, a contradiction in terms creeps into his programme as he ruthlessly threatens to wipe them all out, 'as a child wipes a slate', should they fail to implement universal peace and happiness. Wells satirises the corruption of salvationary collectivist ends by the increasingly monstrous means of contemporary political 'supermen', Right and Left (mass purges of Soviet intelligentsia began in 1936; the Nazis liquidated opposition groups after their 1933 *coup d'état*).

Inevitable catastrophe is visualised in a spectacularly centrifugal flinging off of the building's fabric and inhabitants from the Earth's surface, as Fotheringay stops the rotation of the Earth (in a misguided bid to suspend time altogether like a latter-day Joshua to effect his plans for reform). The frame returns to the Immortals. Indifference says we told you so: 'Once an ape, always an ape.' Having failed to listen to reason about inertia, Fotheringay whirls about amidst chaos in space. However, Fotheringay undoes his wish. The closing temporal reversal runs back to the film's beginning in the pub, with the crucial difference that normal causation now prevails. Fotheringay's renewed attempt to conjure the lamp fails, because he has renounced uncontrollable power (though retaining a dim memory of things being otherwise). Indifference insists that Player's experiment proves that all power does is bring out humankind's petty 'Egotism and elementary lust' and that they will 'never get out of their mess'. But Player remains optimistic that each tiny 'flash of indignation' which ignites in earthlings 'when they think things are false and wrong' will eventually accumulate into the critical mass of *collective* action. If he tries again, allowing 'thought and wisdom' to 'keep pace with the growth of power', his fellow Immortals might be surprised 'in an age or so'. The film's provisional viewpoint is thus not dissimilar to Wells's statement that 'Human history becomes more and more a race between education and catastrophe.'[125] It acquiesces to the inevitability of present disaster, as did *TTC*, while holding on to evolutionary hope.

The New Faust

It is arguable that, like the faultline between entertainment and message in *TTC*, *MWCWM* suffers from the strain between fantastic spectacle and Wellsian set-piece debates, as well as sometimes pulling the film-novel's satirical punch. Unlike *TTC* it was certainly not a great critical hit at the time, though doing rather better commercially, especially in the USA.[126] Compared to the sheer creative energy of Wells's early intuitions about the possibility of new subjects and modes for visual narration, his actual achievement in terms of film-making in the mid-1930s inevitably seems disappointing. Symptomatically, Wells also reworked 'The Story of the Late Mr Elvesham' from forty years earlier as *The New Faust: A Film Story* (*NF*) along with *FOTG* for Korda although these never went into production.[127] Given the production difficulties and mixed success of *TTC* and *MWCWM*, it is perhaps unsurprising. Another possible spoiler is Robert Stevenson's *The Man Who Changed His Mind*, also known as *The Brainsnatchers* (1936).[128] It starred Karloff in his latest mad-scientist role as Dr Laurience, who discovers a method of transferring 'thought content' into other bodies and, therefore, exchanging identities. The film's parallel metacinematic themes, which include (literal) image capture, impersonation and perpetual youth, could also have been developed from Wells's original variation on the *Doppelgänger* trope.

Wells had wished to live over again to 'devote [himself] entirely to working for the cinema'. In this autobiographical context, *NF* is unconsciously revealing. It epitomises both the aspiration and the failure to regenerate his talent in fully cinematic terms. He was 70 at the time he reworked his story, about as old as Elvesham, while the author of the original was closer to his victim, Arthur Reston, at 27.[129] Their mind-swap is mediated by the diabolic McPhister,[130] using occult technology recalling the 'bodysnatching' associations of early recording media. He tempts Elvesham with a notion of posthumous survival, resembling the detachment of the self in *Der Student von Prag* or the parasitic transfer of consciousness into a new host in *Das Testament des Dr Mabuse*. Modernistically, Elvesham recognises that a man is 'but a system of memories'. Hence, the 'I' could be shifted between bodies by transferring the imprinted images which constitute it. Significantly, the film story describes a kind of montage which (parallel to Wells's own life) displays Elvesham's recollections from Victorian childhood to sexual awakening and the motivations behind his ambition.[131]

By becoming an 'unending man', Elvesham seeks to escape the lifecycle's termination of experience and knowledge, to take power as a modern megalo*mediac* or 'serialised Napoleon' (*NF*, pp. 122–23). He even has a chillingly eugenic vision of breeding a race of lower-class 'hosts' specifically for rebirthing élite consciousnesses (*NF*, p. 128). As in the original story, Elvesham tricks Reston into becoming his adopted heir, so that he can 'bequeathe' his own property to a regenerated self, by offering to sponsor the young scientist's ambitious research. Reston, therefore, consents to undergo McPhister's SPR-like telepathic 'experiment'. (Elvesham slyly prepares his staff for his victim's horrified reaction by warning them that he may awake 'a little groggy and queer' (*NF*, p. 126).) The process takes place under studio 'reflectors capable of throwing an intense light on their faces and shoulders', but at the crucial moment Wells literally draws a curtain across this opportunity for metacinematic effects, leaving only vague hints about hypnosis, drugs and electromagnetic fields. Nevertheless, the result would have demanded a virtuoso performance from actors expressing underlying personalities against physical appearance, i.e. a young man 'with faintly senile pose and movements' and the reverse, an old one with determined and vigorous demeanour (*NF*, pp. 126 and 138). In *The Man Who Changed His Mind* the identity switch is also effected by mysterious machines, its subjects invisible in sealed chambers. Its after-effects similarly necessitate actors 'playing' against their ages to suggest contradictions between subject and bodily host.

Wells's film story also brings out how his early tales prefigure our audience identification with screen figures, imagining ourselves in their charismatic skins, acting desires vicariously through absent presences. Elvesham, as Arthur 2, inherits both his body and Marguerite, his glamorous fiancée. Conversely, she senses his creepiness, manifested in Arthur 2's strange new demeanour: 'It's queer how *present* he [Elvesham] seems to me' (*NF*, pp. 129–30). But sexuality, what *KWWAK* criticised as the screen's 'one old, old story', proves the undoing of Elvesham's superhuman ambitions. In another, more ironic kind of doubling, he becomes obsessed by Marguerite as the reincarnation of the lost love seen in his memory montage. Arguably, McPhister's frustration at Elvesham's failure to transcend the generative imperative is also an ambivalent comment on Wells's narrative's own deterioration into romantic distraction: 'It exasperates me to see the incurable littleness and spiritlessness of man. Will you *none* of you escape from this love story?' (*NF*, p. 133) Elvesham's unnatural second life begins to echo his first, as he is locked into the compulsion to repeat (like a proto-*Groundhog Day* (1993)) and his host's youthful hormones take him over.

Wells's cross-cutting to Elvesham 2's awakening reprises the 1896 text's subjective effect of looking in the mirror to find yourself prematurely imprisoned in geriatric flesh (see *NF*, p. 134). However, Reston quickly takes control of his fantastic situation, feigning amnesia so that he can impersonate his patron effectively to get back his own likeness. In another reversal, this has an increasingly unnerving effect on Arthur 2, whom he battens on to like the Student of Prague's detached reflection: 'I am going to be your great friend … always at your side, always watching over that body you stole from me' (*NF*, p. 137). This gives Reston a secret psychological grip on Arthur 2, dependent on the former's advice to play his own part as fiancé and scientist convincingly. Elvesham realises he is in a corporeal trap of his own making. This is compounded by bungled attempts at murder ('You silly old ass. If you get that body of mine hanged or sent to jail …' (*NF*, p. 142)), until Reston finally tricks him into thinking that he has accidentally infected the body Elvesham occupies with the typhoid with which he intends killing his own. Elvesham therefore consents to reversing the process and McPhister reveals his true identity as he dies, pleading desperately for another host. Wells echoes the famous opening of Murnau's *Faust* (1926), when Mephistopheles envelopes a plague-infested town in his shadowy wings: 'He becomes a black shape like a velvet pall brooding over the old man.' It is also now that repeated close-ups of fidgeting digits achieve their macabre pay-off: 'Only Elvesham's fine wrinkled white hand, resting on the chair-arm, is visible. On his finger is his diamond ring. It clings twitching to the chair-arm for a moment … relaxes and falls limp' (*NF*, p. 144).

Whether Wells's final published film story could have been turned into a successful movie is debatable, but both theme and form are undoubtedly symptomatic of his belated striving to reinvent himself in terms of the cinematic promise of his first creative flush. By 1936, he expressed himself as 'more than a little disillusioned with films'. He still believed in their potential, but felt exhausted by the uphill struggle of reshaping an already established industry and collective product to his purpose, falling back on the less technological medium of print, which he trusted more not to compromise his art and intentions:

> They *could* be magnificent art, but all the art has still to be learnt and the temptation to go back to writing books with nothing between you and your reader but the printer – no producers, directors, art directors, camera men, actors and actresses, cutters and editors – is almost irresistible.[132]

It is indicative that, despite such unsatisfactory experiences, Wells did not give up entirely on writing for the cinema. Indeed he returned to scripting a kind of sequel to *TTC* for Korda in the last year of his life. Provisionally entitled, 'The Way the World is Going', this was to have dealt with the possible future of humanity in the post-atomic aftermath of the Second World War.[133]

Both of Wells's films for Korda might have enjoyed another life in a new medium as TV serials (or, in *MWCWM*'s case, even as a film musical!) if Frank Wells and Ivor Montagu's negotiations with the American Barbizon Productions Corporation had borne fruit at the end of the 1950s.[134] Nevertheless, the virtually incalculable ways in which Wells's visual imagination stimulated cinema and television programmes more widely and fruitfully through the efforts of newer talents, adapting, extending and reworking his storylines and techniques, are the subject of the next chapter.

5
Afterimages: Adaptations and Influences

Wells's texts remain an inexhaustible rhizome for intelligent and visually self-aware SF on film and television. To trace the mutation of their influence through post-war films and programmes fully would require a separate study. Suffice it to say that this chapter samples a representative range of both adaptations and influences, focusing on Hollywood versions of several of his best-known scientific romances, as well as less obvious offshoots on British and continental European screens, big and small.

'The Future Ain't What It Used to Be': Hollywood Versions of *The Time Machine*

As we saw in Chapter 1, the concept of a time machine and its synergy with film is a highly effective means for visualising transformations and consequences on an evolutionary scale. By such defamiliarising means, the novella challenges the notion of the white, middle-class, Victorian, male, colonial subject as the measure of human development. The scenario is also, by its very nature, infinitely 'revisitable'. Consequently, adapting Wells's text necessarily presents directors with a basic choice: to treat it either as a 'period piece', for faithful reproduction in every detail (including a 'future past' of 802,701, which seems less plausible than in 1895), or as a critical template for each subsequent social era to see its own conflicted image reflected in the future it imagines for itself, with varying degrees of (un)conscious insight into the sources and motives of its own *Angst*.[1] Hollywood adaptations certainly seem to treat Wells's text as a means both for representing advances in cinematic technology, through their ever more virtual visualisation of time travel, and for projecting topical issues contemporary to their circumstances of making. However, this process involves a peculiar temporal duality: the boundary continually shifts between the retrospectively knowable past (since the novella was published) and whatever hypothetical future succeeds its present. This can be demonstrated by comparing the 1960 George Pal adaptation with the 2002 version directed by Wells's great-grandson, Simon Wells. Both versions use state-of-the-art technology to visualise the process of time-travelling in a highly self-reflexive way, which also alludes to their own prehistory within the developing medium. This inevitably gives rise to a cumulative and 'dialogic' layering of both literary and cinematic intertextuality.

Wells's view that technologised humanity must organise itself in balance with both its natural environment and its own impulses in order to sustain the dynamic and successful evolution of the species was famously influenced by T. H. Huxley's 1893 lecture. The key problem, as articulated in TM, was, on one hand, avoiding 'entropy' through complacent overachievement and, on the other, degeneration into ruthless appetite through internecine competition. As Huxley put it:

> Social progress means a checking of the cosmic process at every step and the substitution for it of another, which may be called the ethical process; the end of which is not the survival of those who may happen to be the fittest ... but of those who are ethically the best.[2]

Effectively, both the 1960 and 2002 films are extrapolations of this basic 'ethical' thesis, reprojected through their contemporary topical contexts.

However, producer/director George Pal was primarily attracted to TM for the opportunities it provided for state-of-the-art special effects, demonstrating just how far ahead Wells was of what was only *potential* in 1895, as R. W. Paul instinctively understood.[3] As well as devising a cinematic equivalent for the novella's narrative structure, with Alan Young as framing character David Filby (to whom the Time Traveller, George (Rod Taylor), tells his tale after coming back from the future),[4] Pal recreated Wells's 'science fiction by gaslight'[5] Victorian setting with convincing authenticity. His film's wonderfully antique vehicle with its radar-like rotating disc (largely down to art director Bill Ferrari) carries a brass maker's plate, 'Manufactured by H. George Wells'. This alludes metafictionally to Wells's subtitle – 'An Invention'– as both futuristic machine and ekphrastic fiction defamiliarising vision (as well as Wells's middle name, as MWCWM had done). Pal consequently foregrounds the novella's implicit analogy between Time Traveller and film spectator by numerous devices. As George[6] cranks the lever to 'free the world for movement' (as Benjamin might put it), he settles back in his plush seat, delighted by watching a marvellous moving spectacle outside his own time, but visually proximate in space, which places us vicariously in his position. Moreover, much of what he sees is initially mediated through the transparent frames of his laboratory roof, the camera mimicking his point of view. Many of Wells's examples of accelerated motion were duly visualised in Pal's Oscar-winning special effects, more or less directly, using time-lapse and stop-motion animation (as well as model shots, early 'blue screen' double-printing and matte painting) in ways which allude to devices from early scientific or trickfilms analogised or anticipated in the novella itself. Details of both plant growth and animal locomotion are temporally condensed: flowers open and close and a snail rockets across the floor (see Chapter 1 above).[7] As George speeds up, the sun blurs across the sky and the alternation of light and darkness picks up Wells's suggestion of the crude flickering of early projectors and effects such as double exposure. Time certainly appears 'spatialised', while inanimate phenomena such as landscape and architectural structures begin to mobilise, in a process of seasonal and then epochal change.

Pal also made crucial additions elaborating the novel's techniques and themes. Most famously, a dummy (in Filby's draper's window opposite) indexes changing feminine fashions and gender roles, but also alludes intertextually to the history of film adaptations of Wells's work. Such a mannequin first indicated the passage of time in Carol Reed's 1941 film of *Kipps*. Reed jumped editorially between seasonal displays from 1900 to 1905, with superimposed dates. Pal's extrapolation from it was in turn reworked in the 2002 version.[8] In the movement of pedestrians, Pal deliberately recalls both Wells's Mrs Watchett, shooting across the laboratory, and the jerky, speeded-up novelty of early film, significantly over a tinkling 'nickelodeon' piano score (Russell Garcia's music is contrastingly electronic in futuristic scenes).

The film's 'retrospectively known history' (which SF novelist David Duncan's Georges-Méliès-Award-winning screenplay foregrounds as the future up to the time of its 1960 making) focuses on the appropriately topical threat of what Wells knew as nationalistic, militarised science. Pal's sceptical doctor suggests that the Time Traveller shouldn't waste his genius on dubious applications, but should invent super-weapons to help win the Boer War (a key reason for relocating the present to 1900). This is a significant departure from the novella's biologisation of class in a mechanised society, but nonetheless extends concerns pervasive in Wells's later work. By 1960 (with the Cuban missile crisis brewing), the arms race and humanity's potential for self-extinction entered their most dangerous nuclear phase. Wells predicted this in *The World Set Free* (1914) and reiterated it in one of his last statements about *TM* in 1938 on the eve of another war that concluded with real atomic bombing. The Victorian idea of the solar system's looming 'heat death' had been discredited, so there was no natural cause to prevent humanity's descendants 'living in comfort and sunshine, for millions of years yet', provided that we did not blow the planet to pieces ourselves.[9]

Hence, in a series of brief stopovers, George visits key moments in the twentieth century's escalating warfare: the mobilisation of the population in the first 'total war' of 1914; the 1940 Blitz; and the 'logical' extension into the hypothetical near future of 1966 subject to nuclear attack. George barely survives the apocalyptic consequences, shocked to witness the fragility of his human world and its Victorian confidence in permanent progress: 'The work of centuries gone in an instant.' It is obvious that the remoter scenario of what replaces it, born from the aftermath of nuclear holocaust, reflects contemporary Cold War anxieties (Pal had already produced an alleged 'Red Menace' version of *WOTW*).[10] As in Wells's text, Pal's Eloi appear to live in a pastoral Utopia from which want and danger have been eliminated, but they are in reality parasitic drones, lacking mutual attachment or social responsibility. However, the Eloi now automatically descend into an underground 'shelter', conditioned by the Pavlovian blast of an air-raid siren over millennia. Consequently, although the film preserves Wells's satire against the neglect of the human inheritance of knowledge and skill (symbolised by the ruinous 'Palace of Green Porcelain' and crumbling books), it jettisons his class allegory, based on evolution and ethics. Pal substitutes a much simpler explanation for how this entropic 'posthuman' world, with its bifurcation into degenerated species, came about. His machine-minding, subterranean Morlocks are no longer the ancestrally victimised working class taking insurrectionary revenge by devouring in turn those who once consumed their labour, just as his Eloi are no longer descendants of their exploiters. Their twisted symbiosis is attributed to contingencies of a post-nuclear order, perhaps also because class was too suspiciously left-wing a topic to broach openly in a Hollywood recently terrorised by McCarthyism. Though retaining Wells's cannibalistic reversion, the Morlocks' mutation is due to radioactive fall-out (metaphorically, if not literally), rather than socio-biological change. Nevertheless, Pal's dystopic revelations retain a Wellsian flavour of the potentially tragic failure of the human project, of would-be gods whose overreaching mortality is laid bare.[11] However, only his Eloi remain *recognisably* human enough (especially as personified in elfin 'romantic interest', 17-year-old Yvette Mimieux as Weena) for the Time Traveller and, by proxy, the cinema audience to invest sympathy and the desire to redeem them.

John Huntington argues that Pal's film thus erases 'the very conflicts that define Wells's work', making the Morlocks merely scary monsters and the Eloi simply 'badly educated'.[12] Indeed, the latter are shown as *potentially* rehumanisable in every way: Weena falls in love and assists George's plans for resistance; he inspires Eloi males to fight back; and the Eloi can still use technology – Weena shows George electronic recording 'rings' through which historical memory and intellectual curiosity might be restored. Having recounted his story to Filby, George goes 'back to the future', armed with all the necessary kit (weapons, tools and books) to rescue them from bondage. (Thus he also undercuts any pacifist message which the film might otherwise suggest by restarting the cycle of aggression that led to the arms race originally and brought humanity to this state.) Pal even planned a sequel to narrate this implied outcome, though it was never made.[13]

Huntington concludes that Pal relocates the narrative's conflict from *within* capitalism itself to its opposition to communism. He even casts the Morlocks as allegorical Soviets; they hold the Eloi, like the people of satellite states (such as Pal's homeland, Hungary) in totalitarian thrall. Wells's text finishes open-endedly, appalling predestination set in paradoxical tension with the reader's will to alter conditions that seem to render its future inevitable by taking action to reform their own present. However, as Huntington puts it, bleak foreshadowing 'of catastrophe, individual, social, racial, cosmic' is missing from Pal's film. Like Nunez in 'The Country of the Blind', 'George seeks a society he can dominate', though without encountering any ironic twist preventing him. Whereas Wells's text critiques the contradictions of his own society, the values of Pal's adopted one appear to pass unquestioned. His future can be redeemed by being heroically returned to the present, replacing 'intellectual tension with melodramatic conventions that inspire unreflective affirmation'.[14] Joshua Stein also argues that Wells's projected future radically subverts the authority and expectations of late Victorian Britain's imperial patriarchy, while Pal's film endorses America's ideology of 'manifest destiny', using time as its new form of frontier.[15] George sets out not to scout for Utopia, but concerned with individualistic free will, pondering 'Can man control his destiny?' No passive observer, he is a 'man of action, bringing the pioneer spirit back to his long-lost cousins'. In waistcoat and tight trousers, he even resembles Western gunslinger, more than Victorian boffin.[16] George's attempt to revive the feminised Eloi's 'manly', 'can do' spirit identifies him with transatlantic libertarianism, but also makes him a future Crusoe, an emblematic coloniser who finds a whole 'breeding population' of Man Fridays to transform into his ruling image.[17]

It is certainly arguable that Pal ducks Wells's central thesis, though, strangely, retaining its conspicuous symbol in the Morlock-faced sphinx surmounting the entrance to their Cold War underworld. This suggests underlying traces of a subtext which doesn't square with any right-wing agenda. For those who know Wells's text, it acts as a prompt to consider the film in dialogic relation with it. For the Victorians, Thomas Carlyle's eponymous essay was 'the Sphinx riddle of To-day': how to organise industrial labour along socially just lines to prevent the catastrophe of class war.[18] The middle-class status of Wells's Time Traveller is also explained by this. A professional inventor himself, familiar with the conditions and processes of new science and industry, he can potentially arbitrate between mechanical drudges and leisured élite.

Moreover, there are other contraindications against a simplistically

MacCarthyist reading, conscious or not. Firstly, possession of the deterrent fails to protect Western civilisation from its ideological 'other' (just as it fails in the Pal–Haskin version of *WOTW*). Instead, nuclear weapons plunge the world back into primal chaos, then social entropy. Secondly, if the Morlocks (their air vents now serving as conspicuous visual puns on intercontinental ballistic missile launch silos) are, as Stein suggests, mutated descendants of missile defence crews, 'still protecting their charges but taking a very literal fee',[19] this implies a more coded political message – the notion of an 'enemy within'. Eloi bondage is therefore not to allegorical Soviet occupation but to a mirror-image tyranny: the very Cold War military–industrial complex which drastically eroded democracy and freedom of expression in order, paradoxically, to protect such Western values and which 'devoured' the professional lives of many high-profile Hollywood victims who dared to speak openly against it.

The Time Machine (2002)

Simon Wells's remake is a clear example of a postmodern phenomenon which John Clute and Peter Nicholls call 'recursive science fiction'. In literary SF this is a metafictional and intertextual trend delving into its own 'growing storehouse' of plots and themes and mixing real and fictional characters freely,[20] but it is also proliferating in film versions of *TM*. Simon Wells was arguably following Nicholas Meyer's precedent in *Time After Time* (1980), as well as Pal's play on Wells's middle name and identity. In Meyer's screenplay, Wells himself is not just the author of a text, but the inventor of a 'real' time machine. In this, he pursues Jack the Ripper into the sexually liberated present of the film's making, topically recasting the novel's Morlockian depredation and themes of changing mores and gender roles. John Logan's screenplay for Simon Wells restores his great-grandfather's historical status as writer of the source text, but makes it the inspiration for another real time machine created by 'Alexander Hartdegen',[21] a fictional turn-of-the-century scientist, who has a picture of his literary progenitor on his laboratory wall. Lack of ontological 'compossibility' between these elements does lead to some faultlines and paradoxes. Time travel is dismissed by Vox, the twenty-first-century New York Public Library computer hologram (played by Orlando Jones) as pure fantasy. He even briefly displays Pal's vehicle[22] and assumes that Hartdegen is the usual nerdish 'Trekkie' (indicated by a weary facial aside to the audience). Moreover, Hartdegen travels on in his impossible machine to the year 802,701 populated by parallel versions of the very Eloi and Morlocks whom he now fails to recognise as actualities, even though they are 'foreknown' to him in fiction (as Renzi points out).[23] Alternatively, it is also arguable that Simon Wells tried to defuse the notoriously 'fractured' causal logic of time-travel narratives.[24] He attempted instead a knowing, postmodern playfulness, in which Wells's text is enfolded in his film's imaginary universe, but also metafictionally invoked in dialogic relation to its latest progeny, recast from its own structural and thematic template.

In visual terms, Simon Wells's film is a measure of cinema's technical advancement since 1960, especially in its self-conscious 'opticality' during the equivalent time-travelling sequences. The special effects (supervised by James E. Price) were achieved by a new programme of CGI, developed especially. The sequence is less a direct visualisation of Wells's ekphrastic description than a reworking (and, arguably, outdoing) of Pal's previous mediation of it. (Similarly, Simon Wells deployed state-of-the-art 'animatronics' and prosthetics, making Pal's Morlocks look like pantomime figures, with electric bulbs for eyes. Terrifying hunting scenes also resemble Tim Burton's 2001 remake of *Planet of the Apes*, from Frenchman Pierre Boulle's *TM*-influenced satire about primate ascendancy, first filmed by Hollywood in 1968 (dir. Franklin Schaffner).) The same basic roster of speeded-up natural-historical processes and architectural change is presented, though this time the camera finally departs from the Time Traveller's intra-diegetic viewpoint, for a tour de force sweeping through the stratosphere out into space, via all the technology of media and communications developed since 1960, including satellites, shuttles and space stations. Likewise, the library hologram represents possibilities just over the horizon of our present. Hartdegen recognises Vox's descent from his own age's machinery of illusion: 'Some kind of stereopticon'. The superencyclopaedic 'compendium of human knowledge' is also an evident projection of Wells's speculations into electronic media presence, coupled with his foreseeing of a cybernetic internet, or 'World Brain'. This was the ultimate stage of the evolution of technology into an integrated global information network, the democratically accessible cerebral cortex and nervous system of Wells's coming World State.[25]

Nevertheless, the same question applies as it did to Pal: does the 2002 film also represent an aesthetic and intellectual advance in terms of the treatment of Wells's themes and debates? Again the period setting is roughly contemporary to Wells's novella (1900 in both films), but Hartdegen's motivation is personalised. In a kind of 'Eurydicean' detour about loss, he invents his machine, not out of disinterested scientific curiosity about a fourth dimension, but to travel back and prevent his fiancée's murder. However, in something of a post-Wellsian cliché, he is unable to change the past and, in despair, fast-forwards into 2030. The topical present of the film's making finally becomes manifest as he finds consumerism overreaching itself and creating potential planetary disaster. The first thing he sees is a *WTSW*-like giant advertising screen, with the appropriate slogan,

'THE FUTURE IS NOW'. This 'previews' the delights of new lunar leisure colonies. However, 'terra-forming' excavations shatter the moon's geo-gravitational stability, so it rains down in massive fragments on the Earth, as Hartdegen learns in another brief 'stopover' matching Pal's Armageddon scene. Hence Simon Wells substitutes ecological for nuclear causality. Hartdegen escapes to the far future when humanity's descendants have long adapted to living with the consequences. Again, our Time Traveller appears to find a pastoral Utopia, but this time inhabited by 'ethnic' New Agers, living in enviably sustainable harmony with their post-industrial environment (they even build windmills). Though it transpires that these Eloi are still preyed upon by mutant descendants of the shelter-dwellers, there is no remaining trace of their social symbiosis, nor indeed of Wells's post-human degeneration. They provide for themselves, practise a sophisticated culture and retain all the empathy and social ties marking *homo sapiens*. Mara (played by pop starlet Samantha Mumba) is the film's equivalent to Weena, though even less like Wells's female protagonist than was Pal's. Apart from conspicuous sexual dimorphism, she is robustly active, cares for her son, nurses Hartdegen after he crash-lands and passes on the 'Old Language' (fossilised English, forming a potential linguistic bridge back to the present). Again, this makes the Morlocks (at least at first) seem merely monstrous predators and the Eloi innocent victims, without ancestral culpability or ambiguous otherness. (Interestingly, both Pal and Simon Wells, though raising the issue of changing gender roles in numerous ways, present the Morlocks as effectively male: the captured Mara is kept alive solely as breeding stock, with a retro-frisson of classic Hollywood heroine–monster miscegenation.)[26]

Jeremy Irons steals the show, in ultimate 'Goth-Metal' make-up. As the world-weary Übermorlock, he effectively reprises his role as Scar, mellifluous boss of the slavering hyenas in Disney's *Lion King* (1994). The Übermorlock is the hyper-evolved product of a eugenic caste system (the potential horror of genetic engineering was trailed in the teacher's threat to 'resequence' a child's DNA, during the library stopover). His bleached albinism (perhaps recalling that of the sociopathic Griffin) contrasts with the Eloi's 'melting-pot' skin tones, a postcolonial colour symbolism that parodies Nazi racial programmes. The Übermorlock may be a controversial interpolation, but nonetheless picks up Wells's ambivalent speculations about 'superhuman' élitism in many other texts. In an interview accompanying the DVD, Simon Wells refers to the Übermorlock as suggesting the Faustian mutation of the technocratic mind represented by Hartdegen, especially its double-edged tendency to manipulate natural processes and conditions in the name of progress. There are certainly ironic hints of *Döppelganger* mirroring between the two: when Hartdegen accuses him of perverting nature, the Übermorlock replies, 'And time travelling isn't?', perhaps in distant evocation of the morally equivocal Nebogipfel, Wells's original 'Chronic Argonaut'. The Übermorlock is also a patent exposition device, explaining how the species' predicament came about. With a sigh of regrettable necessity (turning his reptilian back), he admits that only exercising his telepathic power restrains the voracious appetites of his lower orders enough to sustain the expedient economic balance, otherwise they would 'exhaust the food supply in months'. This speech suggests that blind consumerism, which precipitated the original ecological disaster, has survived in Moreauesque satirical form.[27] (Telepathy, incidentally, also allows the Übermorlock to transmit images influencing the Eloi's unconscious minds, like the form of induced visualisation that Wells imagined in his 1893 essay 'The Dream Bureau'.)[28]

However, the 2002 plot, though ethically more complex than Pal's, leaves even less room for inconclusiveness.[29] Hartdegen, like George before, inevitably reverts to type as Hollywood action hero, rejecting this grim symbiosis as the permanent condition of posterity. The past may be fixed, but he can still alter the future, sacrificing his 'perverse' machine to blow up the troglodytes' lair and rescue the Eloi. Symbolically, the future is genetically *re*humanised by the baby he produces with Mara. The accumulated history of thought and information is also restored by reintroducing them to the library hologram, whose 'central memory core' has miraculously survived intact.

By presenting their respective Eloi as the best hope for restoring humanity to the future and their respective Time Travellers' affiliations as unambivalent, both the Pal and Simon Wells adaptations are effectively 'partial derivatives', Gary Westfahl's term for versions gutting the novella's central dialectic.[30] It remains a perpetual risk that films of *TM*, by taking account of real history since its publication and projecting their own topical futures from contemporary issues, may either creatively extend Wells's template of sociobiological satire or fatally undermine its deeper, more ambiguous warnings.

A Martian Sends a Filmscript Home? Wars of the Worlds

Like *TM*'s topical template, *WOTW* has been reworked in different media at moments of greatest international anxiety: the Munich Crisis (Orson Welles); the Cold War (Pal/Haskin); post–9/11 (Spielberg/Cruise). It has attracted avant-garde and popular film-makers from many countries, for its optical speculations as much as its eminently transferable subject. Specialist in historical blockbusters Cecil B. De Mille acquired the pre-talkie rights for Paramount in 1925, possibly planning a period version which would thus have been one of Hollywood's first 'postmodern' versions of an alternative past.[31] Soviet montagist Sergei M. Eisenstein expressed an interest during his Hollywood sojourn in 1930. A screenplay was duly written, although Eisenstein eventually decided to pursue his project *Que Viva Mexico* instead.[32] Walter Forde was approached by Gaumont British as a possible director in 1932, with Wells as production adviser and screenplay by Montagu with his son Frank.[33] The tyro Alfred Hitchcock also approached him on the subject around this time, but Wells's enthusiasm for his 'outdated' story's adaptability seems to have waned.[34] Pioneering 'Dynamation' animator Ray Harryhausen (influenced by Willis O'Brien's classic monster film, *King Kong* (1933), but also later working at Pal's 'Puppetoons' studios) storyboarded an adaptation in 1949. Unfortunately, it never went into production, although Harryhausen did create the Selenite world for the 1964 *First Men in the Moon*.[35] However, it was Byron Haskin, with Pal acting as producer, who directed the first actual film version in 1953.[36]

If *TM* epitomised temporally relativised vision, *WOTW* mustered many of the cinematic motifs, themes and techniques that Wells tried out in other stories into a full-scale narrative of interplanetary invasion. In effect, he created a 'blockbuster' genre which developed in both filmic and textual forms in the coming century. William Johnson notes that Wells encoded the DNA sequence, as it were, of all extraterrestrial invasion narratives, with its basic dialectic of war, anarchy, reconstruction – new society.[37]

As Hughes and Geduld argue, Wells switched between ekphrastic 'lenses of varying magnitudes, depending on his desired perspective',[38] resulting in the dramatic dilation and contraction of visual scale and changes of angle, as well as panning and tracking effects, among others. The narrative is, consequently, driven by 'a mobilised virtual gaze' of protean sophistication. Before attacking, the Martians have 'scrutinised and studied' human affairs televisually through advanced monitoring technologies (as in 'The Crystal Egg'), with cold detachment used on oblivious microbes in a drop of water. In reverse perspective, Wells's scientific-journalist narrator joins astronomer Ogilvy to scan suspicious explosions on their planet's surface (*WOTW*, pp. 7 and 10–11).[39] In 'The Land Ironclads', the 1903 story which predicted the decisive role of tanks in the Great War, Wells's gunners use a kind of mobile camera obscura for deadly accuracy (*CSS*, pp. 131–32). Similarly, the futuristic Martian 'heat ray', wielded from their armoured vehicles, is metaphorically described as a camera or projector (twice on pp. 63–64 and again on 111). Warwick Goble's illustrations to the 1897 serialisation in *Pearson's Magazine* highlighted this analogy, showing a crippled tripod sending up clouds of steam, 'As the camera of the heat ray hit the water'.[40] It is a kind of mobile optical device, zooming in on distant targets or sweeping panoramically with devastating effect. Thus, like cinema, it 'spectacularises' everything within its visual field. The Martian vehicle is also suggestive of a portable camera mount, as well as the Delphic tripod, essential to Classical Greek ceremonies of prophetic vision. Similarly, Dziga Vertov's metacinematic documentary, *The Man With the Movie Camera* (1929), would famously superimpose gigantic images of the camera tripod over urban crowds in a way which seems to concretise Wells's suggestion about the potentially titanic power of its gaze in modernity. One of the best elements of Steven Spielberg's 2005 film adaptation (see below) is its reversion to Wells's original design for the Martian war machines. Their lenslike lights under projecting hoods are suggestively juxtaposed with state-of-the-art human visual technologies of all kinds – handheld videos, digital cameras, CCTV monitors, etc.

WOTW's spatial dynamism is undoubtedly due to its quasi-cinematic visualisations. The first tripod is seen rushing across the wooded countryside, 'shot' from an extremely low angle beneath its towering stride, accompanied by lightning bursts – a moving effect which could only be literally visualised on film: 'a moment of bewildering darkness, and then, in a flash like daylight ... this problematical object came out clear and sharp and bright' (*WOTW*, p. 46).[41] The sheer size, speed and power of the Martian machines tracked across the landscape dictate the panoramic treatment of geography. Likewise Wells's intercutting between locations, his choreographic mass movement, apocalyptic destruction, etc., anticipate and outdo disaster and battle scenes in such early epics as *The Last Days of Pompeii*, or *Birth of a Nation*. Wells even uses an aerial sweep from an imaginary balloon to survey the chaos down the Thames valley towards London (see *WOTW*, pp. 105–6), a technique he elaborated in the foreshortened perspectives of *WITA*.[42]

Wells makes space seem as heterogeneous and plastic as he did time. Indeed, his narrator witnesses the rapid collapse of a whole civilisation's supposedly solid and permanent structures under the Martian advance with a kind of 'speeded-up' effect recalling *TM*'s telescoping of aeons of geopolitical change into moments and with a viewpoint as chilling and detached as it is cinematic: 'By ten o'clock the police organisation, and by midday even the railway organisations, were losing coherency, losing shape and efficiency, guttering, softening, running at last in that swift liquefaction of the social body' (*WOTW*, p. 92). During the occupation, proportion is ironically inverted and normality defamiliarised to the degree that 'I found about me the landscape, weird and lurid, of another planet.' The narrator experiences a sense of evolutionary 'dethronement' from atop the cosmic food chain, as human scale is usurped, whence everything becomes tilted, as if seen microscopically 'under the Martian heel' (*WOTW*, p. 144).

WOTW features crowds of refugees soon all too familiar in the coming century from newsreel footage of the displacement of peoples by modern, total war. Metonymic 'close-ups' of objects left in the wake of fleeing masses deftly suggest individual panic and atrocity by association:

> here and there things that the people had dropped – a clock, a slipper, a silver spoon, and the like poor valuables. At the corner turning up towards the post-office, a little cart, filled with boxes and furniture, and horseless, heeled over on a broken wheel. A cash-box had been hastily smashed open, and thrown under the debris. (*WOTW*, p. 57)

Using the same technique as 'Through a Window', *WOTW* also takes advantage of the abrupt suspension of visual dynamism to sustain a dramatically concentrated viewpoint over several chapters, beginning in 'What We Saw From A Ruined House'. Holed up with a hysterical curate (who is convinced that the Martians are the scourge of God), the narrator is restricted to watching grisly goings-on at their base by a break in a wall, as if through a static camera angle. This 'horrible privilege of sight' is thus self-consciously framed as passive, partial, fragmentary. It is also tinged with sickeningly voyeuristic fascination in spite of himself. Wells thus anticipates the ambivalent pleasures of future audiences of the horror film genre (see *WOTW*, pp. 123–35, especially 130).

An Alien Gaze

As in *WTSW*, Wells foregrounded the intermeshing power of the mass media. The Martian advance is preceded, by 'magnified account[s] of [their] depredations', to borrow *IM*'s phrase, via newspapers and telegraph, spreading a panic attack from their virtual arrival before they are actually present.[43] The awesome power of the camera-like heat-ray is broadcast so as to be inescapable and all-penetrating. Critical parallelism between aspects of human and Martian technology is pointed up near the beginning. Set in what became the Surrey commuter belt, Wells foregrounds the intrusion of Victorian transport and communications into its supposedly rural idyll. The narrator views the signal lights for the local railway system connecting them with London in a cinematically suggestive kind of visual match against the heavens. This is proleptic of how the first appearance of the Martian cylinders, as mysterious flashes across the heavens, is not recognised as a danger sign either: 'My wife pointed out to me the brightness of the red, green, and yellow signal lights hanging in a framework against the sky. It seemed so safe and tranquil' (p. 12).[44] Later Wells suggestively echoes the shape of the advancing tripods in the heliographs which defending artillerymen use to transmit optical signals between batteries by reflecting the sun's rays (see pp. 57–58). In this sense, Wells's text warns not so much about any real threat of alien invasion as about the domineering 'invasiveness' of a human civilisation radically mutated by technology, as Liz Hedgecock points out. This is in terms of not just colonialism (see below) but also the machine's relentless intrusion into social, cultural and political space. *WOTW* thus expresses this concept of invasion and exposes its dehumanising threat in its ekphrastic visual form as well as content.[45] Wells's pseudo-'camera-eyed' narrator is implicated in that invasion by putting contemporary human progress under his critical 'alien' gaze, as if placing ourselves under the external viewpoint of a different species. Hence the defamiliarising 'double exposure'[46] of his story, which switches between the 'normality' of white, middle-class, imperial subject and imagined Martian viewpoint.

In *WOTW*'s self-conscious double perspective, Wells also expressed a distinct sense of his own paradoxical status as Conrad's 'Realist of the Fantastic', his writing matching the screen's capacity as a virtual space for representing the familiar and the impossible with equal verisimilitude. The documentary accuracy in his diegetic details of the geography and landmarks of the Home Counties stands in brilliant creative tension with his horror from beyond the skies. *WOTW* inflicted imaginary scientific terror on the complacent, bourgeois civilisation in the British Empire's leafy heartland. Wells famously spent days bicycling around this quarter of Surrey, where he then resided, getting his facts right like a kind of 'location shooting' to give utmost plausibility to scenes of fantastic devastation. Escaping the massacre around the crater of the first landing site, his narrator experiences a crucial dislocation of perspective as he nears home. This furnishes a self-reflexive commentary on the novel's method:

> Now it was as if something turned over, and the point of view altered abruptly. There was no sensible transition from one state of mind to the other. I was immediately the self of every day again – a decent ordinary citizen. The silent common, the impulse of my flight, the starting flames, were as if they had been in a dream. I asked myself had these latter things indeed happened. I could not credit it. (*WOTW*, p. 31)

That sense of epistemological and discursive incongruity between parallel yet intersecting worlds comments on the defamiliarising potential of the new medium. Its technology could both mimic a precognised reality, or reproject it through a radically 'alien gaze':

> At times I suffer from the strangest sense of detachment from myself and the world about me; I seem to watch it all from the outside, from somewhere inconceivably remote, out of time, out of space, out of the stress and tragedy of it all. This feeling was very strong upon me that night. Here was another side to my dream. (p. 32)

Wells also divined that the linking dynamic of these apparently incongruous worlds would be ideologically driven. How the modern media functioned as mechanisms for manipulating anxieties and desires would become all too rooted in political reality. The mass panic caused by Orson Welles's 1938 'Mercury Theatre Troupe' broadcast sprang unconsciously from the understandable jumpiness about invasion induced by topical developments around the time of the Munich Crisis, rather than any intended hoax. Radio was even newer than cinema, bringing distant voices, both reassuring and alienating (from Roosevelt's to Hitler's), right into the home.[47] But Orson Welles took his own cue from the novel itself. Wells invoked its contemporary international context of fear and belligerence. The arms race between the imperial Great Powers fuelled public receptivity to his fantasy. I. F. Clarke has shown that Wells was, in effect, shifting the late Victorian 'invasion novel' to an interplanetary plane. This prolific, alarmist genre dates back to Colonel G. T. Chesney's *The Battle of Dorking* (1871), intended as a wake-up call to defend the British Empire from its newest rival. The choice of location and meticulous detail confirm that Wells drew on Chesney, while defusing his jingoism.[48] Significantly, during the 'phoney war' before their tripods break out, the reporting of the Martians fails to excite 'the sensation that an ultimatum to Germany would have done' (*WOTW*, p. 35). In effect, *WOTW* is a kind of allegory of the 'Aliens R Us' variety.[49] It explores the way in which modern technologies of communication and destruction increasingly alienated an imperialistic humanity from itself in moral and psychological terms.

Victorian colonialism became underpinned by the pseudo-science of social Darwinism. This appeared to justify territorial expansion and the subjugation of others, by means of railways and advanced weaponry such as the Maxim machine gun and ironclad battleship, naturalising it on the grounds of evolutionary competition and racial 'superiority'. Hence, as Adam Roberts argues, Wells's Martians are 'imperialists who use superior technology'. Their 'mechanised brutalities' symbolise his exploration of 'a deeper set of concerns' surrounding earthling violence and anxieties about otherness, from the *double viewpoint* of both coloniser and colonised.'[50] Hence Wells personifies this alterity in the quasi-Martian vision of his narrator which is, simultaneously, the perspective of advanced technologies.

In this way it is possible to see *WOTW* as a virtual exercise in inflicting the experience of 'inferior races' back on the heartland population of the most powerful terrestrial empire. Despite their mutated appearance as cephalopods, the Martians are what Hedgecock calls 'hyper-evolved' parodies of ourselves.[51] This is suggested by the metafictional allusion to Wells's own 1893 essay, 'The Man of the Year Million: A Scientific Forecast', speculating about our 'posthuman' descendants in a manner similar to *TM* (see *WOTW*, p. 127). Moreover, prosthetic technology has played a key role in their development as a species. Rendered superhuman by donning different metal 'bodies', as well as artificially extending their senses, the

Martians act, nonetheless, in ethically *sub*human ways by their ruthless violence against other sentient beings in the quest for dominance. Thus Wells confronts his readers with the true evolutionary implications of colonialism. As so often in his narratives of radical otherness, the complex play of difference and similarity gives way to the shocking recognition that the 'monstrous' alien is actually the secret identity of the self. Niall Ferguson's new history of the twentieth century aptly takes Wells's novel as a prophetic starting point for understanding how human beings could behave with all the ethical inhumanity of Martians towards their own species in genocidal wars fuelled by ethnic hatred and militarised science.[52]

However, from the chastening fragility of what seemed invulnerable about the symbols of terrestrial power in *WOTW* comes a distinctive potential for rethinking progress in terms of *inclusively* human values and on a truly global scale. This is the most radical shift from the tradition initiated by *The Battle of Dorking*. From the burnt-out shell of imperial pride in *WOTW* emerges the prediction of an ethical consciousness, cutting across racial divides and competing national interests in a common agenda for the future. Clearly, it foreshadows Wells's concept of international co-operation in a technocratic 'World State' developed in subsequent writings: '[The Martian invasion] has robbed us of that serene confidence in the future which is the most fruitful source of decadence, the gifts to human science it has brought are enormous, and it has done much to promote the conception of the commonweal of mankind' (p. 179). However, as we shall see, the history of responses to *WOTW*, especially in American fiction, radio and film, are effectively caught up in the same ironic double narrative of domination and hegemony, most revealingly in the relative priority they give to special effects and flag-waving over Wells's anti-imperial allegory.

Parallels and Responses

It is important briefly to consider contemporary popular literary responses to *WOTW* to understand how later media adaptations developed Wells's themes and method. As often as not, they have cashed in on its spectacular possibilities, developing ever more impressive techniques to realise Wells's proto-cinematic spectacle of Martian invasion and defeat. However, they have run into problems devising strategies to deal with *WOTW*'s subtext. Arguably, this is because they are themselves, at least in part, products of a cultural and economic expansion which (especially since the Second World War) has superseded the avowed imperialism of late Victorian Britain that Wells targeted. Consequently, American assumptions of moral immunity to *WOTW*'s critical inflections inevitably founder. Its subtext leaks out of the quarantine imposed by Hollywood film versions, whether they consciously engage with it or not. At the gung-ho extreme, Roland Emmerich's *Independence Day* (1996) deliberately omits *WOTW*'s essentially humbling lesson, that the world's most 'advanced' nation emerges not as victor, but as fortuitous survivor. It is sobered by the realisation that it must face the future with a new sense of common human vulnerability and purpose. However, in Emmerich's film there is no sign of Wells's 'great disillusionment' (*WOTW*, opening page), nor of any recognition that the alien other is the disguised image of the imperial self. It culminates a long tradition of responses reasserting confidence in a specifically American 'manifest destiny' and inventiveness, the ultimate triumph of a post-apocalyptic 'elect'. Hence in the process of liberating humanity from fantastic threats of domination, some film-makers have simultaneously helped extend the hegemony of American values over the globe. This tendency evolved not from the 1938 broadcast adaptation but from a much earlier and largely forgotten literary response.

In 1898, journalist and popular astronomer Garret P. Serviss rapidly penned a sequel to *WOTW*, *Edison's Conquest of Mars*. Originally published in media tycoon William Randolph Hearst's *Evening Journal* (12 Jan.–10 Feb.), Serviss's novel was more directly a response to pirated serialisations in New York and Boston newspapers and correspondingly *switched* Wells's location to the Eastern seaboard. Such serialisations also emphasised sensational action and attempted to eviscerate Wells's reflexive, anti-imperial critique by depicting the Martians as a purely external threat.[53] In Serviss's novel, the Wizard of Menlo Park or Modern Prometheus (as Edison became known for his ever-expanding range of electrical inventions, not least motion pictures) makes such SF motifs as anti-gravity spaceships, radioactive disintegrating rays and spacesuits with telephonic communicators into real devices, to carry the fight back to those alien varmints and whip them good. It was symptomatic of the personality cult growing around Edison and of American faith in the powers of technology. It is easily forgotten that 'The White Man's Burden' (published in *The Times* (1 Feb. 1899), though stereotypically associated with the Raj, was written by Kipling to encourage America, where he was staying, in Vermont, to take up the Anglo-Saxon imperial baton's global responsibilities for the new century. Effectively, Edison's fictional counterpart (in a token coalition against interplanetary terror with British and German super-scientists, Lord Kelvin and Röntgen) repulses Martian domination, at the price of achieving earthly supremacy for his homeland.

The prototype Edgar Rice Burroughs/Flash Gordon 'space opera' *Edison's Conquest* describes 'the avenging counterstroke that the Earth dealt back at its ruthless enemy in the heavens',[54] presenting American technological and political championship as an ethically unproblematic condition of modernity: 'The United States naturally took the lead, and their leadership was never for a moment questioned abroad' (*Edison's Conquest*, p. 12). The initiative is merely an extension of 'manifest destiny'; America's right to act on behalf of the planet universalises its interests as those of humankind as a whole.

The 'otherness' of Serviss's Martians similarly differs sharply from Wells's evolutionary satire. Their hideous appearance is explained not by adaptation but by racist pseudo-science like phrenology. They are anthropomorphic bipeds, but with features distorted by irredeemable 'evil'. They combine all 'the intellectual powers of a man, raised to their highest pitch, with some of the physical features of a beast, and all the moral depravity of a fiend' (*Edison's Conquest*, p. 54).[55] Similarly, their invasion is motivated not by the necessity of escaping a dying planet (Mars is rich and fruitful), but by the lust for conquest. Consequently, past defiance of imperial overlordship is frequently invoked: Chapter 8 is even titled 'The Martians Are Coming', playing on the War of Independence alarm call (*Edison's Conquest*, p. 64). Nevertheless, when the Republic split from Britain, it continued the project of colonial expansion into the North American continent on its own terms. This subsequent history also resurfaces in Freudian slippages connected with the enemy's racial difference, though displaced from a very different popular genre: for example during a scouting expedition, '"This affords good protection," said Colonel Smith, recalling his adventures on the western plains. "We can get close in to the Indians – I beg pardon, I mean the Martians – without being seen"' (*Edison's Conquest*, p. 103). Moreover, the novel concludes with a foreshadowing of the universalisation of American values across a grateful Earth in Emmerich's film. (As *Independence Day*'s president (Bill Pullman) puts it, 'And should we win the day, the Fourth of July will no longer be known as an American holiday, but as the day when the world declared we will not go quietly into the night.') On Edison's victorious return, his expedition finds our planet also radically changed: 'new New York' towers resurgent from the ruins of the original Martian attack as 'capitol of the world' (*Edison's Conquest*, p. 160). Despite the real Edison's misgivings, the novel proved so popular that his fictional nephew Frank carried on such exploits in Weldon Cobb's sequel, *Trip to Mars* (1901).[56]

Mediating *The War of the Worlds*

As the Korean War climaxed and the Soviet Union tested its first hydrogen bomb, Wells's action was shifted and updated by Pal and Haskin to Linda Rosa, an obscure town in California's Chino Hills, before moving to Los Angeles. Though there were intermittent montages of simultaneous Martian attacks around the globe,[57] Britain was demoted, in its post-Second-World-War, decolonising state, to a 'plucky', but ultimately futile, bit-part against the alien *Blitzkrieg*. Haskin and Pal took their precedent from Orson Welles's radio broadcast, adapted by Howard Koch, which had become notoriously inscribed in the popular consciousness.[58] Orson Welles's Martians land at Grover's Mill, New Jersey and advance on New York. This relocation had followed the cue of the pirated serialisations forty years before, for the same sensational plausibility by exploiting details of local topography. As in his use of the *IM* theme in other broadcasting and film work, Orson Welles picked up the formal 'self-reflexiveness' of the novel's eye-witness strategy, to create a kind of metaradio. His drama foregrounded the medium's capacity for simultaneous aural simulation of unfolding actuality, transforming Wells's formula into a broadcast 'realism of the fantastic': the Martian landings were reported as if in a newsflash interrupting a music transmission, which is then itself abruptly terminated when the reporter at the site is apparently struck by the heat ray. The play also uses other 'live' techniques, switching locations for interviews with scientists (notably Orson Welles himself as Professor Pierson of Princeton), federal officials and army chiefs, 'overheard' military communications, and its *coup de radio* (anticipating Ed Murrow's rooftop broadcasts from the London Blitz) describing the Martian advance, as if seen from atop the CBS building itself, before the final reporter is overcome with the 'black smoke'. His voice is replaced by a ham operator forlornly calling into the ether, 'Isn't there anyone on the air? Isn't there anyone ...?'[59] The ekphrastic power, epitomised by leading phrases such as 'paint for you a word picture of the strange scene before my eyes' and 'annihilate the world before your very ears', of transferring Wells's visualisation technique (and liberal mentions of mass mediation through actual 1890s newspapers) was largely responsible for emptying much of the city and surrounding countryside with floods of real refugees replicating those in the fiction.[60] Campaigning anti-Fascist Dorothy Thompson commented astutely in the *New York Tribune* on the sheer force of media suggestion that a handful of voices and sound effects had revealed:

> No political body must ever, under any circumstances, obtain a monopoly of radio ... The power of mass suggestion is the most potent force today ... If people can be frightened out of their wits by mythical men from Mars, they can be frightened into fanaticism by the fear of Reds, or convinced that America is in the hands of sixty families, or aroused to revenge against any minority, or terrorized into subservience to leadership because of any imaginable menace.[61]

Big-budget SF was reborn as a mainstream Hollywood genre in the 1950s. Since the 1930 box-office disaster of *Just Imagine*, America had banished it to the lowly status of Saturday serials and comic strips (expensive sets and designs from Butler's film were literally recycled for *Buck Rogers* and *Flash Gordon*).⁶² It is much more than coincidence that its resurgence corresponds with the onset of the Cold War. In the 1950s, as Stella Bruzzi notes, America's imminently realisable dream of space travel was shadowed by nightmare, the prospective conquest of other worlds mirrored by resurgent fantasies of invasion.⁶³ Within this context of paranoid anxiety, the most significant topical shift in the Pal/Haskin film is the strategic issue of nuclear weapons, the ultimate option considered for halting the advance of the Russian-sponsored North Korean army and its revolutionary Chinese allies.⁶⁴ The Martians' 'black smoke' was a forerunner of the Great War's 'weapon of mass destruction', poison gas, and the escalation of the arms race through the militarisation of science preoccupied Wells throughout his subsequent career. In his view it eventually became the single biggest threat to securing his 'commonweal of mankind', mooted in *WOTW*, or even to the survival of the species at all. Nonetheless, in his 1914 visionary novel, *The World Set Free*, Wells could still imagine a new globalised state arising from the planetary ashes:

> The catastrophe of the atomic bombs which shook men out of cities and businesses and economic relations shook them also out of their old established habits of thought, and out of the ... beliefs and prejudices that came down from the past. To borrow a word from the old-fashioned chemists, men were made nascent; they were released from old ties [and made] ready for new associations.⁶⁵

What he could not foresee was the role that nuclear weapons would actually play after a second global conflict, the geopolitical outcome of which took the planet hostage to a nuclear balance of terror, or 'mutual assured destruction'.

Ambiguously, in the 1953 film, the Californian desert, where the first Martian craft lands, also recalls the topography of the 'Manhattan Project' in nearby New Mexico, where the first atomic test explosions were held.⁶⁶ Hence other changes to Wells's plot cluster around contemporary anxieties about this issue. The cylinders fall as radioactive meteors (initially mistaken for bombs dropped by a Cold War enemy, who didn't require naming). Wells's walking tripods are updated into flying-saucer-like craft, hovering on invisible 'magnetic' legs.⁶⁷ They emit an audible radioactive pulse (conveyed through electronic oscillation on the pioneering soundtrack). Armoured by force fields (visualised by transparent 'lucite' domes), they wield an atomising modification of Wells's heat-ray apparatus. Visually a cross between a periscope and Wells's futuristic camera-projector, this ultimately reduces its victims to nuclear 'shadows' like those found at Hiroshima and Nagasaki. The infiltrating UFO motif (first allegedly sighted in 1947) became a fifties Hollywood cliché, as shown in Robert Wise's *The Day the Earth Stood Still* (1951), Fred F. Sears's *Earth Vs the*

Flying Saucers (1956) and Edward L. Cahn's *Invasion of the Saucermen* (1957), and reached camp overextension in Ed Wood Jr.'s *Plan 9 from Outer Space*. The film starting it all, Christian Nyby's *The Thing From Another World* (1951), ended with the slogan 'Watch the Skies', potently combining air-raid vigilance from the last war with Wells's extraterrestrial unease. Pal/Haskin's special effects (by Gordon Jennings's team) were as state-of-the-art as possible, even if, occasionally, you can literally 'see the wires'. As in 1898 and 1938, conventional weapons prove useless. Finally, only America holds out (Washington DC the sole capital still intact). The nuclear explosions, consequently humanity's last hope, were originally to have been visualised in 3D, but this was abandoned because the studio (rightly) judged it an expensive fad.[68] The box-office 'sensation' of the time, designed to fight off competition from television, it would have been the latest evolution of the 'spectacularisation' principle represented by the technologised vision in Wells's text, requiring the audience to don a kind of alien optical device themselves, in the form of 3D specs.

Wells's narrator's retrospect was divided into two authoritatively extra-diegetic, newsreel-like 'voice-overs'. Paul Frees (who went on to voice the 'talking rings' in Pal's *TM*) and Cedric Hardwicke (who played Theotocopulos in *TTC*) supplied these first and second framing narrators. His other function as central eye-witness was taken up by Gene Barry as Dr Clayton Forrester. No longer just a science journalist, but an 'astronuclear-physicist' at Pacific Tech, Forrester thus also inherits some features of Wells's astronomer, Ogilvy. Forrester first realises what the 'meteors' mean and what is hatching from them.[69] An obligatory heterosexual romance (with Ann Robinson as librarian and Pastor's niece, Sylvia Van Buren) was foisted on Pal/Haskin by Paramount, which felt audiences would be less engaged by Wells's protagonist's search for his wife.[70] Nonetheless, Barre Lyndon's script still preserves and elaborates many of his principal details and motifs, as when the professor and librarian (the clergyman (Lewis Martin) has already been vaporised for mistakenly appealing to Martian godliness as 'higher beings') hide out in the ruined house. This now affords a frisson of inter-species sexual panic (mercifully impossible with Wells's hermaphrodite cephalopods), when a distinctly bipedal Martian gropes the heroine's shoulder with its three-fingered hand, only to be overcome by Forrester. Arguably, the film's aliens act as a focus of phobias about otherness more by suggestion, because they are only momentarily revealed, unlike the original text and Goble's serial illustrations.

As Mark Bould points out, accounts of 1950s American SF films stress themes of anti-communist hysteria and nuclear anxiety, especially those centred on *The Red Planet Mars* (as in Harry Horner's 1952 title). However, as epitomised by *Invasion of the Body Snatchers*, their play on terrorising infiltration can be double-edged: is it really about the threat to the democratic humanity of Rockwellesque American values (Linda Rosa seems a generically similar small town), or about the danger of replicating xenophobia, illiberal conformity and kitsch as a national creed?[71] As with Pal's *TM*, whether the themes and presentation of the 1953 film amount to mere Cold War propaganda is open to dispute. Its Martians have often been read as thinly disguised Soviets, topical emblems of the 'red scare' variety common at the time (Pal/Haskin's briefly glimpsed alien is a rusty hue, unlike Wells's greyish-brown; the light from its unscrewing cylinder is angry orange, not green), promoting McCarthyist paranoia and exacerbating international tension. Pal admitted adopting the deliberate strategy of showing the Martians advancing East to West across the screen, for visual consistency if not symbolism as such.[72] The Russians are also conspicuously absent from montages of nations under attack, as Hardwicke's voice-over ominously intones: 'a great silence fell over half of Europe'. However, somewhat contradictorily the Chinese are commended for bravery. Although Hollywood was infamously subject to witch-hunts enforcing Cold War ideology, there may, nonetheless, be evidence that the film preserves enough of Wells's anti-imperial subtext to resist political conformity to some degree. This may even hint at 'a plague a' both your houses' alluding to the superpower balance of terror, holding the rest of the world to ransom. As a Hungarian, Pal may have been in exile from first Nazi and then Soviet domination, but his homeland suffered throughout the century from being caught between the imperial ambitions of larger states (and would do so again climactically in 1956). Moreover, not every period blockbuster of extraterrestrial encounter took a one-sided position. In *The Day the Earth Stood Still*, for example, humans are forced to co-operate and end their arms race by intervention from an advanced alien federation. Similarly, as Newman observes, their representative, Klaatu (Michael Rennie), backed by firepower from invincible robot Gort, is distinctively reminiscent of *TTC*'s John Cabal and his paradoxically pacifying bombers.[73] The American President seeks to convince Klaatu that Earth is divided between the forces of Good and Evil, but Klaatu dismisses this as dangerous moral absolutism that must be deconstructed for the sake of humanity's survival.

The 1953 *WOTW*'s 'Prologue' footage of military technology evolving since Wells's novel emphasises the escalating destructiveness of two world wars and continuing international rivalry (effectively reprised in the 'stopovers' of Pal's *TM*). The next will be fought with 'the weapons of superscience', it informs us. However, as Newman points out, American forces are even more comprehensively routed than their British counterparts (who, despite Victorian weaponry, knock out a couple of tripods by fluke).[74] Indeed, jealous of their public image, the Californian military declined to collaborate in presenting the US army as helpless (particularly when its soldiers were dying in Korea), forcing Pal and Haskin to enlist extras from across the border in Arizona's National Guard.[75] On the other hand, despite their ultimate inadequacy, there is evidence for Julian Cornell's conclusion that the very institutions of state, church and military which Wells criticises so radically for sustaining Britain's imperial project are depicted in contemporary American forms 'as rational, benevolent and in control'. Thus, unlike Wells's curate, artilleryman and London authorities, 'representations of the central power structures ... are absolved of blame'.[76] Similarly, the film's central 'eye-witness' scientist is assigned a heroic rather than interpretive role. He readily co-operates in identifying and combating an externalised threat, but does not provide any counter-perspective into what the aliens might signify at another level.[77] (Omission of their bloodsucking habit removes another key prompt for construing them as parabolic of capitalist–colonial exploiters.) Nevertheless, the linchpin of superpower defence strategy proves totally ineffective against Martian force fields. This runs counter to the logic of deterrent, causing Forrester to conclude that only a biological weapon might work, unexpectedly supplied by nature in the nick of time.

Conversely, there may be muted echoes of Wells's parody of terrestrial racism and technological dehumanisation. Linda Rosa seems as outwardly innocent of imperial complicities as Wells's leafy Surrey. However, although descending from the sky, the Martians' emergence from a pit deep in the desert earth close by is eerily ambiguous to say the least. It resembles nothing so much as the 'Old Indian Burial Ground' motif familiar in postcolonial Gothic narratives, the symbolic memory site for Native Americans, part of a 'taboo' history of internal imperialism.[78] Stephen Greenblatt argues that the 'othering' of Native Americans from the earliest days of colonisation made them 'serve as a screen onto which Renaissance Europeans, bound by their institutions, project[ed] their darkest and most compelling fantasies', corresponding to monstrous forms assumed by Freud's Id.[79] Moreover, California was one of the last territories absorbed in the USA's south-western push into former Spanish-colonial lands, already wrested from indigenous tribes. Is it possible that 1953's extraterrestrials are, at another level, uncanny nightmare 'others' returning from the mythic frontier of its consciousness to haunt a guilt-ridden empire state which dispossessed their ancestors? Significantly, the impromptu 'peace delegation' (consisting of two Caucasians and a Chicano) which approaches the unscrewing cylinder nervously anticipates that 'Not everything that's human has to look like you or me.' Similarly, Wells's bacterial *deus ex machina* has as much ironic relevance to the devastation of Native Americans by imported diseases such as smallpox as it does to the genocide in British colonies such as Tasmania (see *WOTW*, p. 9). The ending of the 1953 screenplay follows Wells's subversion of apparent victory by the Martian lack of immunities to terrestrial disease. Arguably, Pal/Haskin gives this a kind of 'divine intervention' twist, by crashing dying aliens outside a church – 'Forrester: "You were looking for a miracle! Well now you've got one!"' Their closing quotation is also filleted from Wells's Darwinian conclusion that 'the Martians were destroyed and humanity was saved by the littlest things which God in His wisdom had put upon the earth'. (Significantly, a British reviewer objected less to liberties of shifting action in space and time, protagonists who were 'fugitives from a comic-scientific strip' and 'drivelling dialogue', than to 'an offensive taint of false religiosity'.[80]) However, such closure, achieved by the apparent reassertion of faith in transcendent Christian-American values over 'godless' alien-Communists (as opposed to Serviss and Emmerich's facile technological solutions), is rendered porous by the demonstrable impotency of superpower defence policy and unquiet stirrings from America's repressed colonial past, which appear to replay Wells's subtext, albeit in displaced form. Cornell even argues that the film's 'narrative of besiegement', with the USA itself as humanity's 'last outpost', smuggles in motifs from the Western, as does the denouement's substitution of '*Calvary* for *Cavalry*', for nick-of-time rescue.[81] But this is a particularly double-edged move in view of the tradition of identifying Martians with 'Red Indians' traceable back to *Edison's Conquest*. As with Whale's *IM*, Pal/Haskin's *WOTW* shows visible faultlines between concessions to politico-industrial pressures and the genuinely creative transformation of its source.

One thing is certain: the 1953 version is as aware of its medium as its radio predecessor (Barre Lyndon's original treatment was even to have 'broadcast' the Martian breakout through a montage of television screens around the nation, punctuating the rest of the narrative with similar 'updates' foregrounding the notion of a media 'panic attack'.)[82] The movie picks up Wells's visuality to foreground metacinematically the process of making and watching different kinds of film, as Stewart argues.[83] Its pre-credit monochrome archive footage ends with intercontinental missile testings, succeeded suggestively by a descending Martian spaceship (in a visual match recalling Wells's 'warning lights' against the sky). The 'meteor' catches a cinema queue's attention: the commercial attraction is apparently superseded 'gratis' for the proxy audience framed within the screen we are watching. Paradoxically, this ostensible shift from 'mere fiction' to the greater thrill of a fantastically defamiliarised visual reality promises to trump the historical events documented hitherto.[84]

Wells's double perspective, which exposes us to an imaginary alien gaze, is also reproduced in several ways. After the 'prologue' segues into the lurid titles of an infinitely greater 'WAR OF THE WORLDS', Pal/Haskin's Second Narrator declaims Wells's opening statement about the Martian observation of Earth (albeit omitting his parallels with terrestrial colonialism). The film also shifts briefly into Chesley Bonestell's 'astronomical animation' suggesting aliens 'scanning the universe with instruments beyond our imagination'. As Forrester and Van Buren watch from the ruined house, a Martian optical probe, replacing Wells's steel tentacle, seeks them out. (In a later scene, biologist Dr DuPrey (Ann Codee) uses the most advanced human technology – the electron microscope – to analyse Martian blood cells, revealing their anaemic vulnerability and reversing Wells's metaphor about their scrutinising us like 'microbes'.) The film eventually simulates this returned gaze more directly through the captured viewer, consisting (like the Martians' irises) of three lenses with red, green and blue filters, symbolic of the three-strip system of Technicolor itself.[85] On a laboratory screen, mock-scientific footage is projected of tripled fish-eye shots, portraying this prosthetically enhanced Martian vision as suspiciously like unfocused 3D. Significantly (as in Wells's narrator's critically 'Martianised' perspective and its equivalent association with technology), in a film ostensibly showing 'what *they* would look like', this inset sequence 'turns the tables and the camera on us', as Stewart argues. It is a logical extension of the SF tradition of critically defamiliarised vision which Wells exemplifies. The underlying purpose of its space–time distanciations is always 'to show us new views of ourselves' through 'duress from the extraordinary'.[86] *WOTW*'s viewpoint was used by Wells to raise consciousness of the need for 'the commonweal of mankind', to unite us against imperial rivalries and racial subordination in response to imagined alien attack. In a parallel twist, Jack Arnold's adaptation of a Ray Bradbury story, *It Came From Outer Space* (also 1953), used 'intra-diegetic' camerawork through a pioneering fish-eye effect, to suggest the panic and disorientation of an innocently stranded alien hunted by humans through another desert landscape. It also deconstructed the hysterical preconceptions of the Cold War invasion genre by allowing audiences to share the imaginary viewpoint of the 'other' on the threats posed by 'us'.

Hence *WOTW* has always proved a double-edged sword in Hollywood adaptations. The 1953 film's one Oscar was for special effects, taking up over half its running time and most of the $2,000,000 production costs.[87] If these do not entirely upstage subtler elements, this is overwhelmingly the case in the hi-tech CGI of its *post*-Cold-War remake, *Independence Day*, hardly a sermon against human hubris, evolutionary or evangelical. Whatever line you take on the Pal/Haskin version, it contrasts starkly with Emmerich's triumphalism about US guts and know-how defeating supervideo game 'space invaders'.[88] Significantly, intercutting shows the first alien craft sweeping in over Northern Iraq, suggesting the terrain of the 1991 'First Gulf War' to liberate Kuwait. Though Emmerich playfully references Haskin's film, he also replaces Wells's microbes with an ingenious man-made computer virus, which infects and disables the alien shield systems. This is, in effect, a cybernetic updating of Serviss's plot with 'Gatesian-geek' Geoff Goldblum cast as a latter-day Wizard of Menlo Park (inspired by paternal health concerns: 'I don't want you to catch cold.') Consequently, Emmerich completely suppresses *WOTW*'s essentially humbling lesson to the dominant nation of the day. His film restores a brash tang of America's 'manifest destiny' as global defender of civilisation and its values, but entirely begs the question of America's own imperialism, past and present, as well as the world community's dependent position in relation to its one and only 'hyperpower'. On the other hand, if *Independence Day* retains any liberal credentials, these are backhandedly presented in aliens as ruthless capitalist despoilers, strip-mining planets' resources. Goldblum's character is a committed environmentalist, who cycles everywhere like *WOTW*'s author. Emmerich's even more apocalyptic *The Day After Tomorrow* (2004) has similarly been interpreted as a critique of President George W. Bush's denial of global warming.

Despite *Independence Day*'s conspicuous racial integration (Will Smith playing the heroic black pilot who penetrates the mothership), it is nonetheless telling that the desert-frontier landscape of the 1953 film recurs. Similarly, in terms of visual impact, the implications of Wells's prescient critique of 'spectacularising' technology in the service of a culturally imperialistic medium are replicated with unconscious irony by the global invasiveness of such Hollywood blockbusters, as classic examples of the 'effects-rich, ideas-poor' tradition of screen SF adaptation. Emmerich's own 'fire-power' of state-of-the-art special effects threatens to overwhelm any audience's critical defences through its 'shock and awe' intensity. This is typified by the mothership which looms over the Capitol, apparently expanding beyond the horizons of even the biggest screen to blot out the sun, and the ensuing scenes in which national landmarks are destroyed, on which the film itself was marketed. In a kind of strategic complementarity, Wells and Emmerich reveal attempts to conquer through ruthless force on the one hand and ideological persuasion on the other. In *Independence Day* alien domination is inadvertently mirrored by the drive to global cultural hegemony through American movie-making itself. As Cornell shows, in exploiting *WOTW*'s superficial status as spectacle, but claiming moral immunity to its subtext, Hollywood versions 'have time and again appeared to favour empire building rather than to critique it'.[89]

However, as Hedgecock points out, Tim Burton's *Mars Attacks!* (also 1996) is an astute parody of such forms of media invasiveness, though at several further removes from their common Wellsian source, referencing both the 1962 'Topps' trading cards and alien-invasion B-movies.[90] As if in unconsciously Wellsian testimony to the power of communications, Hollywood SF of the fifties often featured alien hijackings of terrestrial broadcasting to magnify terroristic presence electronically through psychological warfare. Typically, in *Earth vs. the Flying Saucers* (1956), as Vivian Sobchack notes, they spread 'disembodied threats around the world in ever-widening circles of the kind that used to emanate from radio-towers in newsreel animated diagrams'.[91] There follows a stock montage of listeners and viewers instructed to watch out for artificial solar convulsions – a 'free show' of strength demonstrating the uselessness of resistance. Significantly, *The Day the Earth Stood Still* bucked this trend by exposing waves of planetary hysteria generated by the irresponsible reporting of an alien intervention precisely designed to terminate terrestrial warmongering. Looking back on this tendency, Burton's mischievous retro-Martians wield not only literal destructive power through kitsch ray guns, but also manipulate television's ubiquitous addictiveness to pacify goggling earthlings with 'awesome' media thrills.

Independence Day also took on an unexpectedly prophetic quality in light of subsequent global media events. One of its most memorable special effects, the atomisation of a skyscraper by the mothership, gave audiences an eerie sense of déjà vu, of life imitating blockbuster fiction, when they watched the collapse of New York's Twin Towers on television on September 11, 2001. However, this in itself rippled out of Wells's deliberately symbolic targeting of London's monumental architecture and his mediation of the Martian attack. Similarly, like Wells, in the immediate aftermath of Al Qaeda's abominable actions, Martin Amis pointed out the need for a world response based on 'species consciousness', though duly sympathetic to America's victimhood.[92] Thus *WOTW* was also prophetic of the controversy surrounding the resulting 'global war on terror': has this been truly directed by common human interests or by the 'Neo-Con' domestic agenda and planetary assertiveness of the remaining 'hyperpower'? Such a background created understandable nervousness about new, contemporised versions, but also a potential opportunity for more ethical engagement with *WOTW*'s anti-colonial subtext.[93] Spielberg's 2005 adaptation (dropping Wells's definite article) pits a new generation of aliens (never explicitly Martians) against 'one family's fight for survival'. In an intellectual downshifting from Wells's science journalist, Tom Cruise plays Ray Ferrier, an anonymous New York crane driver, divorcé and weekend dad. His crane is silhouetted against the skyline in a proleptic visual match for the coming tripods and their cyborgian interface between flesh and machine. (Ray's disordered home is similarly dwarfed by the dehumanising presence of a technologised cityscape, in the form of a vast interstate flyover.) Although he might initially seem to share the aliens' detached perspective (drastically reversed by Spielberg's camera when he joins humankind 'under their heel'),[94] much of the impressive CGI mayhem is viewed on the ground through the eyes of his eleven-year-old daughter

(Dakota Fanning). The film is the ultimate nightmare version of the 'I go away for the weekend, leave you with the kids and look what happens' scenario, in which domesticated values seem to be reinjected with the US pioneer spirit, via the essential decency of its blue-collar worker. Nonetheless, extraterrestrial invasion seems a rather harsh object lesson for 'slack dad' to relearn responsibilities and regain the respect of his aspirational ex-wife and her middle-class boyfriend.

There is a more proportionate response too. Though Spielberg largely substitutes the gendered alienation of the American class system and the fractured nuclear family for Wells's implied racial divisions, topical references (though only other nations' failed colonial enterprises are explicitly named) are liberally interspersed in the dialogue and effects: Cruise's student son is writing a history paper on France's Algerian War; the aliens' initial assault is briefly mistaken for terrorist bombing; and the family emerge from a basement to find the deserted house they sheltered in is a Boeing 747 crash site (a real airliner was dismembered for the purpose). American insularity is deliberately emphasised: there are no global 'montages' like those of Pal/Haskin; and Ferrier's son's reply, to his cryptic recognition that these 'terrorists' come from 'somewhere else,' is 'Like Europe?' However, Spielberg's aliens are more ambiguous than a simple allegory for Al Qaeda's nefarious sneak-attack against the homeland. Though their pilots 'beam down' on lightning bolts (reworking the dramatic storm in which Wells's tripods first break out), their machines, deposited in deep storage aeons ago, emerge from under the city's foundations, like technologised spectres from our primal past (a likely nod to Nigel Kneale's *Quatermass and the Pit* (see below)). In significant ironisation of the salvationist motifs of the 1953 film,[95] the first tripod erupts from underneath a church, literally causing a schism in the fabric of the building and alluding to the role resurgent fanaticisms play in real clashes between different worlds today. Western references receive similar treatment: Spielberg's tripods wield twin heat rays, like trigger-happy gunslingers meting out Wild West justice. Similarly, an ideologically cycloptic viewpoint is suggested by their single headlight beam. In the ruined house scene, Cruise has to confront not just the terrifying gaze of an external Other (an updating of Pal/Haskin's alien probe), but America's 'enemy within', in the form of right-wing Survivalist, Harlan Ogilvy (Tim Robbins). Spielberg's equivalent to Wells's artilleryman holds a fundamentalist's faith in the virtues of armed response, though this jeopardises the safety of them all. Fanning, rightly described by one reviewer as a kind of precocious 'robo-moppet', emoting to order,[96] nonetheless gives a vulnerable edge to scenes of atrocity, effectively crossing the naïve intra-diegetic perspective of Spielberg's *ET* (1982) with his child-witness of genocide in *Empire of the Sun* (1987). However, despite some framing voice-over from Wells's text, overall the film lacks a sufficiently coherent guiding vision to draw its scattered topical prompts to a critical head for a fully developed, post-9/11 take on his subtext.

The style of Spielberg's *WOTW*, like that of most Hollywood blockbusters, is naturalistic (irrespective of touches of unreality in its plot or acting). Nevertheless, it eclipsed the release of Tim Hines's alternative version in a global blaze of publicity, blasting its rival straight to DVD. Despite Haskin's view that an 'authentic' period adaptation of Wells's novel would lack plausibility and relevance,[97] that is exactly what Hines attempted. His version certainly aims to bring out parallels between the Martians and Britain's colonial war machine. It faithfully follows the detail of Wells's description and dialogue over some three hours, with Anthony Piana as eye-witness narrator. Contemporary military uniforms are prominent and the film's shooting title (to camouflage it on location from press spoilers) was 'The Great Boer War'. Also unlike Spielberg, Hines chose a deliberately non-naturalistic style, recalling tinted and flickering footage from primitive silent film. This foregrounds the political and technological context of Wells's narrative in a way theoretically appropriate to such a self-consciously proto-cinematic novel, but also renders its human action almost as stylised as the flat-looking CGI footage of its Martians. Sadly, stodgy playing, uninspired camerawork and lax editing do not match Hines's aesthetically original concept, making his version at best a brave but under-budgeted curiosity.

Almost forty years after *WOTW*, Wells himself revisited the theme of invasion in his *Star Begotten: A Biological Fantasia* (*SB*) (working title: 'The Coming of the Martians'), more explicitly based on the 'Aliens R Us' principle. *SB* needs to be more fully acknowledged as an important influence on cultural phenomena as diverse as John Wyndham's fiction, Nigel Kneale's teleplays, Kubrick's *2001*, David Bowie's media persona and *The X-Files*, among other responses. This time very different Martians seek to colonise Earth in an infiltrative but symbiotic fashion. Gradually altering our genes by transmitting cosmic rays over millennia, their intervention produces terrestrially adapted alien–human hybrids, speeding up evolution more benignly than Moreau's 'beast folk'. These ultimate deconstructions of self and other are designed to inherit our earth, but will also save us from self-destruction through superior intellect and cooperative spirit, dedicating their technological inheritance to mutual progress. As explained self-mockingly through Wells's character Laidlaw:

> Some of you may have read a book called *The War of the Worlds* – I forget who wrote it. Jules Verne, Conan Doyle, one of those fellows. But it told how the Martians invaded the world, wanted to colonize it

and exterminate mankind. Hopeless attempt! ...
   Suppose they say up there, 'Let's start varying and modifying life on earth. Let's change it. Let's get at the human character and the human brain and make it Martian-minded. Let's stop having children on this rusty old planet of ours, and let's change men until they become in effect *our* children. (pp. 50–51)

This is another Wellsian allegory of radically altered viewpoint, but is also riddled with allusions to media influencing minds and bodies at a distance (the rays themselves are described as targeted sub-atomic 'broadcasting'). Similarly, Harold Rigamey's articles, '*The Voice of the Stars*', argue that Martians are signalling to humankind with some kind of interplanetary telecommunications system (see *SB*, p. 115).[98]

WOTW's rampaging monsters are updated with a more ambiguous vision in Joseph Davis's dreams. However, it is still mediated through a 'portal' with cinematically distorting effects which condenses the whole history of ekphrastic and philosophically defamiliarising imagery in Wells's writing:

> These dream-Martians were no longer repulsive creatures, grotesques and caricatures, and yet their visible appearance was not human. They had steadfast, dark eyes, very widely separated, and their mouths were still and resolute. Their broad brows and round heads made him think of the smooth wise-looking head of seals and cats and he could not distinguish clearly whether they had shadowy hands and arms or tentacles. There was always a lens-like effect about his vision, as though he saw them through the eyepiece of some huge optical instrument. Ripples passed across the lens and increased the indistinctness, and ever and again flickering bunches of what he assumed were cosmic rays exploded from nothingness across the picture and flashed out radiating to the periphery and vanished. He felt that his dreams were taking him into a world where our ideas of form and process, of space and time, are no longer valid. (pp. 102–3)

There was a reinvigorated topicality about this theme in 1937 which bears on (and may even have prompted) Orson Welles's adaptation of Wells's original Martian saga. (In *SB*, the US public's robustly sceptical response to the theory of covert alien presence contrasts ironically with the hysteria actually generated by the *WOTW* broadcast only a year later (see *SB*, pp. 120–1).) *SB* also anticipates the 'brainwashing' paranoia of Cold War media campaigns, of which Hollywood's alien/replicant conspiracy films, such as Don Siegel's *Invasion of the Body Snatchers* (1955), were symptomatic. Lord Thunderclap, Tory press baron, twigs what lies behind the planetary threat from 'Reds' of all kinds: 'Moscow – Bernard Shaw – New Dealers – Atheists – Protocols of Zion, all of that – mere agents. It's *Mars* that is after us' (p. 128).⁹⁹ He plans an immediate anti-Martian witch-hunt, until advised that the public might think he's finally gone barking, causing circulation to plummet (pp. 130 and 135).

Similarly, *SB* seems to be the source for key concepts of politics and mediation in Orwell's *Nineteen Eighty-Four* (which, as we saw, is also traceable back to Ostrog's panoptic surveillance technology). Alluding to *WOTW*'s opening metaphor, optimist Professor Keppel thinks that this new breed of aliens, monitoring human affairs as transparently as amoebae under a microscope, have benign rather than menacing intentions: 'If there is such a thing as a Martian, rest assured ... he's humanity's big brother' (see *SB*, pp. 52 and 84). Conversely, the phrase recurs capitalised to personify humanity's regressive urge to seek refuge in the 'protection' of dictatorial creeds: 'My Country Right or Wrong, the Church, the Party, the Masses, the Proletariat. Our imagination hangs on to some such Big Brother idea almost to the end' (*SB*, p. 157).

Big Brother, with his Telescreen, also brings up the question of the disseminal mutation of Wells's alien fictions through subsequent phases and forms of post-war media culture. (As Frayling points out, the notion of mutation itself became particularly coupled with anxieties about 'the unexpected and unintended consequences of atomic research', which dominated SF horror 'in the form of giant mutant barnyard creatures, disfigurement, awakened prehistoric monsters or radioactive zombies', from the 1950s onwards.)¹⁰⁰ John Wyndham's *The Midwich Cuckoos* (1957), for example, in which village women incubate a brood of telepathic alien–human hybrids, that behave with a ruthless 'hive mind', germinated from *SB*. The novel's obstetric and generational anxieties were memorably visualised in Wolf Rilla's influential 1960 film version, *Village of the Damned* (remade by Hollywood in 1995). Rilla's changelings' eerie powers were, significantly, manifest in their irradiating eyes. Their 'master race' uniform blonde hairstyles also had a curious synchronicity with the countercultural, 'beatnik' look of Pal's post-atomic Eloi. Bert I. Gordon, who made an exploitative schlock-horror out of Wells's satire of small-scale thinking, *Food of the Gods* (1976), first tried out the theme in his 1965 *Village of the Giants* (1965), which expresses a similar generational anxiety about rampaging teenagers, magnified by a mysterious growth stimulant.¹⁰¹ David Bowie's allusion to the coming 'homo superior', in his 1972 song 'Oh You Pretty Things', in turn gestured back, through Wyndham, to Wellsian evolutionary ambivalence about 'posthuman' futures. It also hatched Bowie's globally transmitted, pop-cultural persona of androgynous 'starman', rock idol for a whole generation to identify with against the perceived values of their parents.

The most important pioneer of British small-screen SF, Nigel Kneale, creatively fused themes and motifs from both *SB* and *WOTW*. Significantly,

Kneale grew up on Wells as 'a wonderfully visual writer', whose scientific romances were 'full of striking images'.[102] Kneale scripted the BBC's metatelevisual adaptation of *Nineteen Eighty-Four* (1954) and (with Jan Read) Nathan Juran's 1964 *First Men in the Moon*. Kneale's screenplay brings out Wells's anti-imperialism sharply through Bedford's white supremacist venality. He (literally) imported *WOTW*'s devastating colonial germs, through Cavor's cold: the Selenites are wiped out on their own planet like Native Americans with smallpox. Kneale also interpolated a framing narrative set in a (then) very near future, but nonetheless true to Wells's aspirations for international scientific co-operation: the 1960s space mission, shocked to discover the Victorian astronauts' genocidal legacy, is conducted by the United Nations. (Kneale recalled the 'virtual' space race with NASA, the film-makers beating them to the moon by a mere five years.)[103]

However, it was Kneale's partnership with Austrian émigré producer and director Rudolph Cartier that proved one of the most significant factors in creating distinctively televisual prime-time drama in the 1950s when 'the telly' was just becoming a genuine mass medium from the BBC's Alexandra Palace studios. It was also a recent alien arrival in the most familiar and domestic of spheres, as if Wells's rarity, 'The Crystal Egg', was now finding its way into millions of living rooms. As Sconce shows, the intrusion of a nine- or fifteen-inch screen into the home gave rise to anxiety about a new electronic presence combining broadcast sound and moving images:

> The ability of this box in the living room to 'talk' and 'see'... made the medium something more than merely an inanimate technology. Television exuded a powerful presence in the household, serving in the active imagination as a fantastic portal to other worlds or even as a sentient entity brooding in the corner ... Early television owners recognised that this medium had a qualitative 'presence' that distinguished it from radio, a presence that made the medium even more fantastic and perhaps more sinister as well.[104]

This unease was encapsulated by Kneale and Cartier's *Quatermass* trilogy, one of the first serials to explore television's technical parameters as a medium using the camera as visual narrator (rather than just transmitting live 'boxed' theatre or 'illustrated radio') and to stake small-screen SF's claim as a serious genre. As Kneale put it, 'It was television about television, which was new ... it had the sense of a show within a show.'[105] All three series are, effectively, metatelevisual, Wellsian parables of humankind's insidious dangers to itself. The title of their first six-parter, *The Quatermass Experiment* (1953), as John R. Cook and Peter Wright point out, connotes both subject matter and creative approach, to challenge viewers' 'perceptions of a changing medium and a changing world'.[106] Moreover, the trilogy's sections are shot through with developments of Wellsian motifs and concerns focusing on topical ambiguities of dehumanisation by science and technology, 'otherness' and genetic hybridity, in a Cold War context of British decolonisation, nascent consumerism and, increasingly, client status to superpower ascendancy (the nation's abortive independent space mission is symptomatic of its decline). All three parts are based around forms of extraterrestrial invasion by stealth uncovered by scientific investigator, Professor Bernard Quatermass. Their *SB*-like style of suggestiveness was better suited to small-screen intimacy and slow-burning episodic drama than *WOTW*'s rapid and continuous spectacle. Kneale used special effects only in climactic and highly motivated ways. The first series reflects themes of ethically unchecked research into 'the unknown' and possible ecological disaster, bound together by Wells's genetic hybridity motif. As Peter Hutchings points out, Quatermass himself is also a morally ambiguous figure, both personifying encroaching scientific modernity and potentially complicit with the alien threat, though ultimately able to solve their problems.[107] In this sense, Kneale provides an implicit critique of Wells's vision of the scientist as heroic architect of the coming World State. In the post-war situation of military–industrial complexes, the *Quatermass* trilogy addressed the irony that, as Kneale commented, 'we're living in a world dominated by scientists and technocrats who care nothing about anything outside their own narrow sphere. These people are monsters and they're beginning to run things.'[108]

The Quatermass Experiment is also framed by rivalry between imported B-movie sensationalism and the more reflective use of a home-grown medium, working within the same genre. Kneale disliked the term 'science fiction', because of its dominant association with Hollywood movies and their nationalistic trivialisation of its staple issues. (Indeed, it wasn't until Hammer filmed *Quatermass* that British cinema SF re-emerged as a serious cinematic genre after pre-war experiments such as *TTC*.)[109] In Episode 4, infected astronaut Victor Carroon hides at a matinée showing of *Planet of the Dragons*, in which Space Lieutenant rescues his girl from stereotype monsters. 3D format betrays 2D content, just as corny dialogue betrays colonial desire to export 'smalltown' American values into other worlds. As Space Lieutenant monologues, a police 'wanted' image of Carroon is projected over him, captioned 'Have you seen this man?' The proxy audience is symbolically pulled back out into a less escapist, but more questioning fantastic visual 'reality' on the screen, as Johnson argues.[110] Similarly, *Quatermass* deals with its vegetative alien other, not by macho slaying (as in such American invasion films as *The Thing From Another World*, to which Kneale also alludes) but by appealing to the residual humanity of its ingested victim, causing him/it to self-sacrificially destruct.

The Quatermass Experiment's famously metatelevisual climax showed the gigantic life form gestating from its astronaut host apparently transmitted in real time by remote camera. Like Orson Welles's *WOTW* strategy of interrupting 'live' radio, the invader is caught on a BBC outside broadcast from Westminster Abbey, now eerily evacuated of the crowds seen at Elizabeth II's Coronation (televised just a month before). Hence, as Hutchings points out, a highly constructed state event was implicitly subverted by a very different use of the medium for a new Realism of the Fantastic, produced from electrifying tension between its documentary and fictional poles.[111] Equally, the fact that Kneale and Cartier were also searching out new 'alien' forms of representation, in a popular medium pre-imagined as challenging traditional cultural hierarchies in *WTSW*, is signalled iconoclastically by using the specific location of Poet's Corner for Carroon's metamorphosis.

Self-reflexively Wellsian tropes continued in *Quatermass II* (broadcast 22 Oct.–26 Nov. 1955), with more integrated location inserts and the superior technical facilities of Lime Grove to increase plausibility. Quatermass investigates a meteorite shower over a remote town. This turns out to be pods containing life forms, advance guard of another colonisation. Once hatched, they merge into an amoeba-like organism, which takes over high-ranking human minds to serve its ends. What saves the series from mere paranoia about the threat of some externalised ideological other, like its American equivalent, *Invasion of the Body Snatchers*, is that these aliens are also reflective of a dehumanising enemy within. Quatermass tracks down the gestalt creature to a secret government installation of geodesic domes. This alludes to contemporary germ warfare and atomic weapons research centres such as Porton Down or Aldermaston. In effect, the story is symbolic not so much of Soviet infiltration as of the parasitic growth of a scientised 'secret state', purporting to defend the institutions of British democracy in the very act of undermining them. As Kneale said, '"Is it really to keep the Russians away, or is it something else?" I decided my story would be about the "something else"'.[112] The plant pioneers synthetic foodstuffs, but not for human consumption. Significantly, Kneale's alien/quisling plot is foiled only when Quatermass manages to foment a workers' uprising suggestive of the protest movement spearheaded by the Campaign for Nuclear Disarmament (CND), which led to profound social and cultural changes in late fifties and early sixties Britain. Television reviews noted the series' unsettling blend of mundane realism and the fantastic, tracing it back to a specific source: 'grafting of the extraordinary to the commonplace is an old trick – H. G. Wells used it to great effect – and I congratulate Mr Kneale on perceiving there is no better'.[113]

In *Quatermass and the Pit* (22 Dec. 1958–26 Jan. 1959) invasion has already occurred in prehistory. The series benefited from impressively scaled film-sets from the newly acquired Ealing studios which convincingly grounded Quatermass's unearthing of the buried source of 'paranormal' manifestations in the everyday location of a Knightsbridge Tube extension site: an ancient spacecraft filled with insect-like Martian corpses (their tripedal form hinting at Wellsian origins), alongside suspiciously hominid bipeds.[114] As tele-playwright Stephen Gallagher puts it, Kneale 'brought out the latent fantastical in the world we all know ... he made a kind of science fiction that was both world class *and* firmly rooted in British culture. There's a direct line of descent from Wells's fighting machines wailing on Primrose Hill to the demonic force released at Hobb's End.'[115] The series is another parable about humankind's threat to its own survival, because of post-war resurgence in xenophobia. (Significantly, the spacecraft is originally thought to be an unexploded Nazi rocket.) Kneale himself described it as 'a race-hatred fable' and it even features news bulletins alluding to the anti-immigration riots in Notting Hill in the summer of 1958. The series also climaxes with scenes of *IM*-like 'telekinetic' phenomena and social disorder: under compulsion from a vast demonic hologram projected into the sky, a hysterical mob turn on anyone perceived as other.[116] Its *living* alien monsters, like those of Wells or Freud, are most definitely us.

That is proved by palaeontologist Dr Roney, who invents a kind of psychic time machine. This 'optic-encephalograph' allows Quatermass (and the television viewer) to witness the shocking truth about the past's latent legacy by literally peering back into our collective unconscious through translating brain waves into images.[117] Earthling aggressiveness is an evolutionary consequence of genetic tampering by extraterrestrials (such ethical 'Martianisation' had been implicit from the very beginning of Kneale's trilogy, hinted at in its signature theme: Gustav Holst's 'Mars, Bringer of War'). The aliens evacuated their planet after genocidal conflict five million years ago. As Quatermass puts it, this was 'a race purge ... a cleansing of the hives ... a ritual slaughter to preserve a fixed society'. They then surgically reprogrammed our apemen ancestors to conquer this world by proxy, Kneale synthesising motifs from *SB* with *IODM*. The discovery sparks sobering reflection about modern humanity's 'demonic' self-destructiveness and inability to cope with difference except as something to be exterminated, a Janus nod to both *WOTW* and the still fresh historical reality of the *Endlösung*. As Quatermass cautions straight to camera, 'We *are* the Martians. If we cannot control the inheritance within us this will be their second dead planet.' Behind the whole series is the looming threat of nuclear suicide. (He resists American-induced pressure to use space research for planting missile bases on the moon, anticipating the 'Star Wars' project of the Reagan era.) Quatermass sees defence policy as Pyhrric futility, a 'dead man's deterrent', in which annihilated Britain might wreak posthumous vengeance on its enemies.

Quatermass and the Pit's fusion of spectrality and alien incursion has strong echoes of the liaison between spiritualist and technological explanations for bizarre phenomena found in many early Wells stories. As Kneale wrote in 1963, 'ghosts and science belong together' because of the way technology had come to haunt the contemporary imagination with its potentially deathly presence.[118] His highly creative programmes in turn helped Wellsian ideas infuse Chris Carter's *The X-Files* (Fox Television, 1993–2002), the most globally successful and influential of recent American television SF. Kneale was even asked out of retirement to script for it, although he declined.[119] A postmodern, highly knowing and intertextual mosaic of extraterrestrial and paranormal themes, the central pairing of Fox Mulder and Dana Scully, as believer and sceptic respectively, owes much to the tension between the incredible and the rational in Kneale's scientific investigator. (The fourth *Quatermass* serial (ITV Oct.–Nov. 1979), with its blend of megalithic sites and modern mystics (the Planet People), who believe a tractor beam from deep space will transport them to heaven, is particularly evocative of *The X-Files*.) This, in turn, harks back to the paradoxes of Wells's writing as 'Realist of the Fantastic' and its parallels with the 'uncanniness' and defamiliarised vision of evolving media.[120] Moreover, the framing of *The X-Files* narrative, subsuming all its other subjects and motifs, is the quest to find conclusive proof of extraterrestrial life. In pursuit of this, Mulder and Scully encounter all kinds of conspiracies and counter-conspiracies, involving collaboration and/or resistance between interplanetary colonists and a shadowy military–industrial oligarchy, who may or may not be developing an alien–human hybrid specifically adapted to take over our world. Once again this is a continuing mutation of ethically double-edged narratives such as *WOTW* and *SB*, with their indeterminate play between external difference and latent resemblance, between self and other, between plausibility and invention. *Quatermass* also mediated Wellsian influence on the tone and preoccupations of the new hybrid SF–horror-film genre, with its monstrous Gigeresque fusions of machine and organism, started by Dan O'Bannon's script for Ridley Scott's *Alien* (1979), secretly gestating from its human host.[121]

Underground Influence

Wells's less obvious pervasion of fifties and sixties Hollywood is epitomised by Pal's ongoing fascination with his themes and motifs, in creative partnership with Haskin. Their *Naked Jungle* (1954) has much in common with Wells's 1905 story about evolutionary competition from mutant insects, 'The Empire of the Ants' (although Bert I. Gordon's radioactive-waste-fed 1977 film is the first named version, also harking back to the pulp post-atomic precedent, Gordon Douglas's *Them!* (1954)). 1955's *The Conquest of Space* reverses *WOTW* for the attempted earthling colonisation of an uninhabited Mars. *Atlantis, the Lost Continent* (1960) is a kind of proto-totalitarian dystopia. Though set in Classical times, it nonetheless features futuristic technologies such as a crystal 'death-ray' and 'beast-men', surgically hybridised in a 'House of Fear' imported from *IODM*. Pal even negotiated with Associated International Pictures, who owned the rights to *WTSW*, but disagreed over how it should be adapted.[122] He and Haskin also filmed Frank M. Robinson's SF thriller, *The Power*, in 1967, which extended Wellsian themes about the ethics of superhumanity. Its murderous *Übermensch*, Adam Hart, is a kind of psychic 'Man of the Year Million', leapfrogging ahead genetically hundreds of generations. The picture begins with an *IM*-like X-ray anatomisation of a human body. Telekinetic power is suggestively connected with media technology. Its invisible presence is first manifest at a séance-like session at the space research institute, where levitating object suddenly cuts to revolving record. The absent Hart manipulates machines to slay suspicious colleagues, as well as altering their perceptions, significantly figured in a menacing stop-motion sequence where toys in a shop window come to life. Camerawork and pulsing soundtrack continuously suggest an unseen voyeur, although Hart's actual identity is only revealed at the end. Invisibility also featured in one of Pal's last (unmade) projects for filming Philip Wylie's SF gender satire, *The Disappearance*. This may owe something to both *Stella* and *The War of the Wenuses* as much as to Wells, because its men and women become literally unseeable to each other through mutual misunderstanding.[123]

Perhaps mid-twentieth-century Hollywood's most subversive transmutation of a compendium of Wellsian ideas and scenarios remains Fred McLeod Wilcox's *Forbidden Planet* (1956). The first film in Cinemascope *and* Technicolor, with its experimental electronic theremin soundtrack, even its use of the standard alien saucer motif is ambiguous (we don't realise at first that it is a 'United Planets' spacecraft, crewed by humans). Though famously a reworking of Shakespeare's *The Tempest* (written *c*.1611), *Forbidden Planet* draws less overtly on a tangled intertextual hinterland of Wells fictions and adaptations, not least Erle C. Kenton's *Island of Lost Souls* (1932), adapted by Philip Wylie (with Waldemar Young) from *IODM*. Wells criticised this as a 'mad scientist' travesty of his satire of Victorian anxieties about degeneration and the cultural forces keeping us precariously 'human'. However, as with *Metropolis*, Wells wasn't always the best judge of effective screen developments of his own themes. Bela Lugosi put in one of his best performances as Wells's prohibiting 'Sayer of the Law' and his eponymous experimenter in accelerated evolution by artificial means had been deftly played by erstwhile friend and male lead of the Wells–Montagu shorts, Charles Laughton. Laughton is a memorably whip-cracking, sexually ambiguous voyeur, who dresses for dinner in his fortified jungle compound and oozes the perverse psychology of colonialism. This is epitomised by the scene where Moreau, in tropical uniform and dictator's moustache, secretly observes castaway Edward Parker's encounter with his 'Panther Woman' (Kathleen Burke). Moreau has set him up with his unnatural 'daughter' to test the plausibility of his simulations of humanity from vivisected and genetically re-engineered animals (he tells Parker (Richard Arlen) that Lota is 'pure Polynesian').[124] Panther Woman herself can also be seen as a kind of parody of the manufactured exoticism and double standards of Hollywood's *femmes fatales* and its ambiguous presentation of female sexuality as felinely glamorous and potentially lethal. (The tendency reached its apotheosis in Jacques Tourneur's *The Cat People* (1942), whose heroine becomes a monstrous predator when aroused.) She is the symbolic opposite of Parker's white fiancée Ruth (Leila Hyams). Ruth in turn is menaced by the lust of one of Moreau's doctored male creatures in an equivalent scene, evocative of screen stereotypes of interracial rape going back to *Birth of a Nation*.

Shakespeare may be the common factor between *Island of Lost Souls* and *Forbidden Planet*, but Wells's novel had set the precedent for reworking its 'humanist' Utopian-colonial and sexual themes in SF terms.[125] Though Cyril Hume's screenplay was directly sourced from a story by Irving Block and Allen Adler, *Forbidden Planet* is, at least indirectly, a richly Wellsian narrative about the equivocations of scientific power and alterity. As such it foregrounds the ethical imperative to strive for the necessary self-knowledge to preserve our humanity under the stresses and displacements of technological 'progress'. Its central topos is a kind of 'sleep of reason', in which the latent consequences of the dreams of Renaissance magus Prospero are transformed into futuristic inventor Morbius's nightmares. As with Laughton's Moreau, the objectivity of the male scientist is compromised by his sexual unconscious. Moreau's synthetic Calibans roam the island night outside his barred windows, but Morbius's monster is revealed to be *already inside* his idealised family home, despite its electronic conveniences and armoured shutters. *WOTW*'s unmasking of self as alien other also contributes: according to Darko Suvin, all SF's extraterrestrial menaces can be traced back to Wells's imaginative paradigm, compounding xenophobia and biologism.[126]

The Tempest is famously 'metatheatrical' and it is arguable that the equally self-conscious visuality of Wells's texts contributes to how *Forbidden Planet* translates this into cinematic terms. The film also displays a similar critical reflexivity about SF's generic conventions as they had become set since Wells's time. *Forbidden Planet* identifies their masculinity with flawed Utopianism, by linking the 'inner space' of the Freudian unconscious with questions of control over female sexuality and its mediated image, like those raised by Lang in *Metropolis*. This is done specifically through a technologised 'male gaze', making *Forbidden Planet*'s dialogic relationship with its sources more complex than just a piece of vintage kitsch. Shakespeare's scenario and motifs are translated into what had become their stereotype SF equivalents by the 1950s: Prospero's model island 'commonwealth' becomes a colonised planet (Altair IV) in 2200; his supernatural 'Art' is alien technology left by a mysteriously perished, indigenous civilisation; its moral crux is the ab/use of scientific power to achieve an ideal social system. But the plot is also given a distinctive psychological twist enabling it to critique such pulp parameters. As in Kneale's parodic *Planet of the Dragons*, these tended to objectify women as either erotic objects or as helpless victims for heroic rescue from alien monsters, and thus to be naive about blind spots in their own ways of seeing and the ideologies they promoted.

Unconscious contradictions in Utopian social projects were already hinted at by Shakespeare. Prospero slips an intriguing parapraxis of complicity in the 'evil' impulses and actions of his manimal-like native servant, Caliban, at *The Tempest*'s denouement: 'this thing of darkness I/Acknowledge mine' (Act V, Scene ii). Prospero's own telekinetic presence is 'mediated' through good sprite Ariel acting as his eyes and ears for monitoring the island panoptically and manipulating his enemies. The film's equivalent is Morbius's all-capable robot, his overt technological descendant. But that presence is also ironically displaced through *Forbidden Planet*'s invisible Calibanesque monster and unacknowledged counterpart. The creature's shadowy identification with Morbius himself (played by Walter Pidgeon) is similarly only climactically revealed. With suggestive parallelism, when Morbius is unconscious in sleep, the audience sees vicariously through the awakened monster's eyes during its nocturnal attacks. This deliberately recalls techniques depicting the wish-fulfilling voyeurism and superhuman agency of Griffin in Whale's *Invisible Man*, when his absent presence is rendered by footprints and animated objects. Intra-diegetic camerawork for such effects is typical of *Forbidden Planet*'s visualisations, which critically foreground its own workings.

The plot of monstrous otherness in the self therefore plays out the Freudian notion of the repressed impulses of the Id manifesting themselves in 'morbidly' destructive symptoms of dehumanising and bestial regression ('Morbius' is a psychoanalytically overdetermined complex of echoes, telescoping Moreau, Morpheus, Möbius, morbid, etc.) It also matches specifications for Freud's 'uncanny', specifically as it relates to the transition from Gothic/occult into SF/technological narratives exemplified by early Wells. Like Prospero's cell, Morbius's house appears a microcosm of the perfect, enlightened patriarchal regime (with a conspicuously absent maternal influence on his daughter's upbringing). The psychological enigma revolves around a 'mysterious planetary force' threatening anyone who disturbs its celibate domestic harmony. Just as mysteriously, Prospero and his daughter (Anne Francis) seem immune to it.

Her name, Altaira (from the planet itself), embodies alterity. Sexual comedy is generated by her uninhibited attraction to the male crew of the relief expedition from Earth (based on Miranda's reaction in *The Tempest*, Act I, Scene ii), but also raising issues about the role and image of women in modernity pondered by Wells from *WTSW* to *TTC*. However, what might otherwise be construed as marginal 'love interest' driven by box-office rather than plot considerations (as in many Hollywood versions of Wells novels), gradually turns into the film's core concern, as with Parker's encounter with Moreau's 'daughter' in *Island of Lost Souls*. This 'token female' is essential to its critique of the dubious rationality of patriarchal power-knowledge, as well as of the conventions of its own screen genre, because her discovery of the possibility of autonomous desire raises the highest stakes.

The key lies in Morbius's explanation of the, significantly, buried Krel machines which have boosted his intellect, but not his self-knowledge, beyond mortal dimensions. (In design, their city resembles the underground galleries of New Everytown in *TTC*.) Like many of Wells's protagonists, Morbius is a jealously Faustian monopoliser of dangerous knowledge which he alone thinks he can master. At first this appears to be the legitimate male 'white magic' of Prospero's books, but turns out to be more like the hidden feminine legacy of Sycorax, the native island witch and Caliban's dam, supplanted by his colonial incursion. Morbius's godlike power is, significantly, based on 'telekinesis', the psychic ability to manipulate matter at a distance promising liberation from the body and its impulses – what he high-mindedly calls 'freedom from physical instrumentality'. The unconscious irony is that the artificial boost to his evolution from Krel technology also produces an equal and opposite degenerative reaction, in which repressed animalism literally materialises in the form of violent lusts. (In perhaps the most taboo-breaking manoeuvre in fifties Hollywood, the film hints at a latent incest motif, a pathological subtext all the more 'unspeakable' given the 'wholesome' Disney corporation's involvement in sequences where the monster's silhouette is rendered ambiguously visible by animation techniques.)[127] This is a very Wellsian denouement, because the secret identity of the extraterrestrial or inhuman other is recognised as the consequence of superhuman overreaching in a conflicted self. Though the Krel are long dead, Morbius is compulsively repeating the pattern by which their advanced civilisation perished, through 'projecting' part of himself about which he was in denial: 'My poor Krel. After a billion years of shining sanity, they could hardly have understood what power was destroying them.' Moreover, this is analogised with his apparitional double's ability to overcome physical barriers and its visualisation as a ubiquitous absent-presence.

The Krel IQ Machine, or 'Plastic Educator', is another metacinematic device. This materialises thought holographically and complements the disembodied 'gaze' of Morbius's alter ego during its nocturnal rampages. The 'familiar subject' he shows the relief spaceship's officers by way of random illustration is, parapraxistically, a miniaturised, moving simulation of Altaira. She is literally 'on his mind', an image of dutiful daughterhood he has jealously fashioned and controlled, recalling Maria's mechanically counterfeited likeness in *Metropolis*, emblematic of tensions in the mediation of modern femininity foreseen in *WTSW*. Freud's term for the 'uncanny' is, of course, the German *das Unheimliche*; its root (as in the related English adjective 'homely') defines what we recognise as 'familiar', normal or natural. Like Wells's extreme defamiliarisations of the everyday as Realist of the Fantastic, in psychologically fraught circumstances the *Heimliche* inverts into the disturbingly 'alien'. Hence Morbius's obsessive techno-colonial paternalism is the source of *Forbidden Planet's* uncanny 'symptoms'. When the monster finally turns on them too, Morbius says to Altaira, after she falls for the commander of the rescue spaceship, 'Tell it you don't love this man!', evoking Freud's Id (German *das Es*, 'the it'), in a last-ditch attempt to deny this alter ego as 'not I'. The film's reworking of a psychoanalytic paradigm can also be seen as a metaphor for the positioning of the feminine within 'phallocentric' regimes of vision, power-knowledge and pleasure in the kind of 'genre' SF which *Forbidden Planet* deconstructs.[128] Crucial to that process is not just Block and Adler's overt refashioning of *The Tempest*, but a whole network of visually minded Wellsian intertexts and adaptations into which the film logs freely.

European Wells

As demonstrated by transactions with prime examples from four main branches of pre-war Modernist film-making, *L'Inhumaine*, *Paris qui dort*, *Aelita* and *Metropolis*, respectively, Wells was a fertilising presence across French Cubism and Surrealism, Russian Futurism and German Expressionism. His imagination 'infiltrated' 1920s European art cinema, as Nicoletta Vallorani shows,[129] but strong connections can also be traced more recently, especially following films such as *La Jetée* (1962). Chris Marker's 'still movie' remains the most hauntingly paradoxical synthesis of Wellsian SF and Proustian–Modernist motifs in continental cinema, as Coates argues. Shuffled and reshuffled out of their chronological sequence, Marker's photographs function as 'miniature time machines', for both protagonist and viewer, as George Slusser and Robert Heath put it.[130] A prisoner of World War III, with a preternaturally strong tendency to *mémoire involontaire* because of his fixation with the Eurydicean face of a woman, is experimentally dispatched back to his own uncontaminated past. This is to establish a gateway for vital supplies to a future whose Pyrrhic victors control a ramshackle empire of tunnels under the radioactive desert that was Europe. Unknown to him, he is accompanied back by a guard (in dark goggles suggestive of technological surveillance). Marker references many motifs and themes in *TM* (romantic interludes at Paris's Museum of Natural History with the prisoner's lost love evoke the Time Traveller's visit to the Palace of Green Porcelain with Weena). With climactic but also paradoxical determinism, Marker's film folds chronologically in on itself to reveal that an enigmatic premonition from the prisoner's youth was really about fatal intervention from a future yet to happen. As a boy he witnessed the moment of his own death at the hands of the agent shadowing him to prevent escape from his mission back into another life and will go on doing so in an endless, Sisyphean loop.

It was partly because of *La Jetée*'s critical success that several tyros of France's *nouvelle vague* tried their hands at art-house SF with Wellsian overtones. François Truffaut's only English-language film, for example, was a 1966 adaptation of Ray Bradbury's novel *Fahrenheit 451*, a *WTSW*-like post-literate dystopia of (literally) wrap-round, interactive domestic entertainment media, in which 'firemen' incinerate forbidden books (they were also burned by *WTSW*'s euphemistic 'Sanitary Company' to make industrial commodities). Jean-Luc Godard's *Alphaville* (1965) was a noirishly enigmatic quest narrative, set in a repressive techno-city on another planet, which was also a defamiliarisation of Paris itself on the eve of the *événements* that would shake late-sixties French society. Alain Resnais conflated themes from Wells, Marker and L'Herbier in *Je t'aime, je t'aime* (1967), in which a literal time machine's failure to alter the past stands in visual tension with cinema's resurrection of a lost, Eurydicean love. In 1974 veteran Marcel Carné made *La Merveilleuse Visite*, a version of Wells's fable from the same vintage as *TM* about an angel miraculously falling to earth in a country parish, who inadvertently calls the moral bluff of its piously complacent world-view. In a comic-poetic style Carné called *fantastique social*, his heavenly creature (Gilles Kholer) fetches up on a beach to become a kind of personification of the impact of hippie counter-cultural ideas in conservative, rural Brittany.

Vallorani amply demonstrates hitherto underestimated alternatives to the Hollywood pattern in her own survey of Wells's enduring pervasiveness in European television and film. This confirms that adaptation to an American cultural context tends to dilute his texts' 'subversive potential' more than continental or British versions. She casts his influence as 'a sort of "invisible man" or underground presence, a subtext not immediately recognisable, but nonetheless fundamental'.[131] Wells and his continental forerunner Verne (despite the former's distinction between them) shared a practical overlap of topical modernity and popular appeal, which supplied Europe's infant industry with readily adaptable material.[132] Because Wells's work is now perhaps most globally well-known through film adaptations, it is also arguable, as Vallorani puts it, that 'some of his archetypes re-emerged in European cinema' not necessarily direct from source, but mediated by 'a sort of secondary influence' through Hollywood reworkings.[133]

Hence between the 1930s and 1960s, continental screens, big and small, were 'scattered with references' to Wellsian themes, topics and plots.[134] During this period invisibility, space flight and time travel infuse a broad swathe of European popular culture. Again Lang was a key precedent and transmitter, because all three themes are present in the *Mabuse* films, *Metropolis* and *Die Frau im Mond*, along with other pervasive Wellsian motifs of electronic surveillance, virtual presence and media power.[135] Made after Wells's denunciation of *Metropolis*, Lang was understandably stepping back from his influence in this trailblazing lunar expedition picture. Lang's moon, though famously barren and uninhabited unlike *FMITM*'s, nevertheless becomes colonial *Lebensraum* for Germany's 'new Adam and Eve' who are stranded there. Moreover, it is arguable that Wells's dichotomy between Cavor's disinterested quest for scientific knowledge and Bedford's imperial lust to exploit another new world's mineral wealth is replicated in other ways. Space pioneer Helius (his rocket *Friede* means peace) has high-minded intentions for our satellite, but murderous stowaway Turner (agent of an international cartel) is on a mission to seize its riches for controlling the terrestrial gold standard. Lang's mission launch (famously inventing the countdown) is constructed as a global *WTSW*-like media relay: 'The eyes of the world are upon us; the ears of the world are listening.' Similarly, views of the moon, looming through the rocket's portals, recall the 'simulator' visualisations of *FMITM*'s sphere. Hence Wells's influence remains stronger than it might appear, despite Lang's preoccupation with viable space prototypes making his film seem more Vernian in technical principle.

Because of its fascination with science and technology, what I have called the optical speculativeness of Wells's narrative method was a galvanising force for European experimentation with 'dramatic defamiliarizing effects', as Vallorani puts it.[136] Hence Wells's texts were reframed, wholly or partly, in different national filmic and televisual contexts and this continues to be the case today in France, Italy, Germany, Russia, etc. Despite the fact that a specific version of *WTSW* has yet to be made, numerous European films raid it for scenarios about regaining consciousness in the future. It is often combined with *TM* as influences, as in *Metropolis*. In Cèdric Klapisch's *Peut-être* (1999), a man steps through a portal to meet his millennially conceived son, now an elderly citizen of the Paris of 2070. The film hypothesises whether the outcome of our present civilisation's social project will make our descendants unempathic posthumans, in mind if not body: ecological disaster, caused by technological overreaching, has steeped France in a kind of Sahara and the younger generation revert to sadistic barbarism for kicks. Wim Wenders's *Bis ans Ende der Welt* (1991) is highly self-reflexive speculation about a future in which the media pose both destruction and salvation. It involves a quest for new technology allowing the 'blind' to see by transmitting images telepathically, but in a world ringed by potentially explosive communications satellites and threatened by 'Y2K-like' cybernetic meltdown. Wenders's international co-production, *The End of Violence* (1997), extends the Wellsian themes of surveillance and control to an ambiguous Utopia where crime, or even its media representation, is impossible because everyone is permanently watched. (No doubt Wenders's film passed such concerns on to Steven Spielberg's *Minority Report* (2004), based on Philip K. Dick's narrative about a chillingly omniscient tomorrow: moving holographic advertisements on city walls interact with passing consumers individually by reading their personal biometric data and police psychics 'predetect' potential deviancy when barely at Orwell's 'thoughtcrime' stage.) Antonio Albanese's *Un uomo d'acqua dolce* (*A Freshwater Man*) (1997) reprises Wells's motif of narcoleptic temporal displacement, though limiting it to five years for domestic and psychological comedy, rather than long-term dystopianism as such. Massimo Troisi and Roberto Benigni's *Non ci resta che piangere* (*We Can But Cry*) (1984) combines *TM* with a clever inversion of *FMITM*'s colonial 'New World' theme. They travel back to 1492 Tuscany to prevent Columbus's 'discovery' of America, with all that this implies for changing the course of future history.

Smaller European nations which had post-war 'Utopian' solutions imposed upon them by totalitarian power drew on the subversive adaptability of other Wells narratives. Significantly, a 1981 Polish television version of *WOTW* (*Wojna Światów*, dir. Piotr Szulkin) transformed his allegorical subtext into astute satire of state media during what turned out to be the dying decade of the Soviet empire. As we saw in Chapter 2, *IM* was an ideal vehicle for voicing social criticism intimately bound up with questions of subjective identity and modern techno-ideological forces shaping it. Vallorani confirms that both Wells's theme and form were especially protean in European film and television (especially in societies policed by moral or ideological surveillance), allowing invisible protagonists 'to assume the role of ideal witness' with impunity and serve as metaphors for filming cameras.[137] Alexander Zakharov's *Chelovek-nevidimka* (significantly, the same year as the BBC's 1984 serialisation) stuck closely to Wells's narrative, while raising the need for Gorbachev's coming *perestroika* and *glasnost*. Complementarily, Roberto Benigni's 1988 comedy, *Il piccolo diavolo*, with its anarchic, anti-clerical poltergeist, was a Catholic Italian take on *IM*'s theme of unseen agency and forbidden impulses, reawakening some of the folk archetypes behind Wells's SF reworking. Wellsian themes have had a deep impact in non-European media forms too, mutating into strange, cultural hybrids which even Lewis Carroll could never have foreseen. Since 1970, one of the most popular and long-running series in Japanese *manga* comics and *anime* films and television programmes has been Fujio F. Fujiko's *Doraemon*. The saga of a cyborgian cat from the future, his child companions accompany him on fantastic adventures based on devices enabling them to travel through or manipulate time in every conceivable way.[138] Japanese film-makers have also produced subtler responses to Wellsian tropes, initiated by Hiroshi Teshigara's *The Face of Another* (1966), a highly metaphorical take on the questions of mediation, identity and morality raised in *IM*.

British Television Wells

The metaphor of 'The Door in the Wall' for the screen as multifarious 'portal' into parallel worlds was still potent in 1956 when the BFI produced an experimental film using a new 'aspect ratio' technology known as the 'Dynamic Frame' (a radical development of techniques for shaping the visual field, such as masking and the iris in/out, used by early film-makers such as G. A. Smith and D. W. Griffith). Glenn Alvey Junior chose to adapt and direct Wells's story, of a disenchanted politician obsessed with accessing a lost alternative reality, as demonstration subject for its innovative matting process. As the opening notice proclaimed, this allowed 'the shape and size of the picture [to] change according to the dramatic needs of the story' and seemed particularly appropriate for the effects of confinement and discovery it demanded. There is a sudden expansion of the motherless child's claustrophobic visual and emotional horizons once he passes through the narrow green entrance into a kind of technicolor Eden where everything is equivocally heightened (there are ethereal fountains, but also terrifying monsters). An otherworldly lady shows him the book of 'living pictures' Wells describes, which includes views of his drab home life and forbidding father in monochrome contrast. As in the text, he is suddenly ejected through one of its frames back to a routine drained of all tonal warmth. The film therefore visualises the widespread tendency in Wells for placing and manipulating variable frames-within-frames in his own word pictures. As Montagu noted, potential backers were put off at the trade screening by a Protean excess of rapid metamorphoses 'to parade the full capacity of the invention'. Nevertheless, as Marcus points out, the project indicates how the 'Wellsian imaginary' could still be taken as 'the most appropriate arena for cinematic shape-changing'.[139]

However, it is arguable that Wells's ongoing influence in Britain has been greater and most self-reflexively creative on the small screen. With a film industry unable to rival Hollywood budgets, British programme-makers have proved highly resourceful in developing his themes under tight financial and technical constraints. As we saw, Kneale's *Quatermass* helped shape British television fundamentally, establishing a national taste for original teledrama, but also exploring the visual parameters of this alien presence in the most intimate domestic space. Its phenomenal 1960s successor, *Doctor Who*[140] (revived to acclaim in 2005), transported such scenarios into further dimensions by aid of the Tardis, an obvious small-screen derivative from the proto-cinematic *TM*. Robert Barr had already visualised Wells's text for the BBC in January 1949, eleven years before Hollywood.[141] No doubt Montagu's planned big-screen version (for a Wells 'Film Omnibus', alongside 'Harringay', 'Elvesham', 'The New Accelerator' and 'The Man Who Could Work Miracles') was also partly prompted by Barr's teleplay.[142]

The BBC *TM* is a definitive example of how Wells's posthumous influence encouraged creative use of the medium and helped early television break out of the fixity and staginess of live transmission. Broadcast only twice, on 25 January and 21 February 1949 (but, unfortunately, like most early television unrecorded) Barr's script was more faithful to Wells's plot and themes than Pal's, retaining the controversial biologisation of class and his bleak further vision of the dying solar system, though with necessary excisions for scheduling and less exposition. It was also a technically adventurous, hour-long production, incorporating both filmed inserts and back projection to visualise Wells's descriptions of time travel and a recorded voice-over to access the Time Traveller's thoughts, the first time that British SF TV had made use of such effects. Symptomatically, letters to the *Radio Times* indicate that viewers were divided between finding its scenario 'weird and impossible' and marvelling at its technical achievement.[143] As Cook and Wright also point out, the programme's foregrounding of the scientist's dilemmas (played by Russell Napier, with Mary Donn as Weena) shaped the genre's subsequent development.[144] Similarly, *Doctor Who*'s most famous aliens also owed much to *WOTW*. Their creator, Terry Nation, has admitted that his Daleks are essentially Wells's machine-or-ganism evolutionary interface topically Nazified. Orson Welles's adaptation was given a further metaradiophonic twist in Mark Gatiss's 2005 *Doctor Who* serial (BBC Radio 7, Oct.–Nov.), *Invaders From Mars*. Here the hoax was on the extraterrestrials: real aliens emerge from meteorite pods at the time of Welles's broadcast, but are frightened off on learning from 'newsflashes' that they face stiffer competition for Earth than mere humans.

Despite live television's logistical *and* artistic limitations, great things were still achievable, as in the 1954 two-hour adaptation of *Nineteen Eighty-Four*. It was prescient of Kneale and Cartier to fix on Orwell's satire about the coming power of media-saturated 'hyperreality', with its roots in how Wells critically foresaw the technological gaze in *WTSW*. The BBC production used 'metatelevisual' devices, most notably screens-within-the-screen, anticipating more elaborately self-reflexive practices. Kneale himself reworked such themes and motifs as television penetrated ever deeper into the nation's cultural and political life. His psychedelic dystopia, *The Year of the Sex Olympics* (appropriately one of BBC2's first colour transmissions on 29 July 1968),[145] superseded Orwellian state terror and censorship by making erotics the ultimate 'spectator sport'. Indeed, it showed that hedonism and totalitarian surveillance might fit hand in glove in a satire of the questionable liberties of sixties counterculture, at least as they might be appropriated through media commodification.[146] The Utopian notion of the 'permissive society' begged the question: who was doing the permitting and to what ends? In the caste-based tomorrow of *The Year of the Sex Olympics*, the High-Drives led by TV controller Ugo Priest (Leonard Rossiter), numb away passion and discontent among the 'Low-Drives' through a constant, desensitising flow of orgiastic spectacle. This is a 'repressive desublimation' developed from the media-based 'systematised sensuality' and vicarious experience of *WTSW*, which Huxley had updated for the inter-war age of the Dream Palace as the 'Feelies' in *Brave New World*.[147] It is epitomised by the hypnopaedic slogan of 'apathy control': 'Watch. Not do.' Disgusted by all this, a group of dissidents leave for an island apparently beyond the camera's reach. However, foreshadowing today's 'reality TV', *they* are set up as the ultimate 'Live-Life Show', a 24-hour, sado-voyeuristic thrill, stalked by a planted psychopath. A play seemingly conservative in its position on the 'sexual revolution' in 1968, it now looks eerily ahead of its time in foreseeing the cynical ratings-driven exploitation of much early twenty-first-century broadcasting.[148] As Una McCormack shows, the dystopian tradition, as epitomised by the influence of media-saturated texts such as *WTSW* on sources such as Yvgeny Zamyatin, Huxley and Orwell, has been a major factor in British television SF. Similarly, Wells's techno-ecological catastrophes have been an imaginative template behind the many post-apocalyptic futures marking out its pessimism from its American counterpart, as Catriona Miller argues.[149]

Kneale's metatelevisual futurism was one of the channels through which Wells's influence flowed into *Cold Lazarus*, Dennis Potter's posthumous 1998 BBC/Channel 4 co-production. Set in a denatured tomorrow, dominated by global media empires, it has an explicitly *WTSW*-like scenario with added authorial self-referentiality. The cryogenically frozen head of Potter's scriptwriting protagonist from *Karaoke* (Albert Finney), a series redolent of the cultural effects of recording technology, is revived in the twenty-second century. He furnishes the latest form of televisual nostalgia, a kind of exploitative time travel. Paradoxically, his most intimate memories are tapped into as virtual reality for audiences cut off from the authentic sensory and emotional experiences of a bygone age. Their society has become increasingly cocooned in layers of pacifying mediation. Opposing it are the 'RONs', a secret revolutionary organisation, whose slogan is 'Reality or Nothing'. They threaten to blast through its electronic membranes to let in the alternative, raw actuality outside.

Montagu had planned a series for British Lion Productions adapted from Wells's short stories in 1958. He highlighted the televisual potentials of their optically speculative themes and methods: the displacement of 'Davidson's Eyes' could be made 'visually odd and exciting'; 'cartoon animation' might render the disembodied consciousness and 'poetic' style of 'Under the Knife'; the hallucinatory visual puns of 'Pollock' were ripe for treatment; 'trick work' necessary for 'The Magic Shop' would be challenging, but worth the effort; 'The New Accelerator' would 'mix speeded up and slowed down movement' to capture its 'diverting' paradoxes.[150] Although Montagu's programmes were never made, a short-lived, but highly symptomatic example of tracing a still active influence in contemporary television SF back to its source was the Hallmark cable and satellite channel's 'recursive' mini-series, *The Infinite Worlds of H. G. Wells* (transmitted 5–7 Aug. 2001).[151] Significantly, this adapted several of the same short stories. It showed that their forms of defamiliarised vision were eminently televisable, directing attention at its own medium's workings and effects through Wells's prefigurings of them. At one level the series was an obvious (and slightly shoestring) attempt to cash in on the popularity of *The X-Files* with a home-grown, costume-drama version; at another, it was a surprisingly well-researched and imaginative exhumation of the hoard of malleable ideas, motifs and themes that Wells bequeathed to the media. In its framing narrative, Wells becomes a kind of proto-Fox Mulder (played by Tom Ward), a jobbing investigator, reporting evidence of paranormal and extraterrestrial phenomena in a form of 'faction'. The supporting Scully role is filled by a fictionalised version of Wells's (second) wife, Amy Robbins, or Jane (as he nicknamed her), a New Woman scientist at Imperial College (Katy Carmichael). In 'The Crystal Egg' episode, for example, the Martian televisual transmitter is found in a meteorite. It now acts as a literal doorway to the 'elsewhere' of the Red Planet, abducting terrestrial specimens who rashly peer into it from their domestic sanctuaries, for a Martian mirror image of the College's Natural History collections. In 'The Remarkable Case of Davidson's Eyes', the protagonist's teleported vision (represented by disorientating inserts of an antipodean shipwreck) is induced by exposure to accidental feedback from secret Royal

Navy experiments with Faraday coils for broadcasting radio signals. The programme also explicitly recognises how SPR explanations for telepathic phenomena were superseded by telecommunications in Wells's early writings. 'Mr Brownlow's Newspaper' literally shocks a hapless tube electrician temporarily into the middle of next week, giving him a short-term ability to foresee the future which only appears to be psychic. Minor miracles of wish-fulfilment are worked for customers of a real 'Magic Shop' (a comic portmanteau cramming in other stories such as 'The Truth About Pyecraft'): a fat man becomes 'weightless', by losing his sense of gravity, and a bald one, overgrown with mutant follicles in a parody of *TM*-like speeded-up visual effects (Williamson's *The Marvellous Hair Restorer* (1901) was probably the earliest trickfilm on this theme). The metabolic temporal duality of 'The New Accelerator' is exploited by a rogue scientist to steal a march on rivals. However, an irreversibly high dose condemns him to a lonely lifespan amid silent, living statues, during an interminably slowed-down single afternoon. Significantly, this theme was explicitly reworked in an episode of *The X-Files* in which disaffected teenagers discover a strange fungus which speeds up their bodies, so they can wreak mayhem at school as invisible vectors of force.[152]

Wells's texts have constituted a rich and nurturing rhizome for film, television and other media, which shows no sign of withering well over a century since *TM* first inspired R. W. Paul. Long after the author's death, they continue to fertilise visual creativity and critical self-reflection in new and unpredictable ways and to put out exploratory shoots into futures we can barely imagine.

Conclusion

In 1915, Lindsay forecast that the future 'prophet wizards' of American cinema would use it like a kind of time machine to visualise the Republic's global destiny and outstrip 'the submarine mood of Verne, the press-the-button complacency of Bellamy, the wireless telegraph enthusiasm of Wells'.[1] Nevertheless, all the following characteristics, which the doyen of commentators on modernity Lewis Mumford identified as typifying film in the mid-thirties, were also prominent in Wells's writings as we have seen:

> The moving picture with its close-ups and synoptic views, with its shifting events and its ever-present camera-eye, with its spatial forms always shown through time, with its capacity for representing objects that interpenetrate, and for placing distant environments in immediate juxtaposition – as happens in instantaneous communication – with its ability, finally, to represent subjective elements, distortions, hallucinations, is today the only art that can represent with any degree of concreteness the emergent world view that differentiates our culture from every preceding one.[2]

However, despite the astonishing promise of this early imaginative synergy with film and related media, Wells's subsequent record on screen, through both his own scripting and adaptation by others, presents an indubitable curate's egg. All too often Wells's texts have been visualised in 'dumbed-down' form and not just because they were ahead of the evolutionary state of the industry that attempted to realise them. Indeed, Don G. Smith argues that 'cinema has probably betrayed Wells more than it has any other important author', continually ransacking his work for sensational scenarios, creating global 'event movies' out of them while gutting the inconveniently challenging questions they raised. Smith concludes that because the industry developed on a particular commercial and cultural model, 'In the end the cinema must be viewed as an entity opposed to Wells's ideas.' Although he sought to harness this Leviathan for Wellsism, its 'powers of conformity' were consequently intractable, although whether that is good or bad depends on your political, moral and economic stance.[3] However, Smith's judgement is perhaps too polarised. The real situation is more complex and disseminal. There is certainly a case to answer in many effects-rich, ideas-poor screen versions of Wells and their innumerable spin-offs and liftings. But it is equally arguable (according to commentators such as Brooks Landon) that Wellsian materials and methods furnished intellectual and aesthetic foundations for an alternative SF tradition of critical reflection, rather than just spectacular attractions and lucrative marketing, outside the cinematic mainstream.[4]

The continuing allure of Wells's writing to more creative film-makers goes beyond the mere box-office pull of good yarns into matters more discursively and philosophically fundamental to the nature of film itself, as even some early Hollywood adaptations such as Whale's *IM* realised so brilliantly. The sheer ingenuity and range of optical speculations in Wells's early writings, and their refraction of the manifold political, social and cultural implications of cinema, undoubtedly makes him the unjustly neglected precursor of High Modernist interest in and influence on both avant-garde and popular aspects of the new medium.

Towards the end of his life in 1942, Wells returned to characterising temporal consciousness in terms coupling Einsteinian physics and cinema: 'Our yesterdays and tomorrows, our hopes and fears, life and death, and all the sequences of our individual and specific life are no more than a moving picture set in the frame of Relativity.'[5] His conception of its subjective dynamics since 1895 may well have been shaped by the subsequent interiorisation of time travel in Modernist fiction, with its fondness for *mémoire involontaire*, shuttling in and out of the here and now on some sensory provocation (hence Eisenstein took Joyce's interior monologues as a model for Modernist sound cinema). But Wells's statement was just as likely the culmination of his own long interest in the psychology and mechanics of perception, which induced the rich convergence between his writing and cinema in the first place. As he went on, the continuity of 'our waking life' is an effect like that which the persistence of vision has on framestrips: our present is really a succession of 'discontinuous "Nows"', but experienced so rapidly that they seem like a flowing and unselective movement, edited by the mind into the appearance of coherent reality. Thus 'we piece our lives together as our hearts beat', our ongoing selves merely 'serviceable synthetic illusions', as in numerous Modernist representations of William James's celebrated 'stream of consciousness'.[6]

From the mid-1900s Wells turned increasingly away from fantastic stories and scientific romances to intellectual treatise and social-realist novel. It seems that his specifically cinematic narrative method declined in ratio, until revived by his first tentative moves to remodel himself as a professional screenwriter in the mid-1920s. Perhaps the explanation for this hiatus in sustaining and refining his early practices into his later fiction lies partially in questions of style and audience. Optically speculative techniques were licensed in SF and fantasy by the flexibility of generic conventions, whereas in other kinds of fiction they could appear overtly experimental or even wilfully obscure. SF and fantasy inherently carried less risk of mystifying or losing a popular readership, an issue of cultural access and the 'broadbrow' communication of intellectual property which always concerned Wells. It is possible that had he continued to write with similarly filmic techniques in his social-realist fiction, he would, effectively, have transformed into a Modernist himself, but also forfeited public reach and influence. Nonetheless, in the intervening years Wells stayed abreast of experimentalism at least in his viewing and criticism, if not his literary practice. As I have shown in *KWWAK*, for example, we can clearly see the impact of Joyce's 'cinema-minded' *Ulysses*, as well as leading styles of avant-garde film-making.

Brooks Landon argues, it is indicative of Wells's continuing importance that far from being just an SF subgenre, time-travel films remain the most dramatic and self-reflexive 'manifestation of the cinema's longstanding and inherent preoccupation with the displacement of temporal consciousness'.[7] Virilio believes that future developments surpassing 'Geode' and 'IMAX' will make our viewing experience ever more like sitting in a 'real' time machine: 'a palpable metaphor' for movement in stasis, 'a temporality of running on the spot'.[8] Just as anticipated in *WTSW*, *WITA*, *TTC*, etc., there are complementary spatial dimensions to such simulation. Virilio also argues that a technologically mobilised virtual gaze provides both a kind of 'flying machine' for innocently spectacular vicarious thrills and a lethal form of strategic capability for observing targets and homing in from any height, angle or distance: 'At the turn of the century, cinema and aviation seemed to form a single moment. By 1914, aviation was ceasing to be strictly a means of flying ... it was becoming one way, or perhaps even the ultimate way, of *seeing*.'[9] Indeed, as Wells (following writers such as Verne and George Griffith) realised early on, military history would be inseparable from cinema's evolution, from high-speed photography for improving ballistics, to aerial-reconnaissance filming, spy satellites, combat simulators, remote and infra-red night vision and the pinpoint visual displays of laser-guided 'intelligent' weapon systems.

In 1924, Wells observed (presumptuously, with hindsight) that a single global community was 'swiftly and steadily replacing the practically separate national racial communities of the past'. Parrinder and Partington argue that the SF genre was particularly calculated to advance this by exerting 'a cosmopolitan appeal, since like the new technology and new inventions that it described, it showed little respect for national boundaries'.[10] The cinema and broadcast media, with which Wells's early texts were so synergetic, were prominent among such new technologies with *the potential* to undermine borders. However, as writers of the anti-

Modernist generation such as Orwell noted, they were increasingly used in the 1930s to reinforce ideological differences, especially in the totalitarian states, for captive national audiences unable to access alternative sources.[11] In 1942, a chastened Wells had also become more pessimistic about media-driven progress. Renewed world war and vested interests acted as a brake on internationalising advances in technology. HMV was developing a new long-playing apparatus aiming to record an entire 'opera upon one disc, just as it seems possible that already any scene caught by a motion camera may be televised with a minimum of delay all round the earth'. However, he now thought, 'most of us will never be permitted to see these things arrive in our lifetime'. In his case it was true (Wells died in 1946), though not for his younger contemporaries.[12]

Overcorrection for earlier Utopianism this may have been, but Wells's speculations about forms of electronic vision and presence nonetheless reached well beyond technologies realised in his time and anticipate phenomena now pervasive in our postmodern, cultural condition. A retrospective light is shed on *IM* by Wells's own project for integrating communications and media as it had evolved by *World Brain* (1937), a series of articles advocating a global encyclopaedia. This would link all libraries and information services into one system covering every field of knowledge, i.e. a Wellsian foreseeing of the internet. Fifty years before the practical reality of microchip technology Wells's plea for planetary enlightenment went largely unheard. Nevertheless, in *The Camford Visitation* (1938), he fictionalised the same idea. Like *IM*, this concerns a disembodied voice from the ether invading the hallowed portals of Holy Innocents College to challenge its anachronistic complacency. The visitant is another 'superhuman' intellectual force manifested as pure discourse: '"A sort of Invisible Man," said Trumber.' His fellow dons quote arguments about its impossibility from the 1897 novella. The presence also speaks from 'beyond space and time', like one of the Immortals observing the self-destructive antics of Earthly 'animalcules' in the film version of *MWCWM*. The voice echoed Wells's growing frustration at indifference to his vision of a mediated, technocratic future and, more mutedly, recalls Griffin's apocalyptic rants: 'There is no salvation for races that will not save themselves', it concludes ominously. 'Half the stars in the sky are the burning rubbish of worlds that might have been.'[13] Whether the ubiquitous and Babelian 'voices' of the internet are fostering the kind of democratic planetary enlightenment that will save us now is a matter of debate of course.

From the panoptic surveillance cities of *WTSW*, to the fingerprint-registered population of *A Modern Utopia*, Wells anticipates the ubiquity of CCTV and biometric data. From satellite and digital media, to the worldwide web, mobile videophones and computer games, we are now surrounded with electronic simulations which we inhabit as overlapping sensory-intellectual environments, or interact with 'para-socially' as mediated or wholly generated personae. Phenomena such as the preoccupation with the effects and social impacts of virtual reality in the work of 'Cyberpunk' writers such as William Gibson, as much as the practicality of holographic 'telepresencing' technology (which will soon deliver us to conferences we can't attend, like Yoda in *Star Wars*), have traceable imaginative roots in Wells's writings. Twenty-first-century 'idorus' and 'synthespians', invented or deceased celebrities whose images can be digitised and/or resurrected on screen or even projected on stage amongst live actors in real time, are our latest virtual embodiments of Wells's Sleeper, reawakened to electronic being in a globalising, mediated future that seems to be arriving even sooner than his fiction posited.[14] As Sobchack argues, we are now 'part of a *moving image* culture and live cinematic and electronic lives. That is, informed by and intimately familiar with an increasingly pervasive and qualitatively new techno-logic, our lived bodies' orientation in the world and towards others has changed historically.' Our daily experience adapts accordingly, on sensory, psychological and sociological levels, an ongoing process of 'prosthetic' evolution which Wells would both recognise and treat with all due caution.[15]

Notes

Introduction: Wells's Prescience

1 Terry Ramsaye, *A Million and One Nights: A History of the Motion Picture* (New York: Simon and Schuster, 1926; repr. London: Frank Cass, 1964), p. 162.

2 Although it appeared in book form for the first time in 1895, Wells had been exploring the concept of time travel and elaborating its effects since *The Chronic Argonauts* was serialised in the *Science Schools Journal* (Apr.–June 1888). There were probably *at least* five other versions (see, among others, *The Definitive Time Machine: A Critical Edition of H. G. Wells's Scientific Romance* with introduction and notes by Harry M. Geduld (ed.), (Bloomington, IN: Indiana University Press, 1987), pp. 5–6).

3 Louis considered it a mere novelty. 'It'll last six months or more', he predicted to cameramen their company was quickly dispatching round the world. (See Auguste and Louis Lumière, *Letters: Inventing the Cinema*, ed. Jacques Rittaud-Huttinet et al. (London: Faber, 1995) pp. 32–33.) As David A. Cook puts it, 'the invention of the machines preceded any serious consideration of their documentary or narrative potential'. Precisely because 'the cinema at its material base is a technological form', innovation *necessarily* preceded aestheticisation. (*A History of Narrative Film*, fourth edition (New York and London: Norton 2004), p. 5.)

4 Ian Christie, *The Last Machine: Early Cinema and the Birth of the Modern World* (London: BFI/BBC, 1994), p. 65.

5 Wells acknowledged himself that before George Eastman's invention of flexible film, it would have been impossible for anyone to realise the potentials inherent in cinema's various proto-technologies. He recapped key moments in its scientific and technological prehistory, especially Muybridgian analysis of animal locomotion and its influence (especially through French painter, Ernest Meissonier), Kodak, etc. Eventually, 'Zoetrope and rapid plate met and the moving picture was born' (see H. G. Wells, *The King Who Was a King: The Book of a Film* (London: Ernest Benn, 1929), pp. 8 and 9–10; also Chapter 4).

6 See H. G. Wells, *The Time Machine* (1895; London: Penguin, 2005), p. 68. (Henceforth, all page references to *The Time Machine* (*TM*) will be given in brackets in the text.) The 'seventeen papers' the Time Traveller has written on the subject may allude to the inconclusive 1887 Michelson–Morley experiment. This attempted to use an optical system called an 'interferometer' to determine the speed of light (see Stephen Baxter, '1880s Science and *The Time Machine*', *The H. G. Wells Newsletter*, Vol. 3, no. 9 (Autumn 1995), p. 4. (Wells also recalled the experiment in *The Conquest of Time* (1942; repr. Amherst, NY: Prometheus Books, 1995), p. 89.) Alternatively, they could relate to optical illusions (see Bruce David Sommerville, '*The Time Machine*: A Chronological and Scientific Revision', *Wellsian*, new series, no. 17 (Winter 1994), pp. 11–29, especially 12).

7 H. G. Wells, 'The Owner of the Voice', *A Modern Utopia:* (1905; London: Dent, 1994), pp. 3–4, especially 4.

8 See Mary Anne Doane, *The Emergence of Cinematic Time: Modernity, Contingency and the Archive* (Cambridge, MA and London: Harvard University Press, 2002), especially pp. 1–4.

9 Possibly the first mechanisation of time travel predates Wells – Edward Page Mitchell's 'The Clock that Went Backward' (New York *Sun*, 18 Sept. 1881). Two brothers inherit a family heirloom which transports them in a flashback to the key moment in history when it was manufactured (the siege of Leyden). The story is a self-repeating loop of paradoxes involving intervention from the future shaping the present outcome of past events, on both a genetic and a geopolitical basis. The clock's sixteenth-century inventor also turns out to be the mysterious professor who set it backwards in the now (repr. in *The Crystal Man*, ed. Sam Moskowitz (Garden City, NY: Doubleday, 1973), pp. 71–86). Some of Mitchell's tales were reprinted in Britain, notably in C. Arthur Pearson's magazine *Short Stories*, but evidence that Wells read them remains circumstantial, though tantalising (see introduction to *Crystal Man*, especially pp. lxiii–iv).

French astronomer and spiritualist Camille Flammarion's 1866 novel, which fictionalised the optical wonders of lightspeed physics, offers another precedent. Flammarion imagined spirit beings from the star Capella 'travelling' visually in time even back to the beginning of creation, by riding forwards and backwards through space on rays of light emanating from past events. Lumen explains such 'psychical optics' as 'photographs' or 'living pictures'. Thus Lumen is able to witness individual lifespans reversed, so humans appear to resurrect from the grave, grow young and eventually disappear back into the womb. He also watches historical events, such as the Battle of Waterloo inverted from bloody slaughter to healing and finally peaceful withdrawal from the field. In a final chapter, written for the 1897 English edition, Flammarion discussed how his fantasies of making temporality reviewable and plastic had come to pass in technologies such as time-lapse filming (see *Lumen*, authorised trans. (London: Heinemann, 1897), pp. 38, 89–98 and 220–21). Probably under Flammarion's influence, 'L'Historioscope', by Eugène Mouton, concerns an invention (a kind of electrical telescope) which can look back into history, by tracking light waves from past events as they spread through the ether into space (see his *Fantasies* (Paris: Charpentier, 1883), pp. 223–65). Lewis Carroll's professor's Outlandish Watch, 'which has the peculiar property that, instead of *its* going with the *time*, the *time* goes with *it*', is another example. One watch peg allows travel back as far as a month. The narrator attempts retrospectively to prevent a cycling accident, thus initiating one of the conundrums posed by interference with causality. Though undoing the cause, he still finds the injured cyclist back on his heap of pillows on returning to the present (pp. 410–11). Another peg makes 'the events of the next hour happen in the reverse order', so that a dinner party regresses from washing-up, to forking food out of mouths to fill plates and finally wrapping potatoes back in skins for burial. Dialogue is similarly inverted. (See *Sylvie and Bruno,* Part 1 (Dec. 1889); repr. in Lewis Carroll, *The Complete Illustrated Works of Lewis Carroll* (London: Chancellor Press, 1982), pp. 396–97, 410–11 and 413–15.) Carroll's description is uncannily like watching a reversing trickfilm, such as G. A. Smith's *The Sandwiches* (1899) (see Chapter 1). As W. M. S. Russell points out, though Carroll's fantastic mechanism predates *TM*'s serialised versions, it was, nonetheless, pipped by Wells's *The Chronic Argonauts*, written in 1887 (see his 'Time Before and After: *The Time Machine*', *Foundation: The Review of Science Fiction*, no. 65 (Autumn 1995), pp. 24–40, especially 24–25).

Another story that connects machinery with visual time travel is Brander Matthews's

'The Kinetoscope of Time' (*Scribner's Magazine* (Dec. 1895), pp. 733–44). This allows visual access to moments from past history, but the uncanny exhibitor (who appears to have been present at events to take the footage himself) demands years from the punter's own life in exchange for viewing his future.

10 Paul Coates, 'Chris Marker and the Cinema as Time Machine', *Science Fiction Studies*, vol. 14, no. 3 (1987), pp. 307–15, especially 307.

11 *Démolition* recorded Auguste supervising workmen on the family estate, but became routinely shown backwards. As Terry Ramsaye pointed out when discussing 'reversing' in *TM*, the visual effect predates the Lumières in Edison's 'peepshow' machine: 'One of the earliest novelty effects sought in the Kinetoscope in the days when it was enjoying scientific attention was in exactly this sort of reversal of commonplace bits of action. It continues today a somewhat hackneyed bit of trick camera work ... we saw runners backing up at high speed and backing locomotives swallowing their smoke in reverse gear. Nowadays we see Venuses in half-piece bathing suits spring from the pool and retrace the parabola of the dive to alight on the springboard. Such is the progress of art.' (See Ramsaye, Chapter 12, 'Paul and "The Time Machine", *Million and One Nights*, pp. 147–62, especially 153–54.)

12 See Cecil Hepworth, 'Those Were the Days: Reminscences by a Pioneer of the Earliest Days of Cinematography', *The Penguin Film Review* (Apr. 1948), pp. 33–39, especially 37–38. Such novelties find uncanny parallels not just in *TM*, but stories such as H. G. Wells, 'The New Accelerator' (1901), *CSS*, pp. 487–97.

13 Robert M. Philmus argues that Wells repeats accelerated vision of passing centuries in Denton's musings on human 'progress' in 'A Story of the Days to Come' (1899) (see his *Visions and Revisions: (Re-)Constructing Science Fiction* (Liverpool: Liverpool University Press, 2005), p. 33; also *The Complete Short Stories of H. G. Wells*, ed. John Hammond (London: Phoenix Press, 2000), pp. 333–98, especially 397–98. Henceforth all page references to *The Complete Short Stories of H. G. Wells* (*CSS*) will be given in brackets in the text.)

14 See 'Forms of Time and of the Chronotope in the Novel', in Mikhail Bakhtin, *The Dialogic Imagination: Four Essays*, ed. Michael Holquist (Austin, TX: University of Texas Press, 1981), pp. 84–258.

15 See Stephen Kern, *The Culture of Time and Space 1880–1918* (Cambridge, MA: Harvard University Press, 1983), especially pp. 1–8.

16 See Christie, *Last Machine*, pp. 32–33.

17 One noted physicist paid tribute to Wells's anticipation of relativity in 1914: 'There is thus far an intrinsic similarity ... between space and time, or as the Time Traveller puts it ...: "There is no difference between Time and Space except that our consciousness moves along it." It is interesting that even the terms used by Minkowski to express these ideas "Four-dimensional physics" are anticipated in Mr Wells's fantastic novel.' Quoting the Time Traveller's example of pictures of a man taken at different ages – 'All these are evidently sections, as it were. Three-Dimensional representations of his Four-Dimensioned being, which is a fixed and unalterable thing.' – he concludes, 'Thus Mr Wells seems to perceive clearly the absoluteness, as it were, of the world tube and the relativity of its various sections' (Ludwik Silberstein, *The Theory of Relativity* (London: Macmillan, 1914), p. 134. Silberstein's quotations are from *TM*, pp. 32–33).

18 Kenneth V. Bailey, '"There Would Presently Come Out of the Darkness": H. G. Wells "Filmic" Imagination', *The Wellsian* (Summer 1990), pp. 18–35, especially 18.

19 See Bailey, '"There Would Presently Come Out of the Darkness"', pp. 19–20. Bailey's primary example of a Wells text 'observing' an alien landscape through a kind

of proto-Expressionistic distorting lens is the anamorphic or 'fish eye' effect as Bedford watches the diurnal lunar growth from inside Cavor's sphere: 'The picture was clear and vivid only in the middle of the field. All about that centre the dead fibres and seeds were magnified and distorted by the curvature of the glass.' (*The First Men in the Moon* (1901; London: Penguin, 2005, p. 55). Henceforth, all page references to *The First Men in the Moon* (*FMITM*) will be given in brackets in the text.)

20 Bailey, '"There Would Presently Come Out of the Darkness"', pp. 23–24.

21 See Coates, 'Chris Marker', pp. 307–15, especially 312. Similarly, the protagonist of Wells's 'The Treasure in the Forest' (1895), for example, experiences a shuffling or layering of different spaces and times on each other as if by cinematic superimposition: 'He was still dimly conscious of the island, but a queer dream texture interwove with his sensations.' (*CSS*, pp. 92–98, especially 93.)

22 Vachel Lindsay, *The Art of the Moving Picture* (1915; revised version New York: Liveright, 1922; repr. 1970), p. 12.

23 Geduld even goes so far as to detect anticipations of 'talkie' effects, suggestions of sound-dubbing and fade-ins/outs in *TM* (see his *Definitive Time Machine*, p. 100, note 3). Also see David Y. Hughes and Harry M. Geduld (eds), *A Critical Edition of The War of the Worlds: H. G. Wells's Scientific Romance* (Bloomington, IN: Indiana University Press, 1993), p. 204.

24 See Laura Marcus, 'Literature and Cinema' in Laura Marcus and Peter Nicholls (eds), *The Cambridge History of Twentieth-Century English Literature* (Cambridge: Cambridge University Press, 2005), pp. 335–58, especially 338. Susan Hayward also argues that cinematic narrative is woven together from some quintessentially Wellsian paradoxes. Like magic, 'cinema makes absence presence ... It is also about temporal illusion in that the film's narrative unfolds in the present even though the entire film text is prefabricated (the past is made present). Cinema constructs a reality out of selected sounds and images.' (See her *Cinema Studies: The Key Concepts* (London: Routledge, 2000), p. 1.)

25 Letter of 4 December 1898, in *The Collected Letters of Joseph Conrad* (five vols), ed. Frederick R. Karl and Laurence Davies (Cambridge: Cambridge University Press, 1988–96), Vol. 2, pp. 126–27. (See also Chapter 2.) Allardyce Nicoll also thought cinema, unlike the stage, equally mimetic of the fantastic and the real (see his *Film and Theatre* (London: Harrap, 1936), pp. 187–89). Christie stresses its dual nature as simultaneously 'literal and intensively suggestive' (*Last Machine*, pp. 12–13).

26 Wells's views on the paradoxical grounding of the fantastic events in a mimetic technique were expressed in the preface to a reissue of his scientific romances: 'For the writer of fantastic stories to help the reader to play the game properly, he must help him in every possible unobtrusive way to *domesticate* the impossible hypothesis. He must trick him into an unwary concession to some plausible assumption and get on with the story while the illusion holds.' (See H. G. Wells, *The Scientific Romances of H. G. Wells* (London: Gollancz, 1933), p. viii.)

27 Méliès's account is quoted in John Wakeman, *World Film Directors*, Vol. I (New York: H.W. Wilson, 1987), p. 750. The classic statement of the 'dual tradition' argument is in David Bordwell's *'Citizen Kane', Film Comment*, Vol. VII, no. 2 (Summer 1971), pp. 38–47, especially 39. However, stop-motion substitution had already been used for the beheading in *The Execution of Mary, Queen of Scots*, shot for Edison's kinetoscope around August–September 1894 (see Stephen Herbert and Luke MacKernan (eds), *Who's Who of Victorian Cinema: A Worldwide Survey* (London: BFI, 1996), p. 116).

28 For early dis/appearance films, see Lucy Fisher, 'The Lady Vanishes: Magic and

the Movies', in John R. Fell (ed.), *Film Before Griffith* (Cambridge, MA: Harvard University Press, 1983), pp. 339–54, especially 339.

29 As Wells wrote in 1934, 'Hitherto, except in exploration fantasies, the fantastic element was brought in by magic ... But by the end of the last century it had become difficult to squeeze even a momentary belief out of magic any longer ... an ingenious use of scientific patter might with advantage be substituted. That was no great discovery. I simply brought the fetish stuff up to date, and made it as near actual theory as possible. As soon as the magic trick has been done the whole business is to keep everything else human and real.' (Preface to *Scientific Romances of H. G. Wells*, pp. viii–ix.)

30 Albert J. La Valley, 'Traditions of Trickery: The Role of Special Effects in the Science Fiction Film', in George Slusser and Eric S. Rabkin (eds), *Shadows of the Magic Lamp: Fantasy and Science Fiction in Film* (Carbondale: Southern Illinois University Press, 1985), pp. 141–58, especially 145–46.

31 La Valley, 'Traditions of Trickery', pp. 146–47.

32 See Garrett Stewart, 'The "Videology" of Science Fiction', in Slusser and Rabkin (eds), *Shadows of the Magic Lamp*, pp. 159–207.

33 La Valley, 'Traditions of Trickery', p. 144.

34 See Marcus, 'Literature and Cinema', in Marcus and Nicholls (eds), *Cambridge History of Twentieth-Century English Literature*, p. 337.

35 Wells adopted C. H. Hinton's term 'scientific romance' (see Chapter 1, note 1). For the origins of the term 'science fiction' (which goes back at least as far as William Wilson's treatise about the 'poetry of science', but was first used in the modern sense in 1929 by American Hugo Gernsback, editor of *Amazing Stories*), see Edward James, *Science Fiction in the Twentieth Century* (Oxford: Oxford University Press, 1994), pp. 7–8.

36 From 1891 *Strand Magazine* and its picture companion carried all sorts of pioneering photographic articles about modernity: exotic tours, electric lighting and the life history of commodities, new forms of transport (monorails and proto-Zeppelins) and communications (submarine cables, the latest apparatuses for recording and amplifying sound), the behaviour of urban crowds, etc. *Strand*'s regular photo section, 'Curiosities', featured defamiliarising close-ups submitted by readers (e.g., shot directly down a rifle barrel). Its publisher, George Newnes, was a passionate camera user and ran his own photo-agency. Fascinated with inventions, Newnes narrowly missed being instrumental in creating cinema (he was advised against investing in Wordsworth Donisthorpe's 1889 patent 'kinesigraph'). Both he and C. Arthur Pearson did back the Mutoscope and Biograph Syndicate in 1899, envisioning it as the future medium for illustrated journalism in Britain, though their plans for 'home mutoscopes' to display current events failed to catch on. Newnes also financed the filming of an Antarctic expedition that year (see Herbert and McKernan (eds), *Who's Who of Victorian Cinema*, p. 101).

37 Introduction to *The Country of the Blind and Other Stories*, repr. in *CSS*, pp. 873–74.

38 H. G. Wells, *The King Who Was A King: The Book of a Film* (London: Ernest Benn, 1929), p. 11. (Henceforth all page references to *The King Who Was a King* (*KWWAK*) will be given in brackets in the text.)

39 Wells admitted he was belatedly coming to the professional craft of filmwriting but 'thought it was worth while to come in before it was too late to try [his] hand at the new art'. He gave extravagant praise for the medium's potential as in *KWWAK* (see Chapter 4): 'I think it is the very greatest art, with the possibility of becoming the greatest art form that has ever existed. What I think is so extraordinary in the last four or five years is the way in which voice production has reached a point of perfection

and the photographing of the face for dramatic effect – so that you can have more personal drama on the film than you can have on the stage ... it seems to me that the film is likely to oust both the opera and the stage in the long run.' Wells was determined to explore the latent possibilities in film form, which he had not realised at the beginning.

Asked about whether film would replace the novel, Wells replied: 'I should think it would have a very considerable reaction – I do think it will develop a literary collateral of the stage or novel. I think a time will come when it will be possible to write treatments in such a way that they will be read as plays are read', with the reader visualising the scene and action on their own internal screens, as it were. (The interview was reprinted in the British version of *The Era* (11 Dec. 1935), p. 20 under the title 'Shape of Wells to Come: Korda's New Assistant and the American Press'). However, Margery Rowland's riposte put up a spirited defence of stage drama as a non-naturalistic mode, nonetheless dependent on physical presence (see 'Mr Wells is Wrong: You Cannot Compare Stage and Screen,' *Era* (11 Dec. 1935), p. 3).

40 See Tim Armstrong, *Modernism, Technology and the Body* (Cambridge: Cambridge University Press, 1998), especially pp. 77–105.

41 As part of defending his return to 'cinematic' writing in the late 1920s, Wells argued that the divisive notions of High- and Low-brow 'need to be supplemented by Broad-brow', so that their complementary prejudices about being 'cheap and obvious', on the one hand, and 'arty', on the other, could be subsumed in an engagement with the medium *simultaneously* popular and formally innovative (See Introduction to KWWAK, p. 22)

42 'As the still underrated H. G. Wells put it, 'the frame within which the writer sees "reality" has splintered and got into the picture'. (Dennis Potter, 'Realism and Non-Naturalism 2', *The Official Programme of the Edinburgh International Television Festival 1977* (Aug. 1977), p. 36.) Potter referred indirectly to Wells's socially critical view of the implicit ideological investments which Victorian culture made in the seamless illusion of bourgeois realism: 'Throughout the broad smooth flow of nineteenth-century life in Great Britain, the art of fiction floated on this same assumption of social fixity. The novel in English was produced in an atmosphere of security for the entertainment of secure people who liked to feel established and safe and good. Its standards were established within that apparently permanent frame and the criticism of it began to be irritated and perplexed, through a new instability, the splintering frame began to get into the picture. I suppose for a time I was the outstanding instance among writers of fiction in English of the frame getting into the picture.' (H. G. Wells, *Experiment in Autobiography*, Vol. 2, pp. 494–95.)

43 H. G. Wells, 'The Literature of the Future', *Pall Mall Gazette* (11 Oct. 1893), p. 3.

44 For ekphrasis's history, see Valerie Robillard and Els Jongeneel (eds.), *Pictures Into Words: Theoretical and Descriptive Approaches to Ekphrasis* (Amsterdam: VU University Press, 1998), especially Introduction, pp. ix–x.

45 Greek *eidetikos* – 'belonging to an image' – from *eidos*, 'form'.

46 See 'A Camera Man', in *Life and Letters* Vol. 2, no. 12 (May 1929), pp. 336–43; repr. as 'Sinclair Lewis' in E. M. Forster, *Abinger Harvest* (London: Arnold, 1936), pp. 127–33, especially 132.

47 Wells's 'uncle' discussed the retoucher's transformative art – 'They are the fairies of photography and fill our albums with winsome changelings.' (See H. G. Wells, 'The Art of Being Photographed' (*Pall Mall Gazette* (1 Dec. 1893), repr. in *Select Conversations With an Uncle* (London: John Lane, 1895), pp. 23–32, especially 27–28.

48 Bailey, '"There Would Presently Come Out of the Darkness"', pp. 20–21.

49 See Grahame Smith, *Dickens and the Dream of Cinema* (Manchester: Manchester University Press, 2003); also Eisenstein, 'Dickens, Griffith and the Film Today' (in Eisenstein, *The Film Form: Essays in Film Theory*, ed. and trans. Jay Leyda (London: Dennis Dobson, 1963), pp. 195–265. For numerous other anticipations of film's discursive strategies by nineteenth-century writers, see Alan J. Spiegel, *Fiction and the Camera Eye* (Charlottesville: University of Virginia Press, 1976) and John R. Fell, *Film and the Narrative Tradition* (Norman: University of Oklahoma Press, 1975).

50 *Longman's Magazine* I (Feb. 1883), pp. 439–62, especially 442 and 462. (Also repr. in Laura Otis (ed.), *Literature and Science in the Nineteenth Century: An Anthology* (Oxford University Press, 2002), pp. 84–87).

51 Wells, *KWWAK*, p. 9.

52 The links between series photography and cinema have been extensively historicised in, among others: Gordon Hendricks, *Eadweard Muybridge: The Father of the Motion Picture* (London: Secker and Warburg, 1977); Rebecca Solnit, *Motion Studies: Time, Space and Eadweard Muybridge* (London: Bloomsbury, 2003); Marta Braun, *Picturing Time: The Work of Étienne-Jules Marey* (Chicago and London: University of Chicago Press, 1992). Stephen Herbert (ed.), *A History of Pre-Cinema*, three vols (London and New York: Routledge, 2000), Vol. I, pp. 39–217, reproduces key images and facsimile documents.

53 Quoted in Paul Israel, *Edison: A Life of Invention* (New York: John Wiley, 1998), p. 292.

54 Also at the 1900 Paris Expo was the Phono-Cinéma-Théâtre, which featured short stage performances by leading stage and opera stars of the time, including Sarah Bernhardt as Hamlet, using film synchronised with the recording cylinder. Léon Gaumont's Chronophone system, which filmed performers miming to music, was developed as early as 1902. Charles Pathé doggedly pursued sound with opera and music-hall '*phonoscènes*' between 1904 and 1912. By 1913, hundreds of German cinemas were equipped with Oskar Messter's pioneering 'Biophon' synchronised sound system (see Herbert and McKernan (eds), *Who's Who of Victorian Cinema*, especially p. 97).

55 Accepted by most film historians, this nonetheless remains contested as fact. Although the Lumières gave their first public demonstration (to the Société d'Encouragement de l'Industrie Nationale, Paris on 22 March), Christopher Rawlence for example, alleges that cinema was actually invented by another Frenchman, Augustin le Prince, who screened moving pictures as early as 1888 in Leeds (see his *The Missing Reel: The Untold Story of the Lost Inventor of Moving Pictures* (London: Collins, 1991)). English inventor Wordsworth Donisthorpe filed a provisional patent in 1876 for the 'Kinesigraph', a device for printing photographs on a continuous strip, to animate them. He proposed combining his apparatus with Edison's Phonograph in *Nature* in January 1878 (see Herbert and McKernan (eds), *Who's Who of Victorian Cinema*, pp. 42–43). Bradford electrical engineer, Cecil Wray, patented a prototype lantern/prism device for projecting kinetoscope pictures on 3 January 1895. Undoubtedly, individuals in many countries were converging on the same technical breakthrough.

56 Cook, *Narrative Film*, p. 1.

57 The 55th London Film Society programme (Apr. 1932), which Wells may have seen, featured *The Eyes of Science* (1930). This echoed Proctor's prophetic words and marked the extent to which advanced optical processes had come to assist scientific research (see *The Film Society Programmes: 1925–1939*, prepared under the direction of the Council of the London Film Society (New York: Arno Press, 1972), p. 223).

58 Wells would eventually see the London Film Society's regular screenings of 'bionomic' films, which involved time-lapse and X-rays to picture the growth and

functions of organisms, natural forms and the human body. The Institut Marey's own *Studies in Rapid Motion* were shown in its seventh programme (Apr. 1926) (see *Film Society Programmes*, p. 26). Virgilio Tosi's *Cinema Before Cinema: The Origins of Scientific Cinematography*, trans. Sergio Angelini (London: British Universities' Film and Video Council, 2005), is the most comprehensive recent study of the roots and forms of early science films.

59 See Christie, *Last Machine*, pp. 99–102.

60 Wells mentions Lilienthal in the context of the 'alien' technology of the Martian flying machine (see *The War of the Worlds* (*WOTW*), p. 1129). *When the Sleeper Wakes*'s chapter 'The Äeropile' also opens with a reference to him, along with other key aviation pioneers (see p. 139).

61 See H. G. Wells, *When the Sleeper Wakes* (1899; London: Dent, 1994), pp. 150–51; also *The War in the Air* (1908; London: Penguin, 2005), p. 11. (Henceforth, all page references to *When the Sleeper Wakes* (*WTSW*) and *The War in the Air* (*WITA*) will be given in brackets in the text.) For more detailed suggestions about cinematic aerial perspectives in this text, see David Seed, 'British Modernists Encounter the Cinema', in Seed (ed.), *Literature and the Visual Media* (Cambridge: D. S. Brewer, 2005), pp. 48–73, especially 63.

62 For the 'operational aesthetic' and technology in early film, see Christie, *Last Machine*, pp. 18–19.

63 These all appeared in the same numbers of *Pearson's Magazine* serialising *WOTW* (Apr.–Dec. 1897), as well as visual distortions using 'A Magic Mirror' and proto-surrealist montages of infants ('Babyland').

64 See the Introduction to *KWWAK*, especially pp. 8–10.

65 Repr. in Geduld (ed.), *Definitive Time Machine*, Appendix I, pp. 135–52, especially 143.

66 Geduld (ed.), *Definitive Time Machine*, p. 158.

67 See Geduld (ed.), *Definitive Time Machine*, p. 176.

68 *Saturday Review*, no. 81 (9 May 1896), pp. 471–72. William Kingdom Clifford also described the camera as 'merely an eye made of glass with a sensitive plate instead of a retina' (*Seeing and Thinking* (London: Macmillan, 1879), p. 45).

69 See Geduld (ed.), *Definitive Time Machine*, p. 166. Significantly, one of *TM*'s key influences, Edwin A. Abbot's *Flatland: A Romance of Many Dimensions, by A Square* (London: Seely & Co, 1884), is about the potential of altered perception. Its hero tries to persuade his fellow planar beings to believe in the existence of a third, creating an amusing analogy to our own blindness to possible dimensions beyond our own three-dimensional vision.

70 See David Y. Hughes and Robert M. Philmus, 'A Selective Bibliography (with Abstracts) of H. G. Wells's Science Journalism 1887–1901', in Darko Suvin and Robert M. Philmus (eds), *H. G. Wells and Modern Science Fiction* (Lewisburg, PA: Bucknell University Press; London: Associated University Presses, 1977), pp. 191–222, especially 193.

71 See J. D. Beresford, *H. G. Wells: A Critical Biography* (London: Nisbet, 1915), pp. 10–11 and 31–33.

72 Van Wyck Brooks, *The World of H. G. Wells* (New York and London: T. Fisher Unwin, 1915), pp. 25–28.

73 H. G. Wells, 'The Rediscovery of the Unique', *Fortnightly Review*, no. 56 (July 1891), repr. in Robert M. Philmus and David Y. Hughes, *H. G. Wells: Early Writings in Science and Science Fiction*, (Berkeley, Los Angeles, London: University of California Press, 1975), pp. 22–31, especially 30. Frequent allusions in other stories show Wells's fondness

for the subject as both metaphor and effect. Indeed, many of them, as Hammond comments, can be read as 'dissolving views' of normal reality transparently overlapped by, or fading out into, shadowy parallel universes of uncertainty, which defamiliarise the one we take for granted (see J. R. Hammond, *H. G. Wells and the Short Story* (Basingstoke: Macmillan, 1992), p. 26).

74 For the lantern's history, see Barbara Main Stafford and Frances Terpak, *Devices of Wonder: From the World in a Box to Images on Screen* (Los Angeles: Getty Publications, 2001), pp. 297–307; for its cultural prominence, Judith Flanders, *Consuming Passions: Leisure and Pleasure in Victorian Britain* (London: Harper Press, 2006), especially pp. 310–12.

75 H. G. Wells, *The Future in America: A Search After Realities* (London: Chapman and Hall, 1906), pp. 6–7.

76 See H. G. Wells, *Star Begotten: A Biological Fantasia* (London: Chatto and Windus, 1937), p. 4.

77 'It can be assumed that it is this wish which prepares the long history of cinema ... to construct a simulation machine capable of offering the subject perceptions which are really representations mistaken for perceptions.' (See Jean-Louis Baudry, 'The Apparatus: Metapsychological Approaches to the Impression of Reality in Cinema', in P. Rosen (ed.), *Narrative, Apparatus, Ideology: A Film Theory Reader* (New York: Columbia University Press, 1986), pp. 299–318, especially 315.)

78 See Geduld (ed.), *Definitive Time Machine*, p. 144. For the ambiguous symbolism of Moses Nebogipfel's 'visionary' name, see H. G. Wells, *The Time Machine: An Invention, A Critical Text of the 1898 London First Edition*, ed. Leon Stover (Jefferson, NC and London: McFarland, 2001), Appendix 1, p. 175.

79 Clifford, *Seeing and Thinking*, pp. 33–34.

80 Kate Flint, *The Victorians and the Visual Imagination* (Cambridge: Cambridge University Press, 2000), p. 283.

81 For Jean Baudrillard's explanation of media simulations as 'the real's hallucinatory resemblance to itself', i.e. that their discourses create a 'hyperreality', at once apparently indistinguishable from actuality and artificially constructed, see his *Selected Writings*, ed. M. Poster (Cambridge: Polity, 1988), pp. 145–47.

82 Christie, *Last Machine*, p. 13.

83 *Dante Gabriel Rossetti: Collected Poetry and Prose*, ed. Jerome McGann (New Haven, CT and London: Yale University Press, 2003), pp. 345–62, especially 347, line 1, and 360, lines 11–12.

84 Paul Virilio refers to the Lumières' *L'Entrée d'un train en gare* in this way in his 'The Last Vehicle', in D. Kampfer and C. Wulf (eds), *Looking Back on the End of the World* (New York: Semiotext(e), 1989), pp. 90–110, especially 110. See also Anne Friedberg, *Window Shopping: Cinema and the Postmodern* (Berkeley, CA: University of California Press, 1993), pp. 2–3.

85 These were usually displays or sets in buildings incorporating all the proto-cinematic technology of stereoscopic illusion (significantly, photographic pioneer Louis Daguerre played a prominent part in their development) including back-lit images painted on semi-transparent screens, realistic backdrops and moving effects of perspective and depth of visual field, to 'transport' the spectator to an elsewhere or elsewhen, historical, topical or fantastic. (For further details of their construction and cultural significance, see Stafford and Terpak, *Devices of Wonder*, pp. 315–24; also Flanders, *Consuming Passions*, especially pp. 252–53 and 263–71.)

86 'I have been prowling about the North of France on a bicycle and paying a visit to the Exposition.' (Letter 'To Elizabeth Healey' (24 May 1900) in David C. Smith

(ed.), *Correspondence of H. G. Wells*, Vol. I (London: Pickering and Chatto, 1998), p. 355.)

87 For Wells, Paul and these attractions, see (among others) Raymond Fielding, 'Hale's Tours: Ultrarealism in the Pre-1910 Motion Picture,' in Fell (ed.), *Film Before Griffith*, pp. 116–30, especially pp. 118–19. Also Herbert and McKernan (eds), *Who's Who of Victorian Cinema*, pp. 111 and 60–61, respectively.

88 See Christopher Frayling, *Mad, Bad and Dangerous to Know? The Scientist and the Cinema* (London: Reaktion, 2005), p. 56.

89 See Ramsaye, *Million and One Nights*, p. 429.

90 Christie, *Last Machine* pp. 27–28.

91 The opening title promised 'to guide your minds across the chasm of years' so that 'you too' could dream of being 'citizens of that great city of death'.

92 E. Burton Holmes was one of the first to introduce moving pictures into his lantern lectures in 1897, also coining the term travelogue (coincidentally the origin of the French term *'documentaire'*).

93 From the 1860s onwards, magic lantern slides frequently signified multi-temporality or overlapping states of consciousness by superimposing or inserting images (often using early photo-montage techniques) to visualise thoughts or fantasies of characters in the main scene, about something happening simultaneously elsewhere, or in the past or future (see, for example, reproductions in Herbert (ed.), *A History of Pre-Cinema*, 3 vols, Vol. III, p. 117; also Maureen Turim, *Flashbacks in Film: Memory and History* (London: Routledge, 1989), pp. 23–25.)

94 'A Conversation with Leo Tolstoy', in Jay Leyda (ed.), *Kino: A History of the Russian and Soviet Film* (London: Allen and Unwin, 1960), pp. 410–11.

95 American production soon relocated to an obscure industrial suburb of Los Angeles, called Hollywood, because California's favourable climate and diverse geography meant virtually any location in the world could be simulated there (see Cook, *Narrative Film*, p. 37).

96 Christie, *Last Machine*, pp. 53–54.

97 Coates, 'Chris Marker', p. 308.

98 For cinema's industrialisation of theatrical fame, see Paul McDonald, *The Star System: Hollywood's Production of Popular Identities* (London and New York: Wallflower, 2000), especially pp. 15–16.

99 See her 'Mary Elizabeth Coleridge: Literary Influence and Technologies of the Uncanny', in Julian Wolfreys (ed.), *Victorian Gothic: Literary and Cultural Manifestations in the Nineteenth Century* (Basingstoke: Macmillan, 2000), pp. 109–28, especially 109–10.

100 The SPR was founded in Cambridge by moral philosopher Henry Sidgwick and classicist Frederic Myers. Wells venerated several members (somewhat ironically) for their 'practical' psychology and mesmerism in *WTSW*'s imagined future (p. 152), including William James and Gurney and Myers, of *Phantasms of the Living*. The *Journal of the Society for Psychical Research* exposed countless fake mediums, but nonetheless pursued the grail of definitive evidence for paranormal phenomena. The SPR's history was documented in Harry Price, *Fifty Years of Psychical Research: A Critical Survey* (London: Longman's Green, 1939). Price summarised findings on 'Broadcasting and the Occult' (including radio transmissions from 'haunted' houses and spiritualism and the BBC) and 'Cinematography and Psychical Research' (especially evidence from *séances* caught on film), on pp. 263–74 and 236–39, respectively.

101 Flint, *Victorians and the Visual*, p. 37.

102 See Marina Warner's introduction to H. G. Wells, *TM*, p. xx.

103 H. G. Wells, *The Invisible Man* (1897; London: Penguin, 2005), p. 32. (Henceforth,

all page references to *The Invisible Man* (*IM*) will be given in brackets in the text.)

104 See Jeffrey Sconce's *Haunted Media: Electronic Presence from Telegraphy to Television* (Durham, NC and London: Duke University Press, 2000), especially pp. 1–20; also Marina Warner, *Phantasmagoria*, pp. 13–14 and *passim*.

Myers invented the term 'telepathy' for thought transmission, probably alluding to the 'uncanny' distanciations of technology. This is also the psychic method of communication used by Wells's Martians (see *WOTW*, Book II, Chapter 2), despite his hostile review of Podmore's SPR study of such phenomena (see Chapter 1, note 57).

105 For X-rays and the paranormal, see Clément Chéroux et al., *The Perfect Medium: Photography and the Occult* (New Haven, CT and London: Yale University Press, 2005), pp. 115–16.

106 See, for example, 'The New Photography', in *British Medical Journal*, Vol. IX, no. 38 (1 Feb. 1896), pp. 289–90. Symptomatically, the story came first (see George Griffith, 'A Photograph of the Invisible', and H. J. W. Dam, 'A Wizard of Today', *Pearson's Magazine*, Vol. I, no. 4 (Apr. 1896), pp. 376–80 and 413–19.

107 See Herbert and McKernan (eds), *Who's Who of Victorian Cinema*, pp. 87–88.

108 Christie, *Last Machine* p. 111.

109 Wells's 1945 parodic self-demolition still connected his first scientific romance and its cinematic overtones with 'cloning' the human image, while answering charges about the logical absurdity of time travel: 'Otherwise it is plain common sense that a man might multiply himself indefinitely, pop a little way into the future and then come back. There would then be two of him. Repeat *da capo* and you have four, and so on, until the whole world would be full of this Time Travelling Individual's vain repetitions of himself.' (H. G. Wells, 'The Betterave Papers' (*The Cornhill Magazine*, no. 965 (July 1945), pp. 354–63), excerpted as 'A Complete Exposé of this Notorious Literary Humbug', in J. R. Hammond (ed.), *H. G. Wells Interviews and Recollections* (London and Basingstoke: Macmillan, 1980), pp. 108–17, especially 114.) The objection that the Time Traveller would duplicate himself was first made in Israel Zangwill's review (see his 'Without Prejudice', *Pall Mall Magazine*, no. 7 (Sept. 1895), pp. 151–60, repr. in Patrick Parrinder (ed.), *H. G. Wells: The Critical Heritage* (London: Routledge and Kegan Paul, 1972), pp. 40–42, especially 41).

110 For SPR research into visual doubling, see Marina Warner, *Fantastic Metamorphoses, Other Worlds: The Clarendon Lectures in English 2001* (Oxford: Oxford University Press, 2002), especially pp. 201–2. Forms of 'otherness' and their secret relationship with the identity of the self are endemic in Wells's fiction. Linda Dryden has recently shown the extent of Wells's participation in the late-Victorian cult of the double, not just through character psychology, but also through the 'schismatic worlds' he created. She also notes how the subject became technologised (see her *The Modern Gothic and Literary Doubles: Stevenson, Wilde and Wells* (Houndmills: Palgrave, 2003), especially pp. 23 and 28).

111 Christie, *Last Machine*, p. 62.

112 On the simulatory tyranny of the camera's gaze, Wells wrote: 'the unwinking Cyclops eye of the instrument ... and its attendant. They make what they will of us ... So history is falsified before our faces, and we prepare a lie for our grand children.' (Wells, 'Art of Being Photographed', pp. 31–32.)

113 See Georg Simmel, *The Metropolis and Mental Life* (1903), in *Simmel on Culture: Selected Writings*, eds David Frisby and Mike Featherstone (London: Sage, 1997), pp. 174–85.

114 Christie, *Last Machine*, p. 11.

115 For the factors in Hollywood's rise, see Cook, *Narrative Film*, p. 41.

116 Christie, *Last Machine*, pp. 141–42.
117 See note 81.
118 See Herbert and McKernan (eds), *Who's Who of Victorian Cinema*, pp. 44–45.
119 See Walter Lippmann, *Public Opinion* (London: Allen and Unwin, 1929), pp. 14–19.
120 Vladimir Ilyich Lenin, quoted in Ivor Montagu, *Film World* (Harmondsworth: Penguin, 1964), p. 108.
121 Christie, *Last Machine*, p. 142.
122 Although many of these devices were pioneered by British film-makers such as G. A. Smith and James Williamson of the 'Hove School' and other Americans, such as Edwin S. Porter, Griffith integrated them into a fully cinematic 'grammar'. Béla Balázs famously summarised the principles that Griffith brought together to create the 'language of film', many of which find correspondences in Wells's own narrative presentation of space and time:

'1. Varying distance between spectator and scene within one and the same scene; hence varying dimensions of scenes that can be accommodated within the frame and composition of a picture.

2. Division of the integral picture of the scene into sections, or 'shots'.

3. Changing angle, perspective and focus of 'shots' within one and the same scene.

4. Montage, that is the assembly of 'shots' in a certain order in which not only whole scene follows whole scene (however shot) but pictures of smallest details are given, so that the whole scene is composed of a mosaic of frames aligned as it were in chronological sequence.' (Béla Balázs, *Theory of the Film* (London: Dennis Dobson, 1953), p. 31.)

123 Quoted in Pierre Sorlin, *The Film in History: Restaging the Past* (Oxford: Blackwell, 1980), pp. viii–ix. An early French cinema show which specialised in (re)presenting famous events was known as the *'Historiographe'* (see Herbert and McKernan (eds), *Who's Who of Victorian Cinema*, p. 39), perhaps recalling Mouton's imaginary historioscope, which can literally see into the past.

124 Cook, *Narrative Film*, p. 70.

The London Film Society programme of November 1929 referred to the method of Soviet montage in *Potemkin* as 'incitement to hysteria by means of rhythmic cutting' (see London Film Society, *Film Society Programmes*, p. 131).

125 See Friedberg, *Window Shopping*, pp. 2–3.

Chapter 1
Optical Speculations in the Early Writings

1 Significantly, Wells's term derived from Charles Henry Hinton, *Scientific Romances* which contained the 1884 essay 'What is the Fourth Dimension?' (London: Swan Sonnenschein, 1888), pp. 3–32, a specific influence on the defamiliarisation of vision in *TM*. However, a pseudonymous letter by 'S' responding to a review of Hinton's pamphlet (see Anon., 'Scientific Romances', *Nature* (12 Mar. 1885), p. 431), first raised the idea of the fourth dimension as what 'we may call time-space' (see 'S', 'Four-Dimensional Space', *Nature* (26 Mar. 1885), p. 481), anticipating Hermann Minkowski's formulation of the concept in his 1907 *Space and Time*, which provided Einstein with a basis for relativity. Wells certainly read *Nature* at the Normal School of Science. S's letter could have been the work of a fellow student, or even Wells himself (see

Introduction to Nicholas Ruddick (ed.), *The Time Machine: An Invention* (Peterborough, Ont.: Broadview, 2001), p. 24). Wells recalled that discussions at his student debating society, helped him lay hold 'of the idea for a four-dimensional frame for a fresh apprehension of phenomena' (*Experiment in Autobiography*, Vol. I, p. 214). (His fellow student E. A. Hamilton Gordon's paper 'The Fourth Dimension' is repr. in Ruddick, *Time Machine*, pp. 219–20.) However, the idea of time as the fourth dimension had been raised as far back as 1754 (see Russell, 'Time Before and After', pp. 24–40, especially 28–29.)

2 See Christie's chapter on this in *Last Machine*, pp. 15–37.

3 'S' also exemplifies four-dimensionality by imagining the visual continuum of an individual life in a way suggesting the overlapping images of chronophotography: 'Let any man picture to himself the aggregate of his own bodily forms from birth to the present time, and he will have a clear idea of a sur-solid in time-space' (see 'S', 'Four-Dimensional Space', *Nature* (26 Mar. 1885), p. 481).

4 Robert M. Philmus and David Y. Hughes argue that Wells may have derived his concept of dynamic temporality as a dimension of consciousness from William James (see Philmus and Hughes (eds), *H. G. Wells: Early Writings in Science and Science Fiction*, p. 48, note 4). James's famous chapter 'The Perception of Time' is certainly suggestive of both the vehicular means and paradoxical visual effect in time-travelling: 'In short, the practically cognized present is no knife-edge, but a saddle-back, with a certain breadth of its own on which we sit perched, and from which we look in two directions into time. The unit of composition of our perception of time is a *duration*, with a bow and a stern, as it were – a rearward – and a forward-looking end …

'Suppose we were able, within the length of a second, to note 10,000 events distinctly, instead of barely 10, as now; if our life were then destined to hold the same number of impressions, it might be 1,000 times as short. We should live less than a month, and personally know nothing of the change of seasons … The motions of organic beings would be so slow to our senses as to be inferred, not seen. The sun would stand still in the sky, the moon would be almost free from change, and so on. But now reverse the hypothesis and suppose a being to get only 1000th part of the sensations that we get in a given time, and consequently to live 1000 times as long. Winters and summers will be to him like quarters of an hour. Mushrooms and swifter-growing plants will shoot into being so rapidly as to appear instantaneous creations; annual shrubs will rise and fall from the earth like restlessly-boiling water springs; the motions of animals will be as invisible as are to us the movements of bullets and cannon-balls; the sun will scour through the sky like a meteor, leaving a fiery trail behind him.' (*The Principles of Psychology*, Vol. 1 (New York: Henry Holt; London: Macmillan, 1890), pp. 609 and 639.) And cf. 'slow-motion' in 'The New Accelerator'.

5 Geduld (ed.), *Definitive Time Machine*, p. 36.

6 Geduld (ed.), *Definitive Time Machine*, p. 158.

7 Coates also compares both the Invisible Man and the Time Traveller to film viewers (see Coates, 'Chris Marker', pp. 308–9).

8 In Pal's film version, Mrs Watchett's accelerated motion is projected, accompanied by tinkling piano, in a way which deliberately alludes to the novelty effects of early silents or even the kinetoscope (see Chapter 5).

9 'The alternation of light and darkness resembles the effect of a projector's maltese cross movements revealing a movie image projected at less than silent speed (16 frames per second).' (Geduld (ed.), *Definitive Time Machine*, p. 100.)

10 See also Wells's instructions to the film-makers of *TTC* which recall this passage in Chapter 4.

11 Surprisingly, Wells's accelerated lunar ecology was omitted from Ray Harryhausen's special effects for Nathan Juran's 1964 film, although Méliès had suggested it with stop-motion and theatrical props.

12 Early reviewers of the novella were impressed by the visual effects of time travel. See for example, Anon., 'Fiction', which quotes the famous passage from Chapter IV, commenting 'Could anything be more finely imagined or more admirably expressed'? (*Saturday Review*, no. 80 (20 July 1895), pp. 86–87.)

13 Ramsaye argued that 'she glided quietly' is particularly revealing, both for its characteristic motion and *absence* of sound. Wells seemed to ignore the fact that the Time Traveller, in recrossing the moment, should have experienced *both* sound and sight reversed (the latter having already been done in 'experimental reversals' of Edison's phonograph), as if Wells were deliberately mimicking silent film: 'It would seem pretty definite that the *Time Traveller* was all eyes and the story all motion picture.' (See *Million and One Nights*, pp. 153–54.)

14 Wells's framing narrator also considers the human future as 'black and blank', like an empty screen (*TM*, p. 91).

15 Kodak first marketed its portable camera in 1890, under the slogan 'You press the button, we do the rest.' (For the significance of the Kodak as symptom of changing paradigms of scientific evidence, see John Timberlake, 'Forgotten Cameras and Unknown Audiences: Photography, *The Time Machine* and The Atom Bomb', in David Cunningham, Andrew Fisher and Sas Mays (eds), *Photography and Literature in the Twentieth Century* (Newcastle: Cambridge Scholars Press, 2005), pp. 11–24.)

Wells may also allude topically to the evocative magnesium flash photography taken of the labyrinthine Paris sewers in 1892 by Vallot, following Nadar's pioneering use of arc-lamps thirty years before. This was the first time modern visual technology had documented the underground levels of a city, a social and spatial stratification appealing to Wells for obvious reasons (see Chris Howes, *To Photograph Darkness: The History of Underground and Flash Photography* (Carbondale: Southern Illinois University Press, 1990), pp. 1–17 and 145–47). The *Strand Magazine* featured a similar photo-reportage. See Anon., 'Underground London' (Vol. 16, no. 92 (Aug. 1898), pp. 138–47). Alternatively, Wells could be alluding to how social reformers had also been documenting the city's metaphorical 'abyss' with the camera, especially its labyrinthine poverty, criminality and exploitation (see Mary Warner Marien, *Photography: A Cultural History* (London: Laurence King, 2002), pp. 131–40).

16 Lindsay, *Art of the Moving Picture*, pp. 137–38.

17 See Virilio in Introduction.

18 Focusing on the optical details of the famous description of speeding through time ('I drew a breath ... room like a rocket' (*TM*, p. 41)), Ramsaye concluded, 'the evidence is such that if the story was not evolved directly from the experience of seeing the Kinetoscope, it was indeed an amazing coincidence'. (See *Million and One Nights*, pp. 152–53; also Geduld (ed.), *Definitive Time Machine*, p. 100, note 3.)

19 See Lez Cooke, 'British Cinema: From Cottage Industry to Mass Entertainment', in Clive Bloom (ed.), *Literature and Culture in Modern Britain, Volume One: 1900–1929* (London: Longman, 1993), pp. 167–88, especially 167.

20 Ramsaye, for example, quoted the *St Louis Post Dispatch* which marvelled at the kinetoscope's ability to petrify fleeting moments and, especially, run time backwards: 'The effect is said to be almost miraculous. In the process of eating food is taken from the mouth and placed on a plate.' The review also proclaimed that it seemed to make the 'wondrous vision' of *Lumen* 'possible to us' (*Million and One Nights*, pp. 159–60). Zangwill's review compared time travel with light-speed space-travel and its relativis-

tic visual effects (though without referring directly to Flammarion). Wells's hero's 'dealing in futures' might thus have avoided 'the fallacy of mingling personally in the panorama' of other times ('Without Prejudice', *Pall Mall Magazine*, no. 7 (September 1895), pp. 151–60, especially 154–55 (repr. in Ruddick, *Time Machine*, pp. 272–76). Though *TM* and *WOTW* were influenced by two of Flammarion's other books (*Omega: La Fin du monde* (1894) and *La Planète Mars* (1892), respectively), there is no indisputable evidence that Wells read *Lumen* (see Bernard Bergonzi, *The Early H. G. Wells: A Study of the Scientific Romances* (Manchester: Manchester University Press, 1961), pp. 74 and 133; Norman Mackenzie and Jeanne Mackenzie, *The Time Traveller: The Life of H. G. Wells* (London: Weidenfeld and Nicolson, 1973), p. 119).

21 The cinematograph's London debut included the reversed 'Demolition of a Wall' (see Cooke, 'British Cinema', p. 167; also Herbert and McKernan (eds), *Who's Who of Victorian Cinema*, p. 108.

22 Paul's patent (no. 19884) was filed on 24 October 1895. According to Ramsaye, his attention was first caught by the 1894 *National Observer* serialisation. Wells's 1924 letter to Ramsaye stated he couldn't remember details, though without denying that the negotiations happened (see Ramsaye, *Million and One Nights*, pp. 152–53).

23 Ramsaye, *Million and One Nights*, pp. 152–53 and 157.

24 Paul began by exhibiting his adapted version of the kinetoscope (which Edison failed to patent in Europe) at Earl's Court. Edison retaliated by cutting off the supply of films, forcing Paul also to develop a portable camera jointly with Birt Acres. Among the first British films, thus shot by Acres between February and June 1895 and exhibited by Paul at Olympia and the Alhambra Music Hall, were actualities such as *Bootblack at Work in a London Street* and *A Rough Sea at Dover*, but also probably the first British fiction photoplays, such as the recently rediscovered *Arrest of a Pickpocket*. Following the Lumières, Paul also devised a projector for mass screening, the 'Theatrograph' (first exhibited on 20 February 1896, at Finsbury Technical College, and later renamed the Animatographe). (For further details, see among others: John Barnes, *The Beginnings of Cinema in England 1894–1901*, Vol. 1: 1894–1896, revised edition (Exeter: Exeter University Press, 1998), pp. 21–56; Herbert and McKernan (eds), *Who's Who of Victorian Cinema*, pp. 107–8; Frank Gray, 'Innovation and Wonder: Robert Paul in 1896', in Frank Gray (ed.), *The Hove Pioneers and the Animal in Cinema* (Brighton: University of Sussex, 1996), pp. 19–23.)

25 Paul's application was reprinted by Ramsaye in *Million and One Nights*, pp. 155–57. Despite his initial lapse of memory, Wells later claimed that it 'anticipated most of the stock methods and devices of the screen drama' (see Introduction to *KWWAK*, p. 10). He again looked back on it as a lost opportunity (probably with tongue in cheek), in 1941, though this time claiming that they jointly planned to corner the technological basis of cinema itself: 'we took out a provisional patent that would have made us practically the ground landlords of the entire film industry. We nearly patented films! We did not go on with the patent. Happily. Otherwise, we would have found ourselves corruptingly rich, and a heavy incubus on the development of cinema ... I can't answer for Mr. Paul, but I have no doubt all that ill-gotten gain would have demoralized and wasted me completely.' ('The Man of Science as Aristocrat', *Nature*, no. 3729 (19 Apr. 1941), pp. 465–67, especially 467).

Paul did answer for himself. Firstly, in an 1896 interview with *The Era*: '[T]hat weird romance, "The Time Machine,"... had suggested an entertainment to him, of which animated photographs formed an essential part.' A room 'accommodating some hundred people', with oscillating seats would be plunged 'into Cimmerian darkness' with 'a wailing wind'. 'Although the audience actually moved but a few inches, the sensation would be that of journeying through time', with intermittent stoppages during which 'a wondrous picture would be revealed – the Animatographe, combined with panoramic effects.' 'Fantastic scenes of future ages' would first be shown, before the audience 'set forth upon its homeward journey', whereupon their conductor 'would regretfully intimate that he had over-shot the mark, and travelled into the past – cue for another series of pictures.' ('A Chat With Mr. R.W. Paul (By Our Special Commisioner)', *Era* (25 Apr. 1896), p. 17.)

Paul also replied to Wells in *Nature*, reminding him that their patent was less ambitious than the writer made out in 1941, presenting *TM*'s 'main incidents ... by means of animated photographs and dissolving views'. He also claimed that Wells *visited him* at his laboratory at 44 Hatton Gardens. Paul remembered Wells approving the project and talking of 'subjects suitable for the primeval scenes' (not featured in the text), before leaving without discussing future action or arranging to stay in contact. Besides the unresolved practical difficulty of projection, the project was sidelined by public delight in the sheer novelty of cinematography itself and Paul's own subsequent pioneering of narrative film. (See Letter to *Nature*, no. 3730 (17 May 1941), p. 610.)

Nonetheless, Ramsaye argued, they 'plainly had the idea of not only the cutback and close-up but also the fade-in and fade-out, the overlap-dissolving of scenes into each other and all of the other supplemental tonal effects' of atmospherics and lighting common in film by the mid-twenties. They 'forecast something infinitely more complex than any machine – no less than a whole art form' (*Million and One Nights*, pp. 157–58). (For further accounts of Paul's inspiration by Wells, see 'Paul's Time Machine', in Barnes, *Beginnings of Cinema in England*, Vol. 1, pp. 38–41; Christie, *Last Machine*, pp. 28–29; Geoffrey West, *H. G. Wells: A Sketch for a Portrait* (London: Gerald Howe, 1930), pp. 294–96).

26 In *TM*'s lost second version, Nebogipfel and companion are attacked by cavemen. In unpublished manuscript material (dated 4/10/[18]94.) the Time Traveller also overshoots the present into the Puritan era (see Geduld (ed.), *Definitive Time Machine*, p. 153 and Appendix VII, 184–88).

27 Jonathan Bignell, 'Another Time, Another Space: Modernity, Subjectivity, and *The Time Machine*', in Deborah Cartmell, I. Q. Hunter, Heidi Kaye and Imelda Whelehan (eds), *Alien Identities: Exploring Difference in Film and Fiction* (London: Pluto Press, 1999), pp. 87–103, especially 88.

28 Paul's letter to the *Bioscope* suggests there might have been technical problems realising the project: 'My scheme for reproducing Mr Wells' "Time Machine" ... involved machinery for giving spectators a pseudo-impression of movement through time, but at that date things were not ripe for such an exhibition.' (*Bioscope* (19 Feb. 1914), p. 743.)

29 Ramsaye, *Million and One Nights*, pp. 158–99.

30 Christie, *Last Machine*, p. 31.

31 Robert Crossley argues that of all the anticipations of special effects such as stop-motion in early Wells, the novella's description comes closest to the 'virtual reality' of placing readers in the saddle themselves for 'a rough and scary ride through time: hands manipulating the joystick, a blinking light painful to the eye, disorienting sound effects, nausea induced by the swaying of the machine, the persistent fear of falling and expectation of a crash' (see his 'Taking It as a Story: The Beautiful Lie of *The Time Machine*', in George Slusser, Patrick Parrinder and Danièle Chatelain (eds), *H. G. Wells's Perennial Time Machine: Selected Essays from the Centenary Conference 'The Time Machine: Past, Present and Future' Imperial College, London July 26–29, 1995* (Athens, GA and London: University of Georgia Press, 2001), pp. 12–26, especially 17). Alan Mayne

suggests how the Wells/Paul 'simulator' might be practically realised with today's CGI-based virtual reality technology (see his 'The Virtual Time Machine II', in *The Wellsian* no. 20 (Winter 1997), pp. 20–31, especially 27–30). Cf. Brooks Landon on cinema as virtual time travel in *The Aesthetics of Ambivalence: Rethinking Science Fiction Film in the Age of Electronic (Re)Production* (Westport, Connecticut, and London: Greenwood Press, 1992), pp. xiv–xvi and 74–83.

32 Bignell, 'Another Time, Another Space', p. 90.

33 See Erik Barnouw, *The Magician and the Cinema* (Oxford: Oxford University Press, 1981), p. 50; alternatively, Herbert and McKernan (eds), *Who's Who of Victorian Cinema*, p. 142.

34 Bignell, 'Another Time, Another Space', p. 92.

35 For Griffith's term, see Cook, *Narrative Film*, p. 55. The first temporal flashback by editing is often attributed to Griffith's *After Many Years* (1908) (see Don Fairservice, *Film Editing: History, Theory and Practice* (Manchester: Manchester University Press, 2001), p. 69). The OED online records the first use as noun in a filmic context in *Variety* (13 October 1916, 28/4): 'In other words the whole thing is a flash-back of the episodes leading up to her marriage.' However, it was already in use in both mechanics and physics at the turn of the twentieth century. Wells's earliest 'proto-cinematic' use of the idea occurs in 'The Chronic Argonauts' when the clergyman recollects his shock at encountering Nebogipfel's machine: 'immediately all that happened flashed back upon his mind' (See *Definitive Time Machine*, p. 147). *TM*'s overall 'framed' narrative structure can be regarded as a series of 'flashbacks'. Its 'basic narrative rhythm' is 'characterised by growing pace and compression' like film-editing (see Darko Suvin, *Metamorphoses of Science Fiction: On the Poetics and History of a Literary Genre* (New Haven, CT: Yale University Press, 1979), p. 231).

36 Jean-Louis Baudry, 'The Apparatus', p. 315.

37 See Introduction, note 16.

38 Paul might also have been alluding to Mitchell's 'The Clock that Went Backward'. In the fourteenth 'Treehouse of Horror' Hallowe'en episode of *The Simpsons*, '*Stop the World, I Want to Goof Off*' (itself a parody of a famous *Twilight Zone* treatment of the same theme), Bart and Millhouse find a Carrollesque stopwatch which allows them to freeze Springfield's time for similarly delinquent antics.

39 Slow motion would eventually be refined by taking more than the standard 16 (during the silent era) or (subsequently) 24 frames per second then projecting them at normal speed to prevent the flow of images breaking down. (Accelerated motion was achieved by the reverse process of low-speed photography.) James's psychological speculation about accelerated consciousness might also have prompted Wells to reorganise vision accordingly: 'Suppose we were able, within the length of a second, to note 10,000 events distinctly, instead of barely 10, as now; if our life were then destined to hold the same number of impressions, it might be 1,000 times as short ... The motions of organic beings would be so slow to our senses as to be inferred, not seen.' (James, *Principles of Psychology*, Vol. I, p. 639.)

40 Only the watchman atop the Eiffel Tower and passengers arriving by plane escape the ray's effects. The film employs both slow and accelerated motion, as well as freeze-framing. Annette Michelson explores the analogy between mad scientist and film-maker showing the powers of 'that crazy ray, which is the moving picture camera'. (See her 'Dr Crase and Mr Clair', in *October*, no. 11 (Winter, 1979), pp. 30–53, especially 43; also R. C. Dale, *The Films of René Clair*, Vol. I, *Exposition and Analysis* (Metuchen, NJ, and London: Scarecrow Press, 1986), pp. 15–28.)

41 Wells's collaborator, producer Alexander Korda, was instrumental in establishing

the working relationship between fellow Hungarian, Emeric Pressburger, and Michael Powell. *A Matter of Life and Death* was deliberately conceived with the same scale and artistry as *TTC*. (See Ian Christie, *Arrows of Desire: the Films of Michael Powell and Emeric Pressburger* (London: Faber, 1994), pp. 27–28 and 55–57.)

42 Slow-motion techniques were gradually refined into the so-called 'bullet-time' or 'time-slicing' effects of late twentieth-century high-tech features, such as the 'cyberpunk' *Matrix* (though pioneered by photographer Tim MacMillan in the 1980s). This is achieved by taking simultaneous shots from a surrounding battery of cameras to create an impression of three-dimensionality in objects and people frozen in an instant of movement. Subjects can be virtually rotated, as if the eye of the spectator were moving in a different time continuum, but within the same stereoscopic space, exactly like Wells's drugtakers.

43 Geduld argues that a similar effect is suggested by the 'eddying murmur' the Time Traveller hears as his machine starts up (*Definitive Time Machine*, pp. 42 and 100).

44 Bailey, '"There Would Presently Come Out of the Darkness"', p. 29.

45 Significantly, a special edition of *The Door in the Wall and Other Stories* was published in 1911. Jeffrey A. Wolin describes this as 'the first thoroughly integrated example of a photographically illustrated book' (see afterword to reprint (Boston: Godine, 1980), pp. 155–57). Symbolist photographer Alvin Langdon Coburn's semi-dissolved location exposures seem deliberately to draw attention to the photograph's ambiguous status between documentary authentication and poetic fabrication (see Laura Scurriatti, 'A Tale of Two Cities: H. G. Wells's *The Door in the Wall* Illustrated by Alvin Langdon Coburn', in Partington (ed.), *Wellsian: Selected Essays*, pp. 145–65; also Jane M. Rabb (ed.), *Literature and Photography, Interactions 1840–1990: A Critical Anthology* (Albuquerque, NM: University of New Mexico Press, 1995), pp. 122–25).

46 Cf. 'Mr Skelmersdale in Fairyland', likewise haunted by 'inappeasable hunger of the heart' after his vision of miniaturisation in a wondrous parallel world (*CSS*, pp. 456–66, especially 465).

47 Aldous Huxley's connection of the story with hallucinogenics as 'portals' into other states of consciousness may have been triggered by Wells's conviction that cinema could be both cultural narcotic or stimulant, depending on how it was used (see Aldous Huxley, *The Doors of Perception* (London: Chatto and Windus, 1954), p. 49).

48 'Clavopolis' is first visualised as an album of stills which then spring into life (*KWWAK*, pp. 95–96). Alberto Cavalcanti's documentary about the French capital, *Rien que les heures* (1926), uses a similar effect.

49 By the 1870s, James Clerk Maxwell had already laid the basis of broadcasting in his work on electromagnetism. Logie Baird first demonstrated television pictures in 1926, although the BBC did not begin the first regular transmission service from Alexandra Palace until a decade later.

50 Peter Murphy argues that Davidson behaves effectively like someone trapped inside a virtual-reality display helmet (see his 'A Novelist's Account of Visual Immersion – "vr" in the Writings of H. G. Wells', *Interactive Cinema –Panoramic Systems*, http://users.bigpond.net.au/virtual/reportxx.htm

51 The narrator's term for the condition is 'vision at a distance' (*CSS*, p. 70), very close to the root meanings of television (from Gk. *tele*, 'far' or 'distant', + Lat. *videre*, 'to see').

52 See T. P. Marinetti, 'Destruction of Syntax – Imagination Without Strings – Words in Freedom (1913)', in Umbro Apollonio (ed.), *Futurist Manifestos* (London: Thames and Hudson, 1973), pp. 95–106, especially 96.

53 Wells frequently resorted to the metaphor of the magic crystal as an optical

device, like cinema or television, with a potential for defamiliarising the everyday world or as a portal into other, though 'adjacent', realities (see, for example, *The World of William Clissold: A Novel at a New Angle* (London: Ernest Benn, 1926), p. 28). As Hammond comments, access to some viewer of this kind 'is never far from the surface of his fiction' (*Wells and the Short Story*, p. 25). Wells may have based his Martian device on a common Victorian optical toy called a 'peep egg viewer'. Sometimes known as alabaster eggs, these were effectively miniaturised, portable peepshows, often containing souvenir views which could be changed by turning a small lever (for further details and an illustration, see 'Peep Egg Viewer' (Interview with Dr Ralph Wileman, 24 July 2000), http://courses.ncssm.edu/gallery/collections/toys/html/exhibit08.htm) (I am grateful to Paul St George at London Metropolitan University, Computer Animation Department for this lead.)

54 Spectatorial wonder and credulity quickly became self-consciously incorporated into early film-making itself (see Tom Gunning, 'An Aesthetic of Astonishment: Early Film and the (In)credulous Spectator', in Leo Braudy and Marshall Cohen (eds), *Film Theory and Criticism: Introductory Readings* (Oxford: Oxford University Press, 1999), pp. 818–32).

55 Bessel in 'The Stolen Body' also tries to reach out into the other dimension, feeling 'as a kitten ... when it goes for the first time to pat its reflection in a mirror' (*CSS*, p. 519).

56 Significantly, a translator during 'the age of the dream palace' explained the Allegory of the Cave in a similar way: 'A modern Plato would compare his Cave to an underground cinema, where the audience watch the play of shadows thrown by the film passing before a light at their backs. The film itself is only an image of "real" things and events in the world outside the cinema.' (See Plato, *The Republic of Plato*, trans. Francis MacDonald Cornford (London: Oxford University Press, 1941), Chapter XXV, pp. 227–35 and note on p. 228.)

57 Edmund Parish, *Hallucinations and Illusions: A Study of the Fallacies of Perception* (London: Walter Scott, 1897), pp. 66–67.

58 See Flint, *Victorians and the Visual*, pp. 276–9. Wells reviewed Frank Podmore's *Apparitions and Thought Transference: An Examination of the Evidence for Telepathy* (London: Walter Scott, 1894). This considered 'Crystal Vision' in Chapter xv on 'Clairvoyance', pp. 351–70, especially 357–59. (Podmore continued to amass such evidence, including visions of 'alien' (if not extraterrestrial) landscapes, such as the Egyptian pyramids (see new and enlarged edition (London: Walter Scott, 1915), pp. 191–99). Though Podmore reached a similar conclusion to Parish, Wells attacked his scientific basis because his research was unverified by repeated experiment under controlled conditions (see Wells, 'Peculiarities of Psychical Research', *Nature*, no. 51 (6 Dec. 1894), pp. 121–22).

59 'until this day no representation could assure me of the past of a thing except by intermediaries; but with the Photograph, my certainty is immediate; no one in the world can undeceive me. The Photograph then becomes a bizarre *medium*, a new form of hallucination: false on the level of perception, true on the level of time ... a modest, *shared* hallucination (on the one hand "it is not there", on the other "but it has indeed been"): a mad image, chafed by reality.' (See Roland Barthes, *Camera Lucida*, trans. Richard Howard (1982; Frogmore: Fontana, 1984), p. 115.)

60 Wells had already speculated that, with research into sleep psychology, the time was approaching 'to bring the control of dreaming as a fine art into the realm of possibilities'. Future dreamers might be able to order up whatever scenario they wished to consume at a special institute. Still photographs of actualities could be transformed

into moving wish-fulfilment narratives of revenge, romance or escape, visualised in the sleeper's head ('The Dream Bureau', *Pall Mall Gazette* no. 57 (25 Oct. 1893), p. 3). This 'Dream Bureau' was made redundant by the 'waking visions' of the Dream Factory. The élite rule by mesmerising the population in the lost third version of *TM* (Chapter 3, note 6).

61 Anamorphic distortion of objects and people occurs most impressively in Karl Heinz Martin's *Von Morgen bis Mitternacht* (1920), F. W. Murnau's *Der letzte Mann* (1924), Ernö Metzner's *Überfall* (1928) and Alfred Abel's *Narkose* (1929). However, it also featured in novelty photography of the 1890s (as in distorted 'beauty portraits' accompanying Anon.,'Tragedies of a Camera', *Strand Magazine*, Vol. 16, no. 95 (Nov. 1898), the same number carrying Wells's 'The Stolen Body' (see note 76).

In *KWWAK*, Wells used an anamorphic effect of extreme elongation to the vanishing point to suggest defeat of nationalist politics and its symbols: '[The Foreign Secretary] stares blankly out of the picture, a superannuated type of man. His face grows longer. By the use of a distorting lens he is drawn slowly out to an extreme length and attenuation. The Royal Arms and the flag share his fate. So he vanishes' (*KWWAK*, p. 228).

62 For the spiral motif in Ruttmann, see my 'Symphonies of the Big City: Modernism, Cinema and Urban Modernity', in Paul Edwards (ed.), *The Great London Vortex: Modernist Literature and Art* (Bath: Sulis Press, 2003), pp. 34–35. Lang deliberately echoed this at a crucial moment in *M*, to symbolise the city's destruction of childlike innocence by perversely commodified desire.

63 The dreamer's name, 'Hedon' (as in 'hedonist'), suggests the medium's ambiguous ability to treat 'serious' subjects and gratify escapist impulses.

64 See Christie, *Last Machine*, p. 65. In the lost second version of *TM*, a woman's beauty is artificially preserved like the 'immortalised' image of film stars. Indeed, the whole ruling class are subject to this unnatural youth (see Chapter 3, note 6).

65 See Bergonzi, *Early H. G. Wells*, p. 16.

66 For Chapman's concept, see Introduction above.

67 Significantly, the Watchers also resemble the subterranean human tadpoles that Wells imagined as our culminating evolutionary form, after bodily organs and senses have been rendered redundant by 'prosthetic' machinery in his essay 'The Man of the Year Million', *Pall Mall Gazette*, no. 57 (6 Nov. 1893), p. 3, repr. in H. G. Wells, *Journal and Prophecy*, ed. Warren W. Wagar (London: Bodley Head, 1964), pp. 3–8, especially 8.

68 Hammond argues that Wells also puns on the English 'plait', i.e. pleat or zigzag fold, thus suggesting a world (again like film) virtually 'intertwined with our own' (see *Wells and the Short Story*, p. 96). Wells was still revisiting the topos of a photographic 'ghostland', lying 'squint' to normal visual reality as late as 1937 (see *Star Begotten*, p. 156).

69 For the medium as 'psychic camera' picking up rays from the electromagnetic spectrum visible only to the 'etheric body', see Arthur Conan Doyle, *Wanderings of a Spiritualist* (London: Hodder and Stoughton, 1921), pp. 35–36.

70 'The Inexperienced Ghost' was eventually adapted for comic relief in Alberto Cavalcanti's 1945 'portmanteau' horror film, *Dead of Night*.

71 Significantly Wells reworked 'Elvesham' as *The New Faust* (1936), subtitling it *A Film Story* (*Nash's Pall Mall* (Dec. 1936), pp. 124–45) (see below, Chapter 4). It also seems to anticipate the bizarre scenario of Spike Jonze's *Being John Malkovich* (2000), a satire of celebrity, where bodies are literally hired out to other consciousnesses, ending in a dizzying vision of serial immortality.

72 Wells used a similar effect of abrupt recession to the vanishing point in 'How Gabriel Became Thompson' (1894). After Gabriel's plans to educate his wife collapse, 'The New Reformation receded through an illimitable perspective to the smallest speck' (*CSS*, pp. 793–801, especially 800).

73 Max Cowper's one original illustration also emphasised the Regent Street location and featured a mirror behind the figures of Elvesham and Renton to suggest optical doubling (see *Idler*, Vol. IX, no. iv (May 1986), pp. 486–96, especially 486).

74 For Fritz Lang's allusions to 'Elvesham' in the robot/Maria identity switch in *Metropolis* (1926) and again in *Das Testament des Dr Mabuse* (1933), where his dying master criminal snatches a posthumous existence, see Chapters 3 and 2, respectively; also cf. 'The Stolen Body', discussed below.

75 'The Treasure in the Forest' (1895) yields another example overlaying different spaces and times by a kind of superimposition: 'He was still dimly conscious of the island, but a queer dream texture interwove with his sensations' (*CSS*, p. 93).

76 Extensive SPR investigation of such apparitions, 'The best-attested examples being hallucinations representing the figure of the agent himself', had been published in Edmund Gurney, Frederic Myers and Frank Podmore, *Phantasms of the Living*, two vols (London: Trübner and Co., 1886). Similar cases to 'The Stolen Body' are cited in Vol. I, p. 517 and II, pp. 96–100.

In 'How Gabriel Became Thompson', Wells's narrator foresees his radical friend's transformation into Pooteresque husband as 'a kind of "Phantasm of the Living"', visualised by flickering, proto-cinematic insert 'of a fairhaired man with a bees-waxed moustache, dressed in an ample frock coat, and light gloves. It was my prophet – curled and scented. The vision fluttered between me and my bookshelves for a moment and vanished, and I knew at once that my Gabriel, the world-mender, was lost to me for ever' (*CSS*, p. 796).

77 Harringay can't prove that his painting really came to life because of lack of photographic evidence either (*CSS*, p. 41).

78 Writers and scientists like Wells dreamed of rendering the city's social body and workings simultaneously transparent, a perspective that would be enhanced by film. Significantly, the same idea and phrase is used in *WTSW* (see Chapter 3). As Carlo Pagetti shows, Wells's imagination was also caught up in how popular photo-magazines presented London in new spatial dimensions 'as its multifaceted map is observed from the air or explored underground' (see Carlo Pagetti, 'Change in the City: The Time Traveller's London and the "Baseless Fabric" of his Vision', in Slusser et al. (eds), *Perennial Time Machine*, pp. 122–34, especially 127). The *Strand* reported a Nadarian balloon flight by Percival Spencer, illustrated with Kodak pictures. Interestingly, the account stresses eerie silence, panopticism and weightlessness exactly as Bessel experiences them (see Anon., 'London From Aloft', *Strand Magazine*, no. 2 (1891), pp. 492–98). The 'Stolen Body' was published (with illustrations) in Vol. 16, no. 95 (Nov. 1898), pp. 567–76.

79 Cf. Maxim Gorky's 1896 review of his first cinematograph show, which connected its evocative monochrome forms and silence with eerie otherworldliness rather than realism:

'Yesterday I was in the kingdom of shadows.

'If only you knew how strange it is to be there. There are no sounds, no colours. There everything – earth, trees, people, water, air – is tinted in the single tone of grey: in a grey sky there are grey rays of sunlight: in grey faces, grey eyes, and the leaves of the trees are grey like ashes. This is not life, but the shadow of life, and this is not movement but the soundless shadow of movement.' (Repr. in Leyda, *Kino*, pp. 407–9.)

80 Conversely, Bailey argues that Wells uses a 'dissolve' to transit from terrestrial graveyard into Powell and Pressburgeresque cosmic panorama in 'A Vision of Judgement' (1899): 'the old elm tree and the sea view vanished like a puff of steam, and then all about me – a multitude no man could number, nations, tongues, kingdoms, peoples – children of all the ages, in an amphitheatrical space, as vast as the sky'. (*CSS*, pp. 598–602, especially 598; also Bailey, '"There Would Presently Come Out of the Darkness"', p. 19.)

81 Hitchcock adapted Cornell Woolrich's short story 'Rear Window' (1942) (repr. in *Rear Window and Other Stories* (London and NY: Simon and Schuster, 1988), pp. 1–27), originally titled 'Murder from a Fixed Viewpoint'. This features key motifs and plot elements resembling Wells's and may, therefore, form the indirect link between Wells and the film, though it was Hitchcock who made the protagonist a photojournalist. Hitchcock also considered adapting *WOTW*, which contains a similar sequence (see note 84 below).

82 'At a Window', *Black and White*, Vol. VIII, no. 186 (25 Aug. 1894), p. 246.

83 Hammond, *Wells and the Short Story*, p. 45.

84 Wells was similarly injured at the age of seven or eight. He recollected it as a key moment in making him a writer, having 'just discovered the art of leaving my body' into fiction's imaginary elsewheres (see *Experiment in Autobiography*, Vol. I, pp. 76–77).

85 Cf. *WOTW*'s chapter 'What We Saw From A Ruined House'. Holed up, the narrator is restricted to watching the grisly goings-on at the Martian base camp from a break in a wall like a static camera angle. His 'horrible privilege of sight' is passive, partial, fragmentary, tinged with voyeurism and inference based on a kind of sickening, but irresistible fascination. Wells anticipates the captive but ambivalent pleasures of horror film audiences (see *WOTW*, pp. 123–35, especially 140 and Chapter 5).

86 Ford epitomised the same effect of experiencing segments of others' private narratives *en passant* through random events framed by a train window (itself like a lens). The 'touch of pathos and of dissatisfaction' arising from such inconclusiveness, he identified with the culturally ingrained sentiment 'of liking a story to have an end', but it also indicated the incipient cinematisation of modern life. (See his *The Soul of London: A Survey of a Modern City* (1905; London: Everyman, 1995), pp. 28 and 43.)

87 Smith was already experimenting with narrative close-ups in 1900. *Grandma's Reading Glass* features a whole series of incongruously magnified objects, each seen in turn through the lens. His comically voyeuristic *As Seen through the Telescope* features the first risqué close-ups of the body, i.e. a woman's ankle. Such foregrounded mediation is typical of the self-conscious opticality of early films (see Fairservice, *Film Editing*, pp. 21–22, and Christie, *Last Machine*, p. 49).

88 Such 'warning shadows' became a trademark of Expressionist cinema in particular and Wells seemed particularly fond of this highly suggestive and plastic effect. In 'The Red Room' (1896), for example, 'A monstrous shadow' of an old man 'crouched upon the wall and mocked his action as he poured and drank' (*CSS*, p. 191). Wells sustained interest in moving chiaroscuro, as in 'The Cone', where Horrocks takes his victim to experience 'some fine effects of moonlight and smoke' (*CSS*, p. 459).

89 'The Chronic Argonauts' suggests a similarly paradoxical loop in which cause and effect are inverted in endless replay. The 'apparition' of Nebogipfel from the present (1887) precipitates a slaying in the past (1862) by which the house becomes 'haunted', awaiting the future moment when he will move in to build his time machine to travel back (repr. in Geduld (ed.), *Definitive Time Machine*, Appendix I, pp. 135–52).

90 Bruce David Sommerville explains the Traveller's own disappearance into time

as an amusing hoax done by similar illusions achieved with phonograph sound effects and magic lantern projection on to a hidden glass screen (see his *'The Time Machine'*, pp. 11–29, especially 21–22). Ine van Dooren argues his guest may refer to the well-known enlargement trick of 'Pepper's Ghost' (named after its inventor, Regent Street Polytechnic principal John Henry Pepper), or similar phantasmagoric projection (see her 'Travelling Times', in Gray (ed.), *Hove Pioneers*, pp. 12–17, especially 12).

91 Cf. 'Mr Skelmersdale in Fairyland' (1901) which echoes innumerable early trickfilms on this subject from Alice Guy-Blaché's *Fairy of the Cabbage Patch* (1896) onwards. Wells could have based the story on Gamages department store in Holborn, renowned for its huge toy department and just around the corner from R. W. Paul's laboratory in Hatton Gardens.

92 Arthur Melbourne Cooper made several on Paul's animatographe with titles such as *Dolly's Toys* (1901), *The Enchanted Toymaker* (1904) and *Dreams of Toyland* (1908). They feature children's dreams about playthings coming to life and eventually whole miniature worlds of animated objects (see Denis Gifford, *British Animated Films 1895–1985: A Filmography* (Jefferson, NC and London: McFarland, 1987, pp. 6, 8 and 11).

93 Wells first employed this phrase in 'The Chronic Argonauts' to 'avouch' time travel's fantastic reality: '"There is absolutely no deception, sir," said Nebogipfel with the slightest trace of mockery in his voice. "I lay no claim to work in matters spiritual. It is a *bona fide* mechanical contrivance, a thing emphatically of this solid world" ... He rose from his knees, stepped upon the mahogany platform, took a curiously curved lever in his hand and pulled it over. Cook rubbed his eyes. *There* certainly was no deception. The doctor and machine had vanished.' (See Geduld (ed.), *Definitive Time Machine*, p. 147.)

94 Early 'claymation' such as Edwin S. Porter's 1902 *Fun in a Bakery Shop* shaped 'dough' into caricatures of famous faces (see Paul Wells, *Animation: Genre and Authorship* (London and New York: Wallflower, 2002), p. 114). For the logical development of trickfilm into animation and its parallels in Modernist literature, see my *'Ulysses* in Toontown: Vision Animated to Bursting Point in Joyce's "Circe"', in Lydia Rainford and Julian Murphet (eds), *Writing After Cinema: Literature and Visual Technologies* (Houndmills: Palgrave, 2003), pp. 96–121.

95 Metonymy constructs meaning not by comparisons between different things (as in metaphor), but by their physical contiguity; synecdoche, by making part imply whole (see also discussion of *IM* in Chapter 2).

96 Cf. the moving disembodied eyes of the experimental cat in *IM* (pp. 96–97) and the morphing effect of bestial features 'surging up' out of ordinary human faces in Prendick's traumatised perception in the final chapter of *The Island of Doctor Moreau* (1896; London: Penguin, 2005), p. 130. (Henceforth all page references to *The Island of Doctor Moreau* (*IODM*) will be given in brackets in the text.)

97 In Wells's earlier version, 'The Devotee of Art' (*Science Schools Journal* Nov.–Dec. 1888), the protagonist merely dreams his picture comes to life. In the version published the year of the cinematograph's advent, this has literally come to pass: the dream is now a *waking* one.

98 See Gifford, *British Animated Films*, p. 6. 'Harringay' also anticipates artworks on film with a life of their own as with the statue in Jean Cocteau's surrealist *Le Sang d'un poète* (1930).

99 Wells's story brought a traditional form into the age of movies. 'Magic picture stories', through increasing association with both duality and technology, proliferated in Victorian fantasy. A Gothic motif since the late 1700s, by the 1880s they had become a 'deluge' (see K. Powell, 'Tom, Dick and Dorian Gray: Magic Picture Mania in

Late Victorian Fiction', *Philological Quarterly*, no. 62 (1983), pp. 147–70, especially 151 and 163).

100 See, for example, Cooke, 'British Cinema', pp. 186–87. Christie even goes so far as to suggest that lack of renewed interest by Wells and other imaginative writers until the late '20s was too tardy to reverse British film's decline as a world leader (*Last Machine*, p. 136). (For contemporary expectations and debates about Wells's return to direct involvement, see Chapter 4.)

101 'This circumstance', Ramsaye claimed, 'led nearly to the attainment, at a single stroke, of the photoplay construction which has since come only by tedious evolution.' He also went on to argue that Wells and Paul were unhampered by institutionalised conventions of film-making. However, when, more than a decade later, 'the screen reached for the aid of the writing craft', it had established markets and practices restricting freedom of expression. Their project conceived of film 'as a tool and servant in the business of story telling', while writers coming later 'were to be the tools and servants' of entrenched business interests (*Million and One Nights*, pp. 159–60).

102 Ramsaye, *Million and One Nights*, p. 161. Ramsaye argued that if novelists such as Wells 'had followed up their first flitting contact', cinema's technical evolution would have accelerated, producing the equivalent of *Birth of a Nation* a decade earlier (p. 265).

Chapter 2
The Dis/Appearance of the Subject

1 See Plato, *Republic of Plato*, pp. 44–45.

2 Griffin describes his process in Chapter XIX (see *IM*, pp. 88–93). That Wells's science is ultimately fraught with logical contradiction does not invalidate it as a device for initiating imaginative social allegory. (Arnold Bennett's review pointed out that Griffin's transparent eyelids would have gradually rendered him blind. Wells responded that dilution of the reflective membrane behind the retina, necessary for full invisibility, would have done so immediately. (See *Woman*, no. 405 (29 Sept. 1897), p. 9; the review and Wells's letter are reprinted in Harris Wilson (ed.), *Arnold Bennett and H. G. Wells: A Record of a Personal and a Literary Friendship* (London: Rupert Hart-Davis, 1960), pp. 258–59 and 34, respectively.)

Hinton's 1895 story, *Stella*, about a scientist who renders his ward transparent seems to have influenced Griffin's process. Her mentor 'found out how to alter the coefficient of refraction of the body. He made my coefficient equal to one.' Similarly, his method works 'in the border land between chemistry and physics', using spectroscopic technology. His intention in 'taking away visible corporeality' was to take away 'the means of living for herself' (see Hinton, *Scientific Romances*, Second Series (London: Swan Sonnenschein, 1896), pp. 35, 17 and 49, respectively). The experiment makes her a dis/embodiment of her mentor's social philosophy, the denial of egotistical self-reflection. However, Hinton also satirises the social construction of feminine subjectivity and lack of female autonomy in Victorian times (Stella only regains a self-image once she finally achieves a measure of financial independence and equality). Wells's antihero's invisibility leads to diametrically different impulses: to self-aggrandisement and a counterpart masculine power politics. Nevertheless, changes in 'seeing and being seen' in both texts are allegorically designed to break through the limits of normal perception and morality.

There are other technical and thematic parallels, especially aspects that are 'proto-cinematic' or evoke media as 'technology of the uncanny'. Hinton's narrator, 'Churton', first senses Stella's absent presence through objects and furniture subject to her unseen manipulation, then her voice emanating from empty space. The condition of Stella's full invisibility is also nakedness, which she disguises with clothes and veils to 'appear' in public. As in *IM*, the fact that she functions as an 'empty' signifier allows for self-projection by others (Churton falls in love with his imagined ideal, though immune to the charms of women he can see). Stella's lack of social visibility arouses all kinds of bizarre speculations about her identity. She is also exploited by a fake medium to provide supernatural effects at séances. Paradoxically, he is unmasked by an SPR investigator, who unexpectedly provides scientific verification of Stella's even more fantastic reality.

Mitchell's 'The Crystal Man' (New York *Sun* (30 Jan. 1881)) is perhaps the earliest story of scientifically induced transparency. Its processes and motifs may also have influenced Wells, including: bleaching bodily pigments (both retina and red corpuscles); prominent references to albinism; paradoxically superhuman advantages, and tragic isolation. Similarly, descriptions of objects moving without human agency also seem very proto-cinematic (see Mitchell, *Crystal Man*, pp. 1–15, especially 6–7).

3 Ambiguous in/visibility seems to be stressed in the novella by a variety of effects, including the dialect contraction of the protagonist's title to "the 'visible man" (see, for example, *IM*, pp. 68 and 70).

4 George Griffith, 'A Photograph of the Invisible', *Pearson's Magazine*, Vol. I, no. 4 (Apr. 1896), pp. 376–80, especially 380.

5 Dam, 'A Wizard of To Day', pp. 413–19, especially 414–15.

As Allen W. Grove's excellent discussion of the cultural impact of X-rays notes, *IM* epitomised how new visual technology blurred 'the boundaries between public and private, interiors and exteriors, humans and ghosts'. Wells's allusions to crime, spying and spectrality act out the nightmare it created in the Victorian imagination. However, though Grove's case that no other fiction presents 'the wonder, fear and confusion surrounding Röntgen's discovery' so astutely is compelling, there remains much that cannot be accounted for in *IM* without reference to other media, especially cinema and sound recording (see Allen W. Grove, 'Röntgen's Ghosts: Photography, X-rays and the Victorian Imagination', *Literature and Medicine*, Vol. 16, no. 2 (Fall 1997), pp. 141–73, especially 165 and 169).

Significantly, A. A. C. Swinton added X-rays to the roll of great media technologies such as telephony, photography, the phonograph and the possibility of wireless telegraphy, all of which involved potentially uncanny displacements of the subject (see A. A. C. Swinton, 'The New Photography of the Invisible', *Pall Mall Magazine*, Vol. IX, no. 38 (June 1896), pp. 264–68, especially 265–66. Wells was published in both *Pall Mall Gazette* and *Budget* from 1894.)

6 Anon., 'The Photography of the Invisible', *The Quarterly Review*, no. 183 (Apr. 1896), p. 496.

7 Iris Barry, *Let's Go to the Pictures* (1926) (repr. as *Let's Go to the Movies* (New York: Payson and Clarke, 1972), p. 24).

8 Despite the SPR's materialist exposure of staged spirit photographs, it still explored the possibility that (in Michael Solovoy's words from 1891) 'rays of light which the human eye *cannot* see *can* be photographed, and that images invisible to the human eye can affect the sensitized plate' (see Grove, 'Röntgen's Ghosts', pp. 151–56; also the essays and examples in the catalogue to the recent international exhibition, Chéroux et al., *Perfect Medium*, especially pp. 33–34, 92–93, 172–74 and 275).

9 Röntgen made his discovery by accidentally placing his hand between a Crookes tube and a fluorescent surface in November 1895.

10 Appropriately, Derrida made his point on screen, in Ken McMullen's 1982 film *Ghost Dances*. Derrida's *Echographies of Television* (Cambridge: Polity, 2002) extended deconstructive spectrality to television.

11 See Lindsay, *Art of the Moving Picture*, pp. 58–59.

12 Repr. in Michael Cox (ed.), *12 Victorian Ghost Stories* (Oxford: Oxford University Press, 1997), pp. 136–47, especially 142–43 and 146. Fitz-James O'Brien's 'What Was It?' (1857) is another source in which the supernatural is tangible. A sleeper struggles for his life against a nightmare assailant, which cannot be seen until a plaster cast is taken of its body. Like *Stella*, the story moots the possibility of organic beings transparent to light and alludes to invisible manipulations at séances (repr. in Fitz-James O'Brien, *Fantastic Tales of Fitz-James O'Brien*, ed. Michael Hayes (London: John Calder, 1977), pp. 55–67, especially 64–65).

13 Wells later admitted *IM*'s title was a misnomer, because Griffin, like Stella, is, in fact, transparent rather than invisible as such (see David C. Smith, *H. G. Wells, Desperately Mortal: A Biography* (New Haven, CT and London: Yale University Press, 1986), p. 63). Wells's 1894 essay 'Through a Microscope' expressed fascination with transparent organisms (repr. in *Certain Personal Matters* (London: Lawrence and Bullen, 1898), pp. 238–47, especially 240).

14 Geduld (ed.), *Definitive Time Machine*, pp. 136–37.

15 Nicholas Baker's novel *The Fermata* (London: Chatto and Windus, 1994) uses a similar metabolic stimulant for invisibility, as does a plot from *The X-Files*, 'Rush' (season 7, episode 6; see also Chapter 5).

16 See Christian Metz, *The Imaginary Signifier: Psychoanalysis and the Cinema* (Bloomington, IN: Indiana University Press, 1982), pp. 94–97.

17 See Frank McConnell, *The Science Fiction of H. G. Wells* (Oxford: Oxford University Press, 1981), pp. 111–12. Verhoeven's film seems less directly based on Wells than recent pulp rewritings of the theme, such as Thomas Berger's *Being Invisible* (1987). Invisibility becomes furtive wish-fulfilment for slipping into women's changing rooms, etc.

18 See McConnell, *Science Fiction of H. G. Wells*, pp. 114–15.

19 The landlady's reference to the Invisible Man's appearance making him look 'more like a divin' helmet than a human man!' (p. 5) unconsciously hits on the nature of his condition and echoes Wells's 1898 story 'Jimmy Goggles the God', in which a diver is saved from cannibals by the deifying power of his appearance (see *CSS*, pp. 477–86). (The story's motif found cinematic expression in Buster Keaton's *The Navigator* (1924).)

20 McConnell, *Science Fiction of H. G. Wells*, p. 112.

21 In 1942 Wells wrote of the production of social subjects: 'Natural man has, in fact, been replaced in current human society by an *artefact*', as much by the 'artificial integument of clothing', as the checking and moulding of 'inherent behaviour ... by a complex system of education, law and intimidation.' (*Conquest of Time*, p. 60.)

22 For the concept of 'freeplay', see his 'Structure, Sign and Play in the Discourse of the Human Sciences' (1972), in K. M. Newton (ed.), *Twentieth-Century Literary Theory: A Reader*, second edition (Houndmills: Palgrave, 1988), pp. 149–54. For 'trace' and 'metaphysics of presence', see 'Freud and the Scene of Writing', in Jacques Derrida, *Writing and Difference*, trans. Alan Bass (London: Routledge and Kegan Paul, 1981), especially 197–98.

23 In Derrida's *Of Grammatology*, trans. Gayatri Chakravorty Spivak (Baltimore,

MD: Johns Hopkins University Press, 1977), 'phonocentrism' is the bias towards speech, over the reproduction of language in writing and recording technologies, which underpins the Western philosophical tradition and appears to guarantee the 'self-presence' of the subject.

24 See McConnell, *Science Fiction of H. G. Wells*, pp. 123–24.

25 See Sconce, *Haunted Media*, especially pp. 1–20; also Steven Connor, *Dumbstruck: A Cultural History of Ventriloquism* (Oxford: Oxford University Press, 2000), especially pp. 20–21.

26 Flint, *Victorians and the Visual*, p. 34.

27 Bram Stoker, *Dracula* (1897; Harmondsworth: Penguin, 1994), p. 164.

28 *FMITM* refers to Marconi's ongoing experiments with 'electric waves', which he had successfully transmitted across the Channel by 1898; also to Nikola Tesla's alleged reception of radio messages from Mars, the year the novel was written (pp. 15 and 162).

29 For example, Griffin cuts the telegraph wires, in case this rival 'voice' should warn of his escape from Iping (end of Chapter XII). Telegraphy also features frequently in *Stella* (at one point she refers intriguingly to existing only as discourse (see p. 104)).

30 There was a vogue for stop-motion invisibility films in the late 1900s. Possibly the first unmistakably influenced by Wells was Wallace McCutcheon's 1908 comedy *The Invisible Fluid*, for American Mutoscope and Biograph: a mischievous boy runs riot with an inventor's patent atomiser, vanishing objects, pets, people and finally himself. Pathé's 1909, *L'Homme invisible* (accounts differ about whether it was directed by Ferdinand Zecca, Albert Capellani or Louis Gasnier, or possibly Segundo de Chomon, the 'Spanish Méliès'), also known as *The Invisible Thief*, opens with a close-up of Wells's novel itself (showing the famous scene of the bodiless dressing gown), which inspires a criminal to duplicate Griffin's experiment. He discards moving clothes for burglary and scaring off bobbies, but dresses in mask and wig to materialise. The film employed virtually all the special effects (e.g. floating objects and swag) which would be refined by Fulton for Whale's 1933 film. Cecil Hepworth's *Invisibility* (also 1909), in which a husband buys a marvellous powder to evade his nagging wife, is a domestic comedy which has fun with self-propelling shirts and boots, although its trouserless condition may owe more to W. S. Gilbert than Wells (see note 44, below). Gaumont France made its own 'cover version' of *The Invisible Thief* in 1910 to cash in, adding another detail anticipating Whale: a self-pedalling bicycle. (For further details, see Phil Hardy (ed.), *Science Fiction: The Aurum Film Encyclopaedia*, third edition (New York: Aurum Press, 1995), pp. 32–42; Alan Wykes, *H. G. Wells in the Cinema* (London: Jupiter, 1977), pp. 28–30; Don G. Smith, *H. G. Wells on Film: The Utopian Nightmare* (Jefferson, NC and London: McFarland, 2002), p. 61. See also discussion of Vallorani in Chapter 5.)

31 Gilles Deleuze, *Cinema 2: The Time-Image*, trans. Hugh Tomlinson and Robert Galeta (London: Athlone Press, 1989), p. 233.

32 See 'Shape of Wells to Come', *Era* (11 Dec. 1935), p. 20. Wells reiterated that the movie was a key adaptation for him, despite its 'many literary errors': 'The man who reconciled me to films was James Whale. He proved to me with his efficient rendering of my story "The Invisible Man" that, in the cinema, anything is possible.' (Quoted in J. Danvers Williams, 'I Wrote this Film for Your Enjoyment, says H. G. Wells', *Film Weekly* (29 Feb. 1936), pp. 7–8, especially 8.) *The Times* also noted Whale's faithfulness to his novel's 'scientific operations' as a factor persuading Wells to collaborate with Korda (Anon., 'A Film by Mr H. G. Wells', *The Times* (22 Jan. 1934), p. 14).

33 See Armstrong, *Modernism, Technology and the Body*, pp. 220–47.

34 For Eisenstein, W. I Pudovkin and G. V. Alexandrov's joint manifesto on 'The

Sound Film' (Oct. 1928), as well as the broader critical debate about synchronisation, see James Donald, Anne Friedberg and Laura Marcus (eds), *Close-Up 1927–1933: Cinema and Modernism* (London: Cassell, 1998), pp. 79–93. Wells shared Modernist concerns about mortgaging film's space-time fluidities to naturalistic continuity in the late 1920s (see discussion of *KWWAK* in Chapter 4). Technical innovations such as colour and sound should be selective or 'detached ... for the artist to use as he will', to pick out and intensify details, rather than merely for enhanced mimesis of real life (see *KWWAK*, pp. 15–17; also Chapter 4).

35 Significantly, the novella accrued steady royalties over this period, without the sensational impact of the other scientific romances until Whale's film. Wells granted options in the 1920s, eventually selling Universal the rights for $25,000 (see Smith, *Desperately Mortal*, p. 63).

36 Such effects may have been one of the reasons why *IM* had been considered by Universal as its immediate follow-up to *Dracula*, although *Frankenstein* was eventually given priority. (See Mark Gatiss, *James Whale: A Biography, or The Would-be Gentleman* (London: Cassell, 1995) p. 68.)

37 In 'The Work of Art in the Age of Mechanical Reproduction' (1936), in Walter Benjamin, *Illuminations*, ed. Hannah Arendt (London: Fontana, 1973), pp. 217–52, especially 231. Benjamin famously critiqued star charisma not as authentic projection of personality, but the 'phony spell of a commodity' (see *Illuminations*, p. 231).

38 See David Lodge, *The Modes of Modern Writing: Metaphor, Metonymy and the Typology of Modern Literature* (London: Edward Arnold, 1977; paperback, 1979), p. 76. For Lodge's argument about increasing synergy between literary and cinematic metonymy by the thirties, see also p. 214.

39 V. I. Pudovkin, *Filmregie und Filmmanuskript* (Berlin: Verlag der Lichtbühne, 1928), p. 126.

40 Lindsay, *Art of the Moving Picture*, p. 53.

41 Keith Cohen, *Film and Fiction: The Dynamics of Exchange* (New Haven, CT and London: Yale University Press, 1979), pp. 109–10.

42 See Lindsay, *Art of the Moving Picture*, pp. 60–63.

43 *Le Garde-Meuble* was probably by Cohl's disciple Roméo Bosetti, although it is often confused with Cohl's own *Le Mobilier fidèle* (1910), whose scenario it reworks (see Donald Crafton, *Before Mickey: The Animated Film 1898–1928* (Chicago and London: University of Chicago Press, 1993), pp. 154–55).

44 Another possible link with the popular stage was W. S. Gilbert's comic ballad, 'The Perils of Invisibility' (1870). An early reviewer thought Wells was inspired by Gilbert's ironic wish-fulfilment, especially its uncomfortable physical contradictions, whereby nakedness necessary for full disappearance also undermines its advantage by exposing the body to the elements. The sight of empty clothes walking about on their own (as in Gilbert's own illustrations) similarly terrifies local villagers. (See W. S. Gilbert, *The Bab Ballads*, ed. James Ellis (Cambridge, MA: Harvard University Press, 1980), pp. 292–93 and notes on p. 362; also *Spectator* (25 Sept. 1897), p. 408.)

45 According to Barnouw most special effects characteristic of early movies were *already* familiar to magicians (and, consequently, their audiences) 'from a century of scientific magic', which often made use of pre-cinematic optical technologies such as magic lanterns. These included dissolves, fades, substitutions, double exposures, superimpositions, masking, models, back projections and mirrored images. Film only added a few more, such as the very Wellsian (temporal) reversing (see Barnouw, *Magician and the Cinema*, p. 98).

46 Paul Hammond, *Marvellous Méliès* (London: Gordon Fraser, 1974), p. 40.

47 Barnouw, *Magician and the Cinema*, pp. 88–89.
48 The title page of Charles L. Graves and Edward V. Lucas, *The War of the Wenuses* (1898), guys Wells as 'H. G. Pozzuoli', author of 'The Vanishing Lady', a sly allusion to *IM*'s parallels in Mélièsque visual trickery, as well as its likely debt to Hinton's novel. The frontispiece also features a blank 'Portrait of the Invisible Author' taken by spectroscope (repr. in George Locke (ed.), *Sources of Science Fiction: Future War Novels of the 1890s* (London: Routledge/Thoemmes, 1998).
49 See Barnouw, *Magician and the Cinema*, pp. 89–92.
50 See Hammond, *Marvellous Méliès*, p. 124.
51 See Barnouw, *Magician and the Cinema*, p. 98.
52 Maskelyne's partner, David Devant, introduced Paul's 'theatrograph' to Egyptian Hall programmes on 19 March 1896 (just ahead of Paul's own public showings at Olympia). The master himself appeared in Paul's *Maskelyne: Spinning Plates* (1896). Some of Devant's acts were also filmed by Paul and Méliès (Devant sold Méliès his first theatrograph). The Maskelynes quickly started making their own films on their patented 'Mutagraph'. Nevil's experiments with slow motion later led to his analysis of shells for the War Office (see Herbert and McKernan (eds), *Who's Who of Victorian Cinema*, pp. 19–20, 40–41 and 92–93; also Barnouw, *Magician and the Cinema*, pp. 53–54 and 57).
53 Hammond describes the Egyptian Hall visit in *Marvellous Méliès*, p. 15. See also Wells's reference to Maskelyne in 'On Lang and Buchan' (*Saturday Review*, no. 81 (22 Feb. 1896); repr. in *H. G. Wells's Literary Criticism*, ed. Patrick Parrinder and Robert M. Philmus (Brighton: Harvester; Totowa, NJ: Barnes and Noble, 1980), pp. 84 and 86 (note)). It is even possible that Maskelyne is the 'really good conjurer' mentioned by *IM*'s vicar, since Wells could easily have visited Egyptian Hall while studying in London.
54 Hammond, *Marvellous Méliès*, pp. 46–47.
55 Wells felt that the film brought out his text's humour, singling out Una O'Connor's virtuoso performance as shrieking landlady (see Gatiss, *James Whale*, p. 102).
56 See Thomas C. Renzi, *H. G. Wells: Six Scientific Romances Adapted for Film*, second edition (Lanham, MD and Oxford: Scarecrow Press, 2004), p. 88.
57 Griffin places himself between two 'radiating centres' similar to those producing 'Röntgen vibrations' (*IM*, p. 95), presumably electromagnetic rays he has discovered with even more marvellous properties.
58 For examples, see Barnouw, *Magician and the Cinema*, p. 89.
59 Griffin's original devisualisation (see *IM*, p. 99) is rendered even better in BBC One's 1984 television adaptation (scripted James Andrew Hall; dir. Brian Lighthill; broadcast September–October) through 'colour separation overlay' treatment and consequently elaborated by 'bluescreen' and CGI work in versions such as Verhoeven's (explained in Patricia Netzley, *The Encyclopedia of Movie Special Effects* (Westport, CT: Greenwood, 1999), p. 112).
60 See John P. Fulton, 'How We Made the Invisible Man', *American Cinematographer* (Sept. 1934), pp. 200–1 and 214.
61 See Lucien Goldmann, *Towards a Sociology of the Novel*, trans. Alan Sheridan (London: Tavistock, 1975), pp. 137–38.
62 See Georg Lukács, 'Reification and the Consciousness of the Proletariat', in Lukács, *History and Class Consciousness* (1923), trans. Rodney Livingstone (London: Merlin, 1971), pp. 83–110, especially 83.
63 Thomas Richards, *The Commodity Culture of Victorian England: Advertising and Spectacle 1851–1914* (Stamford, CA: Stamford University Press, 1990), pp. 2–3.

64 As a draper's assistant in his youth, clothes were commodities with a particular resonance for Wells. Significantly, Iping is also a real place, just outside Midhurst, West Sussex, where he was apprenticed.

65 Benjamin, *Illuminations*, p. 233.

66 Anne B. Simpson, 'The "Tangible Antagonist": H. G. Wells and the Discourse of Otherness', *Extrapolation*, Vol. 31, no. 2 (1990), pp. 134–47, especially 134.

67 See Gatiss, *James Whale*, pp. vii–viii. Harry M. Benshoff argues that the horror film's evolution was closely involved with ambivalent or displaced portrayals of homosexuality. Latent themes in Expressionism (especially homoerotic doubles) were a major influence on the genre's look and content, as Whale's four classic horrors of the thirties testify. Griffin's disappearance is considered a 'queer thing' by a number of characters in the film. (See Harry M. Benshoff, *Monsters in the Closet: Homosexuality and the Horror Film* (Manchester: Manchester University Press, 1997), especially pp. 20 and 47.)

68 Whale's own initial treatment overlaid Wells's tale with graveyard iconography, suggesting underlying connections with *Frankenstein*. The Invisible Man becomes a macabre healer residing in a vault, who is much more sympathetically tragic than Wells's Griffin. Whale sketched out numerous lines of development, including a prayer to 'THOU WHO ART INVISIBLE' to render his horribly disfigured face unseeable, substituting supernatural for scientific causes. His transformation's side-effects are nonetheless psychopathic. At the protagonist's grotesque suicide, Whale blends Wells's rematerialisation with his own taste for grisly effects. Neatly, the very moment Griffin became visible, the audience would shut their eyes with sheer fright! (See repr. in Gatiss, *James Whale*, Appendix, pp. 172–77).

69 Kemp, whose mind travels 'into a remote speculation of social conditions of the future' and loses itself 'at last over the time dimension' seems a very autobiographical persona, though his rationality is shown self-critically (*IM*, p. 76).

70 Renzi, *Six Scientific Romances*, pp. 85–86 and 90.

71 In Whale's film, Kemp's role also subsumed Marvel the tramp's. The most significant 'diegetic' differences – i.e. in events and consequences – also occur from the point of Jack's coercion of Kemp.

72 Renzi, *Six Scientific Romances*, p. 92.

73 For distribution and exercise of what Foucault called 'power/knowledge' through surveillance, see Michel Foucault, 'Truth and Power', in Paul Rabinow (ed.), *The Foucault Reader: An Introduction to Foucault's Thought* (Harmondsworth: Penguin, 1984), pp. 51–75.

74 The 1930s vogue for mad-scientist pictures often featured equivocal states of visibility with strongly Wellsian overtones. Both Universal's serials *The Vanishing Shadow* (dir. Lew Landers, 1934) and *The Phantom Creeps* (dir. Ford Beebe and Saul A. Goodkind, 1939) feature metacinematic, 'devisualising' devices, allowing protagonists to vanish in and out of the scene of crime. *The Invisible Ray* (dir. Lambert Hillyer, 1936), starring Karloff and Lugosi, also involves a kind of visual 'Time Machine'. 'Janos Rukh' invents a device picking up light rays from Andromeda showing Earth in prehistoric times. But, like Griffin, his researches (into a new element found in a meteor, 'Radium X') eventually turn him psychopathic by cursing him with what Jeff Rovin calls a 'radioactive Midas touch', so he converts his prototype laser from eye-surgery to disintegrator beam (Jeff Rovin, *Classic Science Fiction Films* (New York: Carol Publishing, 1993), p. 30). In an inversion of *IM*, the irradiated scientist also renders himself luminous (perhaps alluding to 'The Stolen Bacillus' (1894), Wells's story about an inept bio-terrorist, who becomes an all-too-visible man dyed blue by the phial he steals, in mistake for

cholera (*CSS*, pp. 3–8)).

75 See McConnell, *Science Fiction of H. G. Wells*, pp. 117–18.

76 Renzi's conclusion that Whale's film is specifically an allegory of financial collapse in the Great Depression misses how it catalyses this crucial interaction between politics, science and the media implicit in the novella. It is likely that what Renzi calls the 'Monster Economic Chaos', arbitrarily wreaking havoc in the lives of ordinary people, lurks somewhere in the film's rich texture of signification. Indeed, as we have seen, the suggestive parallelism between Marx's theory of economic reification and Wells's fantasy of commodities apparently out of control might well support such a topical link between irresponsible science and a capitalist system that had lost 'credibility as benefactor' and become the source of global crisis (Renzi, *Six Scientific Romances*, p. 94). However, other important themes and discursive strategies germinated through transplantation into the medium of film within the hothouse climate of 1930s cultural politics.

77 Topically, the local schoolteacher suspects that Griffin is a bomb-making 'Anarchist in disguise' (*IM*, pp. 22–23). The word 'terrorist' was first used in its modern sense in this period, particularly by Joseph Conrad. *The Secret Agent: A Simple Tale* (1907; Harmondsworth: Penguin, 1990) makes numerous allusions to *IM*, both serious and jocular, in the form of the bomb-toting 'professor's' suicidally fanatical anonymity in the crowd and a pianola which suddenly plays itself.

78 See also Introduction. Conrad wrote, 'Impressed is *the* word, O! Realist of the Fantastic, whether you like it or not. And if you want to know what impresses me it is to see how you contrive to give over humanity to the clutches of the Impossible and yet manage to keep it down (or up) to its humanity, to its flesh, blood, sorrow, folly. *That* is the achievement! In this little book you do it with an appalling completeness.' (*Collected Letters*, Vol. 2, pp. 126–27.)

79 McConnell, *Science Fiction of H. G. Wells*, pp. 115–16.

80 Anarchist bombing was a sensational film subject as far back as Biograph's *A Catastrophe in Hester Street* (1904).

81 See Sebastian Haffner, *The Meaning of Hitler*, trans. Ewald Osers (Cambridge, MA: Harvard University Press, 1979), pp. 8 and 25.

82 The London Film Society screened *Das Testament* in May 1934. Its programme notes drew particular attention to Mabuse's 'invisibility' and posthumous existence as recorded voice (see London Film Society, *Film Society Programmes*, pp. 293–94).

Sarah Kozloff stresses that Lang was one of the pioneers of creatively a-synchronous use of the soundtrack. For example in *M*, the police commissioner's disembodied telephonic voice explains his methods of tracking down the child-murderer over visuals of the police team following up clues (see her *Invisible Storytellers: Voice-over Narration in the American Fiction Film* (Berkeley, CA: University of California Press, 1988), p. 31). Invisibility featured in other pre-war German films, from Lang's own silent epic *Siegfried* (1922–24), where the teutonic hero uses magic powers to help his friend obtain his superhuman love, Kriemhild, to Harry Piel's sound comedy *Ein Unsichtbarer Geht Durch die Stadt* (1934), in which a taxi driver finds an SF invisibility helmet. He uses it to become rich and win a glamorous fiancée, until his friend borrows it to rob banks. A wish-fulfilling fantasy, which seems to owe much to early silents such as *The Invisible Thief*, not surprisingly the whole thing turns out to be a dream.

83 Lang may also have been alluding to other stories by Wells about 'bodysnatching' by mesmeric projections of personality or invisible entities, such as 'The Story of the Late Mr Elvesham' and 'The Stolen Body' (see Chapter 1). For Lang's admiration of and influence by Wells, shared with his wife and collaborator, Thea von Harbou, see

(among others), Patrick McGilligan, *Fritz Lang: The Nature of the Beast* (London: Faber, 1997), pp. 129–30. For extended discussion of the role of recording technology in preserving Mabuse's existence as discourse, see Tom Gunning, *The Films of Fritz Lang: Allegories of Vision and Modernity* (London: British Film Institute, 2000), especially pp. 145 and 150–51.

84 The anonymous reviewer in *The Times* also noted frequent references to the power of telephonic and radio voices (see '"The Invisible Man": A Film of Mr H. G. Wells's Story' (*The Times* (25 Jan. 1934), p. 8).

85 See Christie, *Last Machine*, p. 10.

86 For more examples from the period, see my *British Writers and the Media, 1930–45* (London: Macmillan, 1996), especially pp. 108–10.

87 For details of Welles's radio productions, see Simon Callow, *Orson Welles: The Road to Xanadu* (London: Jonathan Cape, 1995), pp. 202, 320–21 and 399–409. For the influence of German Expressionism's absent presences on his apprentice film-making, see Joseph McBride, *Orson Welles* (New York: Da Capo, 1996), pp. 23–70.

88 Welles's aborted version was to have been another anti-Fascist parable, with Kurtz as charismatic, pseudo-Nietzschean dictator. Marlow's one moment of visibility was turning in facial close-up to confront the viewer directly with the question of his/her own susceptibility to Kurtz's diabolic persuasiveness. In a memo marked 'Camera', Welles noted that the method of shooting required radical technical innovations to make it 'function not only as a mechanical recording device but as a character'. (See Clinton Heylin, *Despite the System: Orson Welles Versus the Hollywood Studios* (Edinburgh: Canongate, 2005), pp. 18–19 and 23–24.)

89 R. C. Sherriff's own account ('everything that I had written was pure and simple Wells ... all that I had done was to dramatise and condense the story to fit the screen') is in *No Leading Lady: An Autobiography* (London: Gollancz, 1968), p. 268. He was dismayed by the bizarre twists which previous screenplays had tried out to 'improve' upon Wells (though this might be explained by the fact that Universal's copy had been lost): one switched the action to Tsarist Russia, another was about a kind of invisible Scarlet Pimpernel, and yet another resorted to invisible Martians (see Sherriff, *No Leading Lady*, p. 255). This was all the more ironic considering that Universal had bought the rights in 1931, with the proviso that Wells retain final script approval. The extent of the adaptation problems is indicated by the fact that the production involved at various stages four directors, ten separate treatments and several changes of cast (for details, see James Curtis, *James Whale: A New World of Gods and Monsters* (Minneapolis, MN: University of Minnesota Press, 2003), pp. 196–201). The psychopathic aspects of the script may have been partly derived from Philip Wylie's lurid *The Murderer Invisible* (1931), to which Universal also had the rights (see Smith, *H. G. Wells on Film*, p. 65).

90 'Whale laughed it off, reasoning that only a lunatic would want to be invisible in the first place' (Gatiss, *James Whale*, p. 99). However, Sherriff strove to convince Wells that adding toxicity to the 'monocaine' would circumvent the problem that Griffin's lack of facial expression would make it too difficult to show a more gradual deterioration in his sanity as a result of his invisible condition (see Curtis, *James Whale*, p. 200).

91 Wells, *Experiment in Autobiography*, Vol. II, p. 561. At a trade reception, he also appeared alongside Whale and Sherriff to declare, 'Hollywood used to buy what they called "film rights" to a story ... and then kick the author out of the studios and guard the door with a dog. I have sent the following telegram to Carl Laemmle ... 'CONGRATULATIONS ON "THE INVISIBLE MAN" WHICH CONSIDER FILMED FLAWLESSLY

CARRYING OUT MY STORY FAITHFULLY.' (Quoted in Curtis, *James Whale*, p. 221.)

92 The lucrative 'franchise' included *The Invisible Woman, The Invisible Man Returns, The Invisible Man's Revenge, The Invisible Agent* and *Abbot and Costello Meet the Invisible Man* (for details, see (among others) Rovin, *Classic Science Fiction Films*, pp. 32–34 and Smith, *H. G. Wells on Film*, pp. 69–94).

Rains went on to play another masked and 'invisible' presence in the 1943 remake of *The Phantom of the Opera*. Wells's novel has spawned more film imitations than virtually any other text. The Internet Movie Database (www.imdb.com) numbers over a hundred and thirty titles with some form of invisibility in them.

There was also a television series in which *The Invisible Man* became a crime-fighter (Official Films–ITP, 1958–59). The most faithful period serialisation remains that by the BBC. The recent American television series (running from 2000) has added little to the genre. (For European film and television adaptations, see also Chapter 5.)

Chapter 3
'Seeing the Future'

1 Lindsay, *Art of the Moving Picture*, pp. 77–78.

2 Wells recollected *WTSW* as a projection of anxieties about the 'monstrous' megalopolis of the 1890s, exaggerating contemporary trends: 'higher buildings, bigger towns, wickeder capitalists and labour more downtrodden than ever and more desperate. Everything was bigger, quicker and more crowded ... It was our contemporary world in a state of highly inflamed distension.' (*Experiment in Autobiography*, vol. 2, 645.) However, if anything seems genuinely prophetic in *WTSW* now, it is Wells's media speculations.

Jules Verne had earlier written a similar dystopia about the Paris of 1961 (a century in the future) in which the French economy is also run by state monopolies and multinationals that oppress workers. This anticipates *WTSW* in foreseeing titanic architecture, electrification, car traffic, 'mass culture' and communications developments such as fax machines – '*la télégraphie photographique*' (see Jules Verne, *Paris au XXe Siècle* (Paris: Hachette, 1994), p. 70). Only recently rediscovered and published, it is therefore notable not as an intertext, but as a parallel response to the emergent modernity of the technologised city.

3 See Introduction, note 32.

4 For widespread recognition of Wellsian sources at the film's release, see Thomas Elsaesser, *Metropolis* (London: BFI, 2000), pp. 12–15; also summaries of contemporary reviews in Ann E. Kaplan, *Fritz Lang: A Guide to References and Resources* (Boston, MA: G. K. Hall, 1981), pp. 152–55.

5 See John Logie Baird, *Television and Me: The Memoirs of John Logie Baird*, ed. Malcolm Baird (Edinburgh: Mercat, 2004), p. 9; also Antony Kamm and Malcolm Baird, *John Logie Baird: A Life* (Edinburgh: National Museums of Scotland, 2002), p. 4.

6 See Wells, *Early Writings in Science and Science Fiction*, pp. 47–48. The world of the second and third versions seems to be a staging post on the way to that of the Eloi and Morlocks, before socially stratified humanity has bifurcated in evolutionary terms. There are other linking motifs with *WTSW*, not least the fact that the ruling class govern by hypnotism in the third version: it is the population who 'awake' from induced sleep, in effect. In the second, the working class rise up from the depths when made aware of their cultural deprivation. (Based on the recollections of Professor A. Morley

Davies quoted in Geoffrey West, *H. G. Wells*, Appendix I, pp. 291–92.)

7   Wells described it as 'the most ambitious and least satisfactory of my earlier books' (*The Sleeper Awakes: The Works of H. G. Wells, Atlantic Edition*, Vol. II (London: T. Fisher Unwin, 1924), p. ix). First published in serial form in *The Graphic* (14 Jan.–6 May 1899), it was also the only novel that Wells both updated and retitled, in 1910, in lieu of another book about the future which he failed to complete (draft material from which was eventually incorporated into *SOTTC* (1933) (see John Lawton's 'Note on the Text', in *WTSW*, pp. xlvi–vii)).

See Nicolletta Vallorani, '"The Invisible Wells" in European Cinema and Television', in Parrinder and Partington (eds), *Reception of H. G. Wells in Europe*, pp. 302–20, especially 308; also Chapter 5.

8   With characteristically self-conscious intertextuality, Wells alludes to the socialist Utopias that his vision undercuts. Graham's trance is induced by overwork on a left-wing pamphlet. Awoken, Graham recalls Edward Bellamy 'the hero of whose Socialistic Utopia had so oddly anticipated this actual experience'. 'Julian West' in Bellamy's *Looking Backward: 2000–1887* (1888) wakes in a future Boston where poverty and social injustice have been eliminated by the state. Similarly, Wells challenges the 'arts and crafts' communism of William Morris's *News From Nowhere* (1890) (see *WTSW*, pp. 51–52 and 120).

Another likely, though unmentioned, source is Jules Verne's 1889 'In the Twenty-Ninth Century – The Day of an American Journalist in 2889' (first published in English). This has much in common with *WTSW*, not just economic and technological advances such as a global informational economy, moving pavements and aerial liners, but, crucially, a cryogenic 'sleeper' from a previous century. (See the reprint in Peter Haining (ed.), *The Jules Verne Companion* (London: Souvenir Press, 1978), pp. 97–116.)

9   Tim Armstrong, 'Technology: Multiplied Man', in David Bradshaw (ed.), *A Concise Companion to Modernism* (Oxford: Blackwell, 2003), pp. 158–78, especially 172. The idea of an instantaneous world communications system had been predicted by the *Illustrated London News* when it reported the laying of the first transatlantic telegraph cable in 1865. This opened the possibility of monitoring 'human affairs over the entire surface of the globe' (quoted in I. F. Clark, *The Pattern of Expectation 1644–2001* (London: Jonathan Cape, 1979), p. 91).

10   Wells became acutely aware of contradictions in cinema's ideological role in depicting luxurious consumption during the Syndicalist strikes. His *Daily Mail* article, 'The Labour Unrest' (13–20 May 1912), criticised 'The Spectacle of Pleasure'. Depictions of the hedonistic rich in features and newsreels stirred social discontent: 'the tendency of newspaper, theatre, cinematograph show, and so forth is to fill his [the worker's] mind with ideas of ways of living infinitely more agreeable and interesting than his own'. '[T]aunting [him] with just that suggestion that it is for that, and that alone, that ... his muscles strain.' (Repr. in Leon Stover (ed.), *When the Sleeper Wakes: A Critical Text of the 1899 New York and London First Edition, with an Introduction and Appendices* (Jefferson, NC and London: McFarland, 2000), pp. 413–14.)

11   See *The Graphic* (1 Apr. 1899), p. 393.

12   The Crystal Palace, which housed the 1851 Great Exhibition of industrial products, was a monument to Victorian commodity advertising. '[T]he first of its kind, a place where the combined mythologies of consumerism appeared in concentrated form ... the capitalist system had not only created a dominant form of exchange but was also in the process of creating a dominant form of representation to go along with it ... consolidating its hold over England not only economically but semiotically. The era of the spectacle had begun' (see Richards, *Commodity Culture*, p. 3 and 17–72). That

'dominant form of representation', subsequently developed through press advertising, posters, photography, etc. (many of which featured in magazines such as *The Graphic*), would boost its spectacle immeasurably through new media technologies such as moving images, as *WTSW* and 'A Story of the Days to Come' realise. (Cf. Flanders, *Consuming Passions*, especially pp. 130–37.)

13 Wells was probably imagining a kind of cassette for film reels. Asked in his 1935 *Era* interview whether 'television will do away with film?', Wells was unsure, but thought 'Quite possibly you will have the film in your own house', without specifying its form ('Shape of Wells to Come', *Era* (11 Dec. 1935), p. 20). Both Lumière and Pathé developed machines for safe home viewing in the cinema's first decades. Britain's Mutoscope and Biograph Syndicate marketed a 'Home Mutoscope', intended for viewing newsfilm in 1900 (see Herbert and McKernan (eds), *Who's Who of Victorian Cinema*, pp. 6, 101 and 106). Albert Robida had depicted a form of hidden video recorder for investigating the fidelity of mistresses in his magazine *La Caricature* in the early 1880s. His *kinétograph* was also a device for playing prerecorded programmes (see Edward Tenner, 'The World's Greatest Futurist', *Harvard Magazine*, Vol. 92, no. 3 (Jan.–Feb. 1990), pp. 36–41, especially 38 and 41).

14 Although Lang's heroine's name does not echo Wells's directly, it was arguably present in shortened and displaced form in the German release. *Metropolis*'s psychological 'backstory' depends on Joh Fredersen and Rotwang's rivalry for Freder's dead mother, 'Hel'. In Paramount's recut for the Anglophone market, all references to this explanatory triangle were, unhelpfully, censored because of closeness to the English 'hell'. Rotwang also originally plans to 'resurrect' Hel artificially by synthesising her features on his android (see Elsaesser, *Metropolis*, p. 30).

15 Guy Debord argued that the reifying 'principle of commodity fetishism ... reaches its absolute fulfilment in the spectacle, where the tangible world is replaced by a selection of images which exist above it, and which simultaneously impose themselves as the tangible *par excellence*'. (See Guy Debord, *The Society of the Spectacle*, trans. from the French (Detroit: Black and Red, 1983), thesis 36.) The spectacle thus becomes the means by which 'the consumer sees "the world of the commodity dominating all that is lived"' as anticipated in *WTSW* and 'A Story of the Days to Come' (Richards, *Commodity Culture*, p. 13).

16 In its references to sound media, *WTSW* seems to draw on the myth of the Tower of Babel, as does Lang's film (admittedly more by visual allusion, as a pre-talkie). *WTSW* features a myriad of apparently competing, but ultimately controlled, disembodied voices, which are a satirical extension of the printed news media of Wells's time. A 'General Intelligence' babble machine shouts continuous government headlines. Others are 'live papers', interactive, inflammatory proto-tabloids, answering direct questions. The illusion of freedom of informational choice is belied by the fact that only richer apartments are connected to whichever international news syndicate the owner selects (see *WTSW*, pp. 175–77 and 178).

In *Looking Backward*, phonographs also replace newspapers and both music and public speeches are transmitted telephonically, 'as if by invisible person in the room' (see Edward Bellamy, *Looking Backward: 2000–1887* (1888; Peterborough, Ontario: Broadview, 2003), pp. 205–6).

17 The OED online defines *ostrog* as Russian for both prison and fortress, appropriately, for a proto-Fascist strongman ruling a 'rationalised' future which extends Jeremy Bentham's principle of the 'panopticon' prison (a key development for Foucault's theory of surveillance culture) to a city-wide scale. London first used electric street lighting in 1878, transforming its night-time environment and its first generating station

was built in Deptford in 1882, thus opening up the urban future of mass-power transmission. However, artificial illumination was not an unqualified blessing, as Wells realised: 'The twentieth century was to experience this light to the full. The glaring of shadowless light that illuminates H. G. Wells's negative Utopias no longer guarantees the security of the individual. It permits total surveillance by the state. The Utopian dream of nights lit up as bright as day was transformed into the nightmare of a light from which there was no escape.' (See Wolfgang Schivelbusch, *Disenchanted Night: The Industrialisation of Light in the Nineteenth Century*, trans. Angela Davies (Oxford, New York and Hamburg: Berg, 1988), especially p. 134.)

18 Ostrog's means also recall European fiction's first 'megalomediac', 'Francis Bennett', owner of the *Earth Herald*, in Verne's 'In the Twenty-Ninth Century'. Caricaturing Bennett's real 'ancestor', Gordon (owner of the American *Forum*, which commissioned Verne), this predicts how informational power might develop over a millennium. Located in megalopolitan 'Centropolis', Bennett is more powerful than nation states owing to his global media empire, based on monopolising a form of television (the 'phonotelephote'). Verne predicted that houses would be equipped with combined television and telephone receivers, bringing subscribers audio-visual news of events as they actually occur. But the world is not enough: Bennett has ambitions for broadcasting to other planets via another medium, the 'telephotogram', see Verne, 'In the Twenty-Ninth Century', pp. 98–99 and 102).

WTSW may also have drawn on earlier foreseeings of television such as that of 'the Jules Verne of caricature', Albert Robida. His *téléphonoscope* visualised a device first theorised by Edison in the 1870s. This transmits live theatre to the home (see text and illustrations in his *Le Vingtième Siècle* (1883; Geneva and Paris: Editions Slatkine, 1981), pp. 54–98). A *Punch* cartoon of 1879 had also responded to Edison, by showing a couple in live contact by sound and image with their distant children (see Herbert and McKernan (eds), *Who's Who of Victorian Cinema*, p. 48). Verne's and Robida's devices (doubling as videophones) also display potential for voyeurism and repressive surveillance (see Verne, 'In the Twenty-Ninth Century', pp. 98–99 and Robida, *Le Vingtième Siècle*, pp. 61–62 and 71–72).

Fictional foreseeings were only just ahead of theoretical and practical developments. German scientist Paul Nipkow patented a scanning disc for conveying images by wire in 1884, but this would be superseded by 'seeing by wireless'. Scottish physicist A. Campbell Swinton proposed combining Nipkow's scanning disc with Karl Ferdinand Braun's cathode ray tube in 1908, to elucidate the basic principles of what he called 'distant electric vision': i.e. conversion of light and shade into electrical signals transmitted from camera to receiver over the same airwaves as radio. This would be the basis of John Logie Baird's thirty-line mechanical system. First demonstrated to the Royal Institution in January 1926, it was capable of transmitting images transatlantically by short wave in February 1928. Vast technical advances since have made television the dominant electronic medium of global virtuality, as Verne and Wells prophesied, with satellite, cable, digital and interactive systems, and latterly the increasing erosion of boundaries with mobile phones, games consoles and internet.

19 Baird made this breakthrough in his laboratory in October 1925. Woody Allen's take on Wells's novel, *Sleeper* (1973), also features a dictator with a telegenic persona, which is little more than a virtual dummy. Allen's film parody astutely extends Wells's ideas, because his leader now literally exists only on screen, his real body having been atomised by a revolutionary's bomb. Nevertheless, the regime secretly strives to clone him 'back into his clothes' from his sole surviving organ, his nose!

20 It seems unlikely to be mere coincidence that 'In the Twenty-Ninth Century'

features a cryogenic experimenter, whose miraculous 'resurrection so impatiently waited for' is to be transmitted live on television (see Haining (ed.), *Jules Verne Companion*, pp. 112 and 115). Not only does this seem to clinch Verne's influence on *WTSW*, but thereby recent critiques of globalised media exploitation and parasitic virtual reality such as that by Dennis Potter (see Chapter 5).

21 Wells's imagined term for television is not as felicitous as our familiar one (first cited from the *Scientific American Supplement* (15 June 1907) by the OED). Nevertheless, as Stover points out, it was technically precise. 'Kineto-tele-photographs' translates as 'moving-at-a-distance-images' (see Stover (ed.), *When the Sleeper Wakes*, p. 218, note 130). 'The Remarkable Case of Davidson's Eyes' came closer (see Chapter 1, note 49).

22 Wells, *Conquest of Time*, pp. 21–22.

23 The subjects of Méliès's film foreseeing television, *La Photographie électrique à distance* (1908), are so shocked at their grotesque enlargement that they wreck its inventor's laboratory.

24 See 'Work of Art', in *Illuminations*, pp. 230–32.

25 Stage methods of expression through body language were of course unsuited to the close-up nature of cinema (and even more so of television), as pioneer film-makers, such as D. W. Griffith, soon learned. They were forced to develop a much subtler vocabulary of acting (see Cook, *Narrative Film*, p. 67). It is arguable that Graham's anxious objectification of himself anticipates the histrionics and hubris of twentieth-century dictators' abuse of the media – 'The picture of a little strutting futility in a windy waste of incomprehensible destinies' (*WTSW*, pp. 205–6).

26 In a 1927 essay, 'The Remarkable Vogue for Broadcasting: Will It Continue?', Wells looked back on half a century 'since the wireless transmission of electric phases was understood to be possible'. He already noted the promised global enlightenment and shrinking of ideological distance – that 'One would live in a new world and ask in all the neighbours' – fading into trivial entertainment, 'official misinformation' and censorship. Nonetheless, he still looks forward to television ending the 'blindness' of radio drama. (See *The Way the World Is Going: Guesses and Forecasts for the Years Ahead* (London: Ernest Benn, 1928), pp. 168–78, especially 170–71 and 173–74.)

27 Besides *WTSW*, Tolstoy's novel seems most obviously to have been influenced by *WOTW* and *FMITM*. For Wellsian inspiration in Soviet SF, see Vera Shamina, 'Russia Revisited', among others, in Parrinder and Partington (eds), *Reception of H. G. Wells in Europe*, pp. 48–62, especially 57. *Aelita* was billed in the Film Society's January 1926 programme (see London Film Society, *Film Society Programmes*, p. 13).

28 Von Harbou's novel was first serialised in *Das illustrierte Blatt*, from August 1926, six months before the film premiered. (See Elsaesser, *Metropolis*, p. 12.)

29 Stewart, '"Videology" of Science Fiction', p. 167.

30 Lang's femme fatale, 'Lio Sha', participates in a conference of her international gang through a 'looking-glass' which is a clear forerunner of Fredersen's screen.

31 'Lang's films ... deal primarily with modernity's systematic nature, its interlocking technologies ... a new landscape of space and time riddled with technological links and devices which seem to extend (and often defy) the human will.' (See Gunning, *Films of Fritz Lang*, especially pp. x–xi.)

32 Stewart, '"Videology" of Science Fiction', p. 167. Lang's interest in surveillance gadgetry, such as pinhole cameras, continued in *Spione* (1928) and culminated in his final German film, *Die Tausend Augen des Dr. Mabuse* (1960). The super-criminal's latest embodiment controls his urban empire through a vast bank of secret television monitors, originally installed by the Nazis.

33 Stewart, in Slusser and Rabkin (eds) *Shadows of the Magic Lamp*, p. 166

34 The process used *Spiegeltechnik* to contrive a new kind of simultaneity of different spaces and dimensions. Named after cameraman Eugen Schüfttan, it involved reflecting miniatures on to glass with a magnifying surface, placed at 45°. Gaps were scraped away from areas where live action in real sets was to take place, thus allowing actors and models to be filmed together without using double-exposure or laboratory manipulation. However, the illusion was not perfected for extensive scenes of crowd movement in futuristic environments until *TTC* (see Paul M. Jensen's introduction to Fritz Lang and Thea von Harbou, *Metropolis: The Screenplay* (London: Faber, 1989), p. 13; also Christopher Frayling, *Things to Come* (London: British Film Institute, 1995), pp. 67–68). (*Illustrations of the Schüfftan Process* was shown at the Film Society in April 1929 and November 1930.))

35 Lang (who had recently visited New York) switched topical locations, partly to reflect anxieties about Weimar Germany's dependence on transatlantic capital under the 1924 Dawes Plan. However, the future of *WTSW* is already subject to 'Americanising' tendencies in both monopolistic economics and architecture. Though published shortly before the Boer War, with British imperialism at its zenith, *WTSW* heralds shifts in global influence much more advanced by 1926.

36 Lanos's serial illustrations blend late-Victorian classical and Gothic, but also show Art Nouveau influence (Europe's 'proto-modern' design style) in curvilinear motifs (see *Graphic* (14 Jan.–6 May 1899), pp. 41–561). Lang, a trained architect, topically incorporated Art Deco *Américain*.

37 For such *raumbildend* motifs in Lang and others, see Lotte H. Eisner, *The Haunted Screen: Expressionism in the German Cinema and the Influence of Max Reinhardt*, trans. Richard Greaves (London: Thames and Hudson, 1969), pp. 119–27.

38 Cf. similar effects in *WOTW*, discussed in Chapter 5.

39 Ford, *Soul of London*, pp. 48–49.

40 'Mr Wells Reviews a Current Film: He Takes Issue with This German Conception of What the City of One Hundred Years Hence Will Be Like', *New York Times* (17 Apr. 1927). Incorporated as 'The Silliest Film: Will Machinery Make Robots of Men?', in his *The Way the World Is Going*, pp. 179–89, especially 179. (Henceforth all page references to *The Way the World is Going* (*WTWIG*) will be given in brackets in the text.)

41 See Chapter II, 'The Probable Diffusion of Great Cities', in H. G. Wells, *Anticipations of the Reaction of Mechanical and Scientific Progress upon Human Life and Thought* (London: Chapman and Hall, 1902) pp. 33–65, especially 39–40 and 58–59.

42 A Fordian point not lost on Aldous Huxley, who made consumerism the basis of *Brave New World* (1932).

43 See McGilligan, *Fritz Lang*, pp. 129–30.

44 Wells probably alluded to Jack London's metaphor from his influential reportage on London poverty, *The People of the Abyss* (1903; London: Journeymen, 1977).

45 According to Bergonzi, Wells's earliest fictional inventor, Nebogipfel, is more 'the scientist as magician or alchemist than the sober investigator of the physical world' (Bergonzi, *Early H. G. Wells*, p. 34). The scene when the superstitious mob break in to lynch him as a warlock could be the prototype of the obligatory storming of the 'mad doctor's' castle in 1930s horror films ('Chronic Argonauts', *Definitive Time Machine*, p. 143). Even 'McPhister', in Wells's late film-story, 'The New Faust' (1936), finally reveals himself to be a modern Mephistopheles (see Chapter 4, below).

46 See Arthur Koestler, *Spanish Testament* (London: Gollancz, 1937), pp. 80–82.

47 The result of Paramount and Metro-Goldwyn-Mayer's offer to subsidise UFA's huge debt to the Deutsche Bank was the preferential distribution company 'Parufamet'

in 1926 (see McGilligan, *Fritz Lang*, pp. 129–30).

48 This may have led to Josef Goebbels's alleged offer to Lang to head the Nazi state film industry in 1933. Anton Kaes argues that the film's mystical *Gemeinschaft* between labour and capital is only possible after the suspiciously semitic Rotwang's control over technology has been removed (see his 'Metropolis: City, Cinema, Modernity', in Timothy O. Benson (ed.), *Expressionist Utopias: Paradise, Metropolis, Architectural Fantasy* (Berkeley, CA: University of California Press, 2001), pp. 146–65, especially 162). For the director's ambivalence about Nazism, see Gösta Werner, 'Fritz Lang and Goebbels: Myth and Facts', *Film Quarterly*, no. 43 (Spring 1990), pp. 24–27.

49 Almost a decade later, a memorandum which Wells circulated to his production team still held up Lang's response to his own dystopias as an antitype: 'The rush and jumble and strain of contemporary life due to the uncontrolled effects of mechanism are not to be raised to the *n*th power. On the contrary they are to be eliminated. Things, structure in general, will be great, yes, but they will not be monstrous ... All the balderdash one finds in such a film as ... *Metropolis* about 'robot workers' and ultra-skyscrapers, etc, etc, should be cleared out of your minds before you work on this film. As a general rule you may take it that whatever Lange [sic] did in *Metropolis* is the exact opposite of what we want done here.' The memorandum was eventually appended to Wells's published script (see *Things to Come – A Film Story Based on the Material Contained in His History of the Future 'The Shape of Things to Come'* (London: Cresset, 1935), pp. 13–16, especially 13). Wells was also keen to repudiate *WTSW*'s ideas about the future in his 1935 *Era* interview (see 'Shape of Wells to Come').

50 As elsewhere, Wells translated '*Übermensch*' literally. The standard rendering became the (latinised) 'superman'.

51 Wells's developing views on manipulative media publicity further subvert his distinctions between Ostrog's and Ponderevo's regimes. Wells decided that the salesman is really 'a propagandist of consumption' and that 'professional advertising' was being extended from 'marketing to politics and the public service' (*The Work, Wealth and Happiness of Mankind* (London: Heinemann, 1932), pp. 221 and 224).

52 Michael Minden, 'The City in Early Cinema: *Metropolis, Berlin* and *October*', in Edward Timms and David Kelly (eds), *Unreal City: Urban Experience in Modern European Literature and Art* (Manchester: Manchester University Press, 1985), pp. 193–213, especially 194.

53 One possible common source for 'Morlock' is a famous passage from Karl Marx, 'The Inaugural Address of the Working Men's International Association' (1864). Marx compared factory-owners' use of unrestricted child labour to devotees of Moloch's cult of human sacrifice (see Karl Marx and Friedrich Engels, *Selected Works*, Vol. 1 (Moscow: Progress Publishers 1969), pp. 11–18, especially 16). Von Harbou's novel features many other idols, evidently based on Wellsian imagery. The factory hooter, 'voice of the city', is described as a '*Behemot-Laut*'. Freder sees a pantheon of deities in the central machine-room, alongside Moloch, including '*den Götterwagen von Dschaggernaut*' (prominent in 'The Lord of the Dynamos' (*CSS*, pp. 71–77, especially 73)). The engine of the '*Paternoster-Maschine*' is compared to Ganesh throughout (see Thea von Harbou, *Metropolis* (1926; Frankfurt am Main, Berlin: Wien, 1984), pp. 15, 25 and 31).

54 In his review, Wells considered Lang's mooted German title '*Neubabelsburg*' (punning on the UFA studios) much more apt (see *WTWIG*, p. 180). In the novel, Fredersen's Central Control Tower is known as '*Der Neue Babel Turm*' (see von Harbou, *Metropolis*, p. 15).

55 Stewart, '"Videology" of Science Fiction', p. 167.

56 The novel's Maria seems to have the uncanny power of being '*an Zwei Orten zu*

gleicher Zeit', because of Rotwang's cloning of her image (von Harbou, *Metropolis*, p. 122).

57 For example, Villiers de l'Isle-Adam's novel *L'Ève future* (1889; Paris: Gallimard, 1993) caricatures Edison as technocratic Pygmalion or modern Faust, creator of android 'Hadaly' ('ideal' in Persian), the perfect moving and speaking image of woman. (Edison marketed a phonographic doll around this time.) Verne provided a Gothic influence in his *Le Château des Carpathes* (1892; Paris: Livre de Poche, 1976) (see Chapter 2). Verne's 'In the Twenty-Ninth Century', also speculates about creating doubles by 'electrical hypnotism' and about soulless artificial beings, manufactured from the 'absolute' element underlying all others (see Haining (ed.), *Jules Verne Companion*, pp. 101 and 107–8).

58 De l'Isle-Adam's 'Edison' similarly employs hypnotism alongside image projection to counterfeit Alicia Clary's living features onto Hadaly (see *L'Ève future*, especially pp. 142, 247–49 and notes). Expressionist film abounds with mesmeric doubling. In another connection with Wellsian themes of visual technology and scientific ethics, Klein-Rogge, the actor playing Rotwang, also played Lang's mad doctor Mabuse, with hypnotic 'gaze' and bodysnatching tendencies.

59 Vallorani, 'Invisible Wells', in Parrinder and Partington (eds), *Reception of H. G. Wells*, pp. 311–12. L'Herbier's film clearly references common sources with *Metropolis*, such as *Le Château des Carpathes* and *L'Ève future*, as well as Robida's foreseeings of television.

60 TSF = '*télégraphie sans fil*': i.e. wireless telegraphy, the basis of radio and television.

61 In 'Amiens in the Year 2000 AD' (1875), Verne foretold a kind of telephonic 'hook-up', enabling a Polish pianist to broadcast music simultaneously round the world (see Verne, 'In the Twenty-Ninth Century', p. 12).

62 Wells could have seen *L'Inhumaine* as part of the London Film Society's thirteenth programme, in February 1927 (see London Film Society, *Film Society Programmes*, pp. 51–52).

63 In the *National Observer* serialisation of *TM*, Wells also briefly entertained mechanical substitution of human identity. His unnamed 'red-haired man' rails against a future of 'Frankenstein machines that have developed souls, while men have lost theirs!' (Geduld (ed.), *Definitive Time Machine*, pp. 167–68).

64 See Stewart, '"Videology" of Science Fiction', p. 166.

65 See J. P. Telotte's *Replications: A Robotic History of the Science Fiction Film* (Urbana and Chicago: University of Illinois Press, 1995), especially pp. 3–5 and 16–17. Telotte traces Futura's screen ancestry in forms of mechanical life deconstructing ontological boundaries between human and artificial entities from Méliès onwards (pp. 54–57).

66 As Gaby Wood notes, conflating replica and revenant 'replicant' encapsulates the 'undead' eeriness of cinematic–mechanical simulation (see *Living Dolls: A Magical History of the Quest for Mechanical Life* (London: Faber, 2002), pp. xvii–xviii).

67 Another serial illustration depicts a stand-off for Graham's attention between Helen and a flirtatious rival. The two women are dressed identically in postures suggesting antithetical doubling (see *Graphic* (11 Mar. 1899), p. 297).

68 See von Harbou, *Metropolis*, p. 113.

69 The first explicitly erotic British film was probably Arthur Esmé Collings's 1896 *Woman Undressing*. Many peepshow loops had voyeuristic appeal going further than skirt-dancing, such as Henri Joly's *Le Bain d'une mondaine* (1895), hence their 'What the Butler Saw' reputation. Méliès began a risqué series in 1897, with *Après le bal – le tub*, starring his mistress. Director 'Léar' (Albert Kirchner) profited equally from striptease (as in *Le Coucher de la mariée* (1896)) and commissions for the Catholic Church, summing up the early industry's moral equivocation. Wells may either have seen such

French films or heard about the scandal they caused at a London music hall in 1897 (see Herbert and McKernan (eds), *Who's Who of Victorian Cinema*, pp. 35, 73, 37, 80 and 112, respectively).

70 See von Harbou, *Metropolis*, pp. 119–20.

71 Seventeen-year-old Brigitte Helm played the roles of both mechanical femme fatale and heroine 'with Gish–Pickford look', by deliberately invoking the dyadic screen image of women as it had developed (see Paul M. Jensen, *The Cinema of Fritz Lang* (Cranbury, NJ: Barnes; London: Zwemmer, 1969), p. 67). For the politics of screen femininity in the Weimar period, see Katharina von Ankum (ed.), *Women in Metropolis: Gender and Modernity in Weimar Culture* (Berkeley, CA and Los Angeles: University of California Press, 1997), especially Janet Lungstrum's '*Metropolis* and the Technosexual Woman of German Modernity', pp. 128–44. It is arguable that via *Metropolis*'s cinematic 'androidisation', *WTSW* remains a latent presence behind sexual–political debate about human–machine interface in the age of 'cyborgs'.

72 Lang quoted in Herbert W. Franke's 'Nachwort' to von Harbou, *Metropolis*, pp. 198–205, especially 201.

73 See Storm Jameson, 'Documents', *Fact*, no. 4 (July 1937), pp. 17–18.

74 Like Pound and other Modernists, Wells held up 'that magnificent production *Berlin*' as a new standard in the treatment of modern themes by 'plotless' means (see *KWWAK*, p. 27, and Chapter 4 for Ruttmann's influence on the 'symphonic montage' of his filmwriting). Alberto Cavalcanti and Dziga Vertov's similarly cross-sectional 'days-in-the-life' of a big city, *Rien que les Heures* (1926) and *The Man with the Movie Camera* (1928), were shown at the Film Society in January 1931 and January 1929, respectively.

75 See Peter S. Fisher, *Fantasy and Politics: Visions of the Future in the Weimar Republic* (Madison, WI: University of Wisconsin Press, 1991), especially pp. 145–49 and 182–201. For films such as *FP1 Antwortet Nicht* (1932), *Der Tunnel* (1933) and *Gold* (1934) designed by Lang's key personnel, see Sabine Hake, *Popular Cinema of the Third Reich* (Austin, TX: University of Texas Press, 2001), pp. 54–57; also Chapter 4.

76 See Alexandra Richie, *Faust's Metropolis: A History of Berlin* (London: Harper Collins, 1998), pp. 453–54.

77 For invasion of private and public space in *High Treason* by telecommunications, see Christine Gledhill, *Reframing British Cinema 1918–1928: Between Restraint and Passion* (London: BFI, 2002), pp. 29–30. Based on independent MP Noël Pemberton-Billing's pacifist drama, the futuristic setting and key role of women did not feature in the stage original, but were almost certainly added because of *Metropolis*. (See Anthony Aldgate, 'Loose Ends, Hidden Gems and the "Moment of Melodramatic Emotionality"', in Jeffrey Richards (ed.), *The Unknown 1930s: An Alternative History of the British Cinema, 1929–39* (London: I. B. Tauris, 1997), pp. 219–36, 260–61, note 7; also discussion of *High Treason*'s similarities with *KWWAK* in Chapter 4).

78 See Donald Albrecht, *Designing Dreams: Modern Architecture in the Movies* (Santa Monica, CA: Hennessey and Ingalls, 1986), pp. 156–60; also Frayling, *Scientist and the Cinema*, pp. 74–75.

Chapter 4
The 'Broadbrow' and the Big Screen: Wells's Film Writing

1 Sylvia Hardy, 'H. G. Wells and British Silent Cinema: The War of the Worlds', in Andrew Higson (ed.), *Young and Innocent? The Cinema In Britain 1896–1930* (Exeter:

University of Exeter Press, 2002), pp. 242–55, especially 242.

2   There is no record of a contract with Pathé even though their 1909 *Invisible Thief* openly foregrounds a copy of its source (see Hardy, 'H. G. Wells and British Silent Cinema', p. 253, note 15).

3   Quoted in Hardy (ed.), *Aurum Film Encyclopedia*, p. 33. Other likely sources are: Kipling's proto-totalitarian 'With the Night Mail: A Story of 2000 AD' (1904, repr. in *Actions and Reactions* (London: Macmillan, 1909), pp. 109–42) and 'As Easy as ABC' (1907, repr. in *Actions and Reactions*, pp. 143–69) (ABC standing for 'Aerial Board of Control', a technocratic dictatorship enforced with airships which may also have influenced *TTC*); Verne's *Robur le Conquérant* (1886) and *Maître du Monde* (1904). It was re-released in 1915 as *The Aerial Torpedo* when real Zeppelin attacks began.

4   See Kim Newman, *Apocalypse Movies: End of the World Cinema* (New York: St Martin's, 2000), pp. 23–24; also Mark Bould, 'Film and Television', in Edward James and Farah Mendlesohn (eds), *The Cambridge Companion to Science Fiction* (Cambridge: Cambridge University Press, 2003), pp. 79–95, especially 79–80.

5   See Appendix 8, 'Stage and Screen Adaptations', in Robert M. Philmus (ed.), *The Island of Doctor Moreau: A Variorum Text* (Athens, GA and London: University of Georgia Press, 1993), pp. 230–35, especially 231. For Chaney's film, see Telotte, *Replications*, p. 56.

6   Anon., Notice (of Gaumont British Contract), *The Times* (9 Jan. 1914), p. 8. Anon., 'Mr Wells and the Cinematograph', *The Times* (10 Jan. 1914), p. 6.

7   Anon., 'Concerning Stoll's 1922 Program', *Kinematograph Weekly* (5 Jan. 1922), p. 89.

8   Producers' views are cited in a letter from Curtis Brown (5 June 1913) in the University of Illinois Wells Archive (quoted by Hardy, 'H. G. Wells and British Silent Cinema', p. 245). For contemporary reviewers' complaints, see Wykes, *H. G. Wells in the Cinema*, p. 33; also John Baxter, *Science Fiction in the Cinema* (New York: A. S. Barnes; London: Zwemmer, 1970), p. 18.

9   See Hardy, 'H. G. Wells and British Silent Cinema', pp. 246–47.

10   Interestingly, when Charlie Chaplin criticised Elvey's cinematography at a private showing, Wells's attitude 'was an affected tolerance'. As if Wells had never got past film's initial fascination, Chaplin recalled him saying, 'There is no such thing as a bad film ... the fact that they move is wonderful.' (See Charlie Chaplin, *My Autobiography* (1964; Harmondsworth: Penguin, 2003), pp. 270–71.)

11   Wilson's judgement on *Birth of a Nation* is quoted in Cook, *Narrative Film*, p. 65. Anon., 'Plays', *Photoplay* (July 1922), p. 58.

12   In 1919 alone Wells received an offer from Sam Goldwyn, for a five-year film option at £1,000 per work, guaranteeing at least £2,000 per annum. By 1933 he had earned £6,750 and $10,000 from British and American companies (see Smith, *Desperately Mortal*, pp. 322–23).

13   Wells's reply to a questionnaire about 'Author or Producer, Which Should Count?' was curt (perhaps prompted by his experience with Stoll): 'I am anxious to oblige, but really I have no views about that matter.' However, he wasn't the only contemporary writer feeling that his work had been travestied (see Anon., 'The Novelist and the Film', *John o' London's*, Vol. IX, no. 226 (4 Aug. 1923), pp. 577–78 and contd. 597, especially 578).

14   Quoted in Danvers Williams, 'I Wrote this Film for Your Enjoyment', *Film Weekly* (29 February 1936), pp. 7–8, especially 8.

15   Wells thought he had spotted 'Chaplinesque' potentials in Lanchester (see Danvers Williams, 'I Wrote this Film for Your Enjoyment', p. 8), perhaps recalling

Mabel Normand's success as female silent clown.

16 Montagu recalled 'desperately working on H. G.'s scraps of paper, trying to think up visual jokes and turn them into scripts' (see Ivor Montagu, *With Eisenstein in Hollywood* (London: Lawrence and Wishart, 1968), pp. 19–20).

17 Ideal's managing director, Simon Rowson, wanted to graft a soundtrack, but Montagu resisted, arguing that further delay would vitiate the motive behind Wells's 'leg-up' to the new talents he was sponsoring: 'Conception occurred in a world of silent films ... Parturition in a world already invaded by sound' (Montagu, *With Eisenstein*, p. 23; see also Hardy, 'H. G. Wells and British Silent Cinema', p. 251). The *Daily Mail* shared Montagu's irritation, commenting that the vogue for sound was depriving the wider public, whereas 'when these comedies were tried out on an ordinary audience in the suburbs the other night the laughter was loud and spontaneous' (Anon., 'Why Not Show Them?', *Daily Mail* (4 July 1929), p. 8).

18 The reviewer in *The Times* singled out this sequence for special comment (Anon., 'New Film Comedies: Humour by Mr H. G. Wells,' *The Times* (12 Sept. 1929), p. 10). *Bluebottles* featured in the London Film Society's 52nd programme (Jan. 1932).

19 Montagu's abundant scrapbook of press clippings confirms this. Critics were duly impressed by both Lanchester and the supporting Charles Laughton (see the BFI's 'Ivor Montagu Collection', Item 25).

20 Jamie Sexton, 'Alternative Film Culture in Britain in the 1920s', in Higson (ed.), *Young and Innocent?*, pp. 291–305, especially 299–301. The *Times* reviewer thought they 'burlesque[d] ... the cruder manners of the screen'. Their critique of avant-gardism was also noted: 'In [Montagu's] employment of trick photography, unusual camera angles and symbolism we observe a criticism of contemporary techniques which blends well with its subject' (Anon., 'New Film Comedies', p. 10).

21 Marcus, 'Literature and Cinema', p. 340.

22 Hardy, 'H. G. Wells and British Silent Cinema', p. 250.

23 Ibid., pp. 251–52.

24 See 'Note to the Reader', in Wells's *Things to Come: A Film Story*, pp. 11–12. (Henceforth, all page references to *Things to Come: A Film Story* (*TTCAFS*) will be given in brackets in the text.)

25 Quoted in Wykes, *H. G. Wells in the Cinema*, p. 75.

26 'Forcword', in L'Estrange Fawcett, *Films: Facts and Forecasts* (London: Geoffrey, 1927), pp. v–vi. Chaplin's 'giant of limitless powers' also suggests a possible allusion to *The Food of the Gods and How It Came to Earth* (1904), a parable about human failure to keep pace with the potentials of social and cultural evolution which Wells would rewrite as a 'film treatment' for Korda in 1935 (see Wells, 'Shape of Wells to Come'; also *H. G. Wells in Love: Postscript to An Experiment in Autobiography*, ed. G. P. Wells (London: Faber, 1984), p. 207).

27 Wells, Preface to *Scientific Romances of H. G. Wells*, p. x.

28 For details, see Rachel Low, *The History of British Film, 1918–1929* (London: George Allen and Unwin, 1971), pp. 198–99. Godal eventually took 'a stranglehold' on the project, signing up stars, director and crew, without raising the money to pay them (unpublished letter, 6 Dec. 1927, in Wells's Archive, cited by Hardy, in Higson (ed.), *Young and Innocent?*, p. 255, note 39).

29 In his 1935 interview, Wells insisted that the media 'have played down too low' to the public, reiterating his confidence in levelling up: 'the public can stand very much better stuff than it ever gets a chance to appreciate'. ('Shape of Wells to Come')

30 *KWWAK* quotes key passages about the extraterrestrial viewpoint of 'certain impersonated abstractions or Intelligences, called 'Spirits' and effects such as the 'zoom

in' to the Earth through parted clouds (from Thomas Hardy, *The Dynasts: A Drama of the Napoleonic Wars in Three Parts, Nineteen Acts, and One Hundred and Thirty Scenes* (London: Macmillan, 1903–8), Part 1, Vol. I, pp. vii and 9.) Wells continued to cite *The Dynasts* as epitomising cinematic writing: 'I think it would go on the screen almost as it is' ('Shape of Wells to Come').

31 Wells was evidently aware of the 'absolute film' movement, with which Ruttmann was associated and which was a significant influence on his *Berlin: Symphony of a Big City*'s characteristic alternation between documentary mimesis and abstract patterning. Wells had the opportunity to see numerous forms of 'absolute films' and abstract animations by Ruttmann, Viking Eggeling and Hans Richter between 1927 and 1929 at the London Film Society (see London Film Society, *Film Society Programmes*, pp. 2 and 66).

32 Hand-tinting had been used in notable contemporary films, such as Eric von Stroheim's *Greed* (1924) (screened in the Society's 11th (Dec. 1926) programme) to pick out symbolic golden objects and suggest materialistic obsession. But this was superseded by more technical processes in the quest for naturalistic full-colour reproduction. Wells may have also seen experimental colour films (see London Film Society, *Film Society Programmes*, pp. 42–43 and 66–67). As noted in Chapter 3, Wells enthused about the method of Ruttmann's *Berlin: Symphony of a Big City*, as an example of how '[u]ndramatic entirely plotless spectacular films' could be 'enormously effective'. He thought it might be possible to use Ruttmann's method to make a film about the Great War, but such subjects possessed 'an established organic integrity', which partly explains why he felt unable to adandon plot altogether for the opposite issue of World Peace (see *KWWAK*, p. 26). *Berlin* itself was screened at the Society in March 1928. The programme drew special attention to the way editing and music were 'welded to form a single rhythm' by symphonic montage (London Film Society, *Film Society Programmes*, p. 87).

33 They attempt to solve their common problem with similar plots about conspiracies of international warmongers versus heroic campaigners. There are further thematic and motific parallels, including protagonists torn between political duty and the peace movement, romantic involvement with the daughter of its leader and climactic acts of expedient assassination to prevent greater conflict (in *KWWAK*, Paul shoots his rival, Prince Michael, just as his Fascist coup seems about to succeed; in *High Treason*, the Peace League head, 'Dr Seymour', shoots the President of Europe, before he can declare war on television).

34 Stephen Dedalus, in the 'Circe' chapter of James Joyce's *Ulysses*, famously says, pointing to his forehead, 'But in here it is that I must kill the priest and the king' (1922; Oxford: Oxford World's Classics, 1998), p. 548.

35 'Woman as Protector and Sustainer' is at least some kind of advance on Mae Marsh as the hapless 'Lily-White' in Griffith's *Man's Genesis*.

36 His scenario may in turn have been influenced by Wells's own tale of human origin, 'A Story of the Stone Age' (1897) (see *CSS*, pp. 290–332).

37 As Bailey points out, actual cinematic realisation would bear an 'uncanny resemblance' to the opening, scripted by Wells devotee Arthur C. Clarke (see Bailey, '"There Would Presently Come Out of the Darkness"'). *2001* also consists of a multistage narrative like *TTC*, moving into near and then successively remoter futures.

38 See, for example, Donald et al. (eds), *Close-Up*, pp. 100, 237 and 240–41. Some of Pabst's other socially critical and anti-militarist films, such as *The Joyless Street* (1925), *Die Drei Groschen Oper* and *Westfront 1918* (both 1930), may also have been seen by Wells (see London Film Society, *Film Society Programmes*, pp. 47, 190 and 200).

39 Paul's phrase may echo Stephen's comment on the claims of past ideologies in the nightmare of history in 'Nestor': '– I fear those big words ... which make us so unhappy' (Joyce, *Ulysses*, p. 31).

40 See Crafton, *Before Mickey*, p. 329. Wells admired both the industrial and aesthetic efficiency of Disney's *Silly Symphonies*, especially in co-ordinating visuals and music. He named Disney 'the most important person in the film industry', after visiting his studios (see Danvers Williams, 'I Wrote this Film for Your Enjoyment', pp. 7–8). In the midst of the Second World War, Wells described the clash of regressive ideologies as a kind of mad cartoon world resembling *Fantasia*'s 'overture' on the 'genetic delirium' of the age of the dinosaurs: 'our mental life today, with its Churches and Powers, its Race delusions and its hegemonies, its American Way of Life and its Dictatorship of the Proletariat ... is a sort of grotesque by Walt Disney, as fantastically unreal' (*Conquest of Time*, p. 63).

41 See Karol Kulik, *Alexander Korda: The Man Who Could Work Miracles* (London: Virgin, 1990), p. 149. Wells also seems to have planned cartoonlike effects within the live action of *MWCWM*, though these were shelved too. Fotheringay interrogates flowers into betraying the Colonel's hiding place. They reply in various voices, including Greta Garbo's (*MWCWMAFS*, pp. 78–79). The London Film Society had screened numerous cartoons, both experimental and popular, by the time *KWWAK* was published: *Krazy Kat*, *Mickey Mouse*, Ruttmann's *Kriemhild's Dream of Hawks*, Lotte Reiniger's 'silhouette' films, etc. (see London Film Society, *Film Society Programmes*).

42 Cf. recommendation for the Steelville car plant: 'The picturing of the factory must be good and exciting. The music must swing into the rhythm of modern machinery' (*KWWAK*, p. 63).

43 Bailey, '"There Would Presently Come Out of the Darkness"', p. 31.

44 For the BBFC's ban on 'controversy', see James C. Robertson, *The British Board of Film Censors: Film Censorship in Britain 1896–1950* (London: Croom Helm, 1985), especially pp. 10 and 54. Ironically, the BBFC would eventually pass *TTC*'s highly realistic 'Blitz' scenes uncut, while taking a very different view of the Left Wing pacifist short, *The Peace of Britain* (see Robertson, *The British Board of Film Censors*, p. 103).

45 Kenneth MacPherson, 'The Novelist Who Was a Scenarist', *Close-Up*, Vol. IV, no. 3 (Mar. 1929), pp. 78–80.

46 Dorothy Richardson, 'Continuous Performance: Almost Persuaded', *Close-Up*, Vol. IV, no. 6 (June 1929), repr. in Donald, Friedberg and Marcus (eds), *Close-Up*, pp. 190–92.

47 Paul Rotha, *The Film Till Now: A Survey of World Cinema* (1930; new edition, Hamlyn, 1967), p. 111.

48 Marcus, 'Literature and Cinema', p. 340.

49 See Jeffrey Richards, '*Things to Come* and Science Fiction in the 1930s', in I. Q. Hunter (ed.), *British Science Fiction Cinema* (London and New York: Routledge, 1999), pp. 16–32, especially 28–29. One film described as such was Anthony Kimmins's *Once in a New Moon* (1934), a comic fable resembling both Wells's *In the Days of the Comet* (1906) and Verne's *Hector Servadac* (1877). An Essex seaside village is gouged off the Earth by a passing comet to become 'Shrimpton-in-the-Universe'. Because its inhabitants won't broaden their horizons, the village does so instead as a new satellite for the Earth. Like many scientific romances in which everyday life is defamiliarised by bizarre phenomena, this results in a kind of social revolution.

50 Wells signed an immediate contract on a penny-postcard. The payment of £10,000 for the film rights of *SOTTC*, plus royalties, indicates how enthralled Korda must have been (see Christopher Frayling, *Things to Come* (London: BFI, 1995), pp. 18

and 20).

51 See Wells's original treatment, *Whither Mankind? A Film of the Future* (*WM*) (repr. as Appendix I in Leon Stover (ed.), *The Prophetic Soul: A Reading of H. G. Wells's Things to Come* (Jefferson, NC and London: McFarland, 1987), pp. 121–79, especially 121–22).

Krishan Kumar argues that *SOTTC* synthesised the classic elements of Wells's technotopian vision: i.e. a world state, based on a form of Saint-Simonian socialism, with economic planning on applied scientific lines. This would be ruled by an intellectual elite, on the principles of efficiency, simplicity and system. The static perfection besetting other Utopias (satirised in the entropy of *TM*) would be avoided through an 'evolutionary dynamism'. (See his *Utopia and Anti-Utopia in Modern Times* (Oxford: Basil Blackwell, 1991), pp. 191–223. *WM* was also based on material from Wells's 1932 socio-economic treatise. Wells had lamented in this that cinema was the most 'startling case of a new, important method of communication gone very seriously astray'. (*Work, Wealth and Happiness of Mankind*, pp. 156–57).

52 Some of its rare concrete images did find their way into the film, however, such as the 'horse-drawn' car and the wasted dome of St Paul's in Book the Second (see H. G. Wells, *The Shape of Things to Come* (1933; London: Dent, 1993), p. 226).

53 Raymond Massey, *A Hundred Different Lives: An Autobiography* (London: Robson Books, 1979), p. 191.

54 Everytown's futuristic costume is more or less unisex, but also practical to accommodate personal televisors on wrists. Designers John Armstrong and the Marchioness of Queensbury added samurai-like '*kata-ginu*' shoulder-pieces, to echo Wells's own term for the Utopian elite in his 1905 text (see *TTC*, 'Release Script', and *WM*, in Stover (ed.), *Prophetic Soul*, pp. 275 and 158, respectively).

55 Quoted in Danvers Williams, 'I Wrote this Film for Your Enjoyment', pp. 7–8, especially 8.

56 Conversely, Wells complained in his diary that Cameron Menzies was 'a sort of Cecil B. de Mille without his imagination' (see *H. G. Wells in Love*, p. 211).

57 See Kulik, *Alexander Korda*, p. 150; also Frayling, *Things to Come*, pp. 15–16.

58 *March of Time*, British issue, no. 7 (Mar. 1936).

59 The *Journal of the British Interplanetary Society* (Feb. 1937) pointed out that G-forces would immediately pulp Wells's astronauts (see Anon., 'Things to Come', repr. in Johnson (ed.), *Focus on the Science Fiction Film*, pp. 41–42). Publicity for the film sidestepped this embarrassment by substituting a rocket ship on posters (see reproduction in Stover, *Prophetic Soul*, plate 2). On the other hand, George Zebrowski argues that the Space Gun's graduated booster system (based on Willy Ley's designs) was misunderstood (Introduction to H. G. Wells, *Things to Come*, ed. Allan Asherman and George Zebrowski (Boston: Gregg, 1975), pp. xxxiii–ix).

60 For overviews of critical and public reactions, see Richards, 'Things to Come', p. 19; Frayling, *Things to Come*, pp. 67–72 and 76–77; Charles Drazin, *Korda: Britain's Only Movie Mogul* (London: Sidgwick and Jackson, 2002), pp. 141–42. Michael Korda calls *TTC* 'an instant box-office failure' (see his *Charmed Lives: A Family Romance* (1979; New York: Harper Collins, 2002), p. 123), whereas Frayling shows that it was moderately successful, if not exactly profitable.

61 Sydney W. Carroll, '"Things to Come": A Stupendous Film', *Sunday Times* (23 Feb. 1936), p. 4. Its sister paper also thought, with such sets and effects, 'Mr. Wells's story, however doubtful his implied arguments may appear and however loose the speeches, cannot fail to carry the spectator away. Any rhetoric against such a background is superb' (Anon., 'New H. G. Wells Film', *The Times* (21 Feb. 1936), p. 12).

62 Repr. in Alistair Cooke, *Garbo and the Night Watchmen* (London: Secker and

Warburg, 1971), pp. 126–30; C. A. Lejeune, 'Film of the Week', *Observer* (23 Feb. 1936), p. 14; Elizabeth Bowen, *Sight and Sound*, no. 17 (Spring 1936), pp. 10–12.

63 Richards, 'Things to Come', pp. 19–20.

64 Quoted in Korda, *Charmed Lives*, p. 123.

65 Richards, 'Things to Come', p. 23. Links between *Metropolis* and *TTC* in fact typify 'symbiosis' between inter-war British and German SF epics, especially their focus on futuristic technology and the heroic role of the scientist/engineer/airman battling international conspiracies of vested interests. Films such as Kurt Bernhardt's *Der Tunnel* (1933) (about a transatlantic link) were remade by British directors such as Maurice Elvey (1935), or in different language versions, such as Karl Hartl's *FP1 Antwortet Nicht/The Secrets of FP1*(1932), about a mid-atlantic flight platform, though with different national–ideological spins and the assistance of German film-makers in exile after the Nazi coup (see Richards, 'Things to Come', pp. 27–28; also Michael Paris, *From the Wright Brothers to Top Gun: Aviation, Nationalism and Popular Cinema* (Manchester: Manchester University Press, 1995) p. 76). *FP1*, in particular, featured much that anticipates *TTC*. Its layered, geometric montage depicting the building of the 'artificial island' seems a visual prototype for Wells's reconstruction scenes. Knock-out gas is used by saboteurs and the project is saved by the alliance between engineer and flyer, with climactic rescue by massed aircraft. As Frayling also points out, Wells may have derived the volunteering of Cabal and Passworthy's children from Elvey's *Tunnel*, in which engineer 'Richard Dix' sacrifices his son to his visionary project (see Frayling, *Things to Come*, p. 56).

66 Symptomatically, *WM* describes the air battle with the Basra fleet taking place 'offscreen', whereas it constitutes one of the film's highlights (see Stover (ed.), *Prophetic Soul*, p. 152).

67 See Frayling, *Things to Come*, pp. 62 and 71–72.

68 *Ballet Mécanique* featured in the Society's 6th programme (Mar. 1926) (London Film Society, *Film Society Programmes*, p. 22).

69 Wells's ideas for New Everytown may also have been influenced by the January 1932 screening of Maximilian von Goldbeck and Erich Kotzer's *The Town of Tomorrow* (1931), a German film employing trick photography, graphics and models to visualise the modernising benefits of planned reconstruction. Moholy-Nagy's international *Architects' Congress* (1933) presented similarly cutting-edge ideas (see London Film Society, *Film Society Programmes*, pp. 211 and 273).

70 Richards, 'Things to Come', p. 18.

71 Newman, *Apocalypse Movies*, p. 30.

72 Wells, of course, did not foresee the current chaos in Iraq. He chose it symbolically as the 'cradle' of civilisation, from which it might be renewed.

73 Massey felt daunted by the demands of playing several versions of himself in different circumstances and ages (see *A Hundred Different Lives*, p. 192).

74 Asked by his American interviewer if *TTC* dealt with the possibility of totalitarian revolution like Sinclair Lewis's novel about Fascist takeover of the USA, *It Can't Happen Here* (1935) (in which media control plays a key part), Wells was arguably evasive (see 'Shape of Wells to Come', p. 20).

75 The film omitted Wells's 'Before the Second World War' sequence which grounded it in documentary footage, with the opening title 'Whither Mankind?' over a global montage of crowds from Depression-hit cities. Nonetheless, he also wanted a counterpart series of *TM*-like dissolves between primitive and modern scenes, suggesting social and technological advance (see *TTCAFS*, pp. 19–20).

76 The huge set at Denham Studios was totally obliterated for the occasion. Wells

could have become familiar with Eisenstein's masterpieces at the London Film Society, which screened *Potemkin* (1925) in November 1929 and *October* (1928) in March 1934.

77 As Stuart Sillars shows, this scene influenced Cecil Day Lewis's 1938 satire 'Newsreel', in which an audience emerges into the reality of an air raid (see his '*Things to Come* and "Newsreel": Versions of Cinematic Influence', in *Notes and Queries*, Vol. 47, no. 1 (Mar. 2002), pp. 91–93).

78 Herman Goering screened *TTC* as a model for Luftwaffe objectives, while Chamberlain took it is as a powerful argument for appeasement (see Korda, *Charmed Lives*, p. 122).

79 Richardson's caricature was accurate enough to get *TTC* banned in Italy, even though Wells stipulated that the Boss should be a more universal and timeless figure (see Stover (ed.), *Prophetic Soul*, p. 137). *The Times*, for example, thought that *TTC*'s actors were 'naturally dwarfed' by the settings, but that Richardson nonetheless managed 'a subtle caricature of a dictator among the ruins' (Anon., 'New H. G. Wells Film', p. 12).

80 See ibid., p. 12.

81 'equation of science with common sense does not really hold good. Modern Germany is far more scientific than England, and far more barbarous. Much of what Wells has imagined and worked for is physically there in Nazi Germany. The order, the planning, the state encouragement of science, the steel, the concrete, the aeroplanes, are all there, but all in the service of ideas appropriate to the Stone Age. Science is fighting on the side of superstition' (George Orwell, 'Wells, Hitler and the World State' (August 1941), in *Complete Works of George Orwell*, ed. Peter Davison, Vol. XII, *A Patriot After All 1940–1941* (London: Secker and Warburg, 2000), pp. 536–41, especially 539. For Nazi hijacking of the cult of the scientist-engineer, see Fisher, *Fantasy and Politics*, especially pp. 145–49 and 182–201).

82 See 'You and the Atom Bomb' and 'What Is Science?' (Oct. 1945), in *Complete Works of George Orwell*, ed. Peter Davison, Vol. XVII, *I Belong to the Left 1945* (London: Secker and Warburg, 2001), pp. 316–28.

83 'New architectural forms appear presently, prevail for a few flashes and pass. Compare the description of time-travelling in the TIME MACHINE' (see Stover (ed.), *Prophetic Soul*, p. 158).

84 Wells had also admired Vertov's *Three Songs of Lenin* (1934) on his recent visit to the USSR, 'One of the greatest and most beautiful films'. The third 'song' was an audio-visual montage of industrial regeneration under Stalin's Five Year Plan. (Quoted in Maria Kozyrena and Vera Shamina, 'Russia Revisited', in Parrinder and Partington (eds), *Reception of H. G. Wells in Europe*, pp. 46–62, especially 54.)

85 See Frayling, *Things to Come*, pp. 72–75. *Lichtspiel Schwarz-Weiss-Grau* was screened at the London Film Society in November 1932 (see *Film Society Programmes*, p. 235).

86 See Frayling, *Things to Come*, p. 67.

87 Pioneering social and industrial documentaries by John Grierson's disciples featured regularly at Film Society screenings. Those with particular relevance to *TTC* include Arthur Elton's *Aero Engine* (1933) and (with Edgar Anstey) *Housing Problems* (1935) (see London Film Society, *Film Society Programmes*, pp. 269 and 331).

88 See Korda, *Charmed Lives*, p. 121. Hardwicke felt that Wells had sacrificed his sense of humour in inverse proportion to his role as world figure: 'I itched to remind him of the G. B. S. dictum that only by ridicule can evil be destroyed.' (*A Victorian in Orbit: The Irreverent Memoirs of Sir Cedric Hardwicke* (London: Methuen, 1961), pp. 197–98.)

89 In *WM*, the speech is transmitted from a giant cinema. The Release Script refers

to the studio as 'the BBC', which launched the first regular television service the year that *TTC* was released (see Stover (ed.), *Prophetic Soul*, pp. 162 and 278).

90 '3D' had been part of moving image research from the beginning. Louis Lumière began with 'Photo-stereo-synthesis plates', like prototype holograms, but by the 1930s was producing stereoscopic films (see Herbert and McKernan (eds), *Who's Who of Victorian Cinema*, p. 87).

91 In a recent radio broadcast, 'Whither Britain?', Wells echoed his original treatment's title and put the case for integrating national interests into a scientific 'commonweal of mankind', very like *TTC*'s: 'Is that Utopian? That is for you to judge. I consider I am talking the plainest common sense. And I cannot help reminding you that once or twice in the past I have been a successful prophet.' (*Listener*, Vol. XI, no. 261 (10 Jan. 1934), pp. 43–44 and contd 83–84, especially 83.)

92 In the film, the presentation of idle masses arguably undermines the anti-Langian impression that Wells aimed to create of the people of the future as 'individualised workers doing responsible co-operative team work' ('Memorandum', *TTCAFS*, p. 14).

93 In *SOTTC*, Theotocopulos's private notebooks suggest more sympathy with his viewpoint that the Air Dictatorship has achieved peace and order at the cost of the aesthetic aspect of life and lost its 'sense of proportion' (see Book the Fourth, pp. 357–65). This seems largely lost in the film.

94 Cooke, *Garbo and the Night Watchmen*, p. 128. *The Times* conceded that Wells had broken with the presumptive logic of Utopian tradition: 'the film no longer accepts quite readily the premise ... that the future will be completely glorious if only the litter of the present can be completely removed'. Nevertheless, they felt that the presentation of Theotocopulos as spokesman for artistic opposition bore the hallmarks of a private grudge rather than genuine debate (Anon., 'New H. G. Wells Film', p. 12).

95 Korda, *Charmed Lives*, p. 122.

96 Kulik, *Alexander Korda*, pp. 151–52; H. G. Wells, *All Aboard for Ararat* (London: Secker and Warburg, 1941), p. 75.

97 See Stover (ed.), *Prophetic Soul*, p. 148.

98 For other post-production excisions and Wells's complaints, see Frayling, *Things to Come*, pp. 77–78.

99 H. G. Wells, *The New Machiavelli* (London: John Lane, 1911), p. 412.

100 *TTCAFS*'s scenes with stereotypically Jewish trader Wadsky were, mercifully, omitted. Conversely, *TTC* failed to follow *WM*'s instruction that the 'Air Council' should be 'of mixed race' (see Stover (ed.), *Prophetic Soul*, p. 149). At worst, Wells aimed at a humane version of Kipling's proto-totalitarian air dictatorship in 'As Easy as ABC', with its slogans 'Transport is Civilization' and 'Democracy is a Disease'.

101 Robert Wohl stresses *TTC*'s uniquely internationalist take on air power, as opposed to its cult role in Fascism (see his *The Spectacle of Flight: Aviation and the Western Imagination, 1920–1950* (Carlton, Victoria: University of Melbourne Press, 2005), pp. 105–6 and 49–108, respectively; cf. Peter Fritzsche, *A Nation of Flyers: German Aviation and the Popular Imagination* (Cambridge, MA and London: Harvard University Press, 1992), pp. 195–200).

102 Wells had just visited Stalin, but failed to persuade him that technocratic revolution had superseded the proletariat. As Richards points out, *TTC* embodies both reactionary and 'modernising' aspects of dictatorship, in its caricature of violent, romantic nationalism in The Boss and idealised authoritarian efficiency personified in Cabal (Richards, 'Things to Come', p. 22).

103 Wells made it clear that *TTC* was not prophecy, but imaginative stimulant to raise debate about urgent issues: 'A film which encompasses all these questions is

NEWS and therefore stands a good chance of being good entertainment. If, at the same time, the film gives the public fresh hope – helps them to see the folly of things as they are, and spurs them on to fresh endeavour – then that is all to the good.' (Quoted in Danvers Williams, 'I Wrote this Film for Your Enjoyment', p. 7.)

104 Anon., 'Mr H. G. Wells's Film "Things to Come"', *Nature*, Vol. 137, no. 3461 (29 Feb. 1936), p. 352. (*TTCAFS* had already been reviewed in no. 3454 (11 Jan. 1936), p. 50.)

105 Richards, 'Things to Come', p. 21.

106 Kulik, *Alexander Korda*, p. 150. Graham Greene's review illustrates this perfectly. He thought the first third 'magnificent' for 'horribly convincing detail', but found its further futures 'vague, optimistic, childlike' (Graham Greene, 'Things to Come', *Spectator* (28 Feb. 1936), repr. in *The Graham Greene Film Reader: Mornings in the Dark*, ed. David Parkinson (Manchester: Carcanet, 1993), pp. 77–79).

107 Wells (ed.), *H. G. Wells in Love*, p. 211.

108 Wells, *Star Begotten*, pp. 170–71. Wells plumbed the depths of disenchantment and self-justification in a letter to James Hodson, after receiving more press cuttings about 'that bloody film', alleging, 'It was mucked up at the end by powers beyond my control ... [I] had to turn [*SOTTC*] over to rhetoric and introduce that space gun foolery simply because I could not get the faintest gleam of invention out of anyone concerned' (4 June 1938, in Smith (ed.), *Correspondence of H. G. Wells*, Vol. 4, *1935–1946*, p. 195).

109 See Susan Sontag, 'The Imagination of Disaster', in Sontag, *Against Interpretation and Other Essays* (London: Eyre and Spottiswoode, 1967), pp. 209–25.

110 See 'Fiction about the Future' (transcript of a broadcast on Australian radio (29 Dec. 1938)), in Parrinder and Philmus (eds), *H. G. Wells's Literary Criticism*, pp. 249 and 250. Postmodern SF film from *Blade Runner* onwards has, arguably, got round this problem with its 'retrofitted' design styles.

111 According to Drazin, Korda was disappointed by the rough cut of *MWCWM* he viewed in July 1935, shelving subsequent production so that it didn't affect the release of *TTC* (see his *Korda*, pp. 143–44).

112 See *MWCWMAFS*, p. 20. (Henceforth all page references to *MWCWMAFS* will be given in brackets in the text.)

113 Michael Spoliansky's score deliberately echoes the rhythm of Paul Abraham Dukas's famous 1897 symphonic poem on this supernatural theme. Spoliansky followed Wells's direction for Fotheringay's signature tune which builds up ominously like his miracle-working: 'petty and comic at first', becoming 'charged with portent and menace' as things get out of control (see *MWCWMAFS*, pp. 9–10).

114 In the novel, this is 'Hades', complete with phantoms. (Mild blasphemies like the landlord's '"'Ere! What the 'ell?"' were also censored.) Winch's materialisation is visualised as if 'through field glasses' to suggest vast distance, but this effect was dropped (see *MWCWMAFS*, pp. 34–35 and 19, respectively).

115 One of the American newspapermen comments on Winch's teleportation as if it were an instance of futuristic transport or communications technology: 'We've got to cut it out, just the same as we should have had to cut out stories about flying, submarines or radio – fifty years ago.' (p. 45) The colonel's remonstration that there hass been enough change in the last century with 'railways, electricity, radio' (he adds photography and steel ships in the film novel (*MWCWM*, p. 71)) draws attention to the same issues.

116 *Nature* reviewed *MWCWMAFS* in these allegoric terms, concluding: 'Mr. Wells uses his new technique to expound his familiar theme of man's inability to use wisely the powers with which science has endowed him, and to bring into sharp relief the moral as well as the material obstacles which beset the transformation of the present

situation of unemployment and impoverishment in the midst of overproduction and sabotage into an era of peace and plenitude for all.' (Anon., 'Man Who Could Work Miracles', *Nature*, Vol. 137, no. 3475 (6 June 1936), p. 929.)

117 See Kulik, *Alexander Korda*, p. 185.

118 See note 30, above.

119 Claude Rains in *The Clairvoyant* (1934, dir. Maurice Elvey) had just played a fraudulent mind-reader, who becomes cursed with real powers of seeing 'things to come', which can be used for trivial or portentous purposes. These range from racing tips to previsions of disasters.

120 The film drops Fotheringay's topical reference to Roosevelt's attempts at reforming American capitalism on more social-democratic lines: 'What price Bill Stoker's New Deal?' (*MWCWMAFS*, p. 51).

121 Fotheringay recognises he is stirred by half-conscious forces, over which he rightly fears losing control: 'I keep thinking of things and wanting things. I can't tell you. Maggie. I got a *bad* imagination. I got a *dangerous* imagination.'

122 *MWCWMAFS* leaves a choice of style between the modernity of Stockholm Town Hall or the architectural paintings of Paul Veronese, just as costumes could have been either futuristic or Renaissance (p. 84). Mendes opted for the latter in both cases to contrast with *TTC*, but also because they reflect Fotheringay's suggestible character better.

123 'it is *Who's Who in America*; it is *Europa* and the *Statesman's Year Book*, assembled' (*MWCWMAFS*, p. 87). The surreal sequence is anticipated in *KWWAK*, where the debating chamber at Dr Harting's lecture expands to incorporate the nations of the Earth: 'The hall is allowed to appear very large, it suggests now the world audience to modern thought, and little groups of nationals appear' (p. 78). Wells's 1931 radio broadcast, 'What I would Do With the World', imagines a similar 'parliament' of world leaders dissolving into a 'babel' of self-interest and replaced by an 'Educational Dictatorship' (see excerpt repr. in Leon Stover (ed.), *The Man Who Could Work Miracles: A Critical Edition of the 1936 New York First Edition* (Jefferson, NC: McFarland, 2003), pp. 130–38, especially 136–37). However, the scene has roots as far back as Wells's 'A Vision of Judgement' and may have influenced the heavenly courtroom in *A Matter of Life and Death* (see Chapter 1, note 80).

124 'Science made miracles, if I didn't. There was plenty and more than plenty. The papers said so. The professors said so. *You* could go anywhere and do anything. And what did you do for *us*? What was *our* share?' (*MWCWMAFS*, p. 88).

125 H. G. Wells, *The Outline of History: Being a Plain History of Life and Mankind*, Vol. II (London: George Newnes, 1920), p. 758.

126 See Drazin, *Korda*, p. 144; Kulik, *Alexander Korda*, pp. 185–86.

127 See J. R. Hammond, *An H. G. Wells Chronology* (Basingstoke: Macmillan, 1999), p. 115. Nevertheless, an exchange of letters with another producer, Leon M. Lion, indicates that the latter thought that *The New Faust* treatment 'would lend itself to the camera'. Lion also suggested Laurence Olivier for the lead role and discussed possible stage versions of *NF* and *MWCWM* (see letter of 14 Nov. 1936 in Smith (ed.), *Correspondence of H. G. Wells*, Vol. 4, *1935–1946*, p. 110 and note). Although Korda did not take up *FOTG* either, his special effects team nonetheless achieved famously convincing gigantism with the genie in *The Thief of Baghdad* (1940; dir. Michael Powell).

128 Stevenson also directed *Non-Stop New York* (1937), a thriller about a murder witness rushing to save an innocent man, set aboard a futuristic airliner. It cashed in on the Wellsian vogue for flight, but also anticipated transatlantic shuttling by Pan-Am and Imperial Airways by two years.

129 Max Beerbohm's *Doppelgänger* caricature of Wells, showing him as a pontificating elder meeting his time-travelling younger self might serve as a kind of comment on the failure of the cinematic promise of *TM* (see repr. in J. B. Priestley, *Man and Time* (London: Aldus Books, 1964), pp. 122–23.)

130 McPhister vanishes spectrally in and out of the shadows at psychological moments.

131 *The New Faust: A Film Story*, *Nash's Pall Mall* (Dec. 1936), pp. 120–45, especially 121–22. (Henceforth all pages references to *NF* will be given in brackets in the text.)

132 Letter to Constance Coolidge (1936), in Smith (ed.), *Correspondence*, Vol. IV, pp. 121–22.

133 See Smith, *H. G. Wells on Film*, p. 183.

134 British Film Institute, 'London Films Production Collection', C/129 ii (3 Dec. 1957–8 Sept. 1959).

Chapter 5
Afterimages: Adaptations and Influences

1 Robert M. Philmus argues that *TM* epitomises SF as an intertextual and dialogic genre of (re)visions, because Wells hypothesises a future which perpetually changes under the traveller's scrutiny and therefore contains alternative possibilities, latent or otherwise, that subsequent texts oppose or elaborate (see his *Visions and Revisions*, especially pp. 49–65).

2 See T. H. Huxley, *Evolution and Ethics* (1896; repr. in T. H. Huxley and Julian Huxley, *Evolution and Ethics 1893–1943* (London: Pilot Press, 1947), pp. 60–102, especially 81.

3 After the success of his *WOTW*, Wells's estate offered Pal the rights to other texts. He selected *TM* because of its filmic suitability, obtaining a cheap option from Wells's son, Frank. Frank had got Pal out of a jam, when Paramount's legal department realised on the eve of *WOTW*'s release that they only owned the silent rights (see Steve Rubin, 'The War of the Worlds', *Cinefantastique*, Vol. 5, no. 4 (Spring 1976), pp. 4–16 and contd 34–47, especially 38). However, Paramount were unimpressed by the project which remained unfilmed until Pal migrated to MGM (see Gail Morgan Hickman, *The Films of George Pal* (South Brunswick, NJ: A. S. Barnes; London: Thomas Yoseloff, 1977), p. 113).

4 The novella's framing narrator remains anonymous until his identity is revealed indirectly as 'Hillyer', the character the Time Traveller glimpses 'pass[ing] like a flash' on his journey back to the present. In relativistic visual counterpoint, Hillyer admits entering his lab at that moment to see him disappearing 'transparently' on his final journey (see Geduld (ed.), *Definitive Time Machine*, pp. 87 and 89).

5 For Sam Moskowitz's apt term for scientific romance by Wells and contemporaries, see the preface to Moskowitz (ed.), *Science Fiction by Gaslight: A History and Anthology of Science Fiction in the Popular Magazines, 1891–1911* (Westport, CT: Hyperion Press, 1971), pp. 11–14, especially 11.

Pal explained his alternative strategy for extending the plausibility of Wells's story: 'We modernized *War of the Worlds* because flying saucers were so topical ... Here the problem was to convince the audience that the time machine was real. So we put it in the past at the turn of the century, and we showed incidents the audience knows did happen, such as the changing of women's fashions, the First World War, the Second World War, etcetera. By that time the people believed it, so they went along and believed that there was such a thing in the future as little blond people on the surface and albino monsters down below.' (Quoted in Hickman, *George Pal*, p. 113.)

6   Taylor had already played a Time Traveller in Edward Bernds's *World Without End* (1956), which borrowed heavily from Wells. A spaceship breaks the Einsteinian 'time barrier', returning to the Earth of 2058, to find *homo sapiens* driven underground by mutants.

7   The methods of special effects by 'Projects Unlimited' (Gene Warren, Wah Chang and Tim Baar) and trick photography by Paul Vogel are explained visually in Clyde Lucas's 1993 documentary *Time Machine: The Journey Back*. Cf. Darrin Scot, '*The Time Machine*', *American Cinematographer*, Vol. 41, no. 8 (Aug. 1960), pp. 490–91 and 496–98, and Hickman, *George Pal*, pp. 121–22.

8   Other details, such as the memorably decomposing Morlock (complete with eye falling from its socket), who has 'just' tried to kill George before he speeds away, were elaborated in Hartdegen's struggle with the Übermorlock.

9   See 'Fiction about the Future', in Parrinder and Philmus (eds), *H. G. Wells's Literary Criticism*, pp. 246–47.

10   Other American time-travel films of the 1960s also took up this theme of a mutant future produced by nuclear fallout (see Newman, *Apocalypse Movies*, p. 103).

11   Wells scholars generally agree that 'Eloi' alludes to the Aramaic form of Matthew, 27: 47-8, when Jesus calls in anguish to 'My God', who appears to have forsaken him ('Eloi, Eloi, lama sabachthani?') This would be ironically appropriate to the Time Traveller's disillusionment with secular doctrines of human progress.

12   John Huntington, *The Logic of Fantasy: H. G. Wells and Science Fiction* (New York and Guildford, Surrey: Columbia University Press, 1982), pp. 54–55.

13   See Hickman, *George Pal*, p. 133. Pal did however co-write a novel based on it, with Joe Morhaim, *The Time Machine II*. George does indeed return to the future to liberate successfully Weena and her tribe, to restore them to his kind of humanity by destroying the Morlocks.

According to Hickman, he also mooted developing another of Wells's narrative strands, omitted in 1960, when the Time Traveller visits the far future. Beyond the era of the Eloi and Morlocks, he finds the remnants of humanity living in caverns, with monstrous insects ruling the Earth (Hickman, *George Pal*, p. 174).

14   Huntington, *Logic of Fantasy*, pp. 54–55. Alternatively, it has been rumoured that Pal did in fact film the further future in which the Time Traveller witnesses the twilight of the Earth. However, the studio 'deemed it too bleak for inclusion in the final cut' (see Kirk Hampton and Carol MacKay, 'Beyond the Endtime: Allegories of Coalescence in Far-Future Science Fiction', in Gary Westfahl, George Slusser and David Leiby (eds), *Worlds Enough and Time: Explorations of Time in Science Fiction and Fantasy* (Westport, CT; London: Greenwood Press, 2002), pp. 65–75, especially 73–75 and note).

15   Joshua Stein, 'The Legacy of H. G. Wells's *The Time Machine*: Destabilization and Observation', in Slusser and Chatelain (eds), *Perennial Time Machine*, pp. 150–59, especially 152.

16   Stein, 'The Legacy of H. G. Wells's *The Time Machine*', p. 153.

17   Stein, 'The Legacy of H. G. Wells's *The Time Machine*', pp. 156–57.

18   See Thomas Carlyle, 'The Sphinx', in Carlyle, *Past and Present* (1843; Oxford: Clarendon, 1918), p. 12. Carlyle surveyed the 'condition of England' and gave rise to the fiction genre of the same name, identified by C. F. G. Masterman, who noted Wells's extension of the tradition (see Masterman, *The Condition of England* (London: Methuen, 1909), p. 149).

19   Stein, 'The Legacy of H. G. Wells's *The Time Machine*', p. 153.

20   See John Clute and Peter Nicholls (eds), *The Encyclopedia of Science Fiction*, second

edition (London: Orbit, 1993), p. 994.

21 Appropriately, leading actor Guy Pearce had just starred in *Memento* (2000), Christopher Nolan's reverse-narrated psychological thriller exploring the nature of memory and time.

22 Pal's 'Filby', Alan Young, also reappears, in a drapery-store cameo role.

23 See Renzi, *Six Scientific Romances*, pp. 37–38.

24 For 'fractured' causal logic, see Stein, 'The Legacy of H. G. Wells's *The Time Machine*, p. 154.

25 The 1937 essay, 'The Idea of a Permanent World Encyclopedia' (Wells's contribution to the new *Encyclopédie Française*), foresees the internet in a universal information system, which subsumes traditional textuality. Claiming that encyclopedism had not kept pace with progress, Wells argued, 'modern facilities of transport, radio, photographic reproduction and so forth are rendering practicable a much more fully succinct and accessible assembly of fact and ideas than was ever possible before'. Moreover, 'the core of such an institution would be a world synthesis of bibliography and documentation with the indexed archives of the world', perpetually keeping human knowledge up to date. Developments in micro-filming would make facsimile projections of the rarest texts and images distributable for simultaneous study on screens all over the world: 'There is no practical obstacle whatever now to the creation of an efficient index to all human knowledge, ideas and achievements, to the creation, that is, of a complete planetary memory for all mankind. And not simply an index; the direct reproduction of the thing itself can be summoned to any properly prepared spot.' (Repr. in H. G. Wells, *World Brain* (London: Methuen, 1938), pp. 58–62, especially 58–60.) Although Wells doesn't anticipate electronic computer networking in its specific forms, he does raise the issue of the revolutionary potentials of such a future global informational resource.

26 Arguably, *TM*'s devolutionary and gender issues have been recently extended in Neil Marshall's 2005 film, punningly entitled *The Descent*. A group of women potholers resort to savagery to survive against a group of cannibalistic troglodytes of *both* sexes.

27 In a parody in *The Simpsons* of *IODM*, 'The Island of Dr. Hibbert' (*Treehouse of Horror XIII*), Homer, the personification of American over-consumption, is appalled to learn that Springfield's citizens have been devolved into manimals, but eagerly volunteers when he learns that their life now consists solely of continuous eating, sleeping and mating.

28 See Chapter 1, note 60.

29 It is possible that the more challenging implications of Simon Wells's narrative were not properly followed through. Simon J. James points out that an uncredited Gore Verbinski (director of the swashbuckler *Pirates of the Caribbean* (2004)) completed the film, after Wells collapsed from exhaustion (see National Film Theatre, H. G. Wells Season, programme notes (Sunday 22 May 2005)).

30 See Chapter 11, 'Partial Derivatives: Popular Misinterpretations of H. G. Wells's *The Time Machine*', in Gary Westfahl, *Science Fiction, Children's Literature and Popular Culture: Coming of Age in Fantasyland* (Westport, CT and London: Greenwood Press, 2000), pp. 129–41. Baxter, 'Further Visions: Sequels to *The Time Machine*', pp. 41–50, discusses similar trends in extensions and spin-offs of Wells's text.

31 De Mille nonetheless retained a hand in the eventual 1953 adaptation, saving it at a crucial moment from being junked by the studio's vice-president. (For a detailed history of planned adaptations before Haskin and Pal, see Rubin, 'The War of the Worlds', pp. 4–16 and contd 34–37; Hughes and Geduld (eds), *Critical Edition of The War of the Worlds*, pp. 237–48; and Smith, *H. G. Wells on Film*, p. 108.)

32 Hickman, *George Pal*, p. 59. Paramount may have also scrapped the project on cost grounds; see Appendix to Sergei M. Eisenstein, *The Film Sense*, ed. Jay Leyda (London: Faber, 1986), p. 175. Also Hughes and Geduld (eds), *Critical Edition of The War of the Worlds*, p. 25.

Eisenstein's own screen practice retained Wellsian analogies. He wrote of a sudden time shift in *Ivan the Terrible* (1945–46): 'And with the ruthlessness of H.G.Wells' "time machine" the same camera boom is wheeled into position to record, with the same objectivity and accuracy as for the stern words of the graying Tzar, the youthful speech and gestures of the newly crowned Tzar.' (See 'Appendix B' to Sergei M. Eisenstein, *Film Form: Essays in Film Theory*, ed. and trans. Jay Leyda (London: Dennis Dobson, 1963), p. 264.)

33 See Anon., 'Mr H. G. Wells and the Screen: "War of the Worlds" as Film', *The Times* (3 Nov. 1932), p. 10. According to Montagu, Wells only remembered that he had sold the rights in perpetuity to Paramount after they had already drafted the script (see Montagu, *With Eisenstein in Hollywood*, p. 34).

A copy of the draft screenplay survives (see BFI, 'Ivor Montagu Collection', Item 25a). It retains Wells's British location, though in a modernised setting, with references to motor lorries, tanks and aircraft, as well as media such as the wireless. Wells's narrator becomes 'Dr Drage', a local GP. The script takes topical account of post-Great-War 'progress' in terrestrial weapons technology: at one point a whole air squadron is wiped out by the heat ray, but, most ironically, it is humans who now wield poison gas (although the Martians are invulnerable to it, high up in their cowled machines).

Significantly, Frank and Montagu also repeat Wells's metaphor of what they call the 'heat ray camera' (see 'New Sequence C', p. 5), deliberately foregrounding its equivalence with cinema as devices creating spectacular effects. Nonetheless, they still expressed anxieties about whether state-of-the-art techniques were yet equal to the task of visualising key moments: 'model shots in sea required by the Thunderer [*sic*] incident' might lack sufficient 'realism' alongside live action ('New Sequence E', note, p. 3). Other sequences extended ideas only sketched in by Wells. His proto-Fascist artilleryman takes Drage down into the sewers to which the resistance has adapted like human rats. They use the trench-warfare strategy of undermining the alien base with explosives, but are rooted out by an even more efficient Martian superweapon: a gigantic flamethrower. However, this parabolic arms race is still terminated not by human ingenuity, but by Martian lack of immunities, diagnosed by Dr Drage.

Montagu and Frank also interested Paramount producer Robert Fellows in their script. Unfortunately, he accepted a new post at Warner Brothers (see Rubin, 'War of the Worlds', p. 6).

34 Ibid.

35 Harryhausen's *WOTW* was to have been set in contemporary America, though sticking closely to Wells's cephalopod and tripod designs. Besides sketches and models, Harryhausen completed a colour test sequence of an alien emerging from its cylinder. *WOTW* remained a subject 'that would haunt me throughout my professional career' (see text and illustrations to Ray Harryhausen and Tony Dalton, *The Art of Ray Harryhausen* (London: Aurum, 2005), pp. 128–38 and 194). *FMITM* was Harryhausen's favourite among his SF films. He had been sketching for a possible adaptation since first reading the novel in the 1930s. *King Kong* producer, Merion C. Cooper, also bought an option on *FOTG* in 1950 and approached Harryhausen to make sketches, although they were never realised because the Wells estate subsequently sold the rights to another company (see Harryhausen and Dalton, *The Art of Ray Harryhausen*, pp. 145–53 and 196). Juran had directed the *FOTG*-like gender satire, *Attack of the 50ft Woman* (1958),

a kitsch SF classic. No doubt Wells's tale of giant mutations by artificial means contributed to the 1950s vogue for radioactively magnified creatures of all kinds.

FOTG was also one of Hitchcock's unrealised projects, according to Ken Mogg (see *The Alfred Hitchcock Story* (London: Titan Books, 1999), p. 182). Similarly, Whale was asked out of retirement to make a version for Columbia in the 1950s (see Curtis, *James Whale*, p. 369).

36 Screenplay by British writer Barre Lyndon. Paramount had already accumulated five draft screenplays over the years for Lyndon to draw on (see Rubin, 'War of the Worlds', p. 9).

37 Johnson, *Focus on the Science Fiction Film*, p. 5.

38 See Hughes and Geduld (eds), *Critical Edition of The War of the Worlds*, p. 204.

39 In his 1894 essay 'Through a Microscope', Wells speculated about human life under observation as we scrutinise microscopic organisms: 'And all the time these creatures are living their vigorous, fussy little lives; in this drop of water they are being watched by a creature of whose presence they do not dream, who can wipe them all out of existence with a stroke of his thumb, and who is withal as finite, and sometimes as fussy and unreasonably energetic as themselves. He sees them, and they do not see him, because he has senses which they do not possess, because he is too incredibly vast and strange to come, save as an overwhelming catastrophe, into their lives.' (Repr. in *Certain Personal Matters* (p. 244.) The flashes seen by Ogilvy allude to contemporary reports of 'A Strange Light on Mars': 'If we assume the light to be on the planet itself, then it must either have a physical or human origin; so it is to be expected that the old idea that the Martians are signalling to us will be revived.' (Anon., 'A Strange Light on Mars', *Nature*, Vol. 50, no. 1292 (2 Aug. 1894), p. 319.)

40 'The War of the Worlds', *Pearson's Magazine*, Vol. IV, no. 19 (July 1897), p. 113. The Martians' invisible beam may also owe something to X-rays, which could not be seen, but whose impact was revealed in burns caused by prolonged exposure. Pal's film shows it rendering victims' skeletons visible, before they vanish altogether, in what has become a cliché of alien weaponry as sent up in *Mars Attacks*.

41 McConnell also claims that *WOTW* anticipated the 'strobing' effect of rapid flashes of light (*Science Fiction of H. G. Wells*, p. 164). Hughes and Geduld compare Wells's use of 'expressionistic' lighting effects to James Whale's moment of monstrous creation in *Frankenstein* (1931) (see *Critical Edition of The War of the Worlds*, p. 207).

42 Probably the first British aerial film (from a balloon by scientist John Mackenzie Bacon) wasn't taken until 1902 (see Herbert and MacKernan, *Who's Who of Victorian Cinema*, p. 20). Wells may have felt his perspective of modern war to be confirmed by Albert Kahn's airship footage of the Great War trenches, shown in the London Film Society's 5th programme (Feb. 1926) (see London Film Society, *Film Society Programmes*, p. 18).

43 For recent historicisation of *WOTW* and the media, especially as impacting through Orson Welles's broadcast, see Robert E. Bartholemew and Hilary Evans, *Panic Attacks: Media Manipulation and Mass Delusion* (Stroud: Sutton, 2004, especially pp. 40–56) and Joanna Bourke, *Fear: A Cultural History* (London: Virago, 2004), pp. 177–88.

44 Electric lighting is also one of the new technologies featuring invasively in *WTSW*.

45 Liz Hedgecock, '"The Martians are Coming!": Civilisation v. Invasion in *The War of the Worlds* and *Mars Attacks!*', in Cartmell et al. (eds), *Alien Identities*, pp. 104–20, especially 104.

46 Richard Law also draws attention to this in 'The Narrator in Double Exposure in *The War of the Worlds*', in Partington (ed.), *Wellsian*, pp. 95–103.

47 Many listeners believed that the Martian invasion camouflaged a sneak attack

by Germany or Japan, using superweapons, as evidenced by Hadley Cantril, Hazel Gaudet and Herta Herzog, *The Invasion From Mars: A Study in the Psychology of Panic* (Princeton, NJ: Princeton University Press, 1940), especially pp. 53–54, 100–1 and 160–62. Their study also compared the broadcast's ingenious building of atmosphere to the dictators' use of media spectacle (p. 75). Hitler recognised its complex of topicality, referring to *WOTW* in a public speech as proving a decadent America's mass gullibility and hysterical fear of air attack. (See Richard Nate, 'Ignorance, Opportunism, Propaganda and Dissent: The Reception of H. G. Wells in Nazi Germany', in Parrinder and Partington (eds), *Reception of H. G. Wells in Europe*, pp. 105–25, especially 109.) Author and dramatist discussed Hitler's response during their joint radio interview, when they eventually met (broadcast by KTSA, San Antonio, Texas, 29 Oct. 1940).

48 See I. F. Clarke, *The Tale of the Next War, 1871–1914* (Liverpool: Liverpool University Press, 1995), pp. 27–33. Clarke lists eight other topical 'terrestrial' invasion novels appearing in 1898, virtually all imperialist 'wake-up calls' with racist overtones, such as *Anglo-Saxons Onward!*, *What Will Japan Do?*, *The Yellow Danger*, etc. (See Clarke, *Voices Prophesying War, 1763–1984* (London: Oxford University Press, 1966), p. 233.)

49 *WOTW* plays a central role in this tradition (see Ziauddin Sardar and Sean Cubitt (eds), *Aliens R Us: The Other in Science Fiction Cinema* (London: Pluto, 2002), especially pp. 6–7).

50 Adam Roberts, *Science Fiction* (London and New York: Routledge, 2000), pp. 63–64.

51 Hedgecock, '"The Martians Are Coming"', pp. 106–8.

52 See Niall Ferguson, *The War of the World: History's Age of Hatred* (London: Allen Lane, 2006), especially pp. xxiii–iv.

53 They included one in the *Evening Journal* itself (15 Dec. 1897–11 Jan. 1898), possibly by its editor, Arthur Brisbane, who commissioned Serviss. (For details of these pirate serialisations and Wells's protests about copyright infringements, see Hughes and Geduld (eds), *Critical Edition of The War of the Worlds*, Appendix II, '*The War of the Worlds* in the Yellow Press', pp. 281–89.)

54 Garrett P. Serviss, *Edison's Conquest of Mars* (1898; repr. in George Locke (ed.), *Sources of Science Fiction: Future War Novels of the 1890s* (London: Routledge/Thoemmes Press, 1998), p. 1. Henceforth all page references to *Edison's Conquest* will be given in brackets in the text. Rice Burroughs's first space potboiler, *Under the Moons of Mars*, was serialised in 1912. The *Flash Gordon* film serial began in 1936, adapted from Alex Raymond's comic strip. (For further discussion of the genre's origins, see Gary Westfahl, 'Space Opera', in James and Mendlesohn (eds), *Cambridge Companion to Science Fiction*, pp. 197–208, especially 198.)

55 This anticipates the scene in *Independence Day* when American scientists find it impossible to negotiate with the implacable aggression of a captured alien.

56 Although Edison originally gave his blessing to the serial, he denounced its crudity as it began to appear (see Israel, *Edison*, p. 369).

57 Renzi argues that this global view is anticipated by *WOTW*'s imaginary observation balloon, analogous to crane or aerial shots (see *Six Scientific Romances*, p. xii).

58 In an interview, Haskin admitted that they relocated *WOTW* and 'transposed it to a modern setting, hoping to generate some of the excitement Welles had done' (quoted in John Brosnan, *Future Tense: The Cinema of Science Fiction* (New York: St Martin's Press, 1978), p. 90).

59 It is likely that Welles was also influenced by the association of radio with spreading Griffin's absent presence in Whale's film. A mobile radio van is similarly quickly on

the scene at the first Martian landing site in the 1953 film.

60 However, Wells protested to CBS, 'I gave no permission whatever for alterations which might lead to the belief that it was real news.' (Quoted in Holmsten and Lubertozzi (eds), *The Complete War of the Worlds*, p. 21.) He was 'deeply incensed by the extensive changes' removing it from its specifically British colonial context, suing CBS for an apology and damages for misleading him (see Hughes and Geduld (eds), *Critical Edition of The War of the Worlds*, p. 244; also discussion with Wells's agent, Jacques Chambrun (31 Oct. 1938), *Correspondence of H. G. Wells*, Vol. IV, p. 204).

61 Quoted in Holmsten and Lubertozzi (eds), *Complete War of the Worlds*, p. 20. A comparable British view is expressed in Anon., 'Radio Play Upsets Americans: "Martian Invasion" of United States Taken Seriously', *Manchester Guardian* (1 Nov. 1938), p. 11.

62 See Frayling, *Scientist and the Cinema*, p. 75.

63 Stella Bruzzi, 'Space Looks', *Sight and Sound* (Sept. 1995), pp. 10–11.

64 In the same year, TTC director William Cameron Menzies's *Invaders from Mars* infiltrate America specifically to sabotage its nuclear programme.

65 H. G. Wells, *The World Set Free* (London: Macmillan, 1914), p. 234. As Newman shows, although Wells did not originate the notion of atomic weaponry as such, the theme quickly became part of the arsenal of sensational and patriotic American movies as early as the year after his novel (see *Apocalypse Movies*, pp. 27–28).

66 As well as recalling Los Alamos, Haskin and Pal may also allude to the alien crash-landing, which allegedly took place at Roswell, New Mexico, in 1948.

67 Art director Al Nozaki's original flying saucer designs were turned down by Pal and Haskin as insufficiently distinctive (see Hickman, *George Pal*, p. 67). Their eventual 'manta-ray' streamlining might well have been lifted from one of Wells's own futuristic prototypes: 'the Asiatic airship was also fish-shaped ... on the lines ... of a ray or a sole' (*WITA*, p. 182).

68 See Hickman, *George Pal*, pp. 69–70.

69 Even more explicitly in line with Cold War anxiety, the protagonist in Lyndon's original treatment was a pilot, patrolling for signs of hostile activity (see Rubin, 'War of the Worlds', p. 10).

70 Pal apologised for this in an interview (see George Pal, 'Filming *War of the Worlds*', *Astounding Science Fiction* (Oct. 1953), pp. 100–11.

71 Bould, 'Film and Television', p. 85. Based on Jack Finney's *Collier's* serial, Siegel's film about alien pods secretly absorbing human life forms and personalities as they sleep seems equivocal in terms of totalitarian and McCarthyist readings. The rational explanation for fear of duplication, 'an epidemic of mass-hysteria' sweeping the community, induced by anxiety about the state of the world, is ambiguous to say the least. (See also Ernesto G. Laura, 'Invasion of the Body Snatchers' (1957; repr. in Johnson (ed.), *Focus on the Science Fiction Film*, pp. 71–73.)

72 Pal quoted in Rubin, 'War of the Worlds', p. 9.

73 Newman, *Apocalypse Movies*, p. 31. The film was based on Harry Bates's novel, *Farewell to the Master*, serialised in *Astounding Science Fiction*. Ironically, *The Day the Earth Stood Still* is an old movie showing on television in the morally absolutist *Independence Day*.

74 See Newman, *Apocalypse Movies*, p. 122.

75 See Rubin, 'War of the Worlds', p. 36.

76 See Julian Cornell, 'All's Well that Ends Wells: Apocalypse and Empire in *The War of the Worlds*', in Robert Stam and Alessandra Raengo (eds), *A Companion to Literature and Film* (Oxford: Blackwell, 2004), pp. 423–47, especially 435–36.

77 Peter Fitting argues that film adaptations of *WOTW* reduce the aliens' reflexive, colonial otherness, though cannot erase it altogether (see his 'Estranged Invaders: *The War of the Worlds*', in Patrick Parrinder (ed.), *Learning from Other Worlds: Estrangement, Cognition and the Politics of Science Fiction and Utopia* (Liverpool: Liverpool University Press, 2000), pp. 127–45, especially 132).

78 Stephen King, who uses this motif prominently in several of his fictions, draws attention to the racial undertones of Pal's *WOTW* in his own study of the horror genre (see *Danse Macabre* (London: Warner Books, 1993), p. 178).

79 Stephen J. Greenblatt, *Learning to Curse: Essays in Early Modern Culture* (New York and London: Routledge, 1990), p. 22.

80 The reviewer was nonetheless impressed by Pal's effects ('The fire spitting cobra is indeed a formidable feature') and pseudo-documentary narrative. Overall though, they judged that the film had missed the 'secret' of the story's success. Whether this was because it failed to capitalise on proto-cinematic vision or omitted its anti-colonial message is unclear (see Anon., 'Film Adaptation of H. G. Wells Story: "The War of the Worlds"', *The Times* (2 Apr. 1953), p. 2).

The religiosity of Lyndon's original treatment was far stronger, however, but perhaps also more ambiguous: Pastor Collins's one-man peace mission resembled a multi-denominational 'crusade', including Catholic priest, rabbi and nuns (see Rubin, 'War of the Worlds', p. 12).

81 Cornell, 'All's Well That Ends Well', p. 439. Ironically, Harry Horner's *Red Planet Mars* was about the ending of superpower friction by alien Christians!

82 See Rubin, 'War of the Worlds', p. 12.

83 See his '"Videology" of Science Fiction', pp. 170 and 207.

84 Cf. the destruction of 'Everytown's dreamhouse' in the greater spectacle of the bombing in *TTC*.

Reuter's reported that 'breaking news' of the Martian invasion similarly emptied a cinema at Orange County, New Jersey during Orson Welles's broadcast (see 'Mr Wells "Deeply Concerned": "Unwarranted" Rewriting of his Novel' (*Manchester Guardian* (1 Nov. 1938), p. 11).

85 See Rubin, 'War of the Worlds', p. 42.

86 Stewart, '"Vidcology" of Science Fiction', p. 171.

87 Hickman, *George Pal*, p. 70. Pal discussed a possible CBS television series based on *WOTW* in the early 1970s, to cash in on the *Star Trek* vogue (see p. 167 and Rubin, 'War of the Worlds', p. 44). Though one was eventually transmitted in 1988–90, connections with the themes and motifs of Pal's film, let alone Wells's text, were attenuated to the point of unrecognisability.

88 See Jan Mair's 'Rewriting the "American Dream": Postmodernism and Otherness in *Independence Day*', in Sardar and Cubitt (eds), *Aliens R Us*, pp. 34–50; also Michael Rogin, *Independence Day: Or How I Learned to Stop Worrying and Love the Enola Gay* (London: BFI, 1998), especially Chapter 6, 'The Virtual War of the Worlds', which focuses on Emmerich's film as a further symbolic stage in the globalisation of American politics and culture, pp. 73–77.

89 Cornell, 'All's Well That Ends Well', p. 425.

90 Hedgecock, '"The Martians are Coming!"', p. 100.

91 Vivian Sobchack, *Screening Space: the American Science Fiction Film*, second, enlarged edition (New Brunswick, NJ and London: Rutgers University Press, 1999), p. 191. Continuing the tradition, Emmerich's aliens hijack Earth's communication satellite network to co-ordinate their attack, the signal for which also jams terrestrial television.

92 Martin Amis, 'The First Circle of Hell', *Guardian*, 'G2' (18 Sept. 2001), pp. 1–5.

93 The release of the 2002 *TM* was also reputedly delayed so that a scene where meteors from the lunar break up shower down on New York could be excised (see Simon J. James, National Film Theatre, H. G. Wells Season, programme notes (Sunday 22 May 2005)).

94 Spielberg's film is impressively metacinematic. The opening sequence homes in from outer space to microbe view, before dissolving into overhead New York traffic warning lights. The alien attack is partially viewed through handheld video camera, dropped in panic, and screens-within-the-screen, such as the television monitor, used to 'rewind' the lightning to analyse the pilot's descent in slow motion.

95 Spielberg's film is riddled with intertextual references to Pal/Haskin. The first attack takes place on 'Van Buren' street and 1953's lead couple are given cameos as grandparents.

96 Peter Bradshaw, 'Attack of the Bug-Eyed Bores', *Guardian*, Review (1 July 2005), pp. 16–17.

97 'In the original Martians travelled around in what were described as creaky old water towers going around frightening horses and old Englishmen, and somehow that didn't fit in with the wars we'd been through and the flying saucer scare at the time.' (Haskin quoted in Hickman, *George Pal*, p. 65.)

98 These allude back to Cavor's lunar broadcasts in *FMITM*, themselves based on radio pioneer Nikola Tesla's belief that he was receiving signals from extraterrestrials at the time the novel was written.

99 Wells may also have been recalling the association of the Red Planet with Soviet revolution in his friend Alexei Tolstoy's *Aelita*, discussed in Chapter 3.

100 Frayling, *Scientist and the Cinema*, p. 171.

101 Discussed in Smith, *H. G. Wells on Film*, pp. 126–35, and Renzi, *Six Scientific Romances*, pp. 169–85.

102 Quoted in Paul Wells, 'Apocalypse Then! The Ultimate Monstrosity and Strange Things on the Coast ... An Interview with Nigel Kneale', in Hunter (ed.), *British Science Fiction Cinema*, pp. 48–56, especially 55. Also cf. Andy Murray on the tele-playwright's admiration for Wells in *Into the Unknown: The Fantastic Life of Nigel Kneale* (London: Headpress, 2006), p. 84.

Kneale's earliest work in different media certainly recalls multiple Wellsian themes: his story 'The Calculation of N'Bambwe' (*Strand* (Mar. 1944)) concerns a witch doctor's prediction that time will literally stop for the British Empire; his radio play, *You Must Listen* (16 Sept. 1952), foregrounds electronic absent presences by featuring uncanny 'interference' from a telephonic voice; his 1953 television adaptation of Stanley Young's *Mystery Story* is about manipulations of space-time (see Murray, *Into the Unknown*, pp. 13, 25–26).

103 For inversion of *WOTW*, see Paul Wells, in Hunter (ed.), *British Science Fiction Cinema*, pp. 48–56, especially 55; also Murray, *Into the Unknown*, p. 84. Though animated by Harryhausen, the Selenites were actually designed by Kneale's artist brother, Bryan.

104 Sconce, *Haunted Media*, p. 131. A recent episode of the revived *Doctor Who* (transmitted 27 May 2006) revisits the coming of the Telly as a literally alien presence provoking Knealean anxieties at the time of the Coronation broadcast. In 'The Idiot's Lantern', by Mark Gatiss, an extraterrestrial feeding on electromagnetic impulses ('The Wire') steals viewers' faces through their screens, a variation on Wells's technological bodysnatching themes appropriate to a new medium of 'talking heads'.

105 Quoted by Paul Wells in Hunter (ed.), *British Science Fiction Cinema*, p. 52. See

also James Chapman, 'Quatermass and the Origins of British Television SF', in Cook and Wright (eds), *British Science Fiction Television*, pp. 21–51.

106 John R. Cook and Peter Wright, '"Futures Past": An Introduction to and Brief Survey of British Science Fiction Television', in Cook and Wright (eds), *British Science Fiction Television*, pp. 5–6, especially 6. The series' landmark status was recently celebrated in a live 'rerun' on BBC Four (2 Apr. 2005).

107 See Peter Hutchings, 'We're the Martians Now: British SF Invasion Fantasies of the 1950s and 1960s', in Hunter (ed.), *British Science Fiction Cinema*, pp. 33–47, especially 40.

108 Bryan Buckingham, 'Interview with Nigel Kneale', *News of the World* (quoted in Murray, *Into the Unknown*, p. 80).

109 For Kneale's views about contemporary SF as cultural ghettoising and the 're-Americanisation' of *Quatermass* in Hammer's cinema version, see (among others) Paul Wells in Hunter (ed.), *British Science Fiction Cinema*, pp. 50–51 and Catherine Johnson, *Telefantasy* (London: BFI, 2005), pp. 34–35.

110 Johnson, *Telefantasy*, p. 37. The first American SF television serial, *Captain Video and his Video Rangers*, had begun in 1949, with similar square-jawed heroics.

111 Hutchings, in Hunter (ed.), *British Science Fiction Cinema*, p. 38.

112 Quoted by Paul Wells, in Hunter (ed.), *British Science Fiction Cinema*, p. 53.

113 *Daily Mail* review, quoted in Murray, *Into the Unknown*, p. 52.

114 *WOTW*'s cylinders also reveal remains of humanoids brought by the Martians as 'packed lunch'. The idea of 'buried' alien intervention, going back to the remote past, is also a classic example of the disseminal mutation of Wellsian motifs, as suggested by the influence on Kubrick's *2001* (and the Arthur C. Clarke story, 'The Sentinel', behind it).

115 Quoted in Murray, *Into the Unknown*, p. 153.

116 See Nigel Kneale, 'Not Quite So Intimate', *Sight and Sound*, Vol. 28, no. 2 (Spring 1959), pp. 86–88, especially 88.

117 Kneale's teleplay, *The Stone Tape* (25 Dec. 1972), featured an equivalent 'audio-psychic' device picking up traces of events inscribed in 'haunted' houses.

118 *Radio Times* article quoted in Murray, *Into the Unknown*, p. 79.

119 Sadly, as with *Doctor Who*, he failed to see the merit in the series and refused (see Murray, *Into the Unknown*, p. 175).

120 Kneale's own serial *Push the Dark Door* (planned for an embryonic British cable station in 1985) echoes media-minded fables such as 'The Door in the Wall', 'Stolen Body', etc., as well as clearly anticipating *The X-Files*. A team, led by television journalist 'Dave Collister', were to use advanced technology to investigate the ambiguous reality of a spectrum of paranormal phenomena for the secret 'Blackstone Corporation'. Kneale nevertheless adapted Susan Hill's 1983 novel *The Woman in Black* (Central, 24 Dec. 1989), which featured a turn-of-the-century psychic investigator named 'Arthur Kipps'. His protagonist, moreover, records supernatural presences with the aid of a phonograph. Nonetheless, Kneale thought Hill's choice of name too impertinently Wellsian and changed it to 'Kidd' (see Murray, *Into the Unknown*, pp. 162–63, 168–70).

121 See O'Bannon quoted in Murray, *Into the Unknown*, pp. 151–52.

122 See Hickman, *George Pal*, p. 158. Jacques Tourneur (of *Cat People*, *Night of the Demon*, etc., fame), was contracted by Associated International Pictures, to film *WTSW* as an alternative to Pal in the mid-1960s. This was an inauspicious project, given the studio's increasingly cut-price production values, and it was probably a mercy that it was never made (see Chris Fujiwara, *Jacques Tourneur and the Cinema of Nightfall* (Baltimore, MD and London: Johns Hopkins University Press, 1998), p. 273).

123 See Hickman, *George Pal*, p. 174.

124 Wells's novel splices speculative ideas from his essays, 'The Limits of Individual Plasticity' (1895) and 'Human Evolution, An Artificial Process' (1896). Although it contains no 'Panther Woman', Moreau does experiment with a number of female 'Beast Folk' (the first vivisection Prendick witnesses is on a female puma, which eventually kills Moreau himself (see *IODM*, Chapter XVII, 'A Catastrophe', pp. 97–101)). The studio changed Prendick to Parker.

125 The best-known and most influential example of an SF reworking of *The Tempest* is of course Aldous Huxley's *Brave New World*. This, as we have seen, is also in close dialogic relation with the media-saturated *WTSW* and other futuristic texts by Wells. Huxley reworked many of the play's issues, motifs and characters with ironic intertextuality into a kind of dystopian satire of trends in modernity and 'technocratic capitalism': mass production ('Fordism'), consumerism (including the sexual variety) and genetic engineering. Although Chantal Zabus's recent study of rewritings of Shakespeare's romance recognises Huxley's mediating influence on dystopias such as *Forbidden Planet*, she overlooks *IODM* and *Island of Lost Souls* (see *Tempests after Shakespeare* (Houndmills: Palgrave, 2002), p. 191).

126 Suvin, *Metamorphoses of Science Fiction*, p. 229.

127 Wells linked his novel with Victorian fears about unspeakably 'bestial reversion' by admitting that it was partly inspired by Oscar Wilde's downfall in his 1924 preface: 'There was a scandalous trial about that time, the graceless and pitiless downfall of a man of genius, and this story was the response of an imaginative mind to the reminder that humanity is but animal, rough-hewn to a reasonable shape and in perpetual internal conflict between instinct and injunction.' (*The Works of H. G. Wells Atlantic Edition*, Vol. II, *The Island of Doctor Moreau, The Sleeper Wakes* (London: T. Fisher Unwin, 1924), pp. ix–xiii, especially ix.) *The Island of Lost Souls* was banned in Britain as 'against nature', probably as much for hints of racial miscegenation and bestiality as for vivisective themes (see Robertson, *British Board of Film Censors*, p. 59).

128 As a curious sidelight, *Forbidden Planet*'s expensive sets and props were recycled for a latter-day *War of the Wenuses* in the form of kitsch classic 'feminisation' of the Boy's Own SF tendency, *Queen of Outer Space* (1958) (see Frayling, *Scientist and the Cinema*, p. 201).

129 Vallorani, '"The Invisible Wells"', p. 306.

130 See Coates, 'Chris Marker', pp. 307–15; also George Slusser and Robert Heath, 'Arrows and Riddles of Time: Scientific Models of Time Travel', in Westfahl et al. (eds), *Worlds Enough and Time*, pp. 11–24, especially 16–18. Cf. Chapter 1 and note on 'Chronic Argonauts' as a ghost story about a haunting from the future. George Slusser and Daniele Chatelain also discuss Chris Marker (see 'A Tale of Two Science Fictions: H. G. Wells in France and the Soviet Union', in Parrinder and Partington (eds), *Reception of H. G. Wells*, pp. 280–301, especially 301, note 73).

131 See Vallorani, '"The Invisible Wells"', p. 303. Although 'ameliorative' time-travel narratives like Spielberg/Zemeckis's *Back to the Future* trilogy proliferated in 1980s America, these were more symptomatic of postmodern knowingness and nostalgia for media-recycled pop culture from the 'pre-lapsarian age' of the 1950s and early 1960s rather than critical confrontation with Reaganite neo-conservatism as such. (See Tom Shales, 'The Re Decade', *Esquire* (Mar. 1986), pp. 67–68; also Andrew Gordon, 'Play It Again, Sam: Ken Grimwood's *Replay* and Time Travel as Reincarnation', in Westfahl et al. (eds), *Worlds Enough and Time*, pp. 139–47).

132 Wells made his famous distinction in the 1933 preface to Renzi, *Scientific Romances*, pp. iv–v.

133 Vallorani, '"The Invisible Wells"', p. 304.

134 Ibid., p. 306.

135 As we have seen, *Mabuse* becomes a posthumous invisible presence through hypnosis and recording technology. Invisibility also features in the 1924 *Siegfried*'s magic cloak.

136 Vallorani, '"The Invisible Wells"', p. 306.

137 Ibid., p. 306.

138 See Jefferson M. Peters, 'The Desire to Control Time in *Doraemon* and Japanese Culture', in Westfahl et al. (eds), *Worlds Enough* and *Time*, pp. 104–11.

139 Montagu, *Film World*, pp. 83–84; also Marcus, 'Literature and Cinema', p. 340. The idea derived from a two-part article by Eisenstein, arguing that screen form should be continuously reshaped to express whatever content the film-maker wished (see 'The Dinamic Square', *Close-Up*, Vol. VIII, no. 1 (Mar. 1931), pp. 2–16, and no. 2 (June 1931), pp. 91–94).

140 Although naturally asked to write for *Doctor Who*, Kneale refused on the grounds that the themes of technological *Angst* appropriate for *Quatermass* were too frightening for children. This did not prevent creative cross-fertilisation of many of Kneale's Wells-influenced themes and motifs (see Murray, *Into the Unknown*, especially pp. 81 and 107–8.) For more connections with Wells, see, among others, Kim Newman, *Doctor Who* (London: BFI, 2005), pp. 3, 23 and 69.

141 Then head of BBC drama, Sydney Newman recalled Pal's period adaptation as the immediate inspiration for *Doctor Who*'s distinctive blend of SF and costume drama, influencing both the Tardis and the character of its inventor. This was also the case in the film spin-offs. (See John R. Cook, 'Adapting Telefantasy: The *Doctor Who and the Daleks* Films', in Hunter (ed), *British Science Fiction Cinema*, pp. 113–27, especially 115–16 and 119.

142 See letter from Angus MacPhail (29 July 1951) in BFI 'Ivor Montagu Collection', Item 404.

143 For listeners' letters, see *Radio Times* (4 Feb. 1949), p. 25. John Swift's article, trailing the first transmission, presented the BBC's conception as a kind of pastiche of Wells's opening symposium of contemporary professionals, who scoff at the possibility of representing such wonders on television ('To the World's End in Sixty Minutes', *Radio Times* (21 Jan. 1949), p. 25). The BBC's regular television columnist, 'The Scanner', considered it a ground-breaking success, although also quoting Barr on the need to iron out technical glitches before the second live transmission ('Experiment with Wells', *Radio Times* (4 Feb. 1949), p. 24). For more details on the programme, see Edward Glenn, 'Fantasy Flashback: *The Time Machine*', *TV Zone*, no. 17 (1991), pp. 28–30.

144 Cook and Wright, '"Futures Past", in Cook and Wright (eds), *British Science Fiction Television*, pp. 5–6.

145 The production used both colour and electronic backgrounds generated by a new process, 'Eidofor', for its effect of visual excess (see Murray, *Into the Unknown*, p. 100).

146 'It was a comment on television and the idea of the passive audience. At that time the population explosion was a very hot topic and it was also the time when *Hair* was on and people were saying "let's put porn on stage." So I put these ideas together and took them to their logical conclusion.' (Nigel Kneale, 'Quatermass and the Pen', interview with Kim Newman and Julian Pentley, *Video Watchdog*, No. 47 (Sept./Oct. 1998), p. 5.)

147 Kneale wrote an unmade screenplay for *Brave New World* in 1964 (see Murray, *Into the Unknown*, pp. 85–86).

148 For further discussion of this irony, see John R. Cook, 'The Age of Aquarius: Utopia and Anti-Utopia in Late 1960s and early 1970s British Science Fiction Television', in Cook and Wright (eds), *British Science Fiction Television*, pp. 93–115, especially 108–12.

149 See Una McCormack, 'Resist the Host: *Blake's 7* – a very British Future' and Catriona Miller, 'British Apocalypses Now – or Then? *The Uninvited, Invasion: Earth* and *The Last Train*', both in Cook and Wright (eds), *British Science Fiction Television*, pp. 174–91 and 263–82, respectively.

150 Montagu wrote detailed synopses of the fifty-six narratives contained in the Wells *Collected Stories* edition (London: Ernest Benn, 1927). (See 'Letter to Stella Jonckheere at British Lion' (31 Dec. 1958), in BFI 'Ivor Montagu Collection', Item 404, especially pp. 5, 7, 8, 13 and 15.)

151 Wells's grandson, Dr Martin Wells, was its co-producer.

152 In *The Simpsons*, 'Stop the World, I Want to Goof Off' (see Chapter 1, note 36), Bart and Millhouse's delinquents' paradise also turns into a nightmare of ageing isolation when they accidentally break their magic stopwatch and can't resynchronise the city's time to their own. For *The X-Files*, 'Rush', see Chapter 2, note 15.

Conclusion

1 Lindsay, *Art of the Moving Picture*, pp. 312–13, and 309, respectively.
2 Lewis Mumford, *Technics and Civilization* (London: Routledge, 1934), p. 342.
3 Smith, *Wells on Film*, pp. 184 and 186.
4 Landon, *Aesthetics of Ambivalence*, especially Introduction, pp. xiv–xvii.
5 Wells, *Conquest of Time*, p. 55.
6 Ibid., pp. 100–1.
7 Landon, *Aesthetics of Ambivalence*, p. 81.
8 See Paul Virilio, 'Cataract Surgery: Cinema in the Year 2000', in Annette Kuhn (ed.), *Alien Zone: Cultural Theory and Contemporary Science Fiction* (London: Verso, 1990), pp. 169–76, especially 170.
9 Paul Virilio, *War and the Cinema: The Logistics of Perception*, trans. Patrick Camiller (London: Verso, 1989), p. 17.
10 Introduction to the *Atlantic Edition of the Works of H. G. Wells*, Vol. I, *The Time Machine, The Wonderful Visit* (London: T. Fisher Unwin, 1924), p. xvii; also Introduction to Parrinder and Partington (eds), *Reception of H. G. Wells in Europe*, p. 3.
11 George Orwell, 'As I Please', *Tribune* (12 May 1944), in *Complete Works of George Orwell*, ed. Peter Davison, Vol. XVI, *I Have Tried to Tell the Truth 1943–1944* (London: Secker and Warburg, 2001), pp. 182–86, especially 182–84.
12 Wells, *Conquest of Time*, p. 84. The first long-playing gramophone records and players were commercially available from 1948. Global television took longer to arrive with the launch of the experimental 'Telstar' in 1962, eventually leading to geostationary satellite relays.
13 H. G. Wells, *The Camford Visitation* (London: Methuen, 1937), pp. 13–14, 34, 42 and 68.
14 For example, Laurence Olivier's posthumous 'appearance' as Nazi scientist, 'Totenkopf', in *Sky Captain and the World of Tomorrow* (dir. Kerry Conran, 2004); or that of the eponymous crooner in the London Palladium musical, *Sinatra* (2006).
15 Vivian Sobchack, 'Towards a Phenomenology of Cinematic and Electronic "Presence": The Scene of the Screen', *Post Script: Essays in Film and the Humanities*, Vol. 10, no. 1 (Autumn 1990), pp. 50–59, especially 50.

Bibliography

Works by Wells Cited

All Aboard for Ararat (London: Secker and Warburg, 1941).
Anticipations of the Reaction of Mechanical and Scientific Progress upon Human Life and Thought (London: Chapman and Hall, 1902).
'The Art of Being Photographed' (1893), repr. in *Select Conversations with an Uncle* (London: John Lane, 1895), pp. 23–32.
'At a Window', *Black and White*, vol. VIII, no. 186 (25 Aug. 1894), p. 246.
'The Betterave Papers' (1945), excerpted as 'A Complete Exposé of this Notorious Literary Humbug', in J. R. Hammond (ed.), *H. G. Wells Interviews and Recollections* (London and Basingstoke: Macmillan, 1980), pp. 108–17.
The Camford Visitation (London: Methuen, 1937).
Collected Stories (London: Ernest Benn, 1927).
The Complete Short Stories of H. G. Wells, ed. John Hammond (London: Phoenix Press, 2000).
The Conquest of Time (1942; Amherst, NY: Prometheus Books, 1995).
The Correspondence of H. G. Wells, four vols, ed. David C. Smith (London: Pickering and Chatto, 1998).
A Critical Edition of The War of the Worlds: H. G. Wells's Scientific Romance, ed. David Y. Hughes and Harry M. Geduld (Bloomington, IN: Indiana University Press, 1993).
The Definitive Time Machine: A Critical Edition of H. G. Wells's Scientific Romance, ed. Harry M. Geduld (Bloomington, IN: Indiana University Press, 1987).
The Door in the Wall and Other Stories (1911; Boston: Godine, 1980).
'The Dream Bureau', *Pall Mall Gazette*, no. 57 (25 Oct. 1893), p. 3.
Experiment in Autobiography: Discoveries and Conclusions of a Very Ordinary Brain (Since 1866), two vols (London: Gollancz/Cresset, 1934).
The First Men in the Moon (1901; London: Penguin, 2005).
The First Men in the Moon: A Critical Text of the 1901 London First Edition, ed. Leon Stover (Jefferson, NC, and London: McFarland, 1998).
The Food of the Gods and How It Came to Earth (London: Macmillan, 1904).
The Future in America: A Search After Realities (London: Chapman and Hall, 1906).
H. G. Wells: Early Writings in Science and Science Fiction, ed. Robert M. Philmus and David Y. Hughes (Berkeley, CA, Los Angeles, London: University of California Press, 1975).
H. G. Wells in Love: Postscript to An Experiment in Autobiography, ed. G. P. Wells (London: Faber, 1984).
H. G. Wells's Literary Criticism, ed. Patrick Parrinder and Robert M. Philmus

(Brighton: Harvester; Totowa, NJ: Barnes and Noble, 1980).
'The Idea of a Permanent World Encyclopedia' (1937; repr. in H. G. Wells, *World Brain* (London: Methuen, 1938)), pp. 58–62.
The Invisible Man (1897; London: Penguin, 2005).
The Invisible Man: A Grotesque Romance. A Critical Text of the 1897 New York First Edition, ed. Leon Stover (Jefferson, NC, and London: McFarland, 1998).
The Island of Doctor Moreau (1896; London: Penguin, 2005).
The Island of Doctor Moreau, The Works of H. G. Wells, Atlantic Edition, vol. II, (London: T. Fisher Unwin, 1924).
The Island of Doctor Moreau: A Variorum Text, ed. Robert M. Philmus (Athens, GA and London: University of Georgia Press, 1993).
Journalism and Prophecy, 1893–1946: An Anthology, ed. W. Warren Wagar (London: Bodley Head, 1966).
The King Who Was a King: The Book of a Film (London: Ernest Benn, 1929).
'The Literature of the Future', *Pall Mall Gazette* (11 Oct. 1893), p. 3.
'The Man of Science as Aristocrat', *Nature*, no. 3729 (19 Apr. 1941), pp. 465–67.
'The Man of the Year Million', *Pall Mall Gazette*, no. 57 (6 Nov. 1893), repr. in *Journalism and Prophecy*, ed. Warren W. Wagar, pp. 3–8.
The Man Who Could Work Miracles: A Critical Edition of the 1936 New York First Edition, ed. Leon Stover (Jefferson, NC: McFarland, 2003).
The Man Who Could Work Miracles: A Film Story Based on the Material Contained in his Short Story 'The Man Who Could Work Miracles' (London: Cresset, 1936).
Mankind in the Making (London: Chapman and Hall, 1903).
A Modern Utopia (1905; London: Dent, 1994).
The New Faust: A Film Story, Nash's Pall Mall (Dec. 1936), pp. 120–45.
The New Machiavelli (London: John Lane, 1911).
'The Origin of the Senses', *Saturday Review*, no. 81 (9 May 1896), pp. 471–72.
The Outline of History: Being a Plain History of Life and Mankind, Vol. II (London: George Newnes, 1920).
'Peculiarities of Psychical Research', *Nature*, no. 51 (6 Dec. 1894), pp. 121–22.
The Scientific Romances of H. G. Wells (London: Gollancz, 1933).
The Shape of Things to Come (1933; London: Dent, 1993).
'Shape of Wells to Come: Korda's New Assistant and the American Press', *The Era*, British edition (11 Dec. 1935), p. 20.
The Sleeper Awakes, The Works of H. G. Wells, Atlantic Edition, Vol. II (London: T. Fisher Unwin, 1924).
Star Begotten: A Biological Fantasia (London: Chatto and Windus, 1937).
Things to Come, ed. Allan Asherman and George Zebrowski (Boston: Gregg, 1975).
Things to Come – A Film Story Based on the Material Contained in His History of the Future 'The Shape of Things to Come' (London: Cresset, 1935).
Things to Come, 'Release Script' (repr. as Appendix II, in Stover, *Prophetic Soul*, pp. 181–297).

'Through a Microscope: Some Moral Reflections' (1894), repr. in *Certain Personal Matters: A Collection of Material, Mainly Autobiographical* (London: Lawrence and Bullen, 1898), pp. 238–45.
The Time Machine (1895; London: Penguin, 2005).
The Time Machine: An Invention, ed. Nicholas Ruddick (Peterborough, Ont.: Broadview, 2001).
The Time Machine, An Invention: A Critical Text of the 1895 London First Edition, ed. Leon Stover (Jefferson, NC and London: McFarland, 1996).
The Time Machine, The Works of H. G. Wells, Atlantic Edition, Vol. I (London: T. Fisher Unwin, 1924).
The War in the Air (1908; London: Penguin, 2005).
The War of the Worlds (1898; London: Penguin, 2005).
The War of the Worlds, serialisation in *Pearson's Magazine* (Apr.–Dec. 1897).
The War of the Worlds: A Critical Text of the 1898 London First Edition, ed. Leon Stover (Jefferson, NC, and London: McFarland, 2001).
The War That Will End War (London: Frank and Cecil Palmer, 1914).
The Way the World Is Going: Guesses and Forecasts for the Years Ahead (London: Ernest Benn, 1928).
When the Sleeper Wakes (1899; London: Dent, 1994).
When the Sleeper Wakes, serialisation in *The Graphic* (14 Jan.–6 May 1899).
When the Sleeper Wakes: A Critical Text of the 1899 New York and London First Edition, ed. Leon Stover (Jefferson, NC and London: McFarland, 2000).
'Whither Britain?' (transcript of radio broadcast), *Listener*, Vol. XI, no. 261 (10 Jan. 1934), pp. 43–44 and contd 83–84.
Whither Mankind? A Film of the Future (original treatment for *TTC*) (repr. as Appendix I in Stover (ed.), *The Prophetic Soul*, pp. 121–79).
The Work, Wealth and Happiness of Mankind (London: Heinemann, 1932).
The World of William Clissold: A Novel at a New Angle (London: Ernest Benn, 1926).
The World Set Free (London: Macmillan, 1914).

Primary Texts by Others

Abbot, Edwin A., *Flatland: A Romance of Many Dimensions, by A Square* (London: Seely & Co., 1884).
Anon., 'A Strange Light on Mars', *Nature*, no. 1292 (2 Aug. 1894), p. 319.
Anon., 'London From Aloft', *Strand Magazine*, Vol. II (Nov. 1891), pp. 492–98.
Anon., 'The New Photography', *British Medical Journal*, Vol. IX, no. 38 (1 Feb. 1896), pp. 289–90.
Anon., 'The Photography of the Invisible', *The Quarterly Review*, no. 183 (Apr. 1896), p. 496.
Anon., 'The Prince's Derby Shown by Lightning Photography' [article on R. W. Paul's Theatrograph] *Strand Magazine*, vol. 12 (Aug. 1896), pp. 134–40.
Anon., 'The Tragedies of a Camera', *Strand Magazine*, Vol. 16, no. 95 (Nov. 1898), pp. 545–52.

Anon., 'Underground London', *Strand Magazine*, Vol. 16, no. 92 (Aug. 1898), pp. 138–47.
Baker, Nicholas, *The Fermata* (London: Chatto and Windus, 1994).
Bellamy, Edward, *Looking Backward: 2000–1887* (1888; Peterborough, Ont.: Broadview, 2003).
Belloc, Hilaire, *The Servile State* (London and Edinburgh: T. N. Fowlis, 1912).
Carlyle, Thomas, *Past and Present* (1843; Oxford: Clarendon, 1918).
Carroll, Lewis, *The Complete Illustrated Works of Lewis Carroll* (London: Chancellor Press, 1982).
Clarke, Arthur C., 'The Sentinel' (1948; repr. in *2001, A Space Odyssey* (London: Arrow, 1990)), pp. 237–50.
Clifford, William Kingdom, *Seeing and Thinking* (London: Macmillan, 1879).
Conrad, Joseph, *The Collected Letters of Joseph Conrad*, five vols. ed. Frederick R. Karl and Laurence Davies (Cambridge: Cambridge University Press, 1988–96).
Conrad, Joseph, *The Secret Agent: A Simple Tale* (1907; Harmondsworth: Penguin, 1990).
de l'Isle-Adam, Villiers, *L'Ève future* (1889; Paris: Gallimard, 1993).
Dam, H. J. W., 'A Wizard of Today', *Pearson's Magazine*, Vol. I, no. 4 (Apr. 1896), pp. 413–19.
Doyle, Arthur Conan, *Wanderings of a Spiritualist* (London: Hodder and Stoughton, 1921).
Flammarion, Camille, *Lumen* (1886; London: Heinemann, 1897).
Ford, Ford Madox, *The Soul of London: A Survey of a Modern City* (1905; London: Everyman, 1995).
Gilbert, W. S., *The Bab Ballads*, ed. James Ellis (Cambridge, MA: Harvard University Press, 1980).
Graves, Charles L., and Edward V. Lucas, *The War of the Wenuses* (1898; repr. in Locke (ed.), *Sources of Science Fiction*).
Griffith, George, 'A Photograph of the Invisible', *Pearson's Magazine*, Vol. I, no. 4 (April 1896), pp. 376–80.
Gurney, Edmund, Frederic Myers and Frank Podmore, *Phantasms of the Living*, two vols (London: Trübner and Co., 1886).
Hamilton, E. A., 'The Fourth Dimension', repr. in Wells, *The Time Machine*, ed. Ruddick, pp. 219–20.
Hardy, Thomas, *The Dynasts: A Drama of the Napoleonic Wars in Three Parts, Nineteen Acts, and One Hundred and Thirty Scenes* (London: Macmillan, 1903–08).
Hill, Susan, *The Woman in Black* (London: Hamish Hamilton, 1983).
Hinton, Charles Henry, 'Stella' (1895; *Scientific Romances*, Second Series (London: Swan Sonnenschein, 1896)).
Hinton, Charles Henry, 'What is the Fourth Dimension?' (1884; *Scientific Romances* (London: Swan Sonnenschein, 1888)), pp. 3–32.
Huxley, Aldous, *Brave New World* (1932; London: Flamingo, 1994).
Huxley, Aldous, *The Doors of Perception* (London: Chatto and Windus, 1954).
Huxley, T. H., *Evolution and Ethics* (1896; repr. in T. H. Huxley and Julian Huxley,

Evolution and Ethics 1893–1943 (London: Pilot Press, 1947)), pp. 60–102.
James, William, *The Principles of Psychology*, Vol. I (New York: Henry Holt; London: Macmillan, 1890).
Joyce, James, *Ulysses* (1922; Oxford: Oxford World's Classics, 1998).
Kipling, Rudyard, *Actions and Reactions* (London: Macmillan, 1909).
Kipling, Rudyard, 'As Easy as ABC' (1907; repr. in Kipling, *Actions and Reactions*), pp. 143–69.
Kipling, Rudyard, 'With the Night Mail: A Story of 2000 AD' (1904; repr. in Kipling, *Actions and Reactions*), pp. 109–42.
Lang, Fritz, and Thea von Harbou, *Metropolis: The Screenplay* (London: Faber, 1989).
Lewis, Sinclair, *It Can't Happen Here* (London: Jonathan Cape, 1935).
Locke, George (ed.), *Sources of Science Fiction: Future War Novels of the 1890s* (London: Routledge/Thoemmes Press, 1998).
London, Jack, *The People of the Abyss* (1903; London: Journeyman, 1977).
Matthews, Brander, 'The Kinetoscope of Time', *Scribner's Magazine* (Dec. 1895), pp. 733–44.
Mitchell, Edward Page, *The Crystal Man*, ed. Sam Moskowitz (Garden City, NY: Doubleday, 1973).
Morris, William, *News From Nowhere, or An Epoch of Rest* (1890; London: Routledge, 1970).
Moskowitz, Sam (ed.), *Science Fiction by Gaslight: A History and Anthology of Science Fiction in the Popular Magazines, 1891–1911* (Westport, CT: Hyperion Press, 1971).
Mouton, Eugène, *Fantasies* (Paris: Charpentier, 1883).
O'Brien, Fitz-James, *Fantastic Tales of Fitz-James O'Brien*, ed. Michael Hayes (London: John Calder, 1977).
Otis, Laura (ed.), *Literature and Science in the Nineteenth Century: An Anthology* (Oxford: Oxford University Press, 2002).
Pal, George, and Joe Morhaim, *The Time Machine II* (New York: Dell, 1981).
Parish, Edmund, *Hallucinations and Illusions: A Study of the Fallacies of Perception* (London: Walter Scott, 1897).
Paul, R. W., 'A Chat With Mr. R. W. Paul (by Our Special Commisioner)', *Era* (25 Apr. 1896), p. 17.
Paul, R. W., Letter to *Bioscope* (19 Feb. 1914), p. 743.
Paul, R. W., Letter to *Nature*, no. 3730 (17 May 1941), p. 610.
Payn, James, *The Eavesdropper: An Unparalleled Experience* (London: Smith, Elder and Co., 1888).
Plato, *The Republic of Plato*, trans. Francis MacDonald Cornford (London: Oxford University Press, 1941).
Podmore, Frank, *Apparitions and Thought Transference: An Examination of the Evidence for Telepathy* (London: Walter Scott, 1894; also new and enlarged edition, 1915).
Priestley, J. B., *Man and Time* (London: Aldus Books, 1964).
Proctor, Richard, 'The Photographic Eyes of Science', *Longman's Magazine*, Vol.

I (Feb. 1883), pp. 439–62.
Rabb, Jane M. (ed.), *Literature and Photography, Interactions 1840–1990: A Critical Anthology* (Albuquerque: University of New Mexico Press, 1995), pp. 122–25.
Robida, Albert, *Le Vingtième Siècle* (1883; Genève and Paris: Editions Slatkine, 1981).
Rossetti, Dante Gabriel, *Collected Poetry and Prose*, ed. Jerome McGann (New Haven, CT and London: Yale University Press, 2003).
'S', 'Four-Dimensional Space', *Nature* (26 Mar. 1885), p. 481.
Serviss, Garrett P. , *Edison's Conquest of Mars* (1898; repr. in Locke (ed.), *Sources of Science Fiction*).
Stephen, Sir Herbert, 'No. 11 Welham Square' (1885; repr. in Michael Cox (ed.), *12 Victorian Ghost Stories* (Oxford: Oxford University Press, 1997)), pp. 136–47.
Stoker, Bram, *Dracula* (1897; Harmondsworth: Penguin, 1994).
Swinton, A. A. C., 'The New Photography of the Invisible', *Pall Mall Magazine*, Vol. IX, no. 38 (June 1896), pp. 264–68.
Tolstoy, Alexei, *Aelita* (1923; trans. Lucy Flaxman (Moscow: Foreign Languages Publishing House, 1962)).
Verne, Jules, 'In the Twenty-Ninth Century – The Day of an American Journalist in 2889' (1889; repr. in Haining (ed.), *Jules Verne Companion*, pp. 97–116.
Verne, Jules, *Le Château des Carpathes* (1892; Paris: Livre de Poche, 1976).
Verne, Jules, *Paris au XXe Siècle* (Paris: Hachette, 1994).
von Harbou, Thea, *Metropolis* (1926; Frankfurt am Main, Berlin: Wien, 1984).
Woolrich, Cornell, 'Rear Window' (1942; repr. in *Rear Window and Other Stories* (London and New York: Simon and Schuster, 1988)), pp. 1–27.

Secondary Texts

Articles, Essays and Reviews

Aldgate, Anthony, 'Loose Ends, Hidden Gems and the "Moment of Melodramatic Emotionality"', in Jeffrey Richards (ed.), *The Unknown 1930s: An Alternative History of the British Cinema, 1929–39* (London: I. B. Tauris, 1997), pp. 219–36.
Amis, Martin, 'The First Circle of Hell', *Guardian*, 'G2' (18 Sept. 2001), pp. 1–5.
Anon., 'A Film by Mr. H. G. Wells', *The Times* (22 Jan. 1934), p. 14.
Anon., 'Concerning Stoll's 1922 Program', *Kinematograph Weekly* (5 Jan. 1922), p. 89.
Anon., 'Fiction', *Saturday Review*, no. 80 (20 July 1895), pp. 86–87.
Anon., 'Film Adaptation of H. G. Wells Story: "The War of the Worlds"', *The Times* (2 Apr. 1953), p. 2.
Anon., 'Man Who Could Work Miracles', *Nature*, no. 3475 (6 June 1936), p. 929.

Anon., 'Mr H. G. Wells and the Screen: "War of the Worlds" as Film', *The Times* (3 Nov. 1932), p. 10.
Anon., 'Mr H. G. Wells's Film "Things to Come"', *Nature*, no. 3461 (29 Feb. 1936), p. 352.
Anon., 'Mr Wells and the Cinematograph', *The Times* (10 Jan. 1914), p. 6.
Anon., 'New Film Comedies: Humour by Mr. H. G. Wells', *The Times* (12 Sept. 1929), p. 10.
Anon., 'New H. G. Wells Film' (review of *TTC*), *The Times* (21 Feb. 1936), p. 12.
Anon., Notice (of Gaumont British contract), *The Times* (9 Jan. 1914), p. 8.
Anon., 'Plays', *Photoplay* (July 1922), p. 58.
Anon., 'Radio Play Upsets Americans: "Martian Invasion" of United States Taken Seriously', *Manchester Guardian* (1 Nov. 1938), p. 11.
Anon., (Review of *TTCAFS*), *Nature*, no. 3454 (11 Jan. 1936), p. 50.
Anon., 'Scientific Romances', *Nature* (12 Mar. 1885), p. 431.
Anon., '"The Invisible Man": A Film of Mr. H. G. Wells's Story', *The Times* (25 Jan. 1934), p. 8.
Anon., 'The Novelist and the Film', *John o' London's*, Vol. IX, no. 226 (4 Aug. 1923), pp. 577–78 and contd 597.
Anon., 'Why Not Show Them?', *Daily Mail* (4 July 1929), p. 8.
Armstrong, Tim, 'Technology: Multiplied Man', in David Bradshaw (ed.), *A Concise Companion to Modernism* (Oxford: Blackwell, 2003), pp. 158–78.
Bailey, Kenneth V., '"There Would Presently Come Out of the Darkness": H. G. Wells's "Filmic Imagination"', *The Wellsian* (Summer 1990), pp. 18–35.
Baudry, Jean-Louis, 'The Apparatus: Metapsychological Approaches to the Impression of Reality in Cinema', in P. Rosen (ed.), *Narrative, Apparatus, Ideology: A Film Theory Reader* (New York: Columbia University Press, 1986), pp. 299–318.
Baxter, Stephen, '1880s Science and *The Time Machine*', *The H. G. Wells Newsletter*, Vol. 3, no. 9 (Autumn 1995), p. 4.
Baxter, Stephen, 'Further Visions: Sequels to *The Time Machine*', *Foundation: The Review of Science Fiction*, no. 65 (Autumn 1995), pp. 41–50.
Benjamin, Walter, 'The Work of Art in the Age of Mechanical Reproduction' (1936), in Benjamin, *Illuminations*, ed. Hannah Arendt (London: Fontana, 1973), pp. 217–52.
Bignell, Jonathan, 'Another Time, Another Space: Modernity, Subjectivity, and *The Time Machine*', in Cartmell et al. (eds), *Alien Identities*, pp. 87–103.
Bordwell, David, '*Citizen Kane*', *Film Comment*, Vol. VII, no. 2 (Summer 1971), pp. 38–47.
Bould, Mark, 'Film and Television', in James and Mendlesohn (eds), *Cambridge Companion to Science Fiction*, pp. 79–95.
Bowen, Elizabeth, Review of *TTC*, *Sight and Sound*, no. 17 (Spring 1936), pp. 10–12.
Bradshaw, Peter, 'Attack of the Bug-Eyed Bores', *Guardian*, Review (1 July 2005), pp. 16–17.

Bruzzi, Stella, 'Space Looks', *Sight and Sound* (Sept. 1995), pp. 10–11.
Cantor, Paul A., '*The Invisible Man* and the Invisible Hand: H. G. Wells's Critique of Capitalism', *The American Scholar*, Vol. 68, no. 3 (Summer 1999), pp. 89–102.
Chapman, Alison, 'Mary Elizabeth Coleridge: Literary Influence and Technologies of the Uncanny', in Julian Wolfreys (ed.), *Victorian Gothic: Literary and Cultural Manifestations in the Nineteenth Century* (Basingstoke: Macmillan, 2000), pp. 109–28.
Chapman, James, 'Quatermass and the Origins of British Television SF', in Cook and Wright (eds), *British Science Fiction Television*, pp. 21–51.
Carroll, Sydney W., '"Things to Come": A Stupendous Film', *Sunday Times* (23 Feb. 1936), p. 4.
Coates, Paul, 'Chris Marker and the Cinema as Time Machine', *Science Fiction Studies*, Vol. 14, no. 3 (1987), pp. 307–15.
Cook, John R., 'Adapting Telefantasy: The *Doctor Who and the Daleks* Films', in Hunter (ed.), *British Science Fiction Cinema*, pp. 113–27.
Cook, John R., 'The Age of Aquarius: Utopia and Anti-Utopia in Late 1960s and early 1970s British Science Fiction Television', in Cook and Wright (eds), *British Science Fiction Television*, pp. 93–115.
Cook, John R., and Peter Wright, '"Futures Past": An Introduction to and Brief Survey of British Science Fiction Television', in Cook and Wright (eds), *British Science Fiction Television*, pp. 5–6.
Cooke, Lez, 'British Cinema: From Cottage Industry to Mass Entertainment', in Clive Bloom (ed.), *Literature and Culture in Modern Britain, Volume One: 1900–1929* (London: Longman, 1993), pp. 167–88.
Cornell, Julian, 'All's Well that Ends Wells: Apocalypse and Empire in *The War of the Worlds*', in Robert Stam and Alessandra Raengo (eds), *A Companion to Literature and Film* (Oxford: Blackwell, 2004), pp. 423–47.
Crossley, Robert, 'Taking It as a Story: The Beautiful Lie of *The Time Machine*', in Slusser et al. (eds), *H. G. Wells's Perennial Time Machine*, pp. 12–26.
Dam, H. J. W., 'A Wizard of Today', *Pearson's Magazine*, Vol. I, no. 4 (Apr. 1896), pp. 413–19.
Danvers Williams, J., 'I Wrote this Film for Your Enjoyment, says H. G. Wells', *Film Weekly* (29 Feb. 1936), pp. 7–8.
Derrida, Jacques', 'Structure, Sign and Play in the Discourse of the Human Sciences', in K. M. Newton (ed.), *Twentieth-Century Literary Theory: A Reader*, 2nd edition (Houndmills: Palgrave, 1988), pp. 149–54.
Eisenstein, Sergei M., 'Dickens, Griffith and the Film Today', in Eisenstein, *The Film Form: Essays in Film Theory*, ed. and trans. Jay Leyda (London: Dennis Dobson, 1963), pp. 195–265.
Eisenstein, Sergei M., 'The Dinamic Square', *Close-Up*, Vol. VIII, no. 1 (Mar. 1931), pp. 2–16, and no. 2 (June 1931), pp. 91–94.
Fielding, Raymond, 'Hale's Tours: Ultrarealism in the Pre-1910 Motion Picture', in Fell (ed.), *Film Before Griffith*, pp. 116–30.
Fisher, Lucy, 'The Lady Vanishes: Magic and the Movies', in Fell (ed.), *Film*

Before Griffith, pp. 339–54.
Fitting, Peter, 'Estranged Invaders: *The War of the Worlds*', in Patrick Parrinder (ed.), *Learning from Other Worlds: Estrangement, Cognition and the Politics of Science Fiction and Utopia* (Liverpool: Liverpool University Press, 2000), pp. 127–45.
Forster, E. M., 'A Camera Man' (1929; repr. as 'Sinclair Lewis' in Forster, *Abinger Harvest* (London: Arnold, 1936)), pp. 127–33.
Foucault, Michel, 'Truth and Power', in Paul Rabinow (ed.), *The Foucault Reader: An Introduction to Foucault's Thought* (Harmondsworth: Penguin, 1984), pp. 51–75.
From Our Own Correspondent, 'Radio Play Upsets Americans: "Martian Invasion" of United States Taken Seriously', *Manchester Guardian* (1 Nov. 1938), p. 11.
Fulton, John P., 'How We Made the Invisible Man', *American Cinematographer* (Sept. 1934), pp. 200–1 and 214.
Glenn, Edward, 'Fantasy Flashback: *The Time Machine*', *TV Zone*, no. 17 (1991), pp. 28–30.
Gordon, Andrew, 'Play It Again, Sam: Ken Grimwood's *Replay* and Time Travel as Reincarnation', in Westfahl et al. (eds), *Worlds Enough and Time*, pp. 139–47.
Gorky, Maxim, 'In the Kingdom of Shadows' (1896), in Leyda (ed.), *Kino*, pp. 407–9.
Gray, Frank, 'Innovation and Wonder: Robert Paul in 1896', in Gray (ed.), *Hove Pioneers*, pp. 19–23.
Greene, Graham, 'Things to Come', *Spectator* (28 Feb. 1936; repr. in *The Graham Greene Film Reader: Mornings in the Dark*, ed. David Parkinson (Manchester: Carcanet, 1993)), pp. 77–79.
Grove, Allen W., 'Röntgen's Ghosts: Photography, X-rays, and the Victorian Imagination', *Literature and Medicine*, Vol. 16, no. 2 (Fall 1997), pp. 141–73.
Gunning, Tom, 'An Aesthetic of Astonishment: Early Film and the (In)credulous Spectator', in Leo Braudy and Marshall Cohen (eds), *Film Theory and Criticism: Introductory Readings* (Oxford: Oxford University Press, 1999), pp. 818–32.
Gunning, Tom, 'Doing for the Eye What the Phonograph Does for the Ear', in Richard Abel and Rick Altman (eds), *The Sounds of Early Cinema* (Bloomington, IN: Indianapolis University Press, 2001), pp. 13–31.
Hampton, Kirk, and Carol MacKay, 'Beyond the Endtime: Allegories of Coalescence in Far-Future Science Fiction', in Westfahl et al. (eds), *Worlds Enough and Time*, pp. 65–75.
Hardy, Sylvia, 'H. G. Wells and British Cinema: The War of the Worlds', *Foundation: The International Review of Science Fiction*, Vol. 28, no. 77 (Autumn 1999), pp. 46–58.
Hardy, Sylvia, 'H. G. Wells and British Silent Cinema: The War of the Worlds', in Andrew Higson (ed.), *Young and Innocent?*, pp. 242–55.
Hedgecock, Liz, '"The Martians are Coming!" Civilisation v. Invasion in *The War of the Worlds* and *Mars Attacks!*', in Cartmell et al. (eds), *Alien Identities*, pp. 104–20.

Hepworth, Cecil, 'Those Were the Days: Reminscences by a Pioneer of the Earliest Days of Cinematography', *The Penguin Film Review* (Apr. 1948), pp. 33–39.

Hodgens, Richard, 'A Brief, Tragical History of the Science Fiction Film', in Johnson (ed.), *Focus on the Science Fiction Film*, pp. 78–90.

Hughes, David Y., and Robert M. Philmus, 'A Selective Bibliography (with Abstracts) of H. G. Wells's Science Journalism 1887–1901', in Darko Suvin and Robert M. Philmus (eds), *H. G. Wells and Modern Science Fiction* (Lewisburg, PA: Bucknell University Press; London: Associated University Presses, 1977), pp. 191–222.

Hutchings, Peter, 'We're the Martians Now: British SF Invasion Fantasies of the 1950s and 1960s', in Hunter (ed.), *British Science Fiction Cinema*, pp. 33–47.

Jameson, Storm, 'Documents', *Fact*, no. 4 (July 1937), pp. 9–18.

Kaes, Anton, 'Metropolis: City, Cinema, Modernity', in Timothy O. Benson (ed.), *Expressionist Utopias: Paradise, Metropolis, Architectural Fantasy* (Berkeley, CA: University of California Press, 2001), pp. 146–65.

Kneale, Nigel, 'Not Quite So Intimate', *Sight and Sound*, Vol. 28, no. 2 (Spring 1959), pp. 86–88.

Kneale, Nigel, 'Quatermass and the Pen', interview with Kim Newman and Julian Pentley, *Video Watchdog*, no. 47 (Sept./Oct. 1998), p. 5.

Kozyrena, Maria, and Vera Shamina, 'Russia Revisited', in Parrinder and Partington (eds), *Reception of H. G. Wells in Europe*, pp. 46–62.

La Valley, Albert J., 'Traditions of Trickery: The Role of Special Effects in the Science Fiction Film', in Slusser and Rabkin (eds), *Shadows of the Magic Lamp*, pp. 141–58.

Laura, Ernesto G., 'Invasion of the Body Snatchers' (1957; repr. in Johnson (ed.), *Focus on the Science Fiction Film*, pp. 71–73.

Law, Richard, 'The Narrator in Double Exposure in *The War of the Worlds*', in Partington (ed.), *Wellsian*, pp. 95–103.

Lejeune, C. A., 'Film of the Week' (Review of *TTC*), *Observer* (23 Feb. 1936), p. 14.

Lukács, Georg, 'Reification and the Consciousness of the Proletariat', in Lukács *History and Class Consciousness* (1923; trans. Rodney Livingstone (London: Merlin, 1971)), pp. 83–110.

MacPherson, Kenneth, 'The Novelist Who Was a Scenarist', *Close-Up*, Vol. IV, no. 3 (Mar. 1929), pp. 78–80.

Mair, Jan, 'Rewriting the "American Dream": Postmodernism and Otherness in *Independence Day*', in Sardar and Cubitt (eds), *Aliens R Us*, pp. 34–50.

Marcus, Laura, 'Literature and Cinema', in Laura Marcus and Peter Nicholls (eds), *The Cambridge History of Twentieth-Century English Literature* (Cambridge: Cambridge University Press, 2005), pp. 335–58.

Marinetti, T. P., 'Destruction of Syntax – Imagination Without Strings – Words in Freedom (1913)', in Umbro Apollonio (ed.), *Futurist Manifestos* (London: Thames and Hudson, 1973), pp. 95–106.

Marx, Karl, 'The Inaugural Address of the Working Men's International Association' (1864; Karl Marx and Friedrich Engels, *Selected Works*, Vol. 1 (Moscow: Progress Publishers 1969)), pp. 11–18.
Mayne, Alan, 'The Virtual Time Machine II', *The Wellsian*, no. 20 (Winter 1997), pp. 20–31.
McCormack, Una, 'Resist the Host: *Blake's 7* – A Very British Future', in Cook and Wright (eds), *British Science Fiction Television*, pp. 174–91.
Michelson, Annette, 'Dr Crase and Mr Clair', *October*, no. 11 (Winter 1979), pp. 30–53.
Miller, Catriona, 'British Apocalypses Now – Or Then? *The Uninvited*, *Invasion: Earth* and *The Last Train*', in Cook and Wright (eds), *British Science Fiction Television*, pp. 263–82.
Minden, Michael, 'The City in Early Cinema: *Metropolis*, *Berlin* and *October*', in Edward Timms and David Kelly (eds), *Unreal City: Urban Experience in Modern European Literature and Art* (Manchester: Manchester University Press, 1985), pp. 193–213.
Murphy, Peter, 'A Novelist's Account of Visual Immersion – "vr" in the Writings of H. G. Wells', *Interactive Cinema – Panoramic Systems*, http://users.bigpond.net.au/virtual/reportxx.htm
Nate, Richard, 'Ignorance, Opportunism, Propaganda and Dissent: The Reception of H. G. Wells in Nazi Germany', in Parrinder and Partington (eds), *Reception of H. G. Wells in Europe*, pp. 105–25.
Orwell, George, 'As I Please' (12 May 1944), in *Complete Works of George Orwell*, ed. Peter Davison, Vol. XVI, *I Have Tried to Tell the Truth 1943–1944* (London: Secker and Warburg, 2001), pp. 182–86.
Orwell, George, 'Wells, Hitler and the World State' (1941), in *Complete Works of George Orwell*, ed. Peter Davison, Vol. XII, *A Patriot After All 1940–1941* (London: Secker and Warburg, 2000), pp. 536–41.
Orwell, George, 'You and the Atom Bomb' and 'What Is Science?' (Oct. 1945), in *Complete Works of George Orwell*, ed. Peter Davison, Vol. XVII, *I Belong to the Left 1945* (London: Secker and Warburg, 2001), pp. 316–28.
Pagetti, Carlo, 'Change in the City: The Time Traveller's London and the "Baseless Fabric" of his Vision', in Slusser et al. (eds), *Perennial Time Machine*, pp. 122–34.
Pal, George, 'Filming *War of the Worlds*', *Astounding Science Fiction* (Oct. 1953), pp. 100–11.
Peters, Jefferson M., 'The Desire to Control Time in *Doraemon* and Japanese Culture', in Westfahl et al. (eds), *Worlds Enough and Time*, pp. 104–11.
Platten, David, 'A Hitchhiker's Guide to Paris: *Paris au XXe Siècle*', in Edmund J. Smyth (ed.), *Jules Verne: Narratives of Modernity* (Liverpool: Liverpool University Press, 2000), pp. 78–93.
Potter, Dennis, 'Realism and Non-Naturalism 2', *The Official Programme of the Edinburgh International Television Festival 1977* (Aug. 1977), p. 36.
Powell, K., 'Tom, Dick and Dorian Gray: Magic Picture Mania in Late Victorian Fiction', *Philological Quarterly*, no. 62 (1983), pp. 147–70.

Proctor, Richard, 'The Photographic Eyes of Science', *Longman's Magazine*, Vol. I (Feb. 1883), pp. 439–62.
Reuters, 'Mr Wells "Deeply Concerned": "Unwarranted" Rewriting of his Novel', *Manchester Guardian* (1 Nov. 1938), p. 11.
Richards, Jeffrey, 'Things to Come and Science Fiction in the 1930s', in Hunter (ed.), *British Science Fiction Cinema*, pp. 16–33.
Richardson, Dorothy, 'Continuous Performance: Almost Persuaded'(1929; repr. in Donald, Friedberg and Marcus (eds), *Close-Up*), pp. 190–92.
Rowland, Margery, 'Mr Wells is Wrong: You Cannot Compare Stage and Screen', *Era*, British edition (11 Dec. 1935), p. 3.
Rubin, Steve, 'The War of the Worlds', *Cinefantastique*, Vol. 5, no. 4 (Spring 1976), pp. 4–16 and contd 34–37.
Russell, W. M. S., 'Time Before and After: *The Time Machine*', *Foundation: The Review of Science Fiction*, no. 65 (Autumn 1995), pp. 24–40.
Sawyer, Andy, '"Backward, Turn Backward": Narratives of Reversed Time in Science Fiction', in Westfahl et al. (eds), *Worlds Enough and Time*, pp. 49–62.
Scanner, The, 'Experiment with Wells', *Radio Times* (4 Feb. 1949), p. 24.
Scot, Darrin, '*The Time Machine*', *American Cinematographer*, Vol. 41, no. 8 (Aug. 1960), pp. 490–91.
Scurriatti, Laura, 'A Tale of Two Cities: H. G. Wells's *The Door in the Wall* Illustrated by Alvin Langdon Coburn', in Partington (ed.), *Wellsian*, pp. 145–65.
Seed, David, 'British Modernists Encounter the Cinema', in Seed (ed.), *Literature and the Visual Media* (Cambridge: D. S. Brewer, 2005), pp. 48–73.
Sexton, Jamie, 'Alternative Film Culture in Britain in the 1920s', in Higson (ed.), *Young and Innocent?*, pp. 291–305.
Shales, Tom, 'The Re Decade', *Esquire* (Mar. 1986), pp. 67–68.
Sillars, Stuart, '*Things to Come* and "Newsreel": Versions of Cinematic Influence', *Notes and Queries*, Vol. 47, no. 1 (Mar. 2002), pp. 91–93.
Simpson, Anne B., 'The "Tangible Antagonist": H. G. Wells and the Discourse of Otherness', *Extrapolation*, Vol. 31 no. 2 (Summer 1990), pp. 134–47.
Slusser, George, and Daniele Chatelain, 'A Tale of Two Science Fictions: H. G. Wells in France and the Soviet Union', in Parrinder and Partington (eds), *Reception of H. G. Wells*, pp. 280–301.
Slusser, George, and Robert Heath, 'Arrows and Riddles of Time: Scientific Models of Time Travel', in Westfahl et al. (eds), *Worlds Enough and Time*, pp. 11–24.
Sobchack, Vivian, 'Towards a Phenomenology of Cinematic and Electronic "Presence": The Scene of the Screen', *Post Script: Essays in Film and the Humanities*, Vol. 10, no. 1 (Autumn 1990), pp. 50–59.
Sommerville, Bruce David, '*The Time Machine*: A Chronological and Scientific Revision', *Wellsian*, new series, no. 17 (Winter 1994), pp. 11–29.
Sontag, Susan, 'The Imagination of Disaster' (1965; repr. in Sontag, *Against Interpretation and Other Essays* (London: Eyre and Spottiswoode, 1967)), pp. 209–25.
Stein, Joshua, 'The Legacy of H. G. Wells's *The Time Machine*: Destabilization

and Observation', in Slusser and Chatelain (eds), *Perennial Time Machine*, pp. 150–59.
Stewart, Garrett, 'The "Videology" of Science Fiction', in Slusser and Rabkin (eds), *Shadows of the Magic Lamp*, pp. 159–207.
Swift, John, 'To the World's End in Sixty Minutes', *Radio Times* (20 Jan. 1949), p. 25.
Tenner, Edward, 'The World's Greatest Futurist', *Harvard Magazine*, Vol. 92, no. 3 (Jan.–Feb. 1990), pp. 36–41.
Timberlake, John, 'Forgotten Cameras and Unknown Audiences: Photography, *The Time Machine* and the Atomic Bomb', in David Cunningham, Andrew Fisher and Sas Mays (eds), *Photography and Literature in the Twentieth Century* (Newcastle: Cambridge Scholars Press, 2005), pp. 11–24.
Tolstoy, Leo, 'A Conversation with Leo Tolstoy', in Leyda (ed.), *Kino*, pp. 410–11.
Vallorani, Nicoletta, '"The Invisible Wells" in European Cinema and Television', in Parrinder and Partington (eds), *Reception of H. G. Wells in Europe*, pp. 302–20.
van Dooren, Ine, 'Travelling Times', in Gray (ed.), *Hove Pioneers*, pp. 12–17.
Virilio, Paul, 'Cataract Surgery: Cinema in the Year 2000', in Annette Kuhn (ed.), *Alien Zone: Cultural Theory and Contemporary Science Fiction* (London: Verso, 1990), pp. 169–76.
Virilio, Paul, 'The Last Vehicle', in D. Kampfer and C. Wulf (eds), *Looking Back on the End of the World* (New York: Semiotext(e), 1989), pp. 90–110.
Wells, Paul, 'Apocalypse Then! The Ultimate Monstrosity and Strange Things on the Coast ... An Interview with Nigel Kneale', in Hunter (ed.), *British Science Fiction Cinema*, pp. 48–56.
Wells, Simon, 'How My Great Grandfather Invented The Time Machine', *Guardian*, Friday Review (31 May 2002), pp. 2–4.
Werner, Gösta, 'Fritz Lang and Goebbels: Myth and Facts', *Film Quarterly*, no. 43 (Spring 1990), pp. 24–27.
Westfahl, Gary, 'Space Opera', in James and Mendlesohn (eds), *Cambridge Companion to Science Fiction*, pp. 197–208.
Wileman, Ralph, 'Peep Egg Viewer' (interview with Dr Ralph Wileman, 24 July 2000) http://courses.ncssm.edu/gallery/collections/toys/html/exhibit08.htm
Williams, Keith, 'Symphonies of the Big City: Modernism, Cinema and Urban Modernity', in Paul Edwards (ed.), *The Great London Vortex: Modernist Literature and Art* (Bath: Sulis Press, 2003), pp. 31–50.
Williams, Keith, 'The Dis/Appearance of the Subject: Wells, Whale and the Invisible Man', in *The Undying Fire* (Journal of the H. G. Wells Society, the Americas) no. 2 (2003), pp. 37–64.
Williams, Keith, '"Seeing the Future": Urban Dystopia in Wells and Lang', in Godela Weiss-Sussex and Franco Bianchini (eds), *Urban Mindscapes of Europe*, European Studies, no. 23 (Amsterdam and New York: Rodopi, 2006), pp. 127–46.

Williams, Keith, '*Ulysses* in Toontown: Vision animated to Bursting Point in Joyce's "Circe"', in Lydia Rainford and Julian Murphet (eds), *Writing After Cinema: Literature and Visual Technologies* (Houndmills: Palgrave, 2003), pp. 96–121.

Books

Albrecht, Donald, *Designing Dreams: Modern Architecture in the Movies* (Santa Monica, CA: Hennessey and Ingalls, 1986).
Armstrong, Tim, *Modernism, Technology and the Body* (Cambridge: Cambridge University Press, 1998).
Baird, John Logie, *Television and Me: The Memoirs of John Logie Baird*, ed. Malcolm Baird (Edinburgh: Mercat, 2004).
Bakhtin, Mikhail, *The Dialogic Imagination: Four Essays*, ed. Michael Holquist (Austin, TX: University of Texas Press, 1981).
Balázs, Béla, *Theory of the Film* (London: Dennis Dobson, 1953).
Barnes, John, *Filming the Boer War* (London: Bishopsgate, 1992).
Barnes, John, *The Beginnings of Cinema in England 1894–1901*, Vol. 1: 1894–1896, revised edition (Exeter: Exeter University Press, 1998).
Barnouw, Erik, *The Magician and the Cinema* (Oxford: Oxford University Press, 1981).
Barry, Iris, *Let's Go to the Pictures* (1926; repr. as *Let's Go to the Movies* (New York: Payson and Clarke, 1972)).
Barthes, Roland, *Camera Lucida*, trans. Richard Howard (1982; Frogmore: Fontana, 1984).
Bartholomew, Robert E., and Hilary Evans, *Panic Attacks: Media Manipulation and Mass Delusion* (Stroud: Sutton, 2004).
Baudrillard, Jean, *Selected Writings*, ed. M. Poster (Cambridge: Polity, 1988).
Baxter, John, *Science Fiction in the Cinema* (New York: A. S. Barnes; London: Zwemmer, 1970).
Benshoff, Harry M., *Monsters in the Closet: Homosexuality and the Horror Film* (Manchester: Manchester University Press, 1997).
Beresford, J. D., *H. G. Wells: A Critical Biography* (London: Nisbet, 1915).
Bergonzi, Bernard, *The Early H. G. Wells: A Study of the Scientific Romances* (Manchester: Manchester University Press, 1961).
Bourke, Joanna, *Fear: A Cultural History* (London: Virago, 2004).
Braun, Marta, *Picturing Time: The Work of Étienne-Jules Marey* (Chicago and London: University of Chicago Press, 1992).
Brooks, Van Wyck, *The World of H. G. Wells* (New York and London: T. Fisher Unwin, 1915).
Brosnan, John, *Future Tense: The Cinema of Science Fiction* (New York: St Martin's Press, 1978).
Callow, Simon, *Orson Welles: The Road to Xanadu* (London: Jonathan Cape, 1995).
Cantril, Hadley, Hazel Gaudet and Herta Herzog, *The Invasion From Mars: A Study in the Psychology of Panic* (Princeton, NJ: Princeton University Press,

1940).
Cartmell, Deborah, I. Q. Hunter, Heidi Kaye and Imelda Whelehan (eds), *Alien Identities: Exploring Difference in Film and Fiction* (London: Pluto Press, 1999).
Chanan, Michael, *The Dream that Kicks: The Prehistory and Early Years of Cinema in Britain* (London: Routledge and Kegan Paul, 1980).
Chaplin, Charlie, *My Autobiography* (1964; Harmondsworth: Penguin, 2003).
Chéroux, Clément, et al., *The Perfect Medium: Photography and the Occult* (New Haven, CT and London: Yale University Press, 2005).
Christie, Ian, *Arrows of Desire: the Films of Michael Powell and Emeric Pressburger* (London: Faber, 1994).
Christie, Ian, *The Last Machine: Early Cinema and the Birth of the Modern World* (London: BFI/BBC, 1994).
Clarke, I. F. (ed.), *British Future Fiction, 1700–1914* (London: Pickering and Chatto, 2001).
Clarke, I. F., *The Pattern of Expectation, 1644–2001* (London: Jonathan Cape, 1979).
Clarke, I. F., *The Tale of the Next War, 1871–1914* (Liverpool: Liverpool University Press, 1995).
Clarke, I. F., *Voices Prophesying War, 1763–1984* (London: Oxford University Press, 1970).
Clute, John, and Peter Nicholls (eds), *The Encyclopedia of Science Fiction*, second edition (London: Orbit, 1993).
Coe, Brian, *Muybridge and the Chronophotographers* (London: MOMI/BFI, 1992).
Cohen, Keith, *Film and Fiction: The Dynamics of Exchange* (New Haven, CT, and London: Yale University Press, 1979).
Connor, Steven, *Dumbstruck: A Cultural History of Ventriloquism* (Oxford: Oxford University Press, 2000).
Cook, David A., *A History of Narrative Film*, fourth edition (New York and London: Norton 2004).
Cook, John R., and Peter Wright (eds), *British Science Fiction Television: A Hitchhiker's Guide* (London and New York: I. B. Tauris, 2006).
Cooke, Alistair, *Garbo and the Night Watchmen* (London: Secker and Warburg, 1971).
Cosandey, Roland, André Gaudrealt and Tom Gunning (eds), *An Invention of the Devil: Religion and Early Cinema* (Sainte Foy, Quebec: Presses de l'Université Laval, 1990).
Crafton, Donald, *Before Mickey: The Animated Film 1898–1928* (Chicago and London: University of Chicago Press, 1993).
Curtis, James, *James Whale: A New World of Gods and Monsters* (Minneapolis, MN: University of Minnesota Press, 2003).
Dale, R. C., *The Films of René Clair*, Vol. I, *Exposition and Analysis* (Metuchen, NJ, and London: Scarecrow Press, 1986).
Daly, Nicholas, *Literature, Technology and Modernity* (Cambridge: Cambridge University Press, 2004).
Debord, Guy, *The Society of the Spectacle*, trans. from the French (Detroit: Black

and Red, 1983).
Deleuze, Gilles, *Cinema 2: The Time-Image*, trans. Hugh Tomlinson and Robert Galeta (London: Athlone Press, 1989).
Derrida, Jacques, *Echographies of Television* (Cambridge: Polity, 2002).
Derrida, Jacques, *Of Grammatology*, trans. Gayatri Chakravorty Spivak (Baltimore, MD: Johns Hopkins University Press, 1977).
Derrida, Jacques, *Writing and Difference*, trans. Alan Bass (London: Routledge and Kegan Paul, 1981).
Doane, Mary Anne, *The Emergence of Cinematic Time: Modernity, Contingency and the Archive* (Cambridge, MA and London: Harvard University Press, 2002).
Donald, James, Anne Friedberg and Laura Marcus (eds), *Close-Up 1927–1933: Cinema and Modernism* (London: Cassell, 1998).
Drazin, Charles, *Korda: Britain's Only Movie Mogul* (London: Sidgwick and Jackson, 2002).
Dryden, Linda, *The Modern Gothic and Literary Doubles: Stevenson, Wilde and Wells* (Houndmills: Palgrave, 2003).
During, Simon, *Modern Enchantments: The Cultural Power of Secular Magic* (Cambridge, MA and London: Harvard University Press, 2002).
Eisenstein, Sergei M., *Film Form: Essays in Film Theory*, ed. and trans. Jay Leyda (London: Dennis Dobson, 1963).
Eisenstein, Sergei M., *The Film Sense*, ed. Jay Leyda (London: Faber, 1986).
Eisner, Lotte H., *The Haunted Screen: Expressionism in the German Cinema and the Influence of Max Reinhardt*, trans. Richard Greaves (London: Thames and Hudson, 1969).
Elsaesser, Thomas, *Metropolis* (London: BFI, 2000).
Evans, Joyce A., *Celluloid Mushroom Clouds: Hollywood and the Atomic Bomb* (Boulder, CO, and Oxford: Westview Press, 1998).
Fairservice, Don, *Film Editing: History, Theory and Practice* (Manchester: Manchester University Press, 2001).
Fawcett, L'Estrange, *Films: Facts and Forecasts* (London: Geoffrey, 1927).
Fell, John R., *Film and the Narrative Tradition* (Norman: University of Oklahoma Press, 1975).
Fell, John R. (ed.), *Film Before Griffith* (Cambridge, MA: Harvard University Press, 1983).
Ferguson, Niall, *The War of the World: History's Age of Hatred* (London: Allen Lane, 2006).
Fisher, Peter S., *Fantasy and Politics: Visions of the Future in the Weimar Republic* (Madison, WI: University of Wisconsin Press, 1991).
Flanders, Judith, *Consuming Passions: Leisure and Pleasure in Victorian Britain* (London: Harper Press, 2006).
Flint, Kate, *The Victorians and the Visual Imagination* (Cambridge: Cambridge University Press, 2000).
Frayling, Christopher, *Mad, Bad and Dangerous? The Scientist and the Cinema* (London: Reaktion, 2005).
Frayling, Christopher, *Things to Come* (London: British Film Institute, 1995).

Friedberg, Anne, *Window Shopping: Cinema and the Postmodern* (Berkeley, CA: University of California Press, 1993).
Fritzsche, Peter, *A Nation of Flyers: German Aviation and the Popular Imagination* (Cambridge, MA, and London: Harvard University Press, 1992).
Fujiwara, Chris, *Jacques Tourneur and the Cinema of Nightfall* (Baltimore, MD and London: Johns Hopkins University Press, 1998).
Gatiss, Mark, *James Whale: A Biography, or The Would-be Gentleman* (London: Cassell, 1995).
Gifford, Denis, *British Animated Films 1895–1985: A Filmography* (Jefferson, NC and London: McFarland, 1987).
Gledhill, Christine, *Reframing British Cinema 1918–1928: Between Restraint and Passion* (London: BFI, 2002).
Goldmann, Lucien, *Towards a Sociology of the Novel*, trans. Alan Sheridan (London: Tavistock, 1975).
Gray, Frank (ed.), *The Hove Pioneers and the Arrival of Cinema* (Brighton: University of Sussex, 1996).
Greenblatt, Stephen J., *Learning to Curse: Essays in Early Modern Culture* (New York and London: Routledge, 1990).
Gunning, Tom, *The Films of Fritz Lang: Allegories of Vision and Modernity* (London: British Film Institute, 2000).
Haffner, Sebastian, *The Meaning of Hitler*, trans. Ewald Osers (Cambridge, MA: Harvard University Press, 1979).
Haining, Peter (ed.), *The Jules Verne Companion* (London: Souvenir Press, 1978).
Hake, Sabine, *Popular Cinema of the Third Reich* (Austin, TX: University of Texas Press, 2001).
Hammond, J. R., *An H. G. Wells Chronology* (Basingstoke: Macmillan, 1999).
Hammond, J. R., *H. G. Wells and the Short Story* (Basingstoke: Macmillan, 1992).
Hammond, J. R., *H. G. Wells: Interviews and Recollections* (London: Macmillan, 1980).
Hammond, Paul, *Marvellous Méliès* (London: Gordon Fraser, 1974).
Hardwicke, Sir Cedric, *A Victorian in Orbit: The Irreverent Memoirs of Sir Cedric Hardwicke* (London: Methuen, 1961).
Hardy, Phil (ed.), *Science Fiction: The Aurum Film Encyclopedia*, third edition (New York: Aurum Press, 1995).
Harryhausen, Ray, and Tony Dalton, *The Art of Ray Harryhausen* (London: Aurum, 2005).
Hayward, Susan, *Cinema Studies: The Key Concepts* (London: Routledge, 2000).
Hendricks, Gordon, *Eadweard Muybridge: The Father of the Motion Picture* (London: Secker and Warburg, 1977).
Herbert, Ray, *Seeing By Wireless: The Story of Baird Television* (Sanderstead: Ray Herbert, 1996).
Herbert, Stephen (ed.), *A History of Pre-Cinema*, three vols (London and New York: Routledge, 2000).
Herbert, Stephen, and Luke MacKernan (eds), *Who's Who of Victorian Cinema: A Worldwide Survey* (London: BFI, 1996).

Heylin, Clinton, *Despite the System: Orson Welles Versus the Hollywood Studios* (Edinburgh: Canongate, 2005).
Hickman, Gail Morgan, *The Films of George Pal* (South Brunswick, NJ: A. S. Barnes; London: Thomas Yoseloff, 1977).
Higson, Andrew (ed.), *Young and Innocent? The Cinema in Britain 1896–1930* (Exeter: University of Exeter Press, 2002).
Holmsten, Brian, and Alex Lubertozzi (eds), *The Complete War of the Worlds: Mars' Invasion of Earth from H. G. Wells to Orson Welles* (Napierville, IL: Sourcebooks, 2001).
Hopwood, Henry Vaux, *Living Pictures: Their History, Photo-Production and Practical Working* (London: Optician and Photographic Trades Review, 1899).
Howes, Chris, *To Photograph Darkness: The History of Underground and Flash Photography* (Carbondale: Southern Illinois University Press, 1990).
Hunter, I. Q. (ed.), *British Science Fiction Cinema* (London and New York: Routledge, 1999).
Huntington, John, *The Logic of Fantasy: H. G. Wells and Science Fiction* (New York and Guildford, Surrey: Columbia University Press, 1982).
Israel, Paul, *Edison: A Life of Invention* (New York: John Wiley, 1998).
Jacobs, Jason, *Intimate Screen: Early British Television Drama* (Oxford: Oxford University Press, 2000).
James, Edward, *Science Fiction in the Twentieth Century* (Oxford: Oxford University Press, 1994).
James, Edward, and Farah Mendlesohn (eds), *The Cambridge Companion to Science Fiction* (Cambridge: Cambridge University Press, 2003).
Jensen, Paul M., *The Cinema of Fritz Lang* (Cranbury, NJ: Barnes; London: Zwemmer, 1969).
Johnson, Catherine, *Telefantasy* (London: BFI, 2005).
Johnson, William (ed.), *Focus on the Science Fiction Film* (Englewood Cliffs, NJ: Prentice-Hall, 1972).
Kamm, Antony, and Malcolm Baird, *John Logie Baird: A Life* (Edinburgh: National Museums of Scotland, 2002).
Kaplan, Ann E., *Fritz Lang: A Guide to References and Resources* (Boston, MA: G. K. Hall, 1981).
Kern, Stephen, *The Culture of Time and Space 1889–1918* (Cambridge, MA: Harvard University Press, 1983).
King, Stephen, *Danse Macabre* (London: Warner Books, 1993).
Koestler, Arthur, *Spanish Testament* (London: Gollancz, 1937).
Korda, Michael, *Charmed Lives: A Family Romance* (1979; New York: Harper Collins, 2002).
Kozloff, Sarah, *Invisible Storytellers: Voice-over Narration in the American Fiction Film* (Berkeley, CA: University of California Press, 1988).
Kulik, Karol, *Alexander Korda: The Man Who Could Work Miracles* (London: Virgin, 1990).
Kumar, Krishan, *Utopia and Anti-Utopia in Modern Times* (Oxford: Basil Blackwell, 1991).

Landon, Brooks, *The Aesthetics of Ambivalence: Rethinking Science Fiction Film in the Age of Electronic (Re)Production* (Westport, CT: Greenwood Press, 1992).
Leyda, Jay (ed.), *Kino: A History of the Russian and Soviet Film* (London: Allen and Unwin, 1960).
Lindsay, Vachel, *The Art of the Moving Picture* (1915; revised version (New York: Liveright, 1922; repr. 1970).
Lippmann, Walter, *Public Opinion* (London: Allen and Unwin, 1929).
Lodge, David, *The Modes of Modern Writing: Metaphor, Metonymy and the Typology of Modern Literature* (1977; London: Edward Arnold, 1979).
London Film Society, *The Film Society Programmes: 1925–1939* (New York: Arno Press, 1972).
Low, Rachel, *The History of British Film, 1918–1929* (London: George Allen and Unwin, 1971).
Luckhurst, Roger, *Science Fiction* (Cambridge: Polity, 2005).
Lumière, Auguste, and Louis Lumière, *Letters: Inventing the Cinema*, ed. Jacques Rittaud-Huttinet et al. (London: Faber, 1995).
MacKenzie, Norman, and Jeanne MacKenzie, *The Time Traveller: The Life of H. G. Wells* (London: Weidenfeld and Nicolson, 1973).
Marien, Mary Warner, *Photography: A Cultural History* (London: Laurence King, 2002).
Marx, Karl, *Capital*, trans. Ben Foukes (Harmondsworth: Penguin, 1990).
Massey, Raymond, *A Hundred Different Lives: An Autobiography* (London: Robson Books, 1979).
Masterman, C. F. G., *The Condition of England* (London: Methuen, 1909).
McBride, Joseph, *Orson Welles* (New York: Da Capo, 1996).
McConnell, Frank, *The Science Fiction of H. G. Wells* (Oxford: Oxford University Press, 1981).
McDonald, Paul, *The Star System: Hollywood's Production of Popular Identities* (London and New York: Wallflower, 2000).
McGilligan, Patrick, *Fritz Lang: The Nature of the Beast* (London: Faber, 1997).
Metz, Christian, *The Imaginary Signifier: Psychoanalysis and the Cinema* (Bloomington, IN: Indiana University Press, 1982).
Mogg, Ken, *The Alfred Hitchcock Story* (London: Titan Books, 1999).
Montagu, Ivor, *Film World* (Harmondsworth: Penguin, 1964).
Montagu, Ivor, *With Eisenstein in Hollywood* (London: Lawrence and Wishart, 1968).
Mumford, Lewis, *Technics and Civilization* (London: Routledge, 1934).
Münsterberg, Hugo, *The Photoplay: A Psychological Study* (1916; repr. as *The Film: A Psychological Study* (New York: Dover Publications, 1970)).
Murray, Andy, *Into the Unknown: The Fantastic Life of Nigel Kneale* (London: Headpress, 2006).
Netzley, Patricia, *The Encyclopaedia of Movie Special Effects* (Westport, CT: Greenwood, 1999).
Newman, Kim, *Apocalypse Movies: End of the World Cinema* (New York: St Martin's, 2000).

Newman, Kim, *Doctor Who* (London: BFI, 2005).
Nicoll, Allardyce, *Film and Theatre* (London: Harrap, 1936).
Paris, Michael, *From the Wright Brothers to Top Gun: Aviation, Nationalism and Popular Cinema* (Manchester: Manchester University Press, 1995).
Parrinder, Patrick (ed.), *H. G. Wells: The Critical Heritage* (London: Routledge and Kegan Paul, 1972).
Parrinder, Patrick, and John Partington (eds), *The Reception of H. G. Wells in Europe* (London and New York: Thoemmes Continuum, 2005).
Partington, John (ed.), *The Wellsian: Selected Essays on H. G. Wells* (London: Equilibris, 2003).
Philmus, Robert M., *Visions and Revisions: (Re-)Constructing Science Fiction* (Liverpool: Liverpool University Press, 2005).
Price, Harry, *Fifty Years of Psychical Research: A Critical Survey* (London: Longman's Green, 1939).
Pudovkin, V. I., *Filmregie und Filmmanuskript* (Berlin: Verlag der Lichtbühne, 1928).
Ramsaye, Terry, *A Million and One Nights: A History of the Motion Picture* (New York: Simon and Schuster, 1926; repr. London: Frank Cass, 1964).
Rawlence, Christopher, *The Missing Reel: The Untold Story of the Lost Inventor of Moving Pictures* (London: Collins, 1991).
Renzi, Thomas C., *H. G. Wells: Six Scientific Romances Adapted for Film*, second edition (Lanham, MD, Toronto and Oxford: Scarecrow Press, 2004).
Richards, Thomas, *The Commodity Culture of Victorian England: Advertising and Spectacle 1851–1914* (Stamford, CA: Stamford University Press, 1990).
Richie, Alexandra, *Faust's Metropolis: A History of Berlin* (London: Harper Collins, 1998).
Roberts, Adam, *Science Fiction* (London and New York: Routledge, 2000).
Robertson, James C., *The British Board of Film Censors: Film Censorship in Britain 1896–1950* (London: Croom Helm, 1985).
Robillard, Valerie, and Els Jongeneel (eds), *Pictures Into Words: Theoretical and Descriptive Approaches to Ekphrasis* (Amsterdam: VU University Press, 1998).
Rogin, Michael, *Independence Day: Or How I Learned to Stop Worrying and Love the Enola Gay* (London: BFI, 1998).
Rotha, Paul, *The Film Till Now: A Survey of World Cinema* (1930; new edition, London: Hamlyn, 1967).
Rovin, Jeff, *Classic Science Fiction Films* (New York: Carol Publishing, 1993).
Sardar, Ziauddin, and Sean Cubitt (eds), *Aliens R Us: The Other in Science Fiction Cinema* (London: Pluto, 2002).
Schivelbusch, Wolfgang, *Disenchanted Night: The Industrialisation of Light in the Nineteenth Century*, trans. Angela Davies (Oxford/New York/Hamburg: Berg, 1988).
Sconce, Jeffrey, *Haunted Media: Electronic Presence from Telegraphy to Television* (Durham, NC and London: Duke University Press, 2000).
Sherriff, R. C., *No Leading Lady: An Autobiography* (London: Gollancz, 1968).
Silberstein, Ludwik, *The Theory of Relativity* (London: Macmillan, 1914).

Simmel, Georg, *The Metropolis and Mental Life* (1903), *Simmel on Culture: Selected Writings*, eds David Frisby and Mike Featherstone (London: Sage, 1997), pp. 174–85.
Skal, David, *Screams of Reason: Mad Science and Modern Culture* (New York: W. W. Norton, 1998).
Slusser, George, Patrick Parrinder and Danièle Chatelain (eds), *H. G. Wells's Perennial Time Machine: Selected Essays from the Centenary Conference 'The Time Machine: Past, Present and Future', Imperial College, London, July 26–29, 1995* (Athens, GA, and London: University of Georgia Press, 2001).
Slusser, George, and Eric S. Rabkin (eds), *Shadows of the Magic Lamp: Fantasy and Science Fiction in Film* (Carbondale: S Illinois University Press, 1985).
Smith, David C., *H. G. Wells, Desperately Mortal: A Biography* (New Haven, CT and London: Yale University Press, 1986).
Smith, Don G., *H. G. Wells on Film: The Utopian Nightmare* (Jefferson, NC; London: McFarland, 2002).
Smith, Grahame, *Dickens and the Dream of Cinema* (Manchester: Manchester University Press, 2003).
Sobchack, Vivian, *Screening Space: The American Science Fiction Film*, second, enlarged edition (New Brunswick, NJ, and London: Rutgers University Press, 1999).
Solnit, Rebecca, *Motion Studies: Time, Space and Eadweard Muybridge* (London: Bloomsbury, 2003).
Sorlin, Pierre, *The Film in History: Restaging the Past* (Oxford: Blackwell, 1980).
Spiegel, Alan J., *Fiction and the Camera Eye* (Charlottesville: University of Virginia Press, 1976).
Stafford, Barbara Main, and Frances Terpak, *Devices of Wonder: From the World in a Box to Images on Screen* (Los Angeles: Getty Publications, 2001).
Stover, Leon, *The Prophetic Soul: A Reading of H. G. Wells's Things to Come, Together with his Film Treatment Whither Mankind and the Postproduction Script* (Jefferson, NC and London: McFarland, 1987).
Suvin, Darko, *Metamorphoses of Science Fiction: On the Poetics and History of a Literary Genre* (New Haven, CT and London: Yale University Press, 1979).
Telotte, J. P., *Replications: A Robotic History of the Science Fiction Film* (Urbana and Chicago: University of Illinois Press, 1995).
Tosi, Virgilio, *Cinema Before Cinema: The Origins of Scientific Cinematography*, trans. Sergio Angelini (London: British Universities' Film and Video Council, 2005).
Turim, Maureen, *Flashbacks in Film: Memory and History* (London: Routledge, 1989).
Virilio, Paul, *War and the Cinema: The Logistics of Perception*, trans. Patrick Camiller (London: Verso, 1989).
Volti, Rudi (ed.), *The Encyclopedia of Science, Technology and Society*, three vols (Chicago and London: Fitzroy Dearborn, 1999).
von Ankum, Katharina (ed.), *Women in Metropolis: Gender and Modernity in Weimar Culture* (Berkeley, CA and Los Angeles: University of California Press, 1997).

Wakeman, John, *World Film Directors*, Vol. I (New York: H. W. Wilson, 1987).
Warner, Marina, *Fantastic Metamorphoses, Other Worlds: The Clarendon Lectures in English 2001* (Oxford: Oxford University Press, 2002).
Warner, Marina, *Phantasmagoria: Spirit Visions, Metaphors and Media into the Twenty-First Century* (Oxford: Oxford University Press, 2006).
Wells, Paul, *Animation: Genre and Authorship* (London and New York: Wallflower, 2002).
West, Anthony, *H. G. Wells: Aspects of a Life* (London: Hutchinson, 1984).
West, Geoffrey, *H. G. Wells: A Sketch for a Portrait* (London: Gerald Howe, 1930).
Westfahl, Gary, *Science Fiction, Children's Literature and Popular Culture: Coming of Age in Fantasyland* (Westport, CT and London: Greenwood Press, 2000).
Westfahl, Gary, George Slusser and David Leiby (eds), *Worlds Enough and Time: Explorations of Time in Science Fiction and Fantasy* (Westport, CT and London: Greenwood Press, 2002).
Whitworth, Michael H., *Einstein's Wake: Relativity, Metaphor and Modernist Literature* (Oxford: Oxford University Press, 2001).
Williams, Keith, *British Writers and the Media, 1930–45* (London: Macmillan, 1996).
Wilson, Harris, *Arnold Bennett and H. G. Wells: A Record of a Personal and a Literary Friendship* (London: Rupert Hart-Davis, 1960).
Wohl, Robert, *The Spectacle of Flight: Aviation and the Western Imagination, 1920–1950* (Carlton, Victoria: University of Melbourne Press, 2005).
Wood, Gaby, *Living Dolls: A Magical History of the Quest for Mechanical Life* (London: Faber, 2002).
Wykes, Alan, *H. G. Wells in the Cinema* (London: Jupiter, 1977).
Zabus, Chantal, *Tempests after Shakespeare* (Houndmills: Palgrave, 2002).

Archival Materials

James, Simon J., National Film Theatre, H. G. Wells Season, programme notes on *The Time Machine* (2002) (22 May 2005).
MacPhail, Angus, Letter from (29 July 1951) in BFI, 'Ivor Montagu Collection', Item 404.
Montagu, Ivor, scrapbook of press clippings, BFI, 'Ivor Montagu Collection', Item 25.
Montagu, Ivor, 'Letter to Stella Jonckheere at British Lion' (31 Dec. 1958), in BFI, 'Ivor Montagu Collection', Item 404.
Montagu, Ivor, with Frank Wells, draft screenplay of *The War of the Worlds* (c.1932), BFI, 'Ivor Montagu Collection' Item 25a.
Wells, Frank, and Ivor Montagu, BFI, 'London Films Production Collection' C/129 ii (3 Dec. 1957–8 Sept. 1959).

Index

Abbot, Edwin A. 190n
Acres, Birt 197n
Adler, Allen 166, 169
Al Qaeda 155, 156
Albanese, Antonio 172
Algerian War 156
Allen, Woody 218n
Alvey Jr, Glenn 173
America/ns/USA 2, 6, 11, 19, 21, 70, 86, 97, 102, 109, 126, 129, 134, 144, 145–46, 147, 149, 150–51, 152, 154, 155, 156, 161, 162, 164, 172, 175, 178, 240n; Arizona National Guard 151; Boston 145; Buffalo 14; Civil War 102; Grover's Mill, New Jersey 147; Linda Rosa, California 146, 150, 151; Los Angeles 146; New Mexico 148; New York 31, 81, 84, 85, 92, 116, 145, 147, 155 (Public Library 135); Pearl Harbor 112; Roswell, New Mexico 240n; San Francisco 44; St Louis 14; Vermont 145; Washington DC 149
Amis, Martin 155
Anschütz, Ottomar 20
Arlen, Richard 166
Armistice 95–96
Armitage, Frederick S 31
Armstrong, Tim 6, 57, 74
Arnold, Jack 153
Art Deco 220n
Art Nouveau 220n
avant-garde 10, 57, 65, 84, 91, 98, 100, 138, 179, 180, 225n

Bacon, John Mackenzie 238n
Bailey, Kenneth V. 3, 104, 185–86n
Baird, John Logie 73, 77, 200n, 218n

Baldwin, Stanley 112
Barbizon Productions Corp 129
Barnouw, Erik 60, 210n
Baron, Auguste 56
Barr, Robert 174
Barry, Gene 149
Barry, Iris 51, 98
Barthes, Roland 35–36, 121, 201n
Baudrillard, Jean 13, 22
Baudry, Jean-Louis 12, 30
BBC 70, 108–09, 162, 174–75, 200n, 211n, 230n, 245n; Alexandra Palace studios 160, 200n
Beaverbrook, Lord 97
Beerbohm, Max 233n
Bell, Alexander Graham 56
Bellamy, Edward 2, 178, 216n, 217n
Benigni, Roberto 172, 173
Benjamin, Walter 58, 64–65, 79, 131, 210n
Bennett, Arnold 206n
Benshoff, Harry M 211n
Bentham, Jeremy 217n
Bergonzi, Bernard 39, 220n
Bergson, Henri 24
Bernhardt, Sarah 51, 56, 189n
Bignell, Jonathan 29–30
Biograph 10, 31, 209n, 213n, 217n
Biró, Lajos 107, 122
Blackton, J. Stuart 59–60
Bliss, Arthur 115
Block, Irving 166, 169
Bonestell, Chesley 153
Booth, Walter R 46, 95
Bould, Mark 149
Boulle, Pierre 136
Bowen, Elizabeth 109
Bowie, David 157, 159
Bradbury, Ray 153, 170

Braun, Karl Ferdinand 218n
Britain/British 11, 19, 21, 28, 56, 71, 96, 98, 102, 103, 106, 107, 109, 110, 146, 152, 157, 161, 162, 163, 170, 174, 244n
British Board of Film Censors 105
British Empire 142, 143, 242n
British Film Institute (BFI) 34, 173
British Lion Productions 176
British Museum 7
British Navy 36
broadcast media 21
Browning, Tod 57–58
Brunel, Adrian 97
Bruzzi, Stella 148
Burke, Kathleen 166
Burroughs, Edgar Rice 145
Burton, Tim 136, 154, 155
Bush, George W. 154
Butler, David 92, 147

Cahn, Edward L. 148
Cameron, Julia Margaret 51
Campaign for Nuclear Disarmament (CND) 162
Capek, Karel 84, 88
Capra, Frank 32; *It's a Wonderful Life* 32
Carlyle, Thomas 51, 55, 134
Carmichael, Katy 176
Carné, Marcel 170
Carroll, Lewis 51, 173, 184n
Carroll, Sydney W. 108
Carter, Chris 164
Cartier, Rudolph 160–64, 175
Catelain, Jacque 89
Cavalcanti, Alberto 200n, 202n
CBS 70, 71, 147, 239–40n, 241n
censorship 19, 20, 21, 104, 219n, 227n, 244n
Chamberlain, Neville 71, 229n
Chaney, Lon 95
Channel 4 (UK) 175
Chaplin, Charlie 99, 106, 224n, 225n
Chapman, Alison 16
Chapman, Edward 112, 124
Chermayeff, Sergei 110
Chesney, Col G.T. 143
China 114
Christ/ianity 75, 85
Christie, Ian 1, 2, 13, 14, 15, 17, 18, 20, 21, 24, 28, 29, 38, 70
Churchill, Winston 20
cinematic time 2–4
Cinematograph Films Act 1927 19
city, the 17–18, 37–38, 81, 84, 87, 90, 202n, 203n
Clair, René 31–32
Clarke, I.F. 143
Clifford, William Kingdom 12, 190n
Clute, John 135
Coates, Paul 2, 3, 16, 169
Cobb, William 146
Coburn, Alvin Langdon 200n
Cocteau, Jean 205n
Codee, Ann 153
Cohen, Edward 110
Cohen, Keith 59
Cohl, Émile 60
Cold War 96, 114, 119, 133, 134, 135, 138, 148, 150, 153, 158, 161, 240n
Collings, Arthur Esmé 222n
colonialism 21, 145–46
Connor, Steve 55
Conrad, Joseph 4, 30, 68, 71, 75, 142, 213n
Constructivism 115
Cook, David A. 9, 183n
Cook, John R. 160, 174
Cooke, Alistair 108–09, 117–18
Cornell, Julian 152, 154
Crichton, Charles 110
Crookes, William 17, 51
Crossley, Robert 198n
Cruise, Tom 138, 155–57
Cuban Missile Crisis 132
Cubism 89

Daguerre, Louis 191n
Dam, H.J.W. 50
Davis, Joseph 12
Dawley, J. Searle 67
de l'Isle-Adam, Villiers 221n, 222n
De Mille, Cecil B 138
Debord, Guy 217n
Defoe, Daniel; *Robinson Crusoe* 134
Deleuze, Gilles 56
Derrida, Jacques 51, 54–55, 207n, 208n
Devant, David 211n
Dick, Philip K. 172
Dickens, Charles 8, 43

Disney Studios 137, 168
Disney, Walt 226–27n
Doane, Mary Anne 2
Donisthorpe, Wordsworth 187n, 189n
Donn, Mary 174
Douglas, Gordon 164–65
Doyen, Eugène-Louis 9–10
Doyle, Arthur Conan 8, 51, 157
Dreyfus Affair 20
Dukas, Paul Abraham 232n
Dumas, Alexander 65
Duncan, David 132
Duncan, F. Martin 9
Durand, Jean 31
Dussaud, François 56

Ealing studios 163
Eastman, George 183n
Eastman-Kodak/Kodak 9, 26, 183n
Edison, Thomas 2, 9, 17, 18, 27, 28, 47, 56, 145–46, 185n, 189n, 196n, 197n, 218n, 221n, 239n; 'kinetoscope' 2, 9, 10, 18, 19, 27–28, 185n, 195n, 196n, 197n
Education Act of 1870 5
Einstein, Albert 3, 194n
Eisenstein, Sergei M. 7–8, 22, 57, 138–39, 179, 236–37n, 245n
Eliot, T.S. 87
Elizabeth II 162
Elvey, Maurice 92, 96, 224n
Emmerich, Roland 145, 146, 152, 153–54, 241n
Expressionism (German) 17, 36, 37, 40, 42, 54, 58, 69, 81, 82, 84, 85, 88, 91, 103, 121–22, 169, 204n, 211n, 222n

Fanning, Dakota 155–56
Feather, Peter 14
Ferguson, Niall 144
Ferrari, Bill 131
film/cinema (techniques/methods/modes/venues): action replay 8; animal locomotion studies 8; animation/cartoons 8, 25, 44, 59, 103, 205n, 227n; autokinesis 59, 64; B-movies 154, 161; blue screen 81, 131, 211n; chronophotography 8–9, 10, 24, 31, 49, 63, 195n;
Cinemascope 165; close-ups 8, 9, 104; computer-generated imagery (CGI) 25, 72, 90, 136, 153, 155, 157, 198n, 211n; cross-cutting 8, 22; cross-fade 12; diorama 13, 14, 29; dissolve 11–12, 203n, 210n, 229n; documentary 22, 80, 82, 84, 91, 103, 111, 112, 114, 140, 200n, 226n, 229n, 230n; double exposure 12, 25, 40, 51, 59, 210n, 219n; dubbing 92; Dynamic Frame 173; early films/actors 79, 197n; fade-out 25; fairground ride 13, 14; film shows 18–19; filmstrip 8; flashback 96, 199n; frame strips 3; freeze-frame 45, 199n; Hollywood 19–20, 21, 47, 57, 58, 64, 65, 66, 67, 71, 72, 92, 95, 96, 106, 130–69, 170, 171, 174, 179; hyperreality 13, 22, 76, 78, 191n; iris in-out 173; magic lantern 8, 11–12, 13, 192n, 204n, 210n; masking 173, 210n; medical operation 9–10; microphotography 9, 27; mix 12; montage 42, 58, 80, 82, 83, 84, 89, 91, 97, 102, 103, 105, 111, 112, 113, 116, 127, 138, 150, 152, 155, 156, 190n, 223n, 226n, 229n, 230n; newsfilms 20–21; nickelodeons (penny gaffs) 19, 33, 90; panorama 13, 14, 29; peepshow 18–19, 185n, 222n; phantom ride 13–14; picture palaces 19, 33; projection 3; propaganda 21; rapid cutting 25; reversing 2, 4, 210n; Schüfftan process 81, 82, 219n; silents 56, 58, 67, 73, 94–99, 195n, 213n, 224n; slow-motion 8, 31, 44, 199n, 211n; soundtrack 56, 57, 99, 100, 148, 165, 213n, 224n; split-screen 104; star system 16, 54, 58, 63, 90; stop-motion 25, 44, 45, 46, 59, 60, 61, 103, 121, 131, 165, 195n, 209n; superimposition 96; switchback 30; Technicolor 153, 165; time-lapse 9, 25, 131, 184n, 189n; time-slicing (bullet time) 32, 199–200n; trickfilms 5, 39, 44, 45, 50, 60, 61, 62, 121, 131, 177, 184n, 204n, 205n

Finney, Albert 175
Finney, Jack 240n
First Gulf War 153
First World War *see* Great War
Flammarion, Camille 184n, 196–97n
Flaubert, Gustave 8
Flint, Kate 13, 16, 35, 55
Ford, Ford Madox 43, 84
Forde, Walter 139
Forster, E.M. 7, 37
Foucault, Michel 67, 217n
Fox studios 96
Fox Television 164
France/French 19, 156, 170, 171, 172, 215n; Cubism 169
Francis, Anne 168
Frayling, Christopher 110, 159, 228–29n
Frees, Paul 149
Freud, Sigmund 22, 151, 163, 166–69 (*see also* uncanny, the)
Friedberg, Ann 13, 22–23
Fujiko, Fujio F. 173
Fulton, John P. 62, 63, 209n
Futurism 35

Gallagher, Stephen 163
Garbo, Greta 227n
Garcia, Russell 132
Gardner, Joan 123
Gatiss, Mark 65, 174, 242n
Gaumont 10; British Gaumont 47, 92, 95, 139
Gaumont, Léon 56, 189n
gaze, the 50
Geddes, Norman Bel 110
Geduld, Harry M. 139
genre(s)/modes: allegory 34, 35, 69, 80, 88, 118, 133, 134, 135, 143, 156, 158, 206n, 232n; analepsis 83; cliché 67, 97, 98, 148; diegesis 91, 136, 142, 149, 153, 156; drama 6; dystopia 10, 18, 36, 73, 74, 84, 85, 90, 109, 117, 133, 165, 170, 172, 175, 215n, 221n; eidetic, the 15; ekphrasis 3, 7, 22, 98, 101, 105, 106, 120, 122, 131, 136, 139, 142, 147, 158; fairytale 49; framed viewpoints 13; Gothic 65, 151, 167, 205n; horror/SF 27, 57, 66, 67, 79, 81, 86, 88, 90, 92, 96, 108, 120, 141, 145, 147, 149, 153, 154, 159, 160, 161, 164, 165, 166, 173, 174, 175, 176, 211n, 241n; journalism 5; magic/conjuring 4, 5, 10, 30, 60, 61, 121, 187n; metaphor 58, 87–88, 205n; metonymy 49, 58, 59, 60, 63–64, 205n; music hall 6; novel 188n; parody 67; popular fiction 6, 17; popular science 10; radio drama 58, 70; romance 49, 66; satire 37, 39, 44, 92, 136, 175, 237n; scientific romance 1, 5, 23, 47, 48, 65, 73, 95, 159–60, 179, 186n, 187n, 227n; short story 5–6, 23, 31–48; social realist novel 179; stream of consciousness 179; striptease 222n; synecdoche 58, 62, 82, 205n; theatre 51; treatise 179; Utopia/nism 2, 22, 73, 101, 110, 116, 120, 123, 133, 134, 137, 166, 167, 172, 175, 181, 216n, 217n, 228n, 231n; vaudeville 61; visual pun 87, 176; Westerns 152, 156
Germany 19, 20, 69, 81, 85, 86, 88, 90, 91–92, 96, 143, 171, 220n, 230n; Nazis 22, 69, 86, 92, 114, 125, 137, 150, 220n, 229n, 230n, 238n (*see also* Expressionism; Hitler)
Gernsback, Hugo 187n
Gibbons, Walter 56
Gibson, William 182
Gilbert, W.S. 210n
Goble, Warwick 139, 149
Godal, Edward 97, 225n
Godal International 99, 106
Godard, Jean-Luc 170
Goebbels, Josef 220n
Goering, Herman 229n
Goldmann, Lucien 63
Goldblum, Geoff 154
Goldwyn, Sam 119
Golem 42, 58, 88, 122
Gorbachev, Mikhail 172
Gordon, Bert I. 159, 164–65
Gorky, Maxim 203n
Great Depression 110
Great War/First World War 19, 21, 22, 46, 47, 65, 73, 96, 104, 110, 112, 114–15, 139, 148, 226n, 238n
Greenblatt, Stephen 151

INDEX

Greene, Graham 232n
Grierson, John 230n
Griffith, D.W. 21, 30, 96, 101, 102, 105, 109, 118, 173, 199n, 219n; *Birth of a Nation* 21–22, 102, 104, 140, 166, 206n; *Intolerance* 22
Griffith, George 50, 180
Grimoin-Sanson, Raoul 14
Gross, Anthony 103
Grove, Allen W. 207n
Guazzoni, Enrico 21
Guernica 112
Gunning, Tom 80

Haffner, Sebastian 69
Haggard, Henry Rider 8
Hallmark cable/satellite channels 176
Hamman, Joë 95
Hammer Studios 161
Hammond, J.R. 190n
Hammond, Paul 43, 60, 61
Hardwicke, Cecil 116, 149, 150, 230n
Hardy, Sylvia 94, 98
Hardy, Thomas 100, 102, 122–23, 225n
Harryhausen, Ray 139, 195n, 237n
Haskin, Byron 135, 138, 139, 146–47, 148, 149, 150, 151, 152, 153, 156, 157, 164, 239n, 240n, 242n
Hayward, Susan 186n
Hearst, William Randolph 145
Heath, Robert 169
Hedgecock, Liz 141–42, 143, 154
Helm, Brigitte 222n
Hepworth, Cecil 2, 61, 95, 209n
Hertz, Heinrich Rudolf 55–56
Heyer, Martha 96
Hickman, Gail Morgan 235n
Hill, Susan 243n
Hines, Tim 157
Hinton, C.H. 49, 50, 194n, 206–07n
Hiroshima 148
Hitchcock, Alfred 43–44, 68, 139, 203–04n, 237n; *Rear Window* 43–44, 203–04n
Hitler 21, 68, 69–70, 86, 92, 119, 125, 143, 239n
HMV 181
Holst, Gustav 163
Horner, Harry 149
hot-air balloons 29

Houghton, Georgiana 51
Hugenberg, Alfred 86
Hughes, David Y. 11, 73, 139
Hume, Benita 92
Hume, Cyril 166
Huntington, John 133–34
Hutchings, Peter 161, 162
Huxley, Aldous 92, 117, 175, 200n, 220n, 243–44n
Huxley, T.H. 131
Hyams, Leila 166
hypnotism/mesmerism 36, 41, 77, 88, 201n, 213n, 215n, 221n, 222n, 244n

Ideal Pictures 97
Iraq 153, 229n
Irons, Jeremy 137
Italy 171, 172, 173

Jacklin, Ross 110
James, Henry 75
James, William 179, 195n, 199n
Jameson, Storm 91
Japan 173, 238n
Jennings, Gordon 149
Johnson, William 139, 161
Jolson, Al; *The Jazz Singer* 56
Jones, Orlando 135
Jonze, Spike 202n
Joyce, James 87, 103, 125, 179, 180
Juran, Nathan 96, 160, 195n

Kaes, Anton 220n
Kaiser Wilhelm II 20
Karloff, Boris 58, 126, 212n
Keats, John 55
Kelvin, Lord 145
Kenton, Erle C. 106, 165–66
Kern, Stephen 3
Kholer, Gilles 170
Kimmins, Anthony 227n
King, Stephen 241n
Kipling, Rudyard 8, 55, 75, 84, 95, 145, 231n
Klapisch, Cèdric 171–72
Kneale, Nigel 156, 157–64, 167, 174, 175, 242n, 243n, 245n
Koch, Howard 147
Kodak 196n, 203

Koestler, Arthur 86
Korda, Alexander 6, 44–45, 47, 106–07, 110, 112, 121, 122, 126, 129, 199n, 209n, 225n, 227n, 232n, 233n
Korda, Michael 112, 116, 118
Korda, Vincent 110, 115
Korean War 146, 148, 150–51
Kosower, Herbert 106
Kozloff, Sarah 213n
Ku Klux Klan 22
Kubrick, Stanley 101–02, 116, 157, 243n; *2001: A Space Odyssey* 101–02, 116, 157
Kulik, Karol 118, 119–20, 122
Kumar, Krishan 227–28n
Kuwait 153

L'Herbier, Marcel 89, 170, 222n
La Valley, Albert J. 4–5
Laemmle, Carl 66
Lanchester, Elsa 97
Landon, Brooks 179, 180
Lang, Fritz 5, 17–18, 36, 38, 40, 69, 108, 109, 167, 171, 202n, 203n, 213n, 217n, 219n, 220n, 221n; *Metropolis* 5, 17–18, 36, 38, 40, 73–93, 96, 109, 115, 116, 117, 120, 165, 167, 168, 169, 171, 202n, 203n, 213n, 217n, 221n, 223n
Lanos, Henri 75
Last Days of Pompeii 15, 140
Laughton, Charles 165–66
Laust, Eugène 56
League of Nations 125
Leblanc, Georgette 89
Le Corbusier 110
Léger, Fernand 89, 110
Leigh, Bruce Gordon 96
Lejeune, C.A. 109
Lenin 21
le Prince, Augustin 189n
Lewis, Sinclair 229n
Lilienthal, Otto 10, 27, 190n
Lincoln, Abraham 102
Lindsay, Vachel 3, 27, 51, 59, 60, 73, 178
Lippmann, Walter 20
Lodge, David 58
Logan, John 135
Lombard, Leslie 60
London 36, 37, 41, 65, 75, 81, 82, 84, 85, 92, 111, 113, 140, 141, 151, 163, 217n; Alhambra 29, 197n; Blitz 112, 147; Coliseum 60; Crystal Palace 75, 216n; Leicester Square 28; New Gallery Cinema, Regent St 98; Olympia 29, 197n; Oxford St 19, 28, 30; Piccadilly (Egyptian Hall) 61, 211n (Circus) 111; Polytechnic, Regent St 28, 40, 204n; Savoy 96; St Paul's 111; Tivoli Palace, Strand 98; Westminster Abbey 162
London Films 87, 107
London Film Society 47, 98, 189n, 213n, 219n, 222n, 223n, 225n, 227n, 229n, 230n, 238n
London, Jack 220n
Lugosi, Bela 165, 212n
Lukács, Georg 63
Lumière brothers 1, 2, 9, 13, 14, 17, 18, 24, 26, 27, 28, 30, 31, 185n, 189n, 197n, 217n, 230n
Lyndon, Barre 149, 152, 238n, 240n, 241n
Lyon, Francis 110

McCarthyism 133, 134, 150, 240n
McConnell, Frank 53–54, 55, 67–68
McCormack, Una 175
McCutcheon, Wallace 17, 209n
Machen, Arthur 39
MacIntyre, John 17
MacLaren, Anne 116
MacLeish, Archibald 70
MacPherson, Kenneth 105
Madrid 112
magazines and newspapers 6, 7; *American Cinematographer* 63; *Bioscope* 198n; *Budget* 207n; *La Caricature* 217n; *Close-Up* 105; *Collier's* 240n; *The Cornhill Magazine* 52; *Daily Mail* 216n, 225n; *The Era* 197n, 216–17n, 221n; *Evening Journal* 145, 239n; *Film Weekly* 119; *Forum* 218n; *Frankfurter Zeitung* 85; *Graphic* 75, 215n, 216n; *Illustrated London News* 216n; *Journal of the British Interplanetary Society* 228n; *Kinematograph Weekly* 95; *Nash's Pall*

Mall 202n; *National Observer* 10, 11, 19, 25, 28, 31, 197n, 222n; *Nature* 119, 194n, 198n, 232n; *New Review* 11, 28; *New York Tribune* 147; *Observer* 109; *Pall Mall Gazette* 207n; *Pearson's Magazine* 17, 50, 139; *Pearson's Weekly* 50; *Photoplay* 96; *Punch* 218n; *The Quarterly Review* 51; *Radio Times* 174; *Science Schools Journal* 183n; *Scientific American Supplement* 218n; *Strand Magazine* 187n, 196n, 203n; *St Louis Post Dispatch* 196n; *Sunday Times* 108; *The Times* 95, 114, 145, 209n, 231n; *Variety* 199n
Manhattan Project 148
Mann, Ned 110, 116, 121
March of Time (newsreel) 107, 109, 110, 232n
Marconi, Guglielmo 55–56, 209n
Marcus, Laura 4, 5, 98, 106, 173–74
Marey, Étienne-Jules 8–9, 10, 16, 27, 31, 49–50, 63
Marinetti, Filippo Tommaso 26, 35
Marker, Chris 169–70
Marsh, Mae 226n
Marshall, Neil 236n
Martians 35, 40, 68, 80, 95, 113, 139–59, 176, 214n, 237n, 238n, 239n, 242n, 243n
Martin, Lewis 149
Marx/ism 22, 63, 64, 212n, 221n
Maskelyne, John Nevil 61, 62, 63, 211n
Massey, Raymond 92, 107, 229n
Matthew, Brander 184–85n
Matuszewski, Boleslaw 9
Maxwell, James Clerk 200n
Mayne, Alan 198n
mechanisms of vision 8
Meissonier, Ernest 183n
Méliès, Georges 4, 5, 20, 30, 39, 47, 50, 59, 61, 94, 104, 195n, 211n, 222n; Georges Méliès Award 132
Mendelson, Erich 110
Mendes, Lothar 122
Menzies, William Cameron 110
mescalin 62
Mescall, John J. 62
Messter, Oskar 9, 189n
Metz, Christian 53

Meyer, Nicholas 135
Michelson, Annette 199n
Michelson-Morley experiment 183n
Miller, Catriona 175
Mimieux, Yvette 133
Minden, Michael 87
Mitchell, Edward Page 184n, 199n, 207n
Modernism 5, 19, 46, 54, 57, 59, 64, 82, 87, 92, 99, 101, 110, 169, 179, 180–81, 209n
Moholy-Nagy, Lázló 115, 229n
Montagu, Ivor 97, 98, 129, 139, 165, 173, 174, 176, 224–25n, 237n
Mosley, Oswald 111
Mouton, Eugène 184n
Mumba, Samantha 137
Mumford, Lewis 178
Munich Crisis 138, 143
Murnau, F.W. 42, 67, 128
Murrow, Ed 147
Mussolini 70, 113
Muybridge, Eadweard 8–9, 16, 18, 32, 49

Nagasaki 148
Napier, Russell 174
Nation, Terry 174
Native Americans 151, 152, 160
Neil, Roy William 96
New Woman, the 90
Newman, Kim 111, 150
Newman, Sydney 245n
Newnes, George 187n
Nicholls, Peter 135
Nicoll, Allardyce 186n
Nietzsche, Friedrich 54, 87
9/11 138, 155, 157
Nipkow, Paul 218n
Normand, Mabel 224n
Nozaki, Al 240n
Nyby, Christian 149

O'Bannon, Dan 164
O'Brien, Fitz-James 207–08n
O'Brien, Willis 139
O'Sullivan, Vincent 39
Olivier, Laurence 233n, 246n
Orwell, George 76–77, 114, 159, 172, 174–75, 180–81

Oscars 153

Pagetti, Carlo 203n
Pal, George 130–35, 136, 137, 138, 139, 146–47, 148, 149, 150, 151, 152, 153, 156, 159, 164, 165, 174, 195n, 234n, 235n, 238n, 240n, 241n, 242n, 245n
Paramount Studios 138, 149, 234n, 237n
paranormal/occult/spiritualism 12, 16–17, 35, 39, 40, 41, 49, 51, 61, 86, 167 (*see also* uncanny, the)
Paris 4, 14, 17, 18, 56, 170, 172, 196n, 215n
Parish, Edmund 35
Parrinder, Patrick 180
Partington, John 180
Pathé 10, 59, 209n, 217n
Pathé, Charles 56
Paul, R.W. 14, 19, 28–29, 30, 35, 46, 47, 48, 95, 99, 131, 177, 197–98n, 205n, 206n
Payn, James 53
Pearce, Guy 235n
Pearson, C. Arthur 187n
Pemberton-Billing, Noël 223n
Pepper, John Henry 204n; Pepper's Ghost trick 204n
Phelps, Elizabeth 39
Philmus, Robert M. 11, 73, 234n
phonograph 9, 32, 55, 56, 69, 75, 76
photography 7, 8, 15, 16, 17, 35–36, 50, 51, 77, 102, 121–22, 196n, 199n, 201n, 202n
Piana, Anthony 157
Piasecki, Pawel 14
Pickford, Mary 38, 98
Pidgeon, Walter 167
Plato 35, 49, 54, 111, 201n
Podmore, Frank 201n
Poe, Edgar Allan 41, 46
Poland 172
pornography 90
Porter, Edwin S 44, 95
Potter, Dennis 7, 44, 175–76, 188n, 218n
Powell, Michael 32, 42
Pressburger, Emeric 32, 42
Price, James E. 136

Priest, Christopher 53
Proctor, Richard 8, 11
propaganda 79, 92, 119
Protazanov, Yakov 5, 79–80
Pudovkin, V. I. 58–59

radio 7, 56, 70–71, 116, 143, 146–47, 152, 162, 174, 218n, 219n, 222n, 232n, 233n, 236n, 239n, 242n
Rains, Claude 58, 65, 69–70, 214n, 233n
Ramsaye, Terry 14, 27, 28, 29, 47–48, 99, 185n, 196n, 197–98n, 205–06n
Rawlence, Christopher 189n
Read, Jan 160
Reagan era 163
Reed, Carol 132
Rennie, Michael 150
Renzi, Thomas C. 62, 66, 67, 135, 212–13n, 239n
Resnais, Alain 170
Revelation, Book of 90
Richards, Jeffrey 106, 109, 110, 119
Richards, Thomas 63, 231n
Richardson, Dorothy 105–06
Richardson, Ralph 113, 124
Riefenstahl, Leni 119
Rilla, Wolf 159
Robbins, Tim 156
Roberts, Adam 143
Robida, Albert 14, 217n, 218n, 222n
Robinson, Ann 149
Robinson, Frank M. 165
Roget, Peter Mark 8
Röntgen, Wilhelm Konrad von 4, 50, 51, 145, 207n (*see also* X-rays)
Roosevelt, President 'Teddy' 20, 71, 143, 233n
Rossetti, Dante Gabriel 13
Rossiter, Leonard 175
Rotha, Paul 106, 114
Rowland, Margery 188n
Royal Institution 114, 218n
Royal Photographic Society 28
Ruhmer, Ernst 56
Russell, Charles 21
Ruttmann, Walther 37–38, 82, 91–92, 225–26n
Rye, Stellan 42, 126

St Albans, England 19

Sanders, George 122
Schaffner, Franklin 136
Sconce, Jeffrey 16, 55, 160
Scott, Margaretta 118, 119
Scott, Ridley 89, 164
Second World War 111, 129, 144, 146
Sears, Fred F. 148
Selig, William N. 20
Serviss, Garret P. 145–46, 152, 154
Sexton, Jamie 98
Shakespeare, William 165; *The Tempest* 165–67, 243–44n
Shaw, Harold 96
Shelley, Mary 67, 88
Sherriff, R.C. 65–66, 71, 214n
Shiel, M.P. 39
Siegel, Don 158–59, 240n
Simmel, Georg 18
Simpson, Anne B. 65
Simpsons, The 199n, 236n, 246n
Slusser, George 169
Smith, Don G. 178
Smith, G.A. 17, 30, 32, 40, 41, 44, 52, 61, 173, 204n
Smith, Grahame 7–8
Smith, Percy 9
Smith, Will 154
Sobchack, Vivian 154, 182
Society for Psychical Research (SPR) 12–13, 16, 17, 40, 51, 52, 176–77, 192–93n, 203n, 207n
Solovoy, Michael 207n
Sommerville, David 204n
Sontag, Susan 120
Soviet Union/USSR 19, 79, 80, 96, 114, 125, 134, 135, 138, 146, 150, 162, 171, 172; Cubo-Futurism 79, 169
Spencer, Percival 203n
Spielberg, Steven 138, 140, 155, 172, 241–42n
Spoliansky, Michael 232n
Stalin 119, 125, 231n
Stead, William 39
Stein, Joshua 134, 135
Stephen, Sir Herbert 52
Stevenson, R.L. 42, 54, 55, 126, 127
Stewart, Garrett 5, 73, 80, 88, 89, 152, 153
Stoker, Bram 55
Stoll studios 47, 96

Surrealism/ists 22
surveillance 18, 21, 34, 53, 76, 80, 159, 170, 172, 175, 181, 217n, 218n, 219n
Suvin, Darko 166
Swinton, A.C. 207n, 218n
Szulkin, Piotr 172

Tasmania 151
Tay Rail Bridge 14
Taylor, Frederick 84
Taylor, Rod 131, 234–35n
television 7, 16, 34, 73, 74, 89, 92, 116, 129, 149, 155, 160, 164, 170, 172, 173–77, 200n, 216–17n, 218–19n, 222n, 230n, 245n, 246n; CCTV 80, 181
Telotte, J.P. 89, 222n
Teshigara, Hiroshi 173
Tesla, Nicola 209n, 242n
Thatcher, Heather 96
Thesiger, Ernest 123
Thompson, Dorothy 147
time travel 24–31
Tolstoy, Alexei 79
Tolstoy, Leo 8
Tourneur, Jacques 166, 243n
trace, the 54
Trans-Siberian Railway 14
Treaty of Versailles 115
Trewey, Félicien 30
Troisi, Massimo 172
Truffaut, François 170
Tucholsky, Kurt 69
Twyford, Cyril 60

uncanny, the 16, 39, 40, 41, 50, 55, 57, 88, 89, 151, 164, 167, 169, 207n (*see also* Freud)
Universal Studios 57, 58, 63, 210n, 212n, 214n
Universum Film Aktiengesellschaft (UFA) 81, 85, 86, 87
Urban, Charles 9

van Dooren, Ine 204n
Vallorani, Nicoletta 73, 89, 169, 170, 171, 172
Veevers, Wally 110, 116
Verhoeven, Paul 54, 72, 208n

Verne, Jules 8, 14, 55, 95, 108, 124, 157, 171, 180, 215n, 216n, 218n, 221–22n, 227n
Veronese, Paul 233n
Vertov, Dziga 140
Virilio, Paul 13, 83, 180
von Harbou, Thea 80, 88, 90, 213n, 221n
voyeurism 16, 18, 53, 80, 88, 141, 165, 166, 167, 204n, 218n, 222n

Wachowski brothers 32
Wall St Crash 85
Ward, Tom 176
Warner, Marina 16
Warwick Trading Company 20
Watkins, Robert Lincoln 9
webcams 34
Wegener, Paul 42, 58, 122
Weld, John 71
Welles, Orson 71, 138, 143, 146–47, 158, 162, 174, 214n, 238n, 239n
Wells, H.G. 1935 interview 56–57; 'broadbrow' 6–7, 94–129, 188n; diary 107, 120; *Doppelgänger* themes 17, 42, 101, 126; draper's assistant 211n; filmscripts 44, 47; film writing 94–129; grandson Simon 130, 135–38, 236n; influence in Europe 169–73; mother 35; newspaper articles 99; on women and modernity 101, 168–69; 'realist of the fantastic' 4, 26, 30, 68, 142, 162, 164, 169, 213n; response to questionnaire 47; review of *Metropolis* 84–85, 109–10; second wife Amy Robbins 176; son Frank 97, 98, 99, 110, 112, 122, 129, 139, 234n, 237n

fiction and published film scripts: 'The Argonauts of the Air' 27; *The Camford Visitation* 181; 'The Chronic Argonauts' 10, 12, 53, 137, 199n, 204n, 205n, 244n; *Complete Short Stories* 6; 'The Cone' 88, 204n; 'The Country of the Blind' 47, 66, 134; 'The Crystal Egg' 15, 16, 18, 33, 35–36, 139, 160; 'The Door in the Wall' 15, 33–34, 74, 97, 173, 243n; 'A Dream of Armageddon' 16, 38, 74; *The Food of the Gods* 10, 126, 225n;

The First Men in the Moon 5, 9, 14, 25–26, 172, 209n; 'How Gabriel Became Thompson' 202n, 203n; 'The Inexperienced Ghost' 40, 52–53; *In the Days of the Comet* 227n; *The Invisible Man* 4, 9, 13, 16, 33, 34, 40, 44, 45–46, 49–72, 78, 106, 141, 163, 165, 172, 173, 181, 205n, 206n, 207n, 208n, 209n, 212–13n; *The Island of Dr Moreau* 95, 106, 163, 165, 205n, 236n; 'Jimmy Goggles the God' 208n; *The King Who Was a King* 6, 22, 48, 94, 96, 97, 98–106, 107, 111, 112, 113, 118, 124, 127, 180, 187n, 202n, 233n; 'The Land Ironclads' 139; 'The Lord of the Dynamos' 88, 221n; 'The Magic Shop' 4, 45; 'The Man Who Could Work Miracles' 4, 44–45, 60–61, 106, *The Man Who Could Work Miracles: A Film Story* 121–26, 227n; *A Modern Utopia* 181; 'Mr Brownlow's Newspaper' 177; 'Mr Skelmersdale in Fairyland' 204–5n; 'The New Accelerator' 11, 18, 31–33, 44, 53, 84, 177; 'The Plattner Story' 15, 16, 17, 33, 39–40, 41–42, 52; 'Pollock and the Porroh Man' 46, 58; 'The Red Room' 40, 52, 106, 204n; 'The Remarkable Case of Davidson's Eyes' 15, 16, 18, 34–35, 53; *The Shape of Things to Come* 106, 110, 115, 116, 118, 119, 120; 'The Star' 35; *Star Begotten* 120, 157–58, 161, 163, 164; 'The Stolen Bacillus' 212n; 'The Stolen Body' 11, 17, 41–42, 97, 202n, 213n, 243n; 'A Story of the Days to Come' 10, 15, 18, 36–37, 75, 88, 216n, 217n; 'The Story of the Last Trump' 97; 'The Story of the Late Mr Elvesham' 15, 17, 40–41, 126, 213n (as *The New Faust: A Film Story*, 126–29, 174); 'A Story of the Stone Age' 226n; 'The Temptation of Harringay' 17, 46–47 ('The Devotee of Art' 205n); *Things to Come – A Film Story* 107, 111–19, 122; *The Time Machine* 1, 4, 7, 10–11, 16, 19, 24–31, 32, 34, 41, 45, 49, 53, 73, 115, 117, 122, 131, 132,

135, 136, 138, 139, 140, 143, 170, 172, 174, 177, 197–98n, 199n, 202n, 222n; 'Through a Window' 15, 42–43, 74, 141; 'The Treasure in the Forest' 186n, 203n; 'The Truth About Pyecraft' 177; 'Under the Knife' 41, 42; 'A Vision of Judgement' 203n, 233n; *The War in the Air* 10, 140, 180; *The War of the Worlds* 4, 10, 67, 71, 113, 133, 139–44, 155, 162, 163, 164, 165, 166, 172, 174, 204n, 234n; *When the Sleeper Wakes* 10, 15, 16, 17, 18, 19, 21, 36, 72, 73–93, 109, 111, 116, 118, 136, 141, 162, 165, 168, 169, 170, 171, 175, 180, 181, 215n, 216n, 217n, 218n, 220n, 221n, 223n; *Whither Mankind? A Film of the Future* 107, 110, 115, 118, 227–31n; *The World Set Free* 132, 148

films and television programmes adapted from Wells: *Bluebottles* 97; 'The Crystal Egg' 176; *Daydreams* 97; 'The Door in the Wall' 173–4; *The First Men in the Moon* 95–96, 139, 171; *The Food of the Gods* 159, 237n; 'The Inexperienced Ghost' 202n; *The Invisible Man* 49–72, 106, 152, 167, 179, 209n; *The Island of Dr Moreau* 95, 106; *Kipps* 96, 132; 'The Magic Shop' 177; *The Man Who Could Work Miracles* 44–45, 106, 113, 121–26, 129, 131, 174, 181; *Marriage* 96; 'Mr Brownlow's Newspaper' 177; 'The New Accelerator' 174, 176; *The Passionate Friends* 96; 'Pollock and the Porroh Man' 176; 'The Red Room' 106; 'The Remarkable Case of Davidson's Eyes' 176; 'The Temptation of Harringay' 174; *Things to Come* 18, 22, 80–81, 82, 86–87, 89, 92, 95, 96, 97, 98, 101, 102, 103, 104, 106–20, 121, 122, 123, 124, 125, 126, 129, 149, 150, 161, 168, 180, 225n, 227n; *The Time Machine* 25, 130–38, 149, 150, 171, 195n; *The Tonic* 97–98; 'The Truth About Pyecraft' 177; 'Under the Knife' 176; *The War of the Worlds* 135, 139–40, 145, 146, 148–57, 161, 172, 237n; *The Wheels of Chance* 96

non-fiction: *Anticipations* 122; 'The Idea of a Permanent World Encyclopedia' 236n; 'The Dream Bureau' 138, 201n; 'Human Evolution, An Artificial Process' 243n; 'The Limits of Individual Plasticity' 243n; 'The Man of the Year Million: A Scientific Forecast' 143, 202n; 'The Origin of the Senses' 11; *The Outline of History* 96; 'The Remarkable Vogue for Broadcasting: Will It Continue?' 219n; 'Through a Microscope' 208n, 238n; *The Way the World is Going* 84

Wells, Isabel 7
Wenders, Wim 172
West, Rebecca 96–97
Westfahl, Gary 138
Whale, James 49–72, 152, 167, 179, 209n, 211–12n, 214n, 237n, 238n, 239n
Wilcox, Fred McLeod 165–69; *Forbidden Planet* 165–69
Wilde, Oscar 41, 54, 244n
Wilson, William 187n
Wilson, Woodrow 96
Wise, Robert 148
Wohl, Robert 231n
Wood Jr, Ed 149
Wood, Gaby 222n
Wray, Cecil 55, 189n
Wright brothers 10
Wright, Peter 160, 174
Wylie, Philip 165
Wyndham, John 157, 159

X-rays 4, 11, 16–17, 41, 50, 51, 62, 189n, 207n, 238n

Young, Alan 131, 235n
Young, Roland 123

Zakharov, Alexander 172
Zamyatin, Yvgeny 175
Zebrowski, George 228n
Zech, Harry 110
Zola, Emile 8

www.ingramcontent.com/pod-product-compliance
Lightning Source LLC
Chambersburg PA
CBHW052047220426
43663CB00012B/2468